# Lecture Notes in Computer Science 8390

*Commenced Publication in 1973*
Founding and Former Series Editors:
Gerhard Goos, Juris Hartmanis, and Jan van Leeuwe

AF895971

More information about this series at http://www.springer.com/series/7409

Dickson K.W. Chiu · Minhong Wang
Elvira Popescu · Qing Li
Rynson Lau · Timothy K. Shih
Chu-Sing Yang · Demetrios G. Sampson (Eds.)

# Advances in Web-Based Learning – ICWL 2013 Workshops

## USL 2013, IWSLL 2013, KMEL 2013 IWCWL 2013, WIL 2013, and IWEEC 2013 Kenting, Taiwan, October 6–9, 2013 Revised Selected Papers

Springer

| | |
|---|---|
| Ming-Hsiung Ying | Chung-Hua University, Taiwan |
| Xiaohui Zhao | Unitec Institute of Technology, New Zealand |
| Mudasser F. Wyne | National University, USA |
| Kuan-Chung Chen | National University of Tainan, Taiwan |
| Eleanna Kafeza | Athens University of Economics and Business, Greece |
| Lei Chen | Hong Kong University of Science and Technology, Hong Kong |
| Chi-hung Chi | Tsing Hua University, China |
| Liya Ding | Macau University of Science and Technology, China |
| Haiyang Hu | Zhejiang Gongshang University, China |
| Wendy W.Y. Hui | University of Nottingham at Ningbo, China |
| Patrick C.K. Hung | University of Ontario Institute of Technology, Canada |
| Hiroshi Igaki | Kobe University, Japan |
| Tsukasa Ishigaki | National Institute of Advanced Industrial Science and Technology, Japan |
| Kengo Katayama | Okayama University of Science, Japan |
| Ichiro Kobayashi | Ochanomizu University, Japan |
| Mario Koeppen | Kyushu Institute of Technology, Japan |
| P. Radha Krishna | SET Labs – Infosys Technologies Ltd., India |
| Carmen Ka Man Lam | Hong Kong Baptist University, Hong Kong |
| Raymond Y.K. Lau | City University of Hong Kong, Hong Kong |
| Chei Sian Lee | Nanyang Technological University, Singapore |
| Ho-fung Leung | Chinese University of Hong Kong, Hong Kong |
| Pierre Levy | The University of Ottawa, Canada |
| Tieyan Li | Institute for Infocomm Research (I2R), Singapore |
| Fu-ren Lin | National Tsing Hua University, Taiwan |
| Wenyin Liu | City University of Hong Kong, Hong Kong |
| Edwin Lughofer | Fuzzy Logic Laboratorium Linz-Hagenberg, Austria |
| Zongwei Luo | University of Hong Kong, China |
| Yinghua Ma | Shanghai JiaoTong University, China |
| Huiye Ma | Eindhoven University of Technology, The Netherlands |
| Akira Maeda | Ritsumeikan University, Japan |
| Mitsunori Matsushita | Kansai University, Japan |
| Farid Meziane | Salford University, UK |
| Atsuyuki Morishima | University of Tsukuba, Japan |
| Koichi Moriyama | Osaka University, Japan |
| Sanaz Mostaghim | University of Karlsruhe, Germany |
| Yoichi Motomura | National Institute of Advanced Industrial Science and Technology, Japan |

# The 2013 International Workshop on Cloud Computing for Web-Based Learning (IWCWL 2013) Chairs' Message

Cloud computing is an active research area on computing and communication technology in recent years. The unprecedented amount of computing and storage resources on cloud systems can be provided to us via the Internet with traditional computers or smart appliances. With these unlimited computing and storage resources, a large number of researches have been focused on applying the traditional Internet services to the cloud computing environments. This workshop concerns the recent developments and applications of web-based learning, as an important Internet service, in the modern cloud-computing environments. The objective of this workshop is to invite authors to submit original research articles that demonstrate and explore current advances in all aspects of cloud computing for web-based learning. Authors are encouraged to submit either theoretical or practical articles to this workshop. After review, we selected six quality papers in IWCWL 2013, respectively, for presentation covering various aspects of cloud computing for web-based learning.

We appreciate the interest and support of all attendees. In particular, we thank the ICWL organizers. The great success of the workshop is indebted to the hard work of all Program Committee members. We also thank all the authors for their contributions.

December 2013

Chu-Sing Yang

# Organization

## IWCWL 2013 Workshop Chairs

| | |
|---|---|
| Chu-Sing Yang | National Cheng Kung University, Taiwan |

## IWCWL 2013 Program Committee

| | |
|---|---|
| Ming-Chao Chiang | National Sun Yat-sen University, Taiwan |
| Chang-Shing Lee | National University of Tainan, Taiwan |
| Steven Chen | Education Business Division of United Daily News, Taiwan |
| Feng-jung Liu | Cheng Shiu University, Taiwan |
| Tien-Wen Sung | Hsing-Kuo University, Taiwan |
| Shih-Pang Tseng | Tajen University, Taiwan |

# The 2013 International Workshop on Web Intelligence and Learning (WIL2013) Chairs' Message

The Internet gathers more and more human activities in the twenty-first century. An abundant amount of data and knowledge is generated by several kinds of Web applications. The Web had become a very important learning tool for formal and informal education. Web intelligence applied artificial intelligence and information technology on the web in order to enrich products and services on the Internet. The web intelligence technology can effectively abstract the valuable information from the Internet for learning. In addition, the web intelligence technology can also analyze the data generated by learning activities in order to improve the adaptivity of learning.

The objective of the workshop is to invite authors to submit original manuscripts that demonstrate and explore current advances in all aspects of Web Intelligence and Learning. Authors are encouraged to submit either theoretical or practical articles to this workshop. After review, we selected six quality papers in WIL 2013, respectively, for presentation covering various aspects of Web Intelligence and Learning.

We appreciate the interest and support of all attendees. In particular, we thank the ICWL organizers. The great success of the workshop is indebted to the hard work of all Program Committee members. We also thank all the authors for their contributions.

December 2013

Jeng-Shyang Pan

# Organization

## WIL 2013 Workshop Chairs

| | |
|---|---|
| Jeng-Shyang Pan | National Kaohsiung University of Applied Sciences, Taiwan |

## WIL 2013 Program Committee

| | |
|---|---|
| Ajith Abraham | Ostrava University of Technology, Czech Republic |
| Jiun-Huei Ho | Cheng Shiu University, Taiwan |
| Mong-Hong Horng | National Kaohsiung University of Applied Sciences, Taiwan |
| Muhammad Khurram Khan | King Saud University, Saudi Arabia |
| Junbao Li | Harbin Institute of Technology, China |
| Yuenan Li | Tianjin University, China |
| Bin-Yih Liao | National Kaohsiung University of Applied Sciences, Taiwan |
| Lianlei Lin | Harbin Institute of Technology, China |
| Jiaqing Qiao | Harbin Institute of Technology, China |
| Lijun Yan | Harbin Institute of Technology Shenzhen Graduate School, China |
| Longjiang Yu | Harbin Institute of Technology, China |
| Yong Xu | Harbin Institute of Technology Shenzhen Graduate School, China |

# The 2013 International Workshop on E-book and Education Cloud (IWEEC 2013) Chairs' Message

The International Workshop on E-book and Education Cloud is aimed at bringing together professionals and researchers who are interested in recent trends in E-books and their connection to Education Clouds. The research papers on exploring the system effectiveness and learning performance of using E-book with teaching and learning strategies on diverse web-based learning environments are particularly welcome.

With the advance of networking, a variety of web applications have emerged on the education field, such as web 2.0, mobile learning, ubiquitous learning, and cloud learning. In response to the prevalence of cloud applications, mobile learning with cloud services has created a new era of e-learning. This new type of mobile learning has further been fueled by diversified handheld devices, which provides a platform for a variety of courseware or e-books. The emergence of cloud services improves the accessibility to information, of which, learning contents can be downloaded through various E-book platforms. This new e-learning infrastructure could impact current e-learning environments. Although some studies have revealed the possibility of coupling e-book learning environments with education clouds, more intensive investigations on the feasibility and evaluations are required. This workshop aims to provide researchers an interactive discussion and hopefully open a new window for the future development of web-based learning. After review, we selected five quality papers in IWEEC 2013, respectively, for presentation covering various aspects of E-book and Education Cloud.

We appreciate the interest and support of all attendees. In particular, we thank the ICWL organizers. The great success of the workshop is indebted to the hard work of all Program Committee members. We also thank all the authors for their contributions.

December 2013

Ting-Ting Wu

# Organization

## IWEEC 2013 Workshop Chairs

| | |
|---|---|
| Ting-Ting Wu | Chia Nan University of Pharmacy and Science, Taiwan |

## IWEEC 2013 Workshop Co-chairs

| | |
|---|---|
| Dunwei Wen | Athabasca University, Canada |

## IWEEC 2013 Program Committee

| | |
|---|---|
| Gwo-Jen Hwang | National Taiwan University of Science and Technology, Taiwan |
| Hong-Ren Chen | National Taichung University of Education, Taiwan |
| Hui-Chun Chu | Soochow University, Taiwan |
| Ming-Chi Liu | National Cheng Kung University, Taiwan |
| Narzikul Shadiev | Samarkand State University, Uzbekistan |
| Qing Tan | Athabasca University, Canada |
| Rustam Shadiev | National Cheng Kung University, Taiwan |
| Shu-Chen Cheng | Southern Taiwan University of Science and Technology, Taiwan |
| Tien-Wen Sung | Hsing Kuo University, Taiwan |
| Zhi-Yuan Su | Chia Nan University of Pharmacy and Science, Taiwan |

# Contents

## International Workshop on E-Book and Education Cloud



## International Workshop on Cloud Computing for Web-Based Learning

## International Workshop on Smart Living and Learning

# International Workshop on Web Intelligence and Learning

# A Web-Based Virtual Lab Platform for Algorithm Learning

Yu Sheng(✉), Wei Zhou, and Jianxin Wang

School of Information Science and Engineering,
Central South University, Changsha, China
{shengyu, zhouweicsu, jxwang}@csu.edu.cn

**Abstract.** Due to the complex in building experiment environment, difficulty to analysis correctness and performance of algorithm in algorithm design experiment in information science courses. In this paper, a web-based virtual lab platform for algorithm learning was designed and developed. In this platform, each resource will be packaged as a web-service, student is able to submit source code of their algorithm developed by multi-programming language to the server and choose corresponding virtual experiment component to build experiment process for testing their algorithm. This platform will enable student to concentrate on the design and optimization of the algorithm. In the last, a virtual experiment system of digital image processing illustrates the effectiveness of the platform.

**Keywords:** Virtual lab platform · Algorithm learning · Heterogeneous resources · Web service

## 1 Introduction

Experimentation is very important for algorithm learning in computer science curricula, which can give students a opportunity to understand how these algorithms work, and to prove the algorithm they redesigned in both functionality and performance. Experiment is a key to an engaging learning experience. However, there are few specified environments for experiment in algorithm design courses. Students need to spend a lot of time to set up the experimental environment by using a program language, even so they are difficult to prove the correctness of the algorithm and analysis of the performance of the algorithm.

Our contributions in this paper are as follows: we proposed a new method to solve those problems in traditional algorithm experiments. Second, due to the use of web-service and Java applet, the platform is easy-to-use for students at any time and in any place. Third, the platform provides a easy way to integrate a variety of heterogeneous resources, Last but not least, the platform provides a high flexibility and high interactivity.

## 2 Related Work

In traditional experiment model, students' algorithm experiment is implemented by two ways: first, student uses a program language such as C, C++, Java to implement, improve and design algorithm of the course, which is a flexible way for algorithm


D.K.W. Chiu et al. (Eds.): ICWL 2013 Workshops, LNCS 8390, pp. 3–10, 2015.
DOI: 10.1007/978-3-662-46315-4_1

experiment. However, students need to spend much time on building development environment. This process will become more complex especially when the need for third part software (such as Matlab). In this mode, it is difficult for students to concentrate on the design and analysis of algorithms. And the students are also difficult to judge whether the algorithm is correct and analysis the performance of the algorithm. Another method is to use Multisim, LabVIEW software to simulation [1]. In this model, students don't have to spend a lot of time to set up the experimental environment. However, this experiment software is generally used in the laboratory computer and students need to learn another program language.

Virtual lab is a hardware and software operating environment which is used for replacing part of or all of the operating steps for traditional experiment. At present, many scholars have done a lot of research on virtual laboratory. In April 2010, Science introduce an introductory chemistry virtual laboratory, Yaron et al. have established a online general chemistry virtual laboratory [2], students can freely choose chemical instruments and reagents chemical experiment in the this laboratory. Bal et al. have established a virtual laboratory of a switched reluctance motor which use of LabView as a user interface and invoke Matlab through the Matlab & Simulink [3]. Li et al. have developed a distributed intrusion detection system based on the virtual machine, and analyzed the experimental results of different virtual machine environment [4]. Li et al. have established a physical virtual experiment, which private virtual experiments of electron, optics and pulley [5]. Our group have done much research and established some virtual lab systems [6–8].

## 3 Platform Design

In this section, we first introduce the design criteria of such a experiment platform for algorithm study, and then introduce the architecture of our platform. The key technical challenges will be presented in the next section.

### 3.1 Design Criteria

The primary goal of our platform is to provide a convenient, flexible and easy to use experiment environment for students' algorithm study, where experimentation has been considered as a key to their learning. As a new solution for algorithm experimentation, the platform must solve those problems in traditional experimentation model. To achieve this goal, we have defined a list of criteria for the platform.

**Open and convenient:** First, the platform must be open to students in 7*24 model, so, when a student has a new idea, he can design and test their idea at any time. Second, the platform should be convenient for the students, thus they don't need to install any software for the experiment.

**Innovative:** The platform should not just provide a replication experiment model for the students. Students should be able to choose the experiment element and set up the experiment process according to the needs of their experiment. They also should be able to design their own algorithm and submit the algorithm the platform for testing and analyzing.

**Visualized:** The platform should provide visual experiment result for students, therefore they can determine the correctness of the algorithm intuitively and compare with the classical algorithm.

## 3.2 Architecture of the Platform

To meet these criteria, this paper uses the Java language development and implementation platform, uses JavaBean technology to develop homogeneous components, encapsulates the heterogeneous components using Web service technology. Its architecture is shown in Fig. 1.

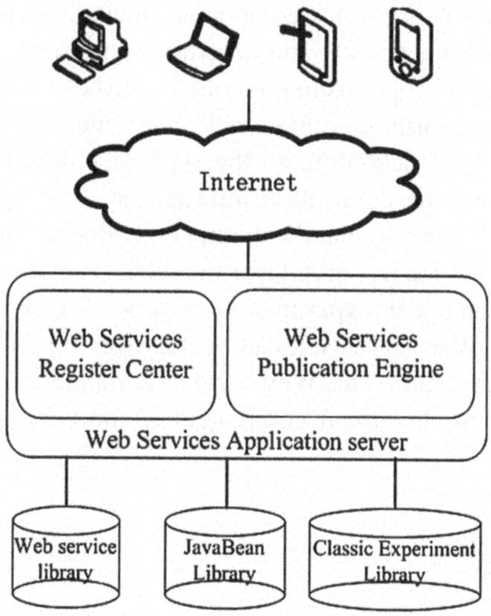


**Fig. 1.** The architecture of virtual laboratory platform

JavaBean components running on the client, which has a higher running efficiency, mainly used for the realization of user and system input and display on the client experiment results and other functions; Web service component is mainly used for the packaging of heterogeneous resources. The virtual experimental platform based on B/S architecture model, consisting of the Applet client, Web server and distributed Web service resources three parts.

Java Applet client provides a graphical interface to the user, through which the user interact with the platform. Users can use it directly through the browser client. After the client starts, it request description information of all the virtual experiment instrument from the service through the network, and use the description information to dynamically update the virtual experiment instrument list. In the platform, users can create a virtual instrument by dragging the mouse, and add the connection line between the virtual instruments to create an experimental process. When the user selects a virtual instrument, the parameters of that instrument can be set or modified in the component parameter configuration panel, and the description of component information can be illustrated in view of virtual instrument panel. After setting the parameters of virtual instrument, the user can start executing experiments and get the results. The platform also provides some functionality, such as preservation experiment, loading experiment, creating experiment and opening a classic experiment. More importantly, the platform provides multiple interface for Web services publishing, users can submit their algorithm source code to platform, the source code will be automatically published as a Web service, and integrated with the current platform.

The Web server provides the Java Applet application, configuration files and other resources for the client, including the service registry and service publishing engine. When the user login to the client, it will obtain the applet application and supporting files from the server. Service registration center saves the description information of JavaBean component and Web service component, including component classification information, the address for accessing and description information. The client starts, to service register center. Service publishing engine publishes the Web services for users. When the user submits algorithm source code from client, the engine automatically publish it as a Web service according to the type of programming language of the source code, and registers the description information of Web service to the service center and pushes to the client, so that the client can update component information list immediately. The Web service resource layer includes Web service component library, JavaBean library and classical experimental library. The Web service component library is a collection of Web services, it can be deployed on different servers to reduce the single server load pressure. The Web service component is the encapsulation of heterogeneous component, JavaBean component is the component encapsulation of Java class.

# 4 Key Technology

## 4.1 Package of Heterogeneous Resource

The Web service communicates through the Internet and SOAP protocol, thus it has strong portability and interoperability. It provides services and resources through the interface, shielding the difference between heterogeneous systems, so as to realize the encapsulation and invocation of heterogeneous resources. When students do experiment of the algorithm courses, they often use a variety of programming language and development tools, such as OpenCV, C/C++, Java and MATLAB etc. In order to realize the communication between the heterogeneous components, the platform using Web services technology to encapsulate them as Web service. As the norm of releasing and invoking of the Web service, The Web service solves the interoperability between heterogeneous components effectively. In order to illustrate the mechanism of service encapsulation of heterogeneous components, the MATLAB module is used for illustrating the process of heterogeneous resources automatic package released.

MATLAB is a scientific computing software. It has powerful computer data processing capabilities, superior graphics rendering and processing capabilities. But it need a specific running environment and is difficult to integrate with other software. Packing MATLAB program is an effective way to solve this problem. But there is no way for packing MATLAB program as web service. An advanced programming language is used as a bridge for the transfer. C/C++ is a most popular language for calling MATLAB.

There are three kinds of interfaces between C/C++ and MATLAB: MEX file, MAT file applications and engine application. The engine application mode is used for the mixed programming in our platform. In this mode, MATLAB is running as a background engine and can be started by the C/C++ program by the engine interface. The MATLAB program will be called by the library file in the engine. There are some common engine library files: engOpen(Open the engine), engClose(Close the engine), engPutVariable(transfer data to MATLAB engine), engGetVariable(Get data from MATLAB engine), engEvalString(Call a MATLAB function). The data type of C/C++ is different of MATLAB's. There is a data type named mxArray is used to indicate the MATLAB data in C/C++. The mxCreateXXX and mxDestroyArray function are also provided for the creating and destroying of data in mxArray type. The MATLAB program can be packaged as a C/C++ component in this way. Then the C/C++ component can be published as a Web service easily.

The gSoap is used as the running environment of C/C++. Firstly, a C/C++ head file is created, which contains the service name, calling method, encoding mode, naming space, etc. Then, the function declaration will be extracted from the C/C++ component and be stored in the head file according to the gSoap format. Assume the name of the header files for ws.h. Then soapcpp2 command provide by gSoap create the files for service publication with ws.h file. Such files will be created: soapC.cpp, soapH.h, soapServer.cpp, soapStub.h, soapObject.h, ws.nsmap. The C/C++ component is also need to modify according to the gSoap format. Lastly, those files and C/C++ component will be compiled by the C/C++ compiler. A CGI file will be created and conFig. to Tomcat. The user can call the Web service supported by MATLAB through CGI.

## 4.2 Scheduling Mechanism in the Platform

In the virtual experiment platform client, the user chooses the virtual experiment instrument components to build an experiment flow by connecting those components. In an experimental flow, various virtual instruments build an organic whole by the connection between them. The connection relationships between components are very complex, in order to ensure the efficient implementation of the order, it is necessary to design a reasonable experimental operation mechanism. In an experimental flow, each virtual experiment device can be abstracted as a node of a, connection between the two pins can be abstracted as a directed edge. In the directed graph, for each node, only all of its parent nodes have executed, transmitted the data to it, it can execute. The Web service components requires mutually data transmission, if A, B are Web service components, A is the parent node of B. WA, WB are Web services corresponding to them. A sends a SOAP request to WA according to the interface information and parameters of service. WA sends SOAP response data back to A after treatment. Then A sends the data to B, B also sends a SOAP request data to the WB according to the interface information and parameters of service, WB sends SOAP response data back to B after treatment. In the whole process, the data are transported between the client and the server four times. Based on analysis, the data transmission can be reduced to two times. A and B can build a Web service composition. If the client request execution of Web service composition, the information for executing will be sent to the server. After the server receives the request, WA and WB will execute in turn, and then returns the results to the client. The execution steps of the experiment process based on combinatorial optimization is shown as follow:

Step 1: check if the experimental topology is empty. If it is empty, the execution flow end;

Step 2: get the experimental component from experimental topology in accordance with the topological order, determine the type of experimental components, if the component is a Web service component, continue with step 1; if the component is a local components, then go to step 3;

Step 3: determine if the local components have precursor. If there is the precursor, go to step 4; otherwise, execute a local component, remove the node from the experimental topology, go to step 1;

Step 4: get all precursor node of local component to build a Web service components list, and delete the precursor node from the experimental topology;

Step 5: build a list of Web service components according to step 4 and send to server;

Step 6: execute the local component according to the results returned by the server, and remove the node from the experimental topology, go to step 1.

## 5 Running Instance

A Butterworth low pass filter experiment in digital signal processing course is used to illustrate the experimental process of the virtual experiment system in this paper.

Firstly, we choose a variety of experimental components required by the experiment. According to the experimental requirements, we selected two cosine wave generators from the signal source component library, and a signal filter (FIR) from the signal processing component library, a Bart low-pass filter coefficient generator and FIR frequency response, and a number of graphics display module from the graphics display component library. Then we connect those components according to the experiment flow. The experiment built by students is shown as Fig. 2.

Secondly, we set the parameter of those components. If an experiment component was clicked by the mouse, its parameter will be shown in the right side of the windows. The user can set the parameter after click on it. In this paper, the parameters of a generator module is set by the table. Its frequency is set to 16, the sampling frequency is set to 64, the phase value is set to 0.

Finally, we execute the experimental process. The result of this experiment will be shown in the experiment result panel. Two input signal waveform were shown in

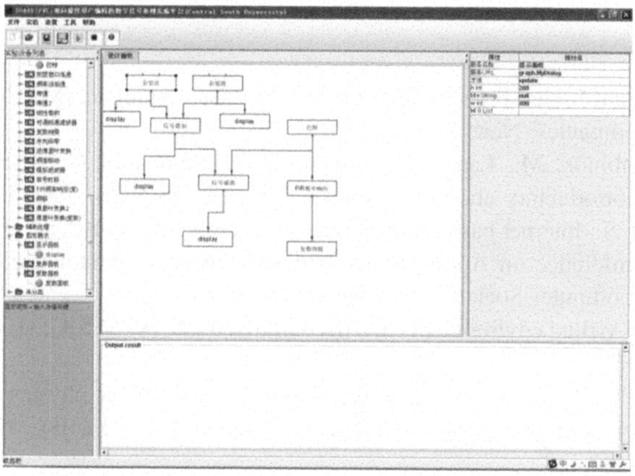


**Fig. 2.** Butterworth LPF experiment

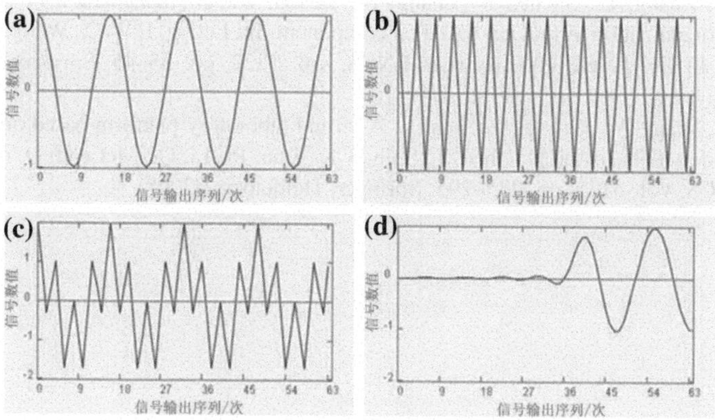


**Fig. 3.** Experiment results

Fig. 3(a), (b), the mixed waveform of two input signal was shown in Fig. 3(c), the waveform filtered by Butterworth low-pass filter was shown in Fig. 3(d).

## 6 Conclusions

This paper has proposed a web-based virtual lab platform for algorithm learning according to those problems existing in traditional experiment mode for algorithm learning. The application and using effect have been illustrated by the digital signal processing experiment system. The platform can provide an algorithm experiment environment for the students, so that students can integrate the algorithm their designed to the platform and analysis of detection and performance without complex configuration of development environment.

## References


1. Mitra, S.K.: Digital Signal Processing-A Computer Based Approach[M], 2nd edn., pp. 1–40. Mcgraw-Hill Companies, New York (2001)
2. Yaron, D., Karabinos, M., Lange, D., Greeno, J.G., Leinhardt, G.: The ChemCollective-virtual labs for introductory chemistry courses. Science **328**(5978), 584–585 (2010)
3. Bal, G., Bayhan, S.: Internet based virtual electric machine lab: switched reluctance motor. In: International Conference on Application of Information and Communication Technologies, pp. 1–5. IEEE Computer Society, Tashkent (2010)
4. Li, P.: Exploring virtual environments in a decentralized lab. ACM SIGITE Res. IT **1**(6), 4–10 (2009)
5. Li, L., Zheng, Y., Zhong, S.: IWVL: a web-based virtual lab for physics teaching in junior high schools. In: Computing and Intelligent Systems. vol. 233, pp. 192–199. Springer, Heidelberg (2011)
6. Sheng, Y., Wang, J., Wang, W., Liu, L.: Design and implementation of collaboration support in virtual experiment environment. In: Luo, X., Spaniol, M., Wang, L., Li, Q., Nejdl, W., Zhang, W. (eds.) ICWL 2010. LNCS, vol. 6483, pp. 399–403. Springer, Heidelberg (2010)
7. Wang, Y., Zhang, L., Sheng, Y., Zhang, H.: Design and implementation of principles of computer organization virtual lab based on component. In: Leung, E.W.C., Wang, F.L., Miao, L., Zhao, J., He, J. (eds.) WBL 2008. LNCS, vol. 5328, pp. 35–45. Springer, Heidelberg (2008)
8. Sheng, Y., Wang, W., Wang, J., Chen, J.: A virtual laboratory platform based on integration of java and matlab. In: Li, F., Zhao, J., Shih, T.K., Lau, R., Li, Q., McLeod, D. (eds.) ICWL 2008. LNCS, vol. 5145, pp. 285–295. Springer, Heidelberg (2008)

# A Genetic Algorithm-Based Multiple Characteristics Grouping Strategy for Collaborative Learning

Hui-Wen Tien[1], Yu-Shih Lin[1], Yi-Chun Chang[2(✉)], and Chih-Ping Chu[1]

[1] Department of Computer Science and Information Engineering, National Cheng Kung University, Tainan, Taiwan (R.O.C)
[2] Department of Computer Science and Information Engineering, HungKuang University, Taichung, Taiwan (R.O.C)
changyc@sunrise.hk.edu.tw

**Abstract.** Literatures have indicated that well-balanced groups facilitate students' learning performance in collaborative learning environments. For instructors, to construct well-balanced groups needs to take efforts and time to consider large number of students and characteristics. Hence, how to automatically construct well-balanced collaborative learning groups has been a popular issue for collaborative learning. This paper proposes a genetic algorithm (GA)-based grouping strategy to assist instructors in constructing inter-homogeneous and intra-heterogeneous collaborative learning groups considering multiple student characteristics. Several data sets with different problem sizes, such as number of students and characteristics, are employed as experimental materials. Experimental results have demonstrated that the proposed grouping method is effective, efficient and robust.

**Keywords:** Collaborative learning · Well-balanced groups · Genetic algorithm (GA) · Multi-objective optimization

## 1 Introduction

Collaborative learning is defined as learners learning together in order to solve problems and accomplish common goals [1], which has validated as one useful technique to enhance students' learning performance in education context [2–4]. Further, adequate groups can assist learners to promote their learning performance through the interactions of group members [5–7]. Numerous researches have indicated the factors that influence collaborative learning success, including inter-group homogeneity, intra-group heterogeneity, grouping criteria and so on [8–10]. The grouping criterion contains different grouping characteristics of students, such as knowledge level, leadership, gender, and so on [10–13]. That is, how to construct adequate groups is one of the important issues in collaborative learning.

Since the number of students and characteristics become larger which results in that grouping problem is harder to solve by instructors, the consideration for all the student characteristics becomes a multi-objective problem. Hence, to cope the aforementioned


D.K.W. Chiu et al. (Eds.): ICWL 2013 Workshops, LNCS 8390, pp. 11–22, 2015.
DOI: 10.1007/978-3-662-46315-4_2

problems, this paper proposes a grouping strategy which adopts Genetic algorithm (GA) [11, 14, 15] with Technique for Order Performance by Similarity to Ideal Solution (TOPSIS) [7, 16] to achieve inter-homogeneous and intra-heterogeneous collaborative learning groups. The reasons adopting GA with TOPSIS in this paper is that GA with TOPSIS is one suitable method to solve grouping problems for multiple objectives problems. Besides, the proposed grouping strategy can facilitate instructors to obtain a better grouping result within a reasonable computation time, even for large scale problems. To evaluate the performance and robustness of the proposed strategy, several experiments with different problem sizes have also been conducted to compare the proposed method with other competing strategies.

The rest of this paper is organized as follows. Section 2 introduces the basic concepts of GA and TOPSIS. Section 3 describes the mathematical and algorithmic formulation of the proposed grouping strategy. Section 4 analyzes the results with different problem sizes. Section 5 presents the conclusions of the proposed strategy.

## 2 Related Work

This section describes the basic concepts of Genetic algorithm (GA), and Technique for Order Performance by Similarity to Ideal Solution (TOPSIS).

GA is proposed by Holland in 1975 [17]. The spirit of GA is "natural selection and survival of the fittest", and it has been widespread used in many complex optimization problems. GA comprises several components processing including chromosome encode, initial population, fitness evaluation and three genetic operator including selection operator, crossover operator and mutation operator. Each operation is detailed in the following section.

TOPSIS is proposed by Hwang and Yoon in 1981 [18]. TOPSIS has solved many decision making multi-objective problems. The procedure of TOPSIS can be described in the following four steps [19, 20]:

Step 1. Constructs a $I \times Q$ decision matrix with respect to $I$ alternatives and $Q$ criteria

Step 2. Determines the positive-ideal solution and negative-ideal solution

Step 3. Uses the m-dimensional Euclidean distance to compute two measures

Step 4. Computes the relative closeness to the ideal solution

## 3 The Proposed Strategy

The details of different components and main features of the proposed method will be shown in this section. Of them one special component focuses on pre-categorizing all students in order to ensure the quality of intra-heterogeneous groups. The other components include the encoding of solutions, initial population, fitness function, the selection, crossover, and mutation. The final subsection describes the elitism. Figure 1 presents the flow of the proposed method.

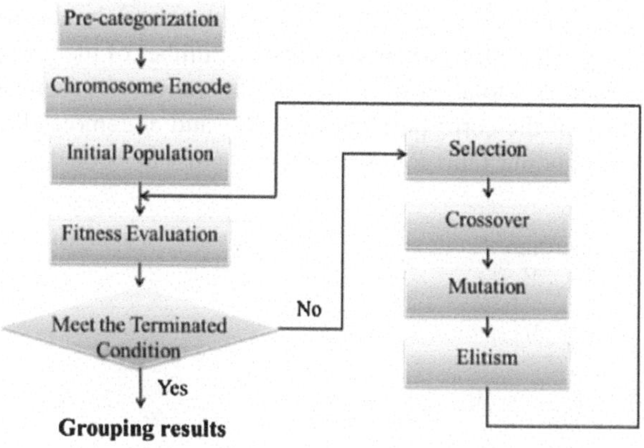


**Fig. 1.** The main flow of the proposed method

### 3.1 Pre-categorizing

To evaluate all features, each characteristic of a student in a class must be a numerical value. However, each characteristic may have different values spreading in a range, which includes following steps:

Step 1. Normalizing every considered characteristic should be taken. After normalization, every characteristic is fitted between 0 and 1. It is calculated as following:

$$Z_{sq} = \frac{X_{sq} - X_q^{min}}{X_q^{max} - X_q^{min}} \tag{1}$$

Step 2. The characteristics of each student are calculated to obtain their represented value $P_s$ which represents their overall performance in the class with $S$ students

Step 3. The mean value $\bar{P}$ and standard deviation $P^{\sigma}$ of the class are derived from all students' $P_s$ value in the class

Step 4. Three categories $L_i$, where $1 \le i \le 3$, which represent low, medium and high performance of the students were divided based on the mean $\bar{P}$ and the standard deviation $P^{\sigma}$. The concept is expressed as Eq. (2) and $N_s$ is denoted as a student, where $1 \le s \le S$

$$\begin{aligned} L_1 &= \{N_s | P_s < \bar{P} - P^{\sigma}\} \\ L_2 &= \{N_s | \bar{P} - P^{\sigma} \le P_s \le \bar{P} + P^{\sigma}\} \\ L_3 &= \{N_s | \bar{P} + P^{\sigma} < P_s\} \end{aligned} \tag{2}$$

Step 5. The number of students in three categories are calculated to obtain their respective ratio $R_{L_i}$, where $1 \le i \le 3$, for the summation fitting the instructor's assignment in which each group has $M$ members. The operations for calculating ratio of three categories is expressed in the following *Ratio-calculating* Algorithm, where $N_{L_i}$ denotes number of members in category $L_i$. Let *TE* denotes total error value of the ratio, $CP_i$ denotes the carrying probability of the corresponding ratio $R_{L_i}$, and $\varepsilon_i$ demotes the carry value of the corresponding ratio $R_{L_i}$, where the $\varepsilon_i$ must be 1 or 0

**Ratio-calculating Algorithm**

Input : $N_{L_1}, N_{L_2}, N_{L_3}, M$

$R_{L_i} = \left\lfloor \frac{N_{L_i}}{\sum_{j=1}^{3} N_{L_j}} M \right\rfloor, where\ 1 \le i \le 3$

$TE = \sum_{i=1}^{3} \left( \frac{N_{L_i}}{\sum_{j=1}^{3} N_{L_j}} M - \left\lfloor \frac{N_{L_i}}{\sum_{j=1}^{3} N_{L_j}} M \right\rfloor \right), CP_i = \frac{N_{L_i}}{\sum_{j=1}^{3} N_{L_j}} M - R_{L_i}$

Let $f: \{1, 2, 3\} \rightarrow \{1, 2, 3\}$ be a function, where $N_{L_{f(1)}} \le N_{L_{f(2)}} \le N_{L_{f(3)}}$

for $j$=1→2 do

  if $R_{L_{f(j)}} = 0$

    $\varepsilon_{f(j)} = 1$

    $R_{L_{f(k)}} = \left\lfloor \frac{N_{L_{f(k)}}}{\sum_{l=j+1}^{3} N_{L_{f(l)}}} \times \left(M - \sum_{l=1}^{j} \varepsilon_{f(l)}\right) \right\rfloor$, where $j < k \le 3$

    $TE = \sum_{k=j+1}^{3} \left( \frac{N_{L_{f(k)}}}{\sum_{l=j+1}^{3} N_{L_{f(l)}}} \times \left(M - \sum_{l=1}^{j} \varepsilon_{f(l)}\right) - R_{L_{f(k)}} \right)$

    $CP_{f(k)} = \frac{N_{L_{f(k)}}}{\sum_{l=j+1}^{3} N_{L_{f(l)}}} \times \left(M - \sum_{l=1}^{j} \varepsilon_{f(l)}\right) - R_{L_{f(k)}}$, for $j < k \le 3$

  else if $TE > 0$ then

    $\varepsilon_{f(j)}$ with a probability $CP_j$ is 1, otherwise is 0

    $TE = TE - \varepsilon_{f(j)}$

$\varepsilon_{f(3)} = TE$

$R_{L_i} = R_{L_i} + \varepsilon_i$ , for $1 \le i \le 3$

Output : $R_{L_1}, R_{L_2}, R_{L_3}$

Furthermore, the students are sorted into three new categories $L_i'$, where $1 \le i \le 3$, according to the ratio shown in Eq. (3), where $N_s'$ denotes sorted students in ascending order.

$$
\begin{aligned}
L_1' &= \left\{ N_s' \middle| 1 \le s \le \left\lfloor \frac{S}{M} \right\rfloor R_{L_1} \right\} \\
L_2' &= \left\{ N_s' \middle| \left\lfloor \frac{S}{M} \right\rfloor R_{L_1} \le s \le \left\lfloor \frac{S}{M} \right\rfloor (R_{L_1} + R_{L_2}) + S \bmod M \right\} \\
L_3' &= \left\{ N_s' \middle| \left\lfloor \frac{S}{M} \right\rfloor (R_{L_1} + R_{L_2}) + S \bmod M \le s \le \left\lfloor \frac{S}{M} \right\rfloor (R_{L_1} + R_{L_2} + R_{L_3}) + S \bmod M \right\}
\end{aligned} \tag{3}
$$

### 3.2 Encoding of the Solution and Initial Population

In GA, a chromosome, i.e. an individual, represents a feasible solution for problem. An individual with S students is represented by a matrix. The number of columns in the matrix corresponds to M members of each group and the number of rows corresponds to G groups. If there are S mod M remainder students, there will be S mod M groups having M + 1 members.

An individual

| Level 1 | Level 2 | Level 3 |
|---|---|---|
| 1 2 | 3 4 5 | 6 7 |
| 8 9 | 10 11 | 12 13 |
| 14 15 | 16 17 | 18 19 |

**Fig. 2.** An example of an individual

In initial population stage, the students are randomly assigned to their corresponding levels according to the ratios of three categories. Hence, each group has three categories members with the ratios. An example of an individual is shown in Fig. 2. The Levels 1, 2 and 3 collect the students belonging to categories $L_1$, $L_2$ and $L_3$, respectively.

### 3.3 Fitness Evaluation

The main goal of the proposed method is to obtain inter-homogeneous and intra-heterogeneous groups. Therefore, it is important to define an adequate evaluation to fit the main goal. In this paper, the fitness evaluation is for evaluating the fitness value of individuals with Q characteristics. The grouping problem is to optimally assign S students, each with Q characteristics, to G groups. To address the problem, a fitness value $F_i$ was shown in Eq. (4), where $\overline{GP}$, $GP^{\sigma}$ and $\omega$ respectively denote the mean value of all groups of an individual, the standard deviation of all groups of an individual, and the weight of $\overline{GP}$ and $GP^{\sigma}$. In Eq. (4), $GP_g$ denotes the relative closeness to the ideal solution for the gth group of an individual, where $1 \leq g \leq G$. Equation (5) expresses the mathematical formulation of $GP_g$, where $W_q$, $E_g$ and $Z^g_{s,q}$ respectively denote the weight of criteria q, the number of members in the gth group, and the value of the qth criterion of the sth learner of the gth group of an individual. The ideal value of $V_q^+$ and $V_q^-$ must be 1 or 0 according to the criteria q, $1 \leq q \leq Q$.

$$F_i = \omega \cdot \overline{GP} + (1-\omega) \cdot (1 - GP^{\sigma}),$$
$$\textit{where } \overline{GP} = \frac{\sum_{g=1}^{G} GP_g}{G} \quad \textit{and} \quad GP^{\sigma} = \sqrt{\frac{\sum_{g=1}^{G} \left(GP_g - \overline{GP}\right)^2}{G-1}} \tag{4}$$

$$GP_g = \frac{\sqrt{\sum_{q=1}^{Q}\left(\frac{\sum_{s=1}^{E_g} Z_{s,q}^{g}}{E_g} - V_q^{-}\right)^2 \cdot W_q}}{\sqrt{\sum_{q=1}^{Q}\left(\frac{\sum_{s=1}^{E_g} Z_{s,q}^{g}}{E_g} - V_q^{+}\right)^2 \cdot W_q} + \sqrt{\sum_{q=1}^{Q}\left(\frac{\sum_{s=1}^{E_g} Z_{s,q}^{g}}{E_g} - V_q^{-}\right)^2 \cdot W_q}}, \quad (5)$$

$$where\ E_g = \begin{cases} M+1, g \leq S\ mod\ M \\ M, \quad others \end{cases}$$

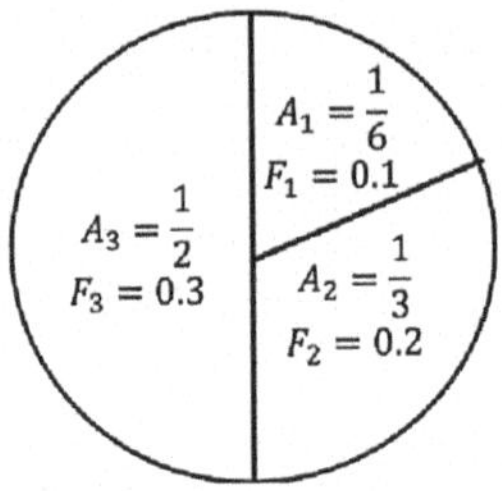


**Fig. 3.** Roulette wheel example

### 3.4 Selection Operator

The objective of selection operator is selecting the better individuals from current population to ensure the more suitable individuals can be preserved in next generation. Roulette wheel selection mechanism [21] is employed in this paper. Figure 3 presents an example of Roulette wheel. An individual i of current population has a portion $A_i$ of all areas in the roulette according to their fitness value $F_i$ and has a random probability to select the corresponding individual in next generation. The larger proportion an individual has in the area, the more probability it can be preserved in next generation.

### 3.5 Crossover Operator

The goal of crossover operator is interchanging genes of individuals to recombine features. C1 operator is one of the famous crossover operator [22]. One version of C1 operator [10] is modified to fit the chromosome data structure in this proposed strategy. There are two steps in the proposed version. Firstly, chooses two parents with crossover probability $P_c$ to do crossover and randomly generates crossover points for each group. Next, offspring preserves the corresponding parent's left part of genes according to the crossover point of each row while the right part of genes are derived from the order of genes in different levels of the other parent.

### 3.6 Mutation Operator

The goal of mutation operator is altering genes to reproduce new individuals [23]. The mutation operator includes two steps in the proposed strategy. In the first step, each level has a probability $P_l$ to do mutation. In the second steps, if a level is selected then two genes are randomly chosen to swap in the selected level.

### 3.7 Elitism

In this stage, the proposed strategy uses the elitist schema to select the best individual to replace the worst one from the population in generation k. Therefore, it can be sure that the population is better in generation $k + 1$ than in generation k and the best individual will be kept in $k + 1$ generation.

## 4 Experiments and Discussions

This paper employs several data sets, such as number of students and characteristics, with different problem sizes as experimental materials to analyze the solution quality, executing time, search speed and stability. Subsect. 4.1 describes the experimental setting. Subsect. 4.2 compares the performance including execution time and search speed of the proposed strategy with other competing methods. Subsect. 4.3 analyzes the solution quality of the proposed strategy. Subsect. 4.4 presents the analyses of robustness.

### 4.1 Experimental Setting

All experiments run on a laptop computer with an Intel Core i7, 2.10 GHz processor, 4 GB RAM using C programming language in CodeBlocks environments. There are five students in each group. The probability of crossover is set to 0.85, the probability $P_l$ is set to 0.15, the population size is set to 20 and the number of generation is set to 100. Each scenario is run 100 times for calculating the average fitness value of the 100 runs in order to get the objective representation of fitness value and execution time of each data set. There are different problem sizes of simulated (uniformly distribution) data sets with four characteristics to compare among random, GA [10] and the proposed method. The first and the second characteristics are set to positive features while the third and the fourth are set to negative features. Each weight of characteristic is set to 0.5.

### 4.2 Performance Comparisons

For random, GA and the proposed strategy, Tables 1 and 2 present the performance results with different number of students and characteristics, where the performance contains fitness value and execution time. Table 1 shows that random method can save more execution time than GA and the proposed method, but it has poorer fitness value than the others with different number of students. In addition, the proposed strategy can use less execution time to obtain the nearer optimal solution than GA method. Table 2 shows that no matter what the number of characteristics is, the proposed strategy is more effective

**Table 1.** Compare the performance among random, GA, and the proposed strategy with increasing number of students

| Number of students | Random | | GA | | The proposed method | |
|---|---|---|---|---|---|---|
| | Fitness value | Execution time | Fitness value | Execution time | Fitness value | Execution time |
| 50 | 0.777272 | 0.00024 | 0.786725 | 0.02818 | 0.787620 | 0.02511 |
| 100 | 0.775255 | 0.00037 | 0.780705 | 0.09021 | 0.783649 | 0.08892 |
| 150 | 0.778487 | 0.00065 | 0.782882 | 0.20064 | 0.786500 | 0.18539 |
| 300 | 0.776038 | 0.00124 | 0.778784 | 0.72348 | 0.783061 | 0.70643 |
| 500 | 0.778968 | 0.00227 | 0.780785 | 2.13675 | 0.785084 | 2.02228 |

**Table 2.** Compare the performance among random, GA, and the proposed strategy with increasing number of characteristics

| Number of characteristics | Random | | GA | | The proposed method | |
|---|---|---|---|---|---|---|
| | Fitness value | Execution time | Fitness value | Execution time | Fitness value | Execution time |
| 10 | 0.680890 | 0.00054 | 0.702620 | 0.03272 | 0.704872 | 0.02982 |
| 20 | 0.689808 | 0.00083 | 0.704013 | 0.04073 | 0.705553 | 0.03615 |
| 30 | 0.696040 | 0.00100 | 0.707440 | 0.04616 | 0.708749 | 0.04256 |
| 50 | 0.694084 | 0.00152 | 0.702103 | 0.06355 | 0.702952 | 0.05873 |

than the other two. To sum, the proposed strategy has the most effective than the other two methods.

Furthermore, in order to compare the search speed of the proposed strategy with GA method, Fig. 4 presents the variations of optimal fitness value within 1000 generations. It shows the proposed strategy is more efficient than GA because that when the optimal fitness value is set to 0.787, the proposed strategy needs 54 generations and GA needs 340 generations to evolution. In other words, GA will spend more time and efforts to get the same fitness value than the proposed strategy.

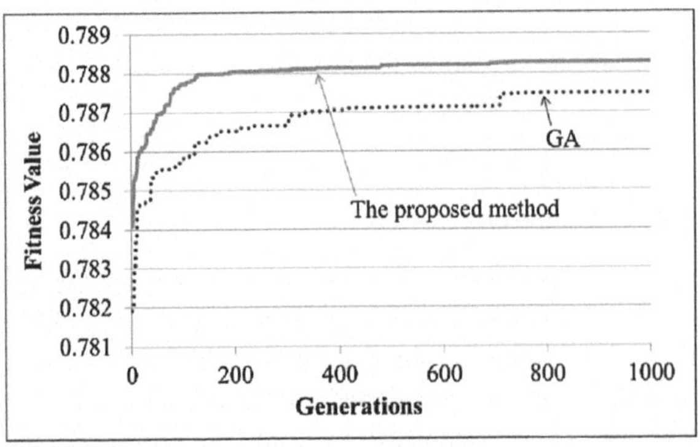


**Fig. 4.** Evolution of optimal fitness of 50 students with GA and the proposed strategy

## 4.3 Comparison of Grouping Results

In this subsection, to compare the grouping results of three methods, Tables 3 and 4 present the standard deviation of the inter-groups and intra-groups against different number of students and characteristics. Table 3 shows that despite different number of students, the proposed method always has smaller standard deviation of inter-groups and larger standard deviation of intra-groups than the random and GA methods. Table 4 shows that no matter what number of characteristics is the standard deviation of inter-groups and intra-groups of the proposed method is better than random and GA methods. In other words, the proposed method has better grouping results than random and GA methods against different number of characteristics.

**Table 3.** Compare standard deviation of inter-groups and intra-group among random, GA, and the proposed strategy with increasing number of students

| Number of students | Random | | GA | | The proposed method | |
|---|---|---|---|---|---|---|
| | Inter-SD | Intra-SD | Inter-SD | Intra-SD | Inter-SD | Intra-SD |
| 50 | 0.021734 | 0.314234 | 0.003427 | 0.355971 | 0.001648 | 0.359978 |
| 100 | 0.018829 | 0.276894 | 0.008167 | 0.304798 | 0.002329 | 0.316636 |
| 150 | 0.018885 | 0.273964 | 0.010420 | 0.300004 | 0.003312 | 0.315074 |
| 300 | 0.019386 | 0.284001 | 0.014084 | 0.302678 | 0.005690 | 0.323426 |
| 500 | 0.017681 | 0.260933 | 0.014189 | 0.273619 | 0.005806 | 0.296865 |

Note: Inter-SD: standard deviation of inter-groups; Intra-SD: standard deviation of intra-groups.

**Table 4.** Compare standard deviation of inter-groups and intra-group among random, GA, and the proposed strategy with increasing number of characteristics

| Number of characteristics | Random | | GA | | The proposed method | |
|---|---|---|---|---|---|---|
| | Inter-SD | Intra-SD | Inter-SD | Intra-SD | Inter-SD | Intra-SD |
| 10 | 0.049219 | 0.088284 | 0.007302 | 0.099160 | 0.003085 | 0.102605 |
| 20 | 0.032909 | 0.059400 | 0.005383 | 0.064895 | 0.002398 | 0.067735 |
| 30 | 0.026397 | 0.050038 | 0.004316 | 0.055073 | 0.001742 | 0.057069 |
| 50 | 0.018552 | 0.033570 | 0.003243 | 0.036931 | 0.001505 | 0.038016 |

Note: Inter-SD: standard deviation of inter-groups; Intra-SD: standard deviation of intra-groups.

## 4.4 Comparisons of Robustness

To analyze the robustness of optimal fitness values obtained from the random, GA and the proposed strategy, two different data sets, such as different number of students and characteristics, will be conducted to compare the proposed strategy with random and GA methods. Each method would run 100 times with each data set then the standard deviation of these 100 optimal fitness values is computed. Figure 5 shows the variations of standard deviation of the optimal fitness values derived from the proposed strategy is significantly better than the other competing methods. The proposed strategy is more stable than the other two with different number of students. Figure 6 shows that

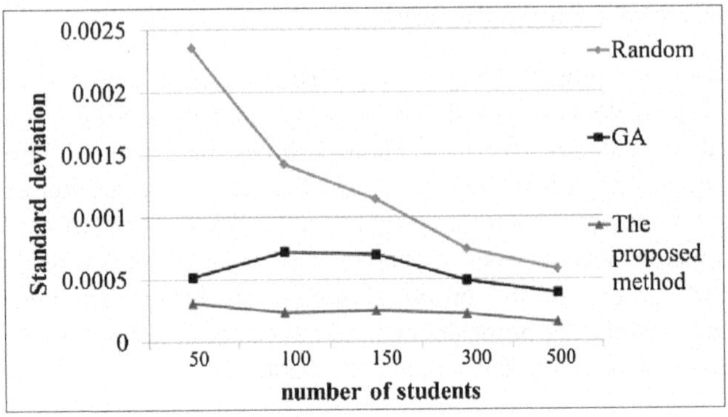


**Fig. 5.** Variations of standard deviation of the optimal fitness values derived by random, GA and the proposed strategy as the number of students increase

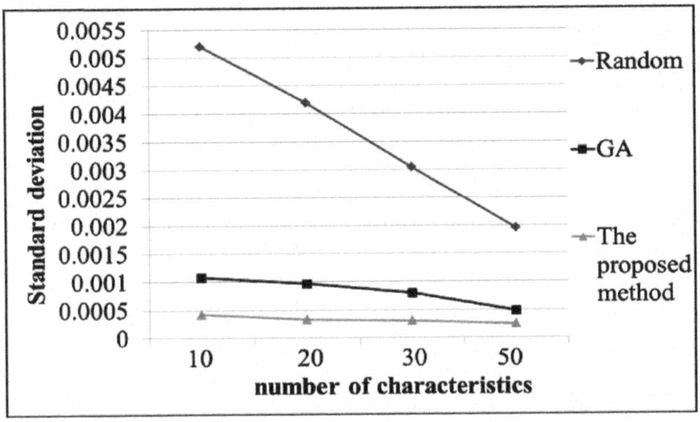


**Fig. 6.** Variations of standard deviation of the optimal fitness values derived by random, GA and the proposed strategy as the number of students' characteristics increases

the variations of standard deviation of optimal fitness values derived from the proposed strategy is more stable than the other two methods.

## 5 Conclusion

This paper has proposed the grouping strategy based on GA to address multiple characteristics grouping problems for cooperative learning environments, which constructs better inter-homogeneous and intra-heterogeneous groups. In this paper, the pre-categorization stage and a well-designed chromosome-like data structure has designed to enhance the performance of the proposed strategy. Furthermore, a novel mutation operator is designed for fitting the chromosome, which improves the performance but doesn't lead to non-convergence of the solution.

To evaluate the proposed strategy, several data sets with different problem sizes, such as number of students and characteristics, were conducted to compare the solution quality, executing time, search speed and stability of the proposed strategy with the other methods. The experimental results have demonstrated the proposed grouping strategy (1) possesses better performance, grouping result and robustness than the random and GA methods, and (2) achieves the goal of obtaining better inter-homogeneous and intra-heterogeneous groups.

**Acknowledgment.** The authors would like to thank Shun-Hsi Chung for his suggestions in this paper. The research is partially supported by the National Science Council of the Republic of China under the grant number NSC 102-2221-E-241-015.

## References

1. Dillenbourg, P.: What do you mean by collaborative learning? In: Dillenbourg, P. (ed.) Cognitive and Computational Approaches Collaborative-Learning, pp. 1–19. Elsevier, Oxford (1999)
2. Dillenbourg, P.: Collaborative Learning: Cognitive and Computational Approaches. Advances in Learning and Instruction Series. ERIC, New York (1999)
3. Dewiyanti, S., et al.: Students' experiences with collaborative learning in asynchronous computer-supported collaborative learning environments. Comput. Hum. Behav. **23**(1), 496–514 (2007)
4. Kreijns, K., Kirschner, P.A., Jochems, W.: The sociability of computer-supported collaborative learning environments. Educ. Technol. Soc. **5**(1), 8–22 (2002)
5. Webb, N.M.: Student interaction and learning in small groups. Rev. Educ. Res. **52**(3), 421–445 (1982)
6. Barkley, E.F., Cross, K.P., Major, C.H.: Collaborative Learning Techniques: A handbook for College Faculty. Jossey-Bass, San Francisco (2004)
7. Wang, Y.-M., Elhag, T.: Fuzzy TOPSIS method based on alpha level sets with an application to bridge risk assessment. Expert Syst. Appl. **31**(2), 309–319 (2006)
8. Dalton, D.W., Hannafin, M.J., Hooper, S.: Effects of individual and cooperative computer-assisted instruction on student performance and attitudes. Educ. Tech. Res. Dev. **37**(2), 15–24 (1989)
9. Hooper, S., Hannafin, M.J.: Cooperative CBI: The effects of heterogeneous versus homogeneous grouping on the learning of progressively complex concepts. J. Educ. Comput. Res. **4**(4), 413–424 (1988)
10. Moreno, J., Ovalle, D.A., Vicari, R.M.: A genetic algorithm approach for group formation in collaborative learning considering multiple student characteristics. Comput. Educ. **58**(1), 560–569 (2012)
11. Yin, P.-Y., et al.: A particle swarm optimization approach to composing serial test sheets for multiple assessment criteria. Educ. Technol. Soc. **9**(3), 3–15 (2006)
12. Hwang, G.-J., et al.: An enhanced genetic approach to composing cooperative learning groups for multiple grouping criteria. Educ. Technol. Soc. **11**(1), 148–167 (2008)
13. Yannibelli, V., Amandi, A.: A deterministic crowding evolutionary algorithm to form learning teams in a collaborative learning context. Expert Syst. Appl. **39**(10), 8584–8592 (2012)
14. Falkenauer, E.: Genetic algorithms and grouping problems. Wiley, New York (1998)

15. Wang, D.-Y., Lin, S.S., Sun, C.-T.: DIANA: A computer-supported heterogeneous grouping system for teachers to conduct successful small learning groups. Comput. Hum. Behav. **23**(4), 1997–2010 (2007)
16. Chen, C.-T.: Extensions of the TOPSIS for group decision-making under fuzzy environment. Fuzzy Sets Syst. **114**(1), 1–9 (2000)
17. Holland, J.H.: Adaptation in Natural and Artificial Systems. The University of Michigan Press, Ann Arbor (1975)
18. Hwang, C.-L., Yoon, K.: Multiple attribute decision making. Springer, New York (1981)
19. Shyur, H.-J., Shih, H.-S.: A hybrid MCDM model for strategic vendor selection. Math. Comput. Model. **44**(7), 749–761 (2006)
20. Yu, X., et al.: Rank B2C e-commerce websites in e-alliance based on AHP and fuzzy TOPSIS. Expert Syst. Appl. **38**(4), 3550–3557 (2011)
21. Weise, T., Global optimization algorithms–theory and application. Self-Published (2009)
22. Reeves, C.R.: A genetic algorithm for flowshop sequencing. Comput. Oper. Res. **22**(1), 5–13 (1995)
23. Goldberg, D.E.: Genetic algorithms in search, optimization, and machine learning. Addison-Wesley Longman Publishing, Boston (1989)

# Adaptation Based on Navigation Type and Learning Style

Nabila Bousbia(✉), Amina Gheffar, and Amar Balla

LMCS: Laboratoire Méthode de Conception de Systèmes,
ESI: Ecole nationale Supérieure d'Informatique, Oued-Smar, Algiers, Algeria
{n_bousbia, a_gheffar, a_balla}@esi.dz

**Abstract.** In this paper, we present an adaptation approach of e-learning content based on the navigation type indicator describing the learner's behavior while browsing an e-learning course. This adaptation approach benefits from the found correlation between this indicator and learning styles, particularly Sequential/Global and Active/Reflective styles. Many studies use leaning styles for adaptation based on educational rules. Thus, we propose for each value of the navigation type indicator, to provide the learner with the appropriate adaptation to the learning style correlated with the indicator value.

**Keywords:** Adaptation · Learning style · Navigation type indicator · Traces

## 1 Introduction

Adaptation in Computer Environments of Human Learning (ILE) is a widely explored research area because it is a very important component in such systems.

Adaptation may concern three elements: content, navigation and presentation and is based on several criteria: the characteristics of the learner (knowledge, learning style…), usage data and environment [1].

The adaptation process in educational systems takes place in three stages: the collection of traces and information on the learner. This information is then processed and analyzed to construct the learner model. According to this model, adaptation will be performed.

It is in this context that several research studies have focused on collecting traces of the learner activities during their interactions with the learning environment to provide learning indicators interpreting the learner's behavior and supplying the learner model to adapt the content.

In this work we present an adaptation method based on a learning indicator. We are interested in web environments, particularly the e-learning platforms, on which several studies have been conducted to interpret the learners' behavior based on their navigation traces.

In this context, we have defined in our earlier work an indicator describing the learners' navigation behaviors based on low-level navigation traces (links followed, clicks, etc.), using a system called IDLS [2]. In this paper, we continue this work by exploiting the possibility to adapt the content using this navigation type indicator.


D.K.W. Chiu et al. (Eds.): ICWL 2013 Workshops, LNCS 8390, pp. 23–31, 2015.
DOI: 10.1007/978-3-662-46315-4_3

Adaptation can focus on the course content, the presentation form or the links provided to each learner. It can be implemented using different techniques. We propose adaptation rules depending on the navigation type. We therefore exploit the state of the art on adaptation based on learning styles because our previous results show that there is a correlation between the navigation type indicator and learning styles [3].

Before presenting our approach, we discuss in the next section the use of learning styles for adaptation.

## 2 Learning Styles and Adaptation

Learning style is considered one of the major individual differences that play an important role in learning. It can provide information on preferences related to the modality of perception, processing and organizing information, reasoning, social aspects, etc. [4].

There are many studies that use learning style as a criterion for adaptation [5–7]. The method generally used is to plan the learning sequence to present to the learner at the beginning of the session, according to the learner's learning style value (known before starting learning). It is then necessary that the course designer or the tutor defines or annotates the adequate resources according to the learners' learning styles.

The main problem with these systems is the detection of the learning style value. Generally, the used detection method of learning styles is done explicitly (dedicated psychological questionnaires that they ask the student to fill in). The resulted LS is then stored once and for all by the system for adaptation.

To solve this problem of LS' identification and update, several studies are currently being done on the detection of LS by analyzing the learner's interaction traces [6, 8–10]. However, the problem of when updating the learning style value remains. Therefore, we propose in this paper an adaptation approach using trace analysis, particularly the navigation type indicator, and learning styles.

## 3 Adaptation Approach

To implement adaptation in an educational hypermedia system we need to answer two questions, first "what to adapt" then "how to adapt".

Answering the question "what to adapt" is to determine the system elements to adapt (e.g. content) according to the chosen criteria of adaptation. Answering the question "how to adapt" is to describe the proposed approach for adaptation.

We propose an approach based on adaptation rules. To define these rules we will determine what can be adapted from the information provided by the navigation type indicator. We first define this indicator, then the adaptations rules and the modifications we made on this indicator.

### 3.1 Navigation Type Indicator

In Bousbia et al. [2] we defined the navigation type indicator which describes the learner's navigation behavior during a learning session at the course level. It can take four values:

- *Overviewing:* this value implies that the learner is covering a large proportion of course pages to acquire an overall view of the course.
- *Flitting:* It reflects a browsing activity without a strategy or a particular goal. The main difference with the *overviewing* value is the lack of focus on the course.
- *Studying:* corresponds to a partial or complete reading of the course pages where the learner spends time on each page.
- *Deepening:* This describes a learner who spends relatively long time on a course, checking details, and seeking Web documents related to the course topics to obtain a deeper understanding of the course.

The calculation of this indicator involves three steps [11]:

1. *Collecting traces:* Trace collection is to capture, using a dedicated tool, the learner's navigation traces when interacting with the educational system.
2. *The calculation of the intermediate indicators:* The calculation of the four values of the navigation type indicator is based on other intermediate indicators:

   - *Average visit duration for a course page Dmc:* used to distinguish a quick reading of the course pages from a complete one. It takes two values: *high*, if the value exceeds a threshold (defined as additional data), or *low* otherwise.
   - *Browsing pattern Fpc:* to distinguish an *overviewing* or *flitting* from a searching activity. Based on Canter's et al. [12] browsing patterns we defined three forms: *(i) Scholar* (This value is retained when the dominant Canter pattern is a path with a few loops or when there is a spike); *(ii) Star* (This form occurs when the learner tends to often return to the same node(s). It often appears in a search query); *(iii) Dispersion*: This is a ring or a mixture of Canter forms; in other words, learners tend to move in all directions.
   - *Semantic proximity between the course content and the pages visited outside the course Prox:* For a given course, this indicator allows estimating the degree of proximity or similarity with the Web pages visited in the same time interval. Its numerical value is compared to a threshold given as additional data. Thus it can take three values: *high, low,* or *null.*
   - *Course duration rate Dc/Ds:* it compares the course visit duration *Dc* to the session total duration *Ds*. It has three values: *low, high or Null,* obtained by comparing the numerical value to a threshold assigned as additional data.

3. *Deducing the value of the navigation type indicator:* The calculation is based on data mining methods and is done by applying a set of rules on intermediate indicators, presented in a decision tree (Fig. 1).

For example, if the intermediate indicator calculation results for a learner's log file are: (Dmc: high, Dc/Ds: high, Fpc: Star, Prox: High), the associated navigation type will be Deepening.

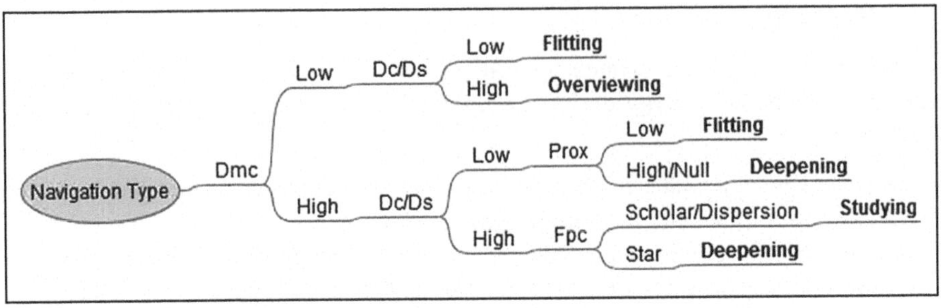


**Fig. 1.** Deduction of the navigation type from intermediate indicators [11].

The main drawback that we face is the time of calculation of the navigation type indicator, which is at the end of the session and for the course level. However, in order to provide effective adaptations the indicators must be performed dynamically and in real time. To solve this problem we propose to calculate the indicator before the end of the training session, at the chapter level instead of the course level.

### 3.2 Calculation of the Navigation Type Indicator at the Chapter Level

When calculating the navigation type indicator we considered that the course has a tree structure. The tree is composed of nodes, consisting of activities. These activities can include sub-activities. Leaf activities point to the resources (hypermedia content). We are particularly interested in HTML pages, thus, we only considered the reading activities of a chapter, or a sub-chapter, etc.

Now, to calculate the navigation type indicator at the "chapter" level we suppose that the activities are chapters and point to the resources (pages), i.e. no sub-chapters.

The test results showed that the intermediate indicator Prox is noisy and does not have a lot influence on the final result [11]. We will therefore neglect this indicator while calculating the navigation indicator at the chapter level.

Thus, based on the decision tree presented in Fig. 1, we propose a new decision tree for the calculation of the indicator at the chapter level (Fig. 2).

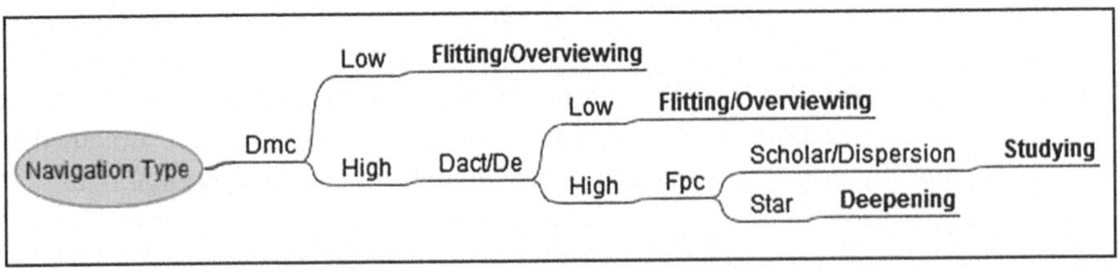


**Fig. 2.** Decision tree for the calculation of the navigation type indicator at the "chapter" level.

As we calculate the navigation type at the chapter level, we consider "Dmc" as the average visit duration for a chapter page. We also replace the course duration rate Dc/Ds, by the chapter duration rate "Dact/De", where "Dact" is the visit duration of the activity (the effective activity time in the chapter for which we calculate the navigation type indicator); and "De" is the time spent on the chapter since the beginning of the session until the time of calculating the indicator. This is the difference between the duration of the session and the time spent on the other chapters:

$$\text{De: Elapsed duration} = T_{\text{session}} - (\text{Time on the previous chapters}).$$

Even with the calculation of the indicator in a shorter time (at the chapter level and in time intervals "t" instead of the whole session) the problem of real-time access to the learner history database persists. Also, the indicator calculation time of the browsing pattern intermediate indicator "Fpc" slows down the system (it requires the application of an algorithm which takes place in two long phases: extraction of the basic forms of Canter et al. [12], and then determining the scholar, star, dispersion forms [11]).

As this indicator mainly depends on the consultation order and we assume that the activities point directly to pages, we can limit its calculation to take into account the values of the path linearity indicator "TL" [11], having the following formula:

$$TL = Npdc/Npc \tag{1}$$

Where:

Npdc: The number of different consulted pages (number of nodes);
Npc: The number of consulted pages (number of steps).

Moreover, since we use the browsing path indicator "Fpc" in only one branch of the decision tree (Fig. 2), we propose to simplify the calculation by reducing its values to two values: scholar and star. Therefore, adapting the results of [11] to our hypothesis, we can say that: if the value of TL is greater than 0.8, the path is linear, Fp will get the value Scholar. Otherwise, Fp will get the Star value.

### 3.3 Adaptation Rules

Our initial goal to address the adaptation issue based on the navigation indicators in an e-learning platform was to analyze and use the definitions of the four navigation type values in order to infer adaptation rules.

For example, by analyzing the interpretation of the *overviewing* type, the student flies to discover the course content and to have an overall view. We can then offer as an adaptation to show the course index to the learner, to include tests to know the learner's level and to suggest paths to follow. But this is small because to translate the needs of a learner from the learner's browsing behavior, we require a lot of experience and knowledge in education and psychology.

To address this problem, we use the state of the art on adaptation based on learning style since our previous results show that there is a correlation between the navigation type indicator and learning styles, particularly Sequential/Global and Active/Reflective styles. Adaptation rules that we propose have the following form:

*If "navigation type value"* **then** *"we propose appropriate adaptations to the learning style correlated with this navigation type".*

The adaptation will be generated by a set of rules according to the values of the navigation type indicator. The use of rules allows their enrichment and updates thereafter.

We propose to combine the overviewing and flitting values in the overviewing value since their definition are close and are both correlated with the global and active learning styles.

Thus, for each value of the navigation type indicator, we provide the learner with the appropriate adaptation to the learning style correlated with the indicator value:

**If** *Overviewing* **then** make appropriate adaptations to the active and global styles.

**If** *Studying* **then** make appropriate adaptations to the reflective and sequential styles.

**If** *Deepening* **then** make appropriate adaptations to the global and reflective styles.

The choice of the appropriate adaptations is wide. Among the existing adaptation strategies in the literature, we are interested in the one of Popescu [9]. In this work, we focus on the adaptation rules suggested for the Sequential/Global and Active/Reflective learning styles of Felder and Silverman learning style model [13]. We reuse these rules because they have the advantage of being generic and based on the definition given in the literature for each learning style. On this basis, we propose the following adaptation rules:

***If*** *Overviewing* ***then*** incorporate interactive animations, simulations, small games; include many exercises, provide communication tools (forum/chat); include lesson plans and abstracts (summaries), embed links related to the discussed topic within the content; place exercises at the end of the chapter, provide advanced organizers or organization chart.

***If*** *Studying* ***then*** include less exercises; include reflection questions; provide contextual annotation tools; include step-by-step content presentations; put links at the end of the course to topics related to the studied concept; highlight the previous and next buttons, hide the plans of the course; propose tests at short intervals.

***If*** *Deepening* ***then*** include less exercise; include reflection questions; provide contextual annotation tools; include course plans and summaries; embed links in relation to the studied subject in the content; place exercises at the end of the chapter; provide advanced organizers or organization chart.

Our main goal here is to provide recommendations on the learning objects and the optimal path based on the current learner's needs, while allowing the learner the freedom to choose paths or links the learner wants.

### 3.4 How to Implement the Solution

We assume that the navigation indicator is calculated after each arbitrary time "t" and its value will be updated in the learner profile. So the adaptation module presents an adapted vision of the studied concept suitable for the learner according to the current navigation type value.

The basic idea is that the adjustments are made from generic documents defined by the teachers for all learners. Teachers (or course designers) create learning activities using dedicated tools available in the e-learning platforms according to the sought learning objective. Educational activity may consist of several documents (HTML pages, documents, images…) related to each other, or contain links to websites or other educational activities.

The activities are created dynamically from basic documents and are presented in different ways depending on the learner profile (Fig. 3).

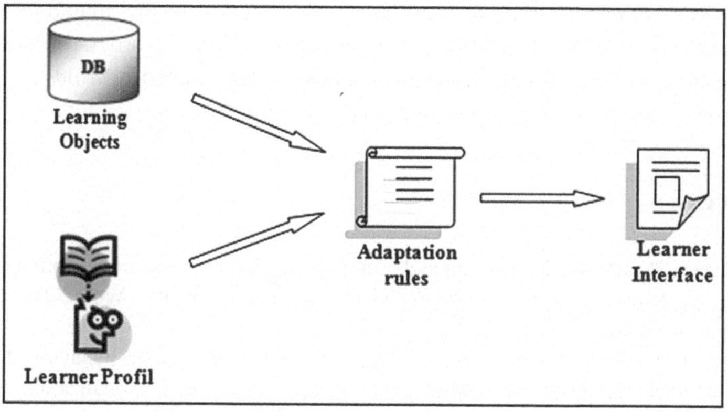


**Fig. 3.** Adaptation process.

The implementation of an adaptation model needs to have a static description of the learning content: the metadata. Without such descriptions, the implementation of the adaptation will not be possible.

For the implementation of the solution, we use the standard LOM and the ontology proposed by Ullrich [14] and enhanced in [15] to describe the semantic information granules (definition, explanation, etc.) and have the same syntax for describing educational learning resources.

When creating the course, the teacher or the tutor indicates the field corresponding to the metadata of the educational type of the various objects and media constituting the course.

Then, during the adaptation phase, to apply the rules that are mainly related to the learner's preferences (e.g. a learner who prefers more explanation and illustration), the system can easily extract the appropriate objects thanks to their metadata.

The adaptation is divided into a set of elementary actions: annotation, insertion, remove or sort learning objects (OPs). It consists in the automatic generation of pages following the various actions taken by the learner.

Depending on the value of the navigation type, the adaptation module applies a set of rules for the navigation type, which will be applied to the baseline scenario in order to adapt the learning situation.

# 4 Conclusion

We proposed in this paper an adaptation approach based on the learner's navigation behavior during an e-learning session. The proposed adaptation rules are based on the value of the navigation type indicator and the correlated learning style value that will indicate the appropriate learning content to present to the learner. So, to make these adaptations possible we calculated the navigation type indicator on the chapter level instead of the whole session to apply adaptation to the learner after each "t" time. This time will be determined after experimentations to find the appropriate period after which the navigation type should be recalculated. We also proposed to describe the learning objects using metadata to facilitate their selection in the adaptation process.

The next step of this work is to test these propositions in order to determine the appropriate time to make adaptation and to perform the adaptation rules.

# References


1. Brusilovsky, P., Millán, E.: User models for adaptive hypermedia and adaptive educational systems. In: Brusilovsky, P., Kobsa, A., Nejdl, W. (eds.) Adaptive Web 2007. LNCS, vol. 4321, pp. 3–53. Springer, Heidelberg (2007)
2. Bousbia, N., Rebaï, I., Labat, J.-M., Balla, A.: Learners' navigation behavior identification based on traces analysis. User Model. User-Adap. Inter.: J. Personalization Res. **20**(5), 455–494 (2010)
3. Bousbia, N., Labat, J.-M., Balla, A., Rebaï, I.: Supervised classification on navigational behaviours in web-based learning systems to identify learning styles. Int. J. Learn. Technol. (IJLT) **6**(1), 24–45 (2011)
4. Dahbi, A.: El kamoun, N., Berraissoul, A.: Conception d'un système hypermédia d'enseignement adaptatif centré sur les styles d'apprentissage: modèle et expérience. Int. J. Technol High. Educ. **6**(1), 55–71 (2009)
5. Cha, H.J., Kim, Y.S., Park, S.-H., Yoon, T.-b., Jung, Y.M., Lee, J.-H.: Learning styles diagnosis based on user interface behaviors for the customization of learning interfaces in an intelligent tutoring system. In: Ikeda, M., Ashley, K.D., Chan, T.-W. (eds.) ITS 2006. LNCS, vol. 4053, pp. 513–524. Springer, Heidelberg (2006)
6. Graf, S.: Adaptativity in learning management systems focussing on learning styles. Ph.D. thesis, Vienna University of Technology, Austria (2007)
7. Piombo, C.: Modélisation probabiliste du style d'apprentissage et application à l'adaptation de contenus pédagogiques indexés par une ontologie. Ph.D. thesis, Institut National Polytechnique de Toulouse, France (2007)
8. Garcia, P., Amandi, A., Schiaffino, S., Campo, M.: Evaluating Bayesian networks' precision for detecting students' learning styles. Comput. Educ. **49**, 794–808 (2007)
9. Popescu, E.: Dynamic adaptative hypermedia systems for e-learning. Ph.D. thesis, Criova, Romania (2008)

10. Chang, Y.-C., Kao, W.-Y., Chu, C.-P., Chiu, C.-H.: A learning style classification mechanism for e-learning. Comput. Educ. **53**(2), 273–285 (2009)
11. Bousbia, N.: Analyse des traces de navigation des apprenants dans un environnement de formation dans une perspective de détection automatique des styles d'apprentissage. Ph.D. thesis, UPMC & ESI (2011)
12. Canter, D., Rivers, R., Storrs, G.: Characterizing user navigation through complex data structures. Behav. Inf. Technol. **4**(2), 93–102 (1985)
13. Felder, R.M., Silverman, L.K.: Learning and teaching styles in engineering education. Engr. Educ. **78**(7), 674–681 (1988)
14. Ullrich, C.: The learning-resource-type is dead, long live the learning- resource-type! Learn. Objects Learn. Des. **1**, 7–15 (2005)
15. Lu, E.J.L., Hsieh, C.J.: A relation metadata extension for SCORM Content Aggregation Model. Comput. Stand. Interfaces **31**(5), 1028–1035 (2009)

# A Novel Recommendation Relevancy Measure for Collaborative Filtering

Bo Shu[1], Zhendong Niu[1(✉)], Chunxia Zhang[1], Xiaotian Jiang[1], Hongping Fu[1], and Wei Chen[2]

[1] School of Computer Science and Technology, Beijing Institute of Technology, Beijing 100081, China
shu.bo.china@gmail.com,
{zniu, cxzhang, hpfu}@bit.edu.cn, 0532yangya@163.com

[2] Agricultural Information Institute, Chinese Academy of Agricultural Sciences, Beijing 100081, China
chenwei@caas.cn

**Abstract.** Recommendation systems help people find their potential interests. In recommendation algorithms relevancy measures play an important role. Current relevancy measures often employ only user-item rating data or combine with contextual information to obtain related users or items. However, in some specific situations, these measures may not guarantee high accuracy or sufficient candidates. This paper solves these problems by proposing a novel recommendation relevancy measure, which indicates how worthy an item can be recommended to a user. In this paper, each interaction between a user and the recommendation system is regarded as a behavior represented with several features. The relevancy measure is achieved with a series of stepwise calculations and combinations on these features and behaviors. We evaluated the effectiveness of this measure against three other popular measures with a public dataset extracted from a commercial search engine. The experiment result shows that it can generate more recommendable items and achieves both high recall and precision.

**Keywords:** Recommendation system · Collaborative filtering · Behavior sequence

## 1 Introduction

Recommendation systems help people find the valuable things, such as web-pages, goods, music, and movies [1]. Current recommendation approaches can be classified into several categories [2, 3]: content-based recommendation, collaborative filtering, model-based recommendation, hybrid approach, etc.

The content-based approaches first analyze the textual information that represents users and items. Then, for each user, the similarities of all items to him are calculated and the top ranked ones are recommended [3].

These approaches often employ the TF-IDF (term frequency-inverse document frequency) weighting scheme to represent a text description and cosine similarity to measure the similarity between two text descriptions [4]. However, this method can


D.K.W. Chiu et al. (Eds.): ICWL 2013 Workshops, LNCS 8390, pp. 32–41, 2015.
DOI: 10.1007/978-3-662-46315-4_4

only be used for text descriptions. For other types of features, such as discrete or continuous feature, we need to define their similarity measures respectively.

Collaborative filtering is based on either users or items [1, 3], and ratings can be either implicit or explicit [5, 6]. The user-based approaches first retrieve the ratings that users rated and then calculate the similarity between users. For each user, the users whose behaviors are most like him are selected and the items enjoyed by these users are recommended. Likewise, item-based approaches use the ratings to calculate the similarity between items. Then, for each user, the items that are most like what he has rated are recommended.

The most common-used similarity or relevancy measures in collaborative filtering are Pearson correlation and cosine similarity. However, as the data scale increases, the data become sparser. The sparser data becomes, the fewer co-rated items are. This makes the two similarity measures becoming more and more unreliable [3]. Since collaborative filtering does not employ contextual information, the accuracy may be impaired.

In order to overcome the limitations of collaborative filtering and the content-based approaches, some recommendation systems take more contextual information into consideration, such as time [7, 8], location [9, 10], etc. Other approaches combine collaborative filtering with content-based methods with different strategies [2, 11]. Many researches show that those hybrid methods can obtain more precise candidates than pure collaborative filtering or content-based approaches [12].

The PTango [11] system, which combines the collaborative filtering and content-based with equal weight, adjusts the weights with the feedback of users. This strategy is similar to boosting [13]. Other similar methods adopt different weighting schemes. For example, [12, 14] adopt weighted majority voting, [15] adopts weighted average voting. In [16], G. Adomavicius proposed a reduction-based recommendation method. It first retrieves the same or similar contextual users of a certain user with content-based method, then uses the user-item rating of the retrieved users to generate the prediction with collaborative filtering method.

The combination of two recommendation approaches indeed presents better performance. However, here is still room for improvement.

In this paper, we adopt the idea of employing contextual information and use all the features of a user. For each of these features, we define a specific similarity measure according to its characteristic. We also notice that the behavior sequence also has order or position information. But due to the computation complexity, in this paper we ignore the order information and treat each behavior sequence as a set.

With all the ideas above, we present a novel recommendation relevancy measure in this paper. Unlike the traditional approaches, this measure treats each interaction of a user with recommendation system as a behavior and forms a behavior sequence for each user. Then it measures how worthy an item can be recommended to a user with a series of stepwise calculations and combinations on these features and behaviors.

The rest of this paper is organized as follows. We propose our algorithm in Sect. 2. In Sect. 3, we show the experimental results, compare our method with other methods and do some analysis. At last we draw the conclusions in Sect. 4.

## 2 Algorithm

### 2.1 Notations and Problem Statement

Let U be the set of users, $U = \{u_1, u_2, \ldots, u_n\}$. We consider each interaction of user $u_i$ with recommendation system as a behavior $b_{ij}$. The behaviors of $u_i$ form a behavior sequence $B_i$, $B_i = \{b_{i1}, b_{i2}, \ldots, b_{im}\}$. Each behavior can be represented by several features, $b_{ij} = <a_{ij1}, a_{ij2}, \ldots, a_{ijd}>$, where d is the number of feature. For example, the behavior of a user's buying a book in an e-commercial website can be described by the following features: user ID, user location, buying time, book title, price, etc. The task of a recommendation system is to calculate on what extent a behavior is worth recommending to a user.

### 2.2 The Similarity Between the Same Kinds of Features

We use different similarity functions to calculate the similarities of different features according to their specific characteristics. The common form of k-th feature similarity function is:

$$sim_{k\langle u_i,u_j\rangle}\left(a_{u_{ik}}, a_{v_{jk}}\right) = f_k\left(a_{u_{ik}}, a_{v_{jk}}\right) \tag{1}$$

For example, in this paper we use Levenshtein distance, which is a special type of edit distance, to measure the similarity between query strings according to [17].

$$Sim_q(q_a, q_b) = 1 - \frac{L(q_a, q_b)}{MaxLen(q_a, q_b)} \tag{2}$$

where $Sim(q_a, q_b)$ is the similarity between query string $q_a$ and $q_b$, $L(q_a, q_b)$ is the Levenshtein Distance between $q_a$ and $q_b$, $MaxLen(q_a, q_b)$ is the length of the longer sequence between $q_a$ and $q_b$. The range of this similarity is [0, 1] and a larger value means the two queries are more similar.

In this paper, we define the similarity of the submitted time of two behaviors as:

$$Sim_t(t_a, t_b) = \frac{1}{1 + |t_b - t_a|} \tag{3}$$

where $t_a$ is the submitted time of behavior $a$ and $t_b$ is the submitted time of behavior $b$.

### 2.3 The Similarity Between Two Behaviors

We define the similarity between two behaviors from different users as the linear combination of the similarities for each feature. That is,

$$simb(b_u, b_v) = \sum\nolimits_{k=1}^{d} w_k sim_k(a_{uk}, a_{vk}) \tag{4}$$

where $b_u$ is a behavior of user $u$, $b_v$ is a behavior of user $v$, and

$$\sum_{k=1}^{d} w_k = 1$$

The range of similarity between two behaviors is [0, 1]. The larger similarity value means the two behaviors are more similar. In this paper we deploy the Delphi method to determine the weights in (4).

## 2.4 The Similarity Between a Behavior and a Behavior Sequence

Supposing that user u has a behavior $b_{ui}$, user v has a behavior sequence $B_v = \{b_{v1}, b_{v2}, \ldots, b_{vm}\}$; bvmg, the similarity between $b_{ui}$ and $b_{vj}$ is $s_j$, then we can define the similarity between $b_{ui}$ and $B_v$ as:

$$simbB_{(b_{u_i},B_v)} = 1 - \prod\nolimits_{j=1}^{m} (1 - s_j)^{\rho-1} * (1 - s_j) \tag{5}$$

where parameter $\rho(\rho \geq 1)$ is a case amplification power [18, 19], which punishes the low similarity and reduces the noise in the data. Like [19], we use $(1 - s_j)^{\rho-1} * (1 - s_j)$ instead of $(1 - s_j)^{\rho}$ in (5) to emphasize the adjustment of $(1 - s_j)$ by itself. When $\rho$ is large enough, any large $s_j$ can sharply increase $simbB_{(b_{u_i},B_v)}$; if any $b_{v_j}$ in $B_v$ is similar to $b_{u_i}$, $simbB_{(b_{u_i},B_v)}$ will be large. According to [18, 19] we set $\rho$ to 2.5 in our experiment. The range of similarity between a behavior and a behavior sequence is [0, 1], and a larger value means that the behavior is more similar to the behavior sequence.

## 2.5 The User Relevancy Measure

Supposing that user u has a behavior sequence $B_u$ consisting of m behaviors and user v has a behavior sequence $B_v$ consisting of n behaviors, we define the recommendation relevancy measure of $B_u$ to $B_v$ as:

$$R(u, v) = \sigma * \frac{1}{m} \sum\nolimits_{i=1}^{m} s_{(b_{u_i},B_v)} \tag{6}$$

where

$$\sigma = \frac{min(|B_u|, |B_v|)}{MaxLen(|B_u|, |B_v|)}$$

The range of $R(u, v)$ is [0, 1]. A Large value means the behaviors of user $v$ is better worth recommending to user $u$. This measure is asymmetric, which means that the items of user $u$ is worth recommending to user $v$ does not mean the items of user $v$ is also worth recommending to user $u$. $\sigma$ is a parameter set to make sure that the similar $|B_v|$ and $|B_u|$ will make $R(u, v)$ large.

## 3 Experiment Result

We evaluate the effectiveness of our recommendation relevancy measure vs. Pearson Correlation Coefficient, content-based method based on textual similarity, and a hybrid method of Pearson Correlation Coefficient and content-based method based on textual similarity as baseline methods in collaborative filtering systems.

### 3.1 Training Data Set

Since the research in this paper works as a component in a commercial search engine, we use the log data from a similar search engine[1] as the test data set. This is a Chinese search engine and most of queries in the log are in Chinese. Each line in the data records a searching and the subsequent click-through action of a user. The format of this data is shown in Table 1. Among them, user ID is automatically assigned by the search engine system according to the Cookie information generated when users get access to the system.

**Table 1.** Format of query long

| Time | UserID | User query | Ranking of the clicked URL | Order of user click | The clicked URL | ... |
|---|---|---|---|---|---|---|
| 20111231083559 | xxx | $q_1$ | 1 | 1 | www.a. com | ... |
| 20111231085927 | yyy | $q_2$ | 10 | 4 | www.b. com | ... |

Like [20], we use user ID to identify each user and the clicked URL to identify each web page. We treat the URLs as items. The order of user click is considered as the rating of this user to the clicked URL. The time and the query submitted by user are regarded as the description of an interaction. The total search and click-through records of a user are regarded as the behavior set of the user.

The log data includes a two-day record of 2011-12-30 and 2011-12-31. We use the earlier 9/10 log data as the training set and the rest as the test set.

The training data set contains 39,190,896 search and click-through records and 5,675,810 user Ids. The test data set contains 4,354,548 search and click-through records and 701,632 user Ids. Figure 1 summarizes the statistics and shows the relationship between the number of clicked URL of a user and the number of users in training set and test set. We can see from it that the users' number decreases as the URLs number of a user goes up. The proportion of the users whose number of clicked

[1] http://www.sogou.com/labs/dl/q-e.html. Corpus Search Engine Click-through Log (SogouQ). 2012-12-15.

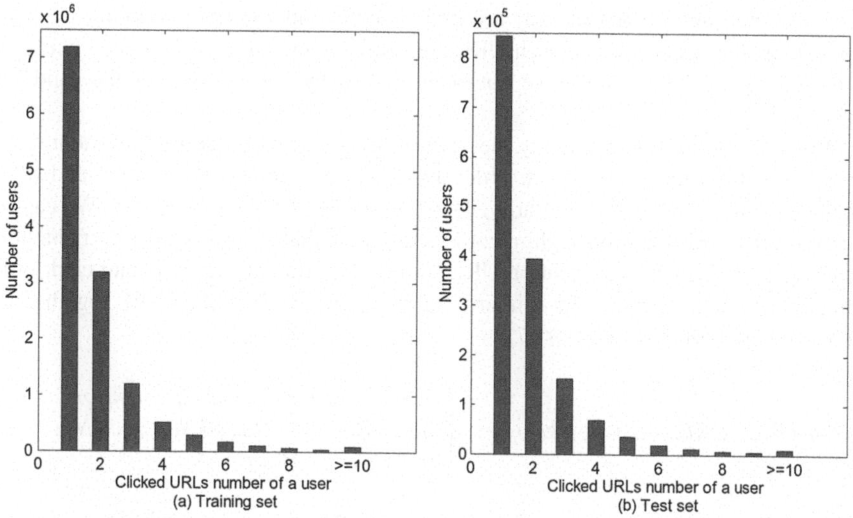


**Fig. 1.** Relationship between the number of clicked URLs of a user and the number of users in training set and test set

URLs is larger than 10 sum up to no more than 1.54 % of the total number of users, so they can be safely discarded. We selected the users with the click-through URLs number varying from 2 to 9 for training and test.

## 3.2 Experiment Design

We conduct user evaluation tests on our recommendation relevancy measure vs. three other similarity measures. First we randomly selected 200 test users from the test set. For each test user, we use the four measures in collaborative filtering system to generate 10 candidate items, then we choose 20 volunteers to evaluate the web pages of the recommended URLs (i.e. candidate items). Each of them evaluated all the URLs. If they think the user will also interest in the web pages after performing the search and click-through behaviors, which means the candidates are worth recommending, they will approve it; otherwise they will reject it. For a candidate URL, we accumulate the occurrence of its approval from all the volunteers. If the occurrence is larger than 9, we consider that this candidate is approved by volunteers.

We use the standard metrics–|precision and recall to–evaluate the performance of the four measures. Precision is defined as the ratio of the number of candidates approved by volunteers over the number of all candidates. Recall is defined as the ratio of the number of candidates approved by volunteers over the expected number of candidates.

The details of the four approaches will be depicted below.

1. We adopt User-Based Top-N Recommendation Algorithm [18, 21] with our recommendation relevancy measure to generate candidate items. First, for each test user we use our recommendation relevancy measure to find up to the 20 most similar

users in training set (some user may not find enough similar users in training set). Then we calculate the occurrence of each URL the similar users have clicked and choose the 10 most frequent URLs that have not been clicked by the test user as the candidate items.

When evaluating the relevancy measure of test users with the users in training set, we use user ID, time, query, click order and URL as features. We use (3) and (2) to calculate the time and query similarity. The granularity of time is set to day. We can see that a search and click-through record actually includes two kinds of behaviors: searching with a query and rating a URL. In our experiment, we associate click order with clicked URL, calculate the similarity of click order with clicked URL together and define the similarity function as (7):

$$sim(URL_a, URL_b, clkNo_a, clkNo_b) = \begin{cases} 1, URL_a = URL_b, clkNo_a = clkNo_b \\ 0.5, URL_a = URL_b, clkNo_a \neq clkNo_b \\ 0, URL_a \neq URL_b \end{cases} \quad (7)$$

where $clkNo_a$ denotes the click order of behavior a. Here we do not take the ranking of the clicked URL into consideration, because this term is determined by the search engine system. In this paper we set the weights of time, query and the combination of clicked URL and click order number as 0.2, 0.5, and 0.3.

2. We also adopt User-Based Top-N Recommendation Algorithm based on Pearson Correlation Coefficient similarity measure to generate candidate items. We calculate the Pearson Correlation Coefficient between a test user and the users in training set, then select 20 users with the highest Pearson Correlation Coefficient, at last we retrieved the 10 most frequent URLs clicked by these users as candidate items.

3. We perform content-based method by calculating the similarity between queries of two search records. For each query search record of a test user we use (2) to find up to 10 most similar queries in training set, search in training set and retrieve the search records that contain those similar queries. The 10 most frequent clicked URLs in those records will be selected as the candidate items.

4. When using hybrid method of collaborative Filtering and Content-based approaches, for each test user, we first deploy the collaborative filtering method with Pearson Correlation Coefficient similarity to retrieve the 10 most similar users in training set, then find the most similar queries submitted by those similar users with (2) and obtain their subsequent clicked URLs, from which we choose the 10 most frequent URLs as the candidate items.

### 3.3 Recall and Precision Analysis

Figure 2 shows experiment results. From it we can make the following observations:

1. The Collaborative filtering based on Pearson Correlation Coefficient similarity measure has the recall of 0.34 and generated the largest candidate set. Although there are only a few users who shared co-clicked URLs with the test user in training set, there are plenty of search records of those users. But the search records of a user often consist of several topics and those topics usually have no explicit relevancy. Although two

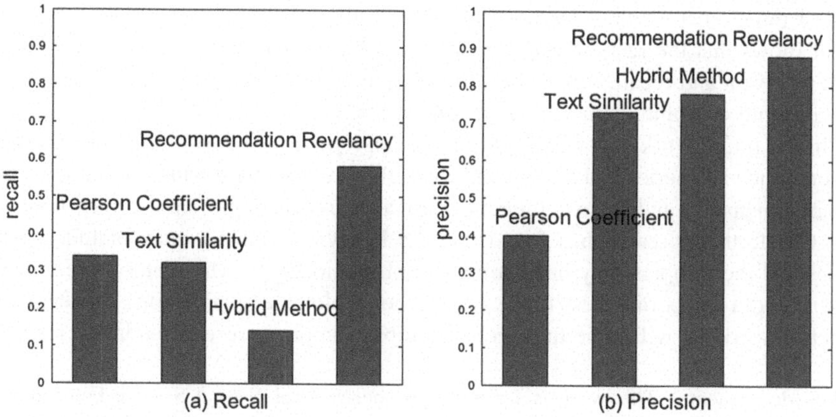


**Fig. 2.** Recall and precision of four methods

users share a topic and some co-clicked URLs, it does not mean the other topics also have strong relevancy. Lots of clicked URLs of the retrieved users in training set are not worth recommending and cannot improve the recall and precision. Lots of candidates and low accuracy leads to the lowest precision at 0.40 for this method.

2. The content-based approach with textual similarity measure obtained many similar queries in the training set, but the search records containing the queries often contain the same clicked URLs as that in the test user's records which are not worthy of recommending. The precision of this method achieves 0.73 and is higher than that of the Pearson method, because it generates enough candidates and these candidates have moderate relevancy with test user.

3. The hybrid approach has the lowest recall at 0.14 for its minimum candidates set. First it uses the Pearson correlation coefficient measure to filter out the users who have no co-clicked URLs with test user. Then text similarity method is used to retrieve the records that have similar queries with the test user. So there are only a few candidates left. Although the candidates have high recommending value that raised the precision to 0.78, it still cannot greatly increase the recall. We can also see from the result that the usage of content-based method, which adopts text similarity, can significantly raise the accuracy of recommending candidates.

4. The Collaborative filtering approach with recommendation relevancy measure takes the information about text similarity of queries, the rating of co-clicked URLs, and time difference into consideration. They ensure this method can find sufficient highly relevant candidates. We also deploy the flexible combination strategy to improve the precision. So our approach achieved the highest recall and precision at 0.58 and 0.88 across all these four approaches.

## 4 Conclusions

In this paper, we present a recommendation relevancy measure for multi-dimensional behavior sequences and evaluated the performances of our method with public data set against three other existing methods in collaborative filtering system. The experiment result shows that the recommendation system which is based on our method has both high precision and recall. This is because we adopt almost all the features that the data contains and combine them with a flexible strategy.

In the future work, we will deploy more appropriate similarity functions for some features such as queries and times. And we will test our method with a training set with higher dimensions and more complicated structure like the log of an e-commercial web site. Our further research has found that the behavior sequence may include several topics and these topics may have some causal relationships. The method presented in this paper did not extract these topics and did not deploy the relationships between them. In future work we will mine these relationships to improve recommendation result.

**Acknowledgements.** This work is supported by the National Natural Science Foundation of China (no. 61250010, 61272361, 61003263), the Program for Beijing Municipal Commission of Education (grant no.1320037010601), the 111 Project of Beijing Institute of Technology and the New Century Excellent Talents in University (grant no. NCET-06-0161).

## References

1. Linden, G., Smith, B., York, J.: Amazon. com recommendations: Item-to-item collaborative filtering. IEEE Internet Comput. **7**(1), 76–80 (2003)
2. Adomavicius, G., Tuzhilin, A.: Toward the next generation of recommender systems: A survey of the state-of-the-art and possible extensions. IEEE Trans. Knowl. Data Eng. **17** (6), 734–749 (2005)
3. Xiaoyuan, S., Khoshgoftaar, T.M.: A survey of collaborative filtering techniques. Adv. Artif. Intell. **2009**, 4 (2009)
4. Pazzani, M.J., Billsus, D.: Content-based recommendation systems. In: Brusilovsky, P., Kobsa, A., Nejdl, W. (eds.) Adaptive Web 2007. LNCS, vol. 4321, pp. 325–341. Springer, Heidelberg (2007)
5. Koren, Y.: Recommender system utilizing collaborative filtering combining explicit and implicit feedback with both neighborhood and latent factor models, 11 October 2011. US Patent 8,037,080
6. Lee, S.K., Cho, Y.H., Kim, S.H.: Collaborative filtering with ordinal scale-based implicit ratings for mobile music recommendations. Inf. Sci. **180**(11), 2142–2155 (2010)
7. Koren, Y.: Collaborative filtering with temporal dynamics. In: Proceedings of the 15th ACM SIGKDD International Conference on Knowledge Discovery and Data Mining, pp. 447–456. ACM (2009)
8. Zheng, V.W., Zheng, Y., Xie, X., Yang, Q.: Collaborative location and activity recommendations with gps history data. In: Proceedings of the 19th International Conference on World Wide Web, pp. 1029–1038. ACM (2010)
9. Sandholm, T., Ung, H.: Real-time, location-aware collaborative filtering of web content. In: Proceedings of the 2011 Workshop on Context-Awareness in Retrieval and Recommendation, pp. 14–18. ACM (2011)
10. Ye, M., Yin, P., Lee, W.-C.: Location recommendation for location-based social networks. In: Proceedings of the 18th SIGSPATIAL International Conference on Advances in Geographic Information Systems, pp. 458–461. ACM (2010)

11. Claypool, M., Gokhale, A., Miranda, T., Murnikov, P., Netes, D., Sartin, M.: Combining content-based and collaborative filters in an online newspaper. In: Proceedings of ACM SIGIR workshop on recommender systems, vol. 60. Citeseer (1999)
12. Pazzani, M.J.: A framework for collaborative, content-based and demographic filtering. Artif. Intell. Rev. **13**(5–6), 393–408 (1999)
13. Zacharias, F.: Introduction. In: Zacharias, F. (ed.) Knowledge Representations for Planning Manipulation Tasks. COSMOS, vol. 16, pp. 1–6. Springer, Heidelberg (2012)
14. Delgado, J.A.: Agent-based information filtering and recommender systems on the internet, Engineering. Nagoya Institute of Technology, Nagoya (2000)
15. Su, X., Greiner, R., Khoshgoftaar, T.M., Zhu, X.: Hybrid collaborative filtering algorithms using a mixture of experts. In: Proceedings of the IEEE/WIC/ACM International Conference on Web Intelligence, pp. 645–649. IEEE Computer Society (2007)
16. Adomavicius, G., Sankaranarayanan, R., Sen, S., Tuzhilin, A.: Incorporating contextual information in recommender systems using a multidimensional approach. ACM Trans. Inf. Syst. (TOIS) **23**(1), 103–145 (2005)
17. Shi, X., Yang, C.C.: Mining related queries from search engine query logs. In: Proceedings of the 15th International Conference on World Wide Web, pp. 943–944. ACM (2006)
18. Breese, J.S., Heckerman, D., Kadie, C.: Empirical analysis of predictive algorithms for collaborative filtering. In: Proceedings of the Fourteenth Conference on Uncertainty in Artificial Intelligence, pp. 43–52. Morgan Kaufmann Publishers Inc. (1998)
19. Lemire, D.: Scale and translation invariant collaborative filtering systems. Inf. Retrieval **8**(1), 129–150 (2005)
20. Peng, X., Niu, Z., Huang, S., Zhao, Y.: Personalized web search using clickthrough data and web page rating. J. Comput. **7**(10), 2578–2584 (2012)
21. Karypis, G.: Evaluation of item-based top-n recommendation algorithms. In: Proceedings of the Tenth International Conference on Information and Knowledge Management, pp. 247–254. ACM (2001)

# Automatic Clustering of Research Articles Using Domain Ontology and Fuzzy Logic

Ramanathan Periakaruppan(✉) and Rethinaswamy Nadarajan

PSG College of Technology, Coimbatore, India
rm_pk@yahoo.com

**Abstract.** Today, one of the key tasks for Web based learning is to retrieve research articles of specific domains. To accomplish this task, data mining techniques and semantic web technologies can be used to retrieve user relevant documents. In this work we extract author supplied keywords from a collection of computer science articles, which has a strong influence on the topic of the article when compared with other words. For these keywords term weight is computed using Fuzzy Logic which uses three criteria namely mapping with concept in domain ontology, keyword frequency in the title and keyword frequency in abstract. Using domain ontology, keywords of each document with their term weights are represented hierarchically as XML documents and they are clustered. The experimental results show that the proposed technique yields better precision and recall rates when compared with some of the existing approaches.

**Keywords:** Information retrieval · Domain knowledge · Fuzzy logic · XML

## 1 Introduction

The main objective of Information Retrieval (IR) system is to provide user relevant documents for a query. Early IR techniques are based on the exact keyword match and they do not consider the semantic relationship between keywords, hence users often find difficult to express right keywords and due to this there is low precision and recall. To improve the searching process, domain or concept based IR systems are widely used [13, 17]. Domain knowledge can be represented using Ontology and they have a significant role in information retrieval process [4, 11, 14]. The term ontology is used for complete domain knowledge information including object relationship and property relationship. In this paper we have used knowledge representation based on hierarchical domain ontology namely ACM CCS classification system because the input documents considered deals with computer science subject classification.

Vector Space Model (VSM) is one of the popular methods of representing a document [16]. The main disadvantage of VSM method is it fails to identify the underlying concepts behind the words and also it has a limitation of high dimensional document representation. Here, we tackle the higher dimensionality problem extracting important keywords from the document. These keywords are used to identify the topic of the document and are supplied by the author of research articles. In order to capture the underlying concept of a word the term weight is calculated based on Fuzzy Logic.


D.K.W. Chiu et al. (Eds.): ICWL 2013 Workshops, LNCS 8390, pp. 42–51, 2015.
DOI: 10.1007/978-3-662-46315-4_5

Three criteria are considered namely matching the keyword semantically with domain knowledge, frequency of keyword in the title and abstract of the document. For mapping with domain knowledge Latent Semantic Indexing (LSI) is used which discovers the underlying semantics. A similar approach was discussed by Paukkeri et al. [15], in which they use fuzzy logic based feature weighting for automatic learning of taxonomy. In our approach the keywords along with their term weight are represented hierarchically as an XML document.

XML document similarity can be measured in terms of structure and semantic which is addressed by many researchers [2, 10, 12, 19]. Jeong et al. [9] addresses the semantic similarity of XML documents based on supervised classifier using neural networks for a limited number of samples. Both semantic and structural similarity was discussed by Ghosh, et al. [6]. However, in this approach, the SVM (Support Vector Machine) has to be tuned with optimal weights. Another hybrid approach was discussed by Tekli et al. [18], which computes similarity based on element/attribute labels not on element/attribute values. A Fuzzy based similarity measure was discussed by Ceravolo et al. [1], in which, the semantic weight of the term is not considered. Structure and Content similarity using LSI was discussed by Tran et al. [20], in which, all the terms in the XML document are considered and hence the dimensions of the input matrix is higher. In this paper, similarity between XML documents is computed based on term weight similarity measure. The term weight attribute present in XML document indicates the significance of a term with respect to a domain topic. Now to cluster XML documents different methods were proposed by many researchers [2, 3, 7, 8] and we have used an agglomerative hierarchical clustering algorithm since it provides data at different levels.

### 1.1 The Contributions

- Automatic identification of the topic of the document in XML format using a Fuzzy Logic approach to compute Term Weight
- Computing semantic similarity between XML documents using term weight
- Clustering XML document based on Similarity measure
- Searching the cluster of XML documents and retrieving results

The rest of the paper is structured as follows. Section 2 describes the automatic identification of the subject of the document. XML similarity computation is explained in Sect. 3. Experimental results are discussed in Sect. 4 while Sect. 5 briefs the conclusion.

## 2 Automatic Identification of Subject of the Document

A classification system is used to associate information with a set of predefined concepts. Examples of popular classification system are ACM hierarchical ontology (ACM CCS), Mathematics Subject classification (MSC), Physics and Astronomy Classification Scheme, Journal of Economic Literature Classification System etc. Automatic identification of the topic of a document is a key issue in information retrieval.

Once the information is organized, the retrieval process can be done effectively. The process of mapping topics of the document with the classification system is given in Fig. 1.

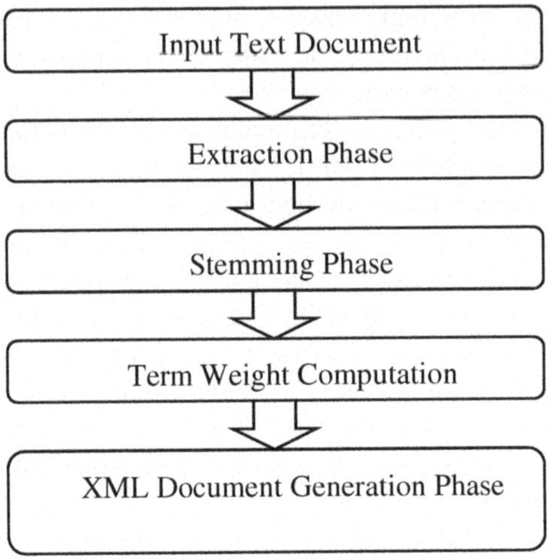


**Fig. 1.** Automatic topic Identification

### 2.1 Input Text Document

The input text document can be any research article, books or any other electronic resources on a particular domain. Here ACM CCS Ontology is considered which deals with the computer science domain.

### 2.2 Extraction Phase

The extraction phase involves identifying important keywords. In a research article the keywords given by the author is considered because they describe the topic of the article in a précised manner. Similarly, the table of contents in a book defines the topic of a book more elaborately than the title. In this phase these keywords are extracted.

### 2.3 Stemming Phase

In Stemming phase, key words are stemmed which we got in extraction phase, using a Porter Stemming algorithm. Each keyword can be a combination of words and each word is stemmed. If the keyword is "Data Structures and Algorithms", the stemmed output is: "Data Structure Algorithm".

### 2.4 Term Weight Computation

In Term Weight computation phase, Fuzzy logic is used based on the following criteria

- Mapping with a domain ontology (ACM CCS) using LSI

- Frequency of keyword in Title
- Frequency of keyword in Abstract

The term weight value is associated with linguistic terms namely "high", "medium" and "low". Each linguistic term describes the membership degree of the corresponding Fuzzy Set. The Fuzzy sets and the corresponding membership functions are shown in Fig. 2.

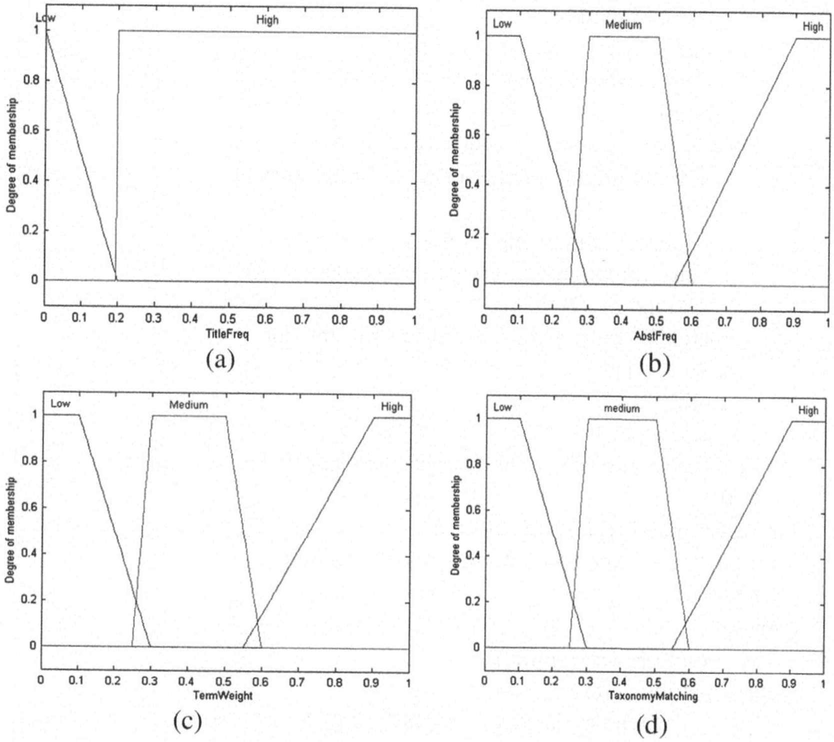


**Fig. 2.** Membership function for (a) Title freqency (b) Abstract freqency (c) Term Weight (d) Concept mapping in domain ontology

The steps in Fuzzification and Defuzzification are as follows:

STEP 1: Significance for each of the criteria is fixed in the range 0 to 1 based on the application is given by

$$Ts + TFs + AFs = 1 \tag{1}$$

where Ts – Significance of mapping with concept in domain ontology, TFs – Significance of Title frequency and AFs – Significance of Abstract frequency

STEP 2: Input variable for mapping with concept in domain ontology is calculated based on LSI and the algorithm is given in Fig. 3.

```
Input: keyword K containing Stemmed words w1,
        w2...,wn.
        Hierarchical classification document D
        Ts – significance of mapping with concept in domain ontology
Step 1: // Exact match //
        If (w1^w2...^wn) found in D then
           Tax_weight ← 1.0
           return ( classification code, Tax_weight)
           exit function
        else
           goto step 2
        endif
 Step 2: // Partial match. Possibility of more than one match //
        q ← minimum number of words to be present
        k ←0
        while(not end of file D) do
      If (any combination of words w1,w2) (q<=i<n)
           found in D) then
      match[k] ← classification hierarchy element
      k ← k + 1;
      endif
        endwhile
 if (k=0) //No partial match// return(false) endif
 r ← 0
 for each match[j] ( 1<= j < k)
 sim[r] ← compute LSI between K and match[j]
 r ← r + 1;
 endfor
 Tax_weight← max(sim[r])
 classification code ← match[j]
              where j is max { sim[m] }, 0 ≤ m ≤ r
 Tax_weight ← Tax_weight * Ts
 return ( classification code , Tax_weight)
 exit function
```

**Fig. 3.** Algorithm for mapping with concept in domain ontology

STEP 3: Input variable for Title frequency is obtained by

$$Title_{freq} = (n_k/N_t) * TFs \tag{2}$$

where $n_k$ is the frequency of keyword in Title, $N_t$ is the total number of words in Title and TFs is the significance of Title frequency

STEP 4: Input variable for Abstract frequency is obtained by

$$Abs_{freq} = (m_k/M_t) * AFs \tag{3}$$

where $m_k$ is the frequency of keyword in Abstract, $M_t$ is the total number of words in Abstract and AFs is the significance of Abstract frequency

STEP 5: The Fuzzy rules based on the above criteria are designed

STEP 6: The output of the Fuzzy system is the Term weight which is a crisp value and this term weight is associated with the keyword for document representation.

### 2.5 XML Document Generation Phase

In XML document generation phase the corresponding XML document is generated based on the term weight computing. Every key word is mapped and the corresponding classification code is taken as XML element and the corresponding semantic weight is considered as the attributes. For the above example the classification code for "Data Structures" is E1 and the Fuzzy term weight is 0.92. This is done for all extracted keywords.

For example if the keywords extracted from the document are "Data Structures", "Arrays" and "Trees" then the corresponding XML document is shown in Fig. 4.

```
<root>
    <E1 weight="0.92">
        <E1.1 weight="0.85"/>
        <E1.7 weight="0.79"/>
    </E1>
</root>
```

**Fig. 4.** XML document with semantic weight

## 3 Computing Semantic Similarity Between XML Documents

Once input documents are represented in XML form, the similarity between XML documents are computed based on Fuzzy set. The computation process is explained with the following example.

Document 1 with the following key words

Communication network
Network architecture and design
Distributed network

Document 2 with the following key words

Network analysis and design
Network communication
Distributed Network management

The corresponding XML documents are generated as explained in the previous sections and are shown in Fig. 5.

| | |
|---|---|
| <root> | <root> |
| <c2 weight=”0.94”> | <c2 weight=”0.95”> |
| <c21 weight=”0.91”> | <c21 weight=”0.80”> |
| <c214 weight=”0.91”/> | <c214 weight=”0.92” /> |
| </c21> | </c21> |
| </c2> | </c2> |
| </root> | </root> |

**Fig. 5.** XML representation of documents 1 and 2.

Now each XML document is represented as Fuzzy set with semantic weight as membership function. The definition of Fuzzy Set representing XML document and the membership function is defined as follows:

$$\mu(w;\,\alpha,\,\beta) = \begin{cases} 0 & \text{if } w \le \alpha \\ w & \alpha < w < \beta \\ 1 & w \ge \beta \end{cases} \tag{4}$$

Where w is the semantic weight and α and β are threshold values which can be set based on applications. Based on (4) with α = 0.10 and β = 0.90, document-1 and 2, shown in Fig. 5 is represented as

$$\begin{aligned} A &= \{ (c2, 1.0), (c21, 1.0), (c214, 1.0)\} \\ B &= \{ (c2, 1.0), (c21, 0.80), (c214, 1.0)\} \end{aligned}$$

The fuzzy similarity measure between A and B is given as

$$\text{Sim}\ (A, B) = \min(\mu_A(t),\ \mu_B(t))/\max(\mu_A(t)\ ,\ \mu_B(t)) \tag{5}$$

Using (5) the similarity between the Fuzzy sets A and B is computed as

$$\text{Sim}(A, B) = (1 + 0.80 + 1)/(1 + 1 + 1) = 2.80/3 = 0.93.$$

Thus a high similarity value between documents A and B is returned even though the keywords are not exactly same.

## 3.1 Clustering XML Documents and Retrieval of Results

Based on the similarity measure explained above document similarity matrix is constructed and it is used for clustering. Agglomerative hierarchical clustering with complete linkage is used because it groups clusters at different levels.

In order to improve the efficiency of searching process an index file is associated with every cluster and this index file contains all parent elements of classification code in the corresponding cluster. For example if the classification code is E112, then the parent element E with cluster id is stored.

The user query is mapped with the hierarchical classification document. The mapping process is same as explained above and the corresponding classification code is returned and the same code is searched in the index file and the corresponding documents within the clusters are returned.

## 4 Experimental Results

Our Experimental results focus on two real time data sets namely Infovis and DBLP. InfoVis-2004 is a contest conducted in the field of information visualization [5], the dataset contains complete metadata for all the papers of 8 years (1995–2002) of InfoVis Conference and their references. DBLP stands for Digital Bibliography Library Project, and the DBLP server provides Bibliographic information on major computer science journals and proceedings. We have used both InfoVis data set and DBLP dataset to compare our algorithm with state-of-art algorithm namely keyword based and with Tran et al. [20] approach. Table 1 presents the detailed information about the datasets.

**Table 1.** Dataset used for document similarity measures

| Data sets | # of Articles | # of Keywords/Article extracted |
|---|---|---|
| InfoVis | 4240 | 5–15 |
| DBLP | 3104 | 4–18 |

In order to analyze the performance of the proposed method, experiment is conducted by varying the parameters of the membership function α and β with three set of values from {{0.1, 0.9}, {0.2, 0.8}, {0.3, 0.7}}. For analyzing the clustering performance, average precision, recall and F-Measure are used.

The following graphs shown in Fig. 6 depict the results received from each dataset. Our approach yields high precision and recall when compared to Tien Tran approach as well as the State-of-Art algorithm keyword based approach.

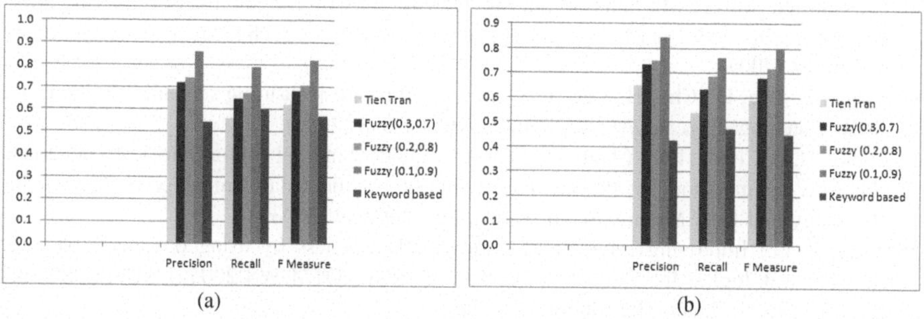


**Fig. 6.** Average precision, recall and F-Meausre for (a) InfoVis dataset (b) DBLP dataset

From the Fig. 6 we observed that for both the dataset Infovis and DBLP, the parameters α and β with the values {0.1, 0.9} yields higher precision and recall values. For the parameters α and β with values {0.2, 0.8} and {0.3, 0.7} yields better precision and recall in that order followed by Tien Tran approach and keyword based approach.

# 5 Conclusion

In this paper we propose a method for retrieving user relevant research articles based on domain knowledge and Fuzzy Set. This ensures the improved efficiency of researcher who uses the web as a resource for research. In the proposed method the term weight is calculated using Fuzzy logic. The experimental result shows an improved information retrieval when compared with other existing approaches. In future extension, we are planning to test our system in a large data set, namely, research corpus, which is in Bibtex record format. In future we also planned to use SKOS based domain ontology so that the accuracy of retrieval process can be still improved.

# References

1. Ceravolo, P., Nocerino, M.C., Viviani, M.: Knowledge extraction from semi-structured data based on fuzzy techniques. In: Negoita, M.G., Howlett, R.J., Jain, L.C. (eds.) KES 2004. LNCS (LNAI), vol. 3215, pp. 328–334. Springer, Heidelberg (2004)
2. Dalamagas, T., Cheng, T., Winkel, K.J., Sellis, T.: A methodology for clustering XML documents by structure. Inf. Syst. **31**(3), 187–228 (2006)
3. Damiani, E., Nocerino, M.C., Viviani, M.: Knowledge extraction from an XML data flow: building a taxonomy based on clustering technique. In: Proceedings of EUROFUSE 2004: Eighth Meeting EURO Working Group on Fuzzy Sets, pp. 133–142 (2004)
4. Dogac, A., Laleci, G.B., Kabak, Y., Cingi, I.: Exploiting web service semantics: taxonomies vs. ontologies. IEEE Data Eng. Bull. **25**(4), 10–14 (2002)
5. Fekete, J.D., Grinstein, G., Plaisant, C.: IEEE InfoVis 2004 Contest. In: The History of InfoVis (2004)
6. Ghosh, P.M., Mitra, P.: Combining content and structure similarity for XML document. In: Proceedings of the International Conference on Pattern Recognition, pp. 1–4 (2008)
7. Gil-García, R., Badia-Contelles, J.M., Pons-Porrata, A.: A general framework for agglomerative hierarchical clustering algorithms. In: Proceedings of 18th International Conference on Pattern Recognition ICPR, vol. 2, pp. 569–572 (2006)
8. Guerrini, G., Mesiti, M., Sanz, I.: An overview of similarity measures for clustering XML documents. In: Web Data Management Practices: Emerging Techniques and Technologies, pp. 56–78 (2007)
9. Jeong, B., Lee, D., Cho, H., Lee, J.: A novel method for measuring semantic similarity for XML matching. Expert Syst. Appl. **34**(3), 1651–1658 (2008)
10. Leung, H.P., Chung, F.L., Chan, S.C.: A new sequential mining approach to XML document similarity computation. In: Proceedings of the 7th Pacific-Asia Conference on Knowledge Discovery and Data Mining, Seoul, Korea, pp. 569–569 (2003)
11. Nagypál, G.: Improving information retrieval effectiveness by using domain knowledge stored in ontologies. In: Meersman, R., Tari, Z. (eds.) OTM-WS 2005. LNCS, vol. 3762, pp. 780–789. Springer, Heidelberg (2005)

12. Nierman, A., Jagadish, H.V.: Evaluating structural similarity in XML documents. In: Proceedings of 5th International Workshop on the Web and Databases (WebDB 2002), Madison, Wisconsin, USA, pp. 61–66 (2002)
13. Pan, H., Tan, X., Han, A., Yin, G.: A domain knowledge based approach for medical image retrieval. Int. J. Inf. Eng. Electron. Bus. **3**, 16–22 (2011)
14. Paralic, J., Kostial, I.: Ontology-based information retrieval. In: 14th International Conference on Information and Intelligent Systems, Varazdin, Croatia, pp. 23–28 (2003)
15. Paukkeri, M.-S.: Learning a taxonomy from a set of text documents. In: Applied Soft Computing, pp. 1138–1148 (2011)
16. Salton, G., Wong, A., Yang, C.S.: A vector space model for automatic Indexing. Commun. ACM **18**(11), 613–620 (1975)
17. Sølvberg, I., Nordbø, I., Aamodt, A.: Knowledge-based information retrieval. Future Gener. Comput. Syst. **7**, 379–390 (1992)
18. Tekli, J., Chbeir, R., Yétongnon, K.: A hybrid approach for XML similarity. In: van Leeuwen, J., Italiano, G.F., van der Hoek, W., Meinel, C., Sack, H., Plášil, F. (eds.) SOFSEM 2007. LNCS, vol. 4362, pp. 783–795. Springer, Heidelberg (2007)
19. Tekli, J., Chbeir, R., Yetongnon, K.: An overview on XML similarity: background, current trends and future directions. Comput. Sci. Rev. **3**(3), 151–173 (2009)
20. Tran, T., Nayak, R., Bruza, P.: Combining structure and content similarities for XML document clustering. In: Proceedings of the 7th Australasian Data Mining Conference (AusDM), vol. 87, pp. 219–226 (2008)

# Model of Teachers' Personalized Decision Making on Activities and Resources in Web-Based Training

Kai-li Wang(✉) and Wen-ya Liu(✉)

School of Educational Technology, Shenyang Normal University, Shenyang 110034, Liaoning, China
wangkl@synu.edu.cn, liuwenya0717@126.com

**Abstract.** Teachers' educational technology competence training takes plural forms, one of which is web-based training. However, for many educational institutions in mainland of China, the online training effect is not satisfied for providing teachers with uniform resources and activities without considering the personal factors when the role of a teacher has changed into an adult learner. In this paper, a preliminary survey is used to figure out the influential factors of training effect, and a decision making model is proposed by KAFR tool, which is developed for observing both the relation between learning styles and learning activities, as well as the relation between learning styles and learning resources. The model could be used in the generation of user model by describing teacher's profile in any adaptive educational system.

**Keywords:** Decision making model · Learning style · Learning activities · Learning resources

## 1 Introduction

In mainland of China, traditional mode and environment for teachers' educational technology competence training are challenged by blending learning emphasizing on participation, activities and interactive activities [1]. However, the training effect is not satisfied because most of the training systems provide teachers with uniform activities and resources during the online training phase. The existing studies have seldom considered providing personalized resources and recommending proper activities for teacher-as-learner from primary and secondary schools. In this paper, teacher's learning style and its relation with learning activities/resources are analyzed, based on which the decision making model is established to adapt to the teachers' needs in online educational technology competence training.

## 2 Observation on Teacher-As-Learner

### 2.1 Learning Style

The study in learning styles was initially developed as the result of interest in individual differences [2–4]. No matter from what perspectives it is defined or described, the


D.K.W. Chiu et al. (Eds.): ICWL 2013 Workshops, LNCS 8390, pp. 52–59, 2015.
DOI: 10.1007/978-3-662-46315-4_6

learning style is considered by researchers as a stable indicator of how a learner performs in the learning environment [5–7]. Comparing with the other elements that influence teachers' decision making, we choose learning style as the independent variable of inferring rule in this study.

### 2.2 Teacher-As-Learner

In educational technology competence training programs, teachers play the role of online adult learners. They have some distinct characteristics: self-guided, experienced, concentrated, and inner motivated. Meanwhile, their learning process and learning motivation are special in such aspects as continual, professional development. That implies that teacher's working domain and experience should be paid more attention during the training process; well organized personalized learning resources and activities may supply domain special experiences, which are positive for the training goal of ultimate application in daily teaching activities.

## 3 Study on Learning Activities and Learning Resources in Web-Based Training

### 3.1 Classification of Learning Activities

Online training is a form of separation between trainer and trainees both in space and in time. Learning activities are the units in which every trainee should be definitely involved. Different learning activities could be chained online in order to fulfill the serial learning tasks. The effective category of these activities is a foundation of the later model construction. Some researchers have contributed to the learning activities categorization, such as in the work of Reigeluth [8], Merrill [9], Jonassen [10], Skinner [11], and Zhang and He et al. [12], with the goal of promoting the acquisition of analytical skills, autonomy, collection of relevant information, group work, etc. Among these research, He's [12] practical results could comprehensively summarize all aspects of learning process. Based on Zhang and He's foundations, the online learning activities in this study are divided into four first-level categories with learning activities in details on each sub-level (see Fig. 1a).

### 3.2 Classification of Learning Resources

The other foundation of the later decision-making model construction is learning resources. For a network resources manager, the volume of the information is immense and rapidly updated, well organized resources by clear classification for the access of information are more convenient. There exist different categorizations of learning resources: from their origin, according to the types of learning outcome or according to the domain of science, etc. Mostly, the resources are categorized by the representing format (text, image, audio, video, animation) of information and the *Technical Specification for Educational Resource Construction Information Model* of CELTSC [13] has also classified the same basic units of educational communication as a standard, which inspire the categorization of learning resources in this study (see Fig. 1b).

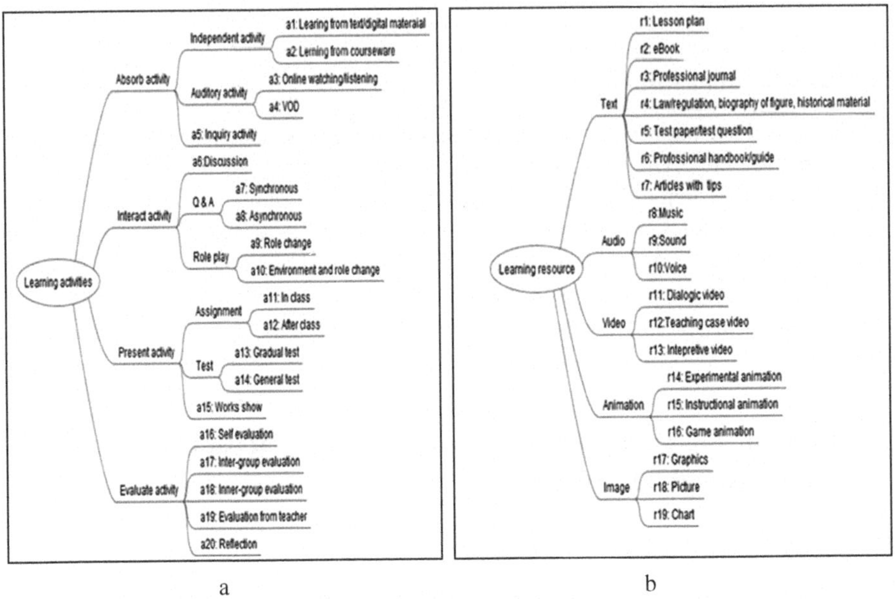


**Fig. 1.** Categorization of online learning activities and resources

# 4 Decision Making Model

## 4.1 Design of the Research Tool

In order to observe teacher's learning style and its relation with their learning activities/ learning resources, a questionnaire integrating index of learning style, a set of learning activities and a set of learning resources is developed. Kolb's KLSI-1984 [14] is used for observing teacher's learning style. One reason to use this index is its long-time world-wide usage with the proof of validity and reliability. The other reason is: according to Kolb's experiential learning theory, learners need four abilities for effective learning: concrete experience abilities, reflective observation abilities, abstract conceptualization abilities, and active experimentation abilities. This classification has the similar angles as for the categorization of the learning activities in this study; there is a similar reason for using Fleming's VARK model to infer relation between learning style and learning resources [15]. The categorization of learning activities and learning resources according to learning style can also be regarded as the hypothesis for the construction of decision making model in this study.

The research tool is a questionnaire composed of general information, learning style-learning activities, and learning style-learning resources. Before large-scale launch of questionnaire, a preliminary result is obtained by a small scale investigation, according to which some ambiguous items in paper questionnaire are revised to be clearer for interviewees, and the KAFR tool is thus generated [16]. In this tool, "KA" module and "FR" module collectively produce a questionnaire for teachers, "K", "A","F" and "R" respectively stand for "Kolb's KLSI-1984", "Learning Activity", "Fleming's VARK model" and "Learning Resource".

## 4.2 Data Analysis

The questionnaire was distributed among the teachers who have been the trainees in teacher's educational technology competence training, attaching a letter to explain the research motivation. These teachers are from 9 elementary and secondary schools of Shenyang, Liaoning province, 150 teacher respondents and 142 (94.67 %) valid ones are retrieved.

The data analysis employs SPSS 17.0 and Microsoft Excel 2007. The concordance coefficient of learning style-learning activities and learning style-learning resources of the KAFR tool are both 0.647, which verifies the hypothesis on the two relations above-mentioned. Learning activities a1–a20 and learning resources r1–r19 are explained in Fig. 1, and the distribution result by KAFR tool is shown in Tables 1 and 2.

**Table 1.** Distribution of learning activities according to learning style

| | Absorb activity | Interact activity | Present activity | Evaluate activity |
|---|---|---|---|---|
| Assimilator | a1 a2 | | a11 a12 a13 a14 | |
| Accommodator | a3 a4 a5 | a6 a9 a10 | | a17 a18 a19 |
| Converger | | a7 a8 | | a19 |
| Diverger | a2 a3 a4 | | a15 | a16 a20 |

**Table 2.** Distribution of learning resources according to learning style

| | Text | Audio | Video | Animation | Image |
|---|---|---|---|---|---|
| Visual | | | r12 r13 | | r16 r17 r18 r19 |
| Aural/ Auditory | | r9 r10 r11 | | | |
| Read/Write | r1 r2 r3 r4 r5 r6 r7 r8 | | | | r20 |
| Kinesthetic | | | | r14 r15 | |

Index of Coupling Degree (ICD) is employed for observing the consistent degree of hypothesis and result by KAFR tool on "learning style-learning activities" (ICD1) and "learning style-learning resources"(ICD2), "n" is the size of valid sample.

$$\mathrm{ICD}_1 = \frac{count(\mathrm{TypeK} = \mathrm{TypeA} = 1)}{\mathrm{n}} \tag{1}$$

$$\mathrm{ICD}_2 = \frac{count(\mathrm{TypeF} = \mathrm{TypeR} = 1)}{\mathrm{n}} \tag{2}$$

"Type K = 1" signifies a learning style observed by KLSI-1984 (Assimilator, Accommodator, Converger or Diverger), Type A signifies the learning style of a teacher who directly choose the activities that are classified in Table 1.

"Type F = 1" signifies a learning style observed by Kolb's KLSI-1984 (Visual, Aural/Auditory, Read/Write, Kinesthetic), Type R signifies the learning style of a teacher who directly choose the resources that are classified in Table 2.

According to the data collected by KAFR tool, ICD1 = 90/142 = 0.634, ICD2 = 100/142 = 0.704. The coupling situation are both satisfied (>=0.6). Thus, this result can be used in the later modeling process.

### 4.3 Construction of Decision Making Model

Sample ratio coefficient(SRC) of every sub-learning activities(or resources) according to every type of learning style can be figured out and sorted from highest to lowest, being marked from "1" to "4". If the highest SRC from the result of questionnaire is coupled with the hypothesis in Sect. 4.1, the correspondent activities can be related into the correspondent learning style. Tables 3 and 4 show the results of coupling.

The relation between learning style and learning activities then could be expressed as:

$$\mathrm{Ai} = \mathrm{f}(\mathrm{K_{LS}}) = \begin{cases} \mathrm{A_{AS}} & = \mathrm{A_j}\ (\mathrm{j} = 1,\ 2,\ 9,\ 11,\ 13,\ 14,\ 18), & \mathrm{K_{LS}}\text{ is assimilator} \\ \mathrm{A_{AC}} & = \mathrm{A_j}\ (\mathrm{j} = 4,\ 5,\ 6,\ 7,\ 18,\ 19), & \mathrm{K_{LS}}\text{ is accommodator} \\ \mathrm{A_C} & = \mathrm{A_j}\ (\mathrm{j} = 7,\ 8,\ 12,\ 19), & \mathrm{K_{LS}}\text{ is a converger} \\ \mathrm{A_D} & = \mathrm{A_j}\ (\mathrm{j} = 2,\ 3,\ 4,\ 5,\ 10,\ 15,\ 16,\ 20), & \mathrm{K_{LS}}\text{ is a diverger} \end{cases}$$

And the relation between learning style and learning resources could be expressed as:

$$\mathrm{Ri} = \mathrm{f}(\mathrm{F_{LS}}) = \begin{cases} \mathrm{R_V} = \mathrm{R_j}\ (\mathrm{j} = 4,\ 8,\ 12,\ 13,\ 16,\ 18,\ 19), & \mathrm{F_{LS}}\text{ is visual} \\ \mathrm{R_A} = \mathrm{R_j}\ (\mathrm{j} = 9,\ 10,\ 11), & \mathrm{F_{LS}}\text{ is aural/auditory} \\ \mathrm{R_R} = \mathrm{R_j}\ (\mathrm{j} = 1,\ 2,\ 3, 5,\ 6,\ 7,\ 20), & \mathrm{F_{LS}}\text{ is a read/write} \\ \mathrm{R_K} = \mathrm{R_j}\ (\mathrm{j} = 14,\ 15), & \mathrm{F_{LS}}\text{ is a kinesthetic} \end{cases}$$

**Table 3.** Coupling of hypothesis and result by KAFR tool (*learning style-learning activities*)

| | | As | Ac | C | D | Hypothesis | Result | Coupled |
|---|---|---|---|---|---|---|---|---|
| Absorb activity | a1 | 1 | 3 | 2 | 4 | Assimilator | Assimilator | YES |
| | a2 | 2 | 3 | 4 | 1 | Assimilator diverger | Assimilator diverger | YES |
| | a3 | 3 | 4 | 2 | 1 | Accommodator Diverger | Converger diverger | Not all |
| | a4 | 4 | 1 | 3 | 2 | Accommodator diverger | Accommodator diverger | YES |
| | a5 | 4 | 2 | 3 | 1 | Accommodator | Diverger | No |
| Interact Activity | a6 | 3 | 1 | 4 | 2 | Accommodator | Accommodator | YES |
| | a7 | 2 | 3 | 1 | 4 | Converger | Converger | YES |
| | a8 | 3 | 2 | 1 | 4 | Converger | Converger | YES |
| | a9 | 1 | 4 | 3 | 2 | Accommodator | Assimilator | No |
| | a10 | 3 | 4 | 2 | 1 | Accommodator | Diverger | No |
| Present activity | a11 | 1 | 2 | 4 | 3 | Assimilator | Assimilator | YES |
| | a12 | 4 | 3 | 1 | 2 | Assimilator | Converger | No |
| | a13 | 1 | 3 | 4 | 2 | Assimilator | Assimilator | YES |
| | a14 | 1 | 3 | 2 | 4 | Assimilator | Assimilator | YES |
| | a15 | 4 | 3 | 2 | 1 | Diverger | Diverger | YES |
| Evaluate activity | a16 | 2 | 4 | 3 | 1 | Diverger | Diverger | YES |
| | a17 | 4 | 1 | 2 | 3 | Accommodator | Accommodator | YES |
| | a18 | 1 | 2 | 3 | 4 | Accommodator | Assimilator | No |
| | a19 | 4 | 2 | 1 | 3 | Accommodator converger | Accommodator converger | YES |
| | a20 | 3 | 2 | 4 | 1 | Diverger | Diverger | YES |

*Note*: As-Assimilator, Ac-Accommodator, C-Converger, D-Diverger.

**Table 4.** Coupling of hypothesis and result by KAFR tool (*learning style-learning resources*)

| | | V | A | R | K | Hypothesis | Result | Coupled |
|---|---|---|---|---|---|---|---|---|
| Text | r1 | 3 | 4 | 1 | 2 | R | R | YES |
| | r2 | 2 | 4 | 1 | 3 | R | R | YES |
| | r3 | 3 | 3 | 1 | 2 | R | R | YES |
| | r4 | 1 | 2 | 4 | 3 | R | V | No |
| | r5 | 4 | 2 | 1 | 3 | R | R | YES |
| | r6 | 3 | 3 | 1 | 1 | R | R | YES |
| | r7 | 3 | 4 | 1 | 1 | R | R | YES |
| | r8 | 1 | 4 | 3 | 1 | R | V | No |
| Audio | r9 | 4 | 1 | 3 | 1 | A | A | YES |
| | r10 | 2 | 1 | 3 | 4 | A | A | YES |
| | r11 | 2 | 1 | 3 | 4 | A | A | YES |
| Video | r12 | 1 | 4 | 2 | 3 | V | V | YES |
| | r13 | 1 | 2 | 4 | 3 | V | V | YES |
| | r14 | 4 | 2 | 3 | 1 | K | K | YES |
| Animation | r15 | 2 | 3 | 4 | 1 | K | K | YES |
| | r16 | 1 | 4 | 3 | 2 | V | V | YES |
| | r17 | 1 | 3 | 2 | 4 | V | V | YES |
| Image | r18 | 1 | 2 | 4 | 3 | V | V | YES |
| | r19 | 1 | 2 | 3 | 4 | V | V | YES |
| | r20 | 2 | 4 | 1 | 3 | R | R | YES |

Thus the decision making model can be generated based on the two relations: the corresponding activities and resources according to a teacher's learning style, this model could recommend the activities and resources before a teacher enters in formal training on a training platform (see Fig. 2).

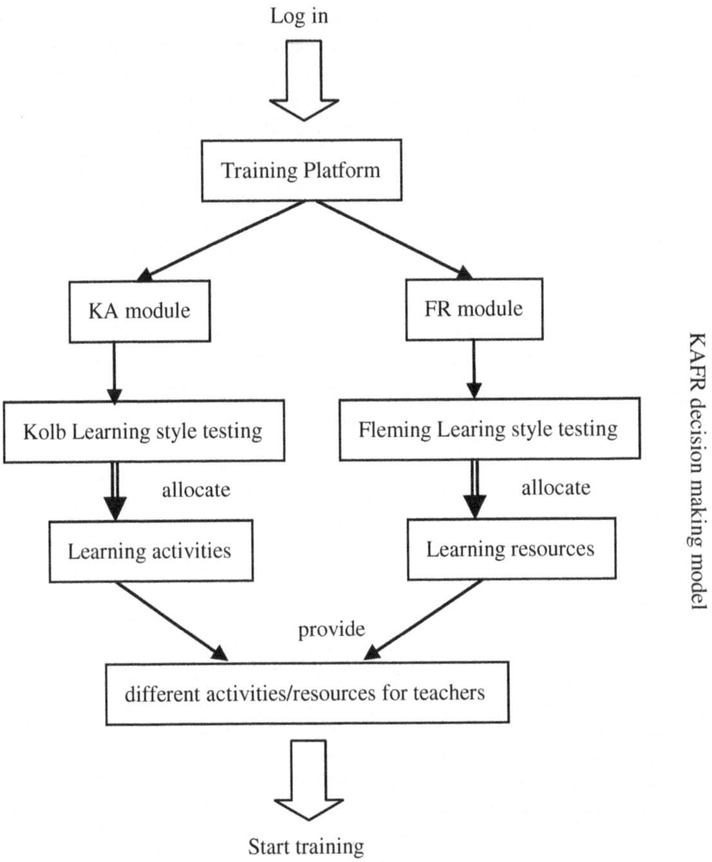


**Fig. 2.** KAFR model implemented in training platform

## 5 Conclusion

Based on the situation of teachers' online training in mainland of China, the duality of teacher's role is analyzed in this paper. Learning style is chosen as a relatively stable indicator that influences teacher's decision making on learning activities and learning resources. After quantitative analysis, the relations are established in decision making model, which could be employed before the formal training on a platform. The future work will be carried out with a larger sample in teachers' community, besides learning style, other factors would be examined.

**Acknowledgment.** This paper is one of the achievements of research program "Design of Personalized Model for Online Teachers' Teaching and Learning" (No. W2012127) supported by the *Project of Humanities and Social Sciences of Education Department of Liaoning Province*.

## References

1. Jun, H., Zhuzhu, W.: Capability building in educational technology for teachers in China. Br. J. Educ. Technol. **41**(4), 607–611 (2010)
2. Brown, S.: Cognitive preferences in science: their nature and analysis. Stud. Sci. Educ. **1975** (2), 43–65 (1975)
3. Entwistle, N.J., Hauley, M.: Personality, cognitive style and students' learning strategies. Higher Educ. Bull. **6**(1), 23–43 (1979)
4. Dunn, R.S., Dunn, K.J.: Learning styles/teaching styles: Should they…can they… be matched? Educ. Leadersh. **36**, 238–244 (1979)
5. Felder, R.M., Spurlin, J.: Applications, reliability and validity of the Index of Learning Styles. Int. J. Eng. Educ. **21**(1), 103–112 (2005)
6. Keefe, J.W.: Learning style: an overview. In: Keefe, J.W. (ed.) Student Learning Styles: Diagnosing and Prescribing Programs, pp. 1–17. National Association of Secondary School Principals, Reston (1979)
7. Kolb, D.A.: Learning styles and disciplinary differences. In: Chickering, A.W. (ed.) The Modern American College: Responding to the New Realties of Diverse Students and a Changing Society, pp. 232–255. Jossey-Bass, San Francisco (1981)
8. Reigeluth, C.M., Stein, F.S.: The elaboration theory of instruction. In: Reigeluth, C.M. (ed.) Instructional Design Theories and Models: An Overview of Their Current Status. Prentice-Hall, Hillsdale (1983)
9. Merrill, M.D.: Component display theory. In: Reigeluth, C.M. (ed.) Instructional Design Theories and Models: An Overview of Their Current Status. Prentice-Hall, Hillsdale (1983)
10. Jonassen, D.H.: Designing constructivist learning environments. In: Reigeluth, C.M. (ed.) Instructional Theories and Models, 2nd edn, pp. 215–239. Lawrence Erlbaum Associates, Mahwah (1999)
11. Skinner, B.F.: The Behavior of Organisms: An Experimental Analysis. Appleton-Century, New York (1938)
12. Zhang, S., He, K., et al.: Research on web-based formative evaluation of learning activities —based on the experience of the K-12 teachers' ET ability training. Modern Educ. Technol. **17**(10), 82–87+90 (2007)
13. CELTSC (2013). http://www.celtsc.edu.cn/qhcms/index.html
14. Kolb, D.A.: Experiential learning: Experience as the source of learning and development. Prentice-Hall, Englewood Cliffs (1984)
15. Leite, W.L., Svinicki, M., Shi, Y.: Attempted Validation of the Scores of the VARK: Learning Styles Inventory With Multitrait-Multimethod Confirmatory Factor Analysis Models. Educ. Psychol. Measur. **70**, 323–339 (2010)
16. Wenya, L., Zhaojun, L., Kaili, W.: The tool design of KAFR model of network teacher training. China Educ. Technol. **314**(3), 74–79 (2013)

# International Symposium on Knowledge Management and E-Learning

# Analyzing Learning Flows in Digital Learning Ecosystems

Maka Eradze, Kai Pata, and Mart Laanpere(✉)

Tallinn University, Narva rd. 25, 10120 Tallinn, Estonia
{Maka.eradze,kai.pata,mart.laanpere}@tlu.ee

**Abstract.** This paper envisages emerging trends and methods in learning analytics for post-LMS era, where learning increasingly takes place in distributed, user-defined digital learning ecosystems. Inspired by the recent developments on uptake framework and Experience API, we propose learning flow as the main unit of analysis while studying learning-related interactions.

## 1 Introduction

Recent changes in online learning environments towards openness and distribution, and the paradigm shift towards learner-centered approach have brought out the need to better understand how learning takes place in such systems. We conceptualize new e-learning systems as dynamic and evolving Digital Learning Ecosystems (DLE) and assume that DLEs may be governed by ecological principles [1]. Knowing empirically which ecological principles are applicable to DLEs, and how they function, would enable designing new type of learning interactions in DLE and managing these as learning environments. But in order to take an in-depth look at how a DLE functions and which ecological principles appear in these systems, new approaches for learning analytics are required. While traditional approaches in educational data mining and learning analytics are based on analyzing frequencies of events (e.g. page views, posts, comments), Suthers et al. [2] have argued that exploratory sequential data analysis of learners' digital footprints might provide better insight to individual and collaborative learning processes. In this paper, we are going to explain why the next generation TEL systems, should contain such new kind of learning analytics tools that support learning interactions based on ecological principles.

Previous research on Technology-Enhanced Learning (TEL) has regarded learning interactions as an important unit of analysis, which has been studied at various perspectives [3–5]. Most of the TEL research is based on the data collected through learner-reported surveys [6, 7], educational data mining techniques [8, 9], qualitative text analysis [10] or social network analysis [11]. We argue that each of the approaches alone is neither sufficient nor relevant for researchers aiming at conducting large-scale learning analytics in Digital Learning Ecosystems (DLE). This paper envisages emerging trends and methods in learning analytics for post-LMS era, where learning


D.K.W. Chiu et al. (Eds.): ICWL 2013 Workshops, LNCS 8390, pp. 63–72, 2015.
DOI: 10.1007/978-3-662-46315-4_7

increasingly takes place in distributed, user-defined digital learning ecosystems. Inspired by Uptake Framework by Suthers and Rosen [2] and recent developments towards Experience API [12], we propose to use learning flow as the main unit for learner interaction analysis.

## 2 Digital Learning Ecosystems

We define DLE as '*an adaptive socio-technical system consisting of mutually interacting digital species (tools, services, content used in learning process) and communities of users (learners, facilitators, experts) together with their social, economical and cultural environment*' [1]. DLE consists of a large and distributed set of dynamically evolving online tools and services, which are selected and used by different groups of learners and facilitators. DLE is a third-generation virtual learning environment, replacing traditional Learning Management Systems in coming decade.

While the second generation of TEL systems presented software systems as an environment where learners and teachers interacted with each other as well as with learning resources, we propose to turn the roles upside down for DLE. In DLE, the "species" or "organisms" are various interacting software tools and services together with their users, while larger technological landscape, social and cultural contexts play the role of the "environment". This is a change of paradigm, which will help us better understand, analyze and design the future tools and services to enhance learning. We are not using ecological concepts as metaphors; we propose to extend the ecosystems theory towards the digital world.

The three main principles of ecology may be translated into DLEs as following:

The first principle in ecology is that the flow of energy and the exchange of matter through open ecosystem is regulated by the interactions of species and the abiotic component (by the web of energy and matter). Reyna [13] conceptualized "teaching and learning" as this energy that empowers digital learning ecosystems to changing "information to knowledge". The permeability of a DLE to the export and/or import of information and knowledge depend on the nature of the 'architecture' of the components of the system (e.g. connectivity, clustering), the characteristics of species, and their diversity and distribution, and interactions between them (such as commensalism).

The second important ecological principle is existence of the feedback loop to and from the environment that enables species to be adaptive to the environment and the environment to change as a result of species. A recent literature in evolutionary theory elaborates the notion of niche construction [14] as an ecological factor that enables organisms to contribute for and benefit from environmental information. If organisms evolve in response to selection pressures modified by themselves and their ancestors, there is feedback in the system. In our approach to DLEs, the "service-species" are activated by users with different roles (learner, facilitator) and their learning intentions. Ecological psychology [15] suggests that learner's/teachers' direct perception of the learning environment's action potentialities (or so-called affordances) varies and this would give the variability to the actual use of services in the e-learning system. The niches for each service-species in the digital ecosystem may be collected from this user-behavior, for example by learning analytics.

The third important principle that we extend from ecology to DLEs is associated with the communicative interactions between species. The digital community is a naturally occurring group of "service-species" populations in e-learning ecosystem who inhabit the same habitat (but use different niches) and form temporary coalitions (communities). For example the mutualisms such as parasitism, symbiosis or commensalism may appear between service species are associated with sharing the re-sources and associate with our first principle (energy and matter exchanges in the network). Other type of interactions, based on communication, which assumes mutual awareness, signaling between agents (or using the accumulated signals left into the environment) may be distinguished as well.

We assume that as a result of applying these three ecological principles on designing the next-generation online learning platforms, an open, loosely coupled, self-organised and emergent DLE can evolve. Yet, this is a hypothesis that should be empirically validated by using new approaches to learning analytics in DLEs.

## 3 Defining Interaction

Interaction is a concept that is common to the systems in nature as well as to human-technology systems. Wagner defines interaction as '*reciprocal events that re-quire at least two objects and two actions. Interactions occur when these objects and events mutually influence each other*' [16]. In natural systems we may differentiate between resource-based interactions between different agents of the systems that generate transformative flows across chains of resource networks, as well as communicative interactions between agents. Suthers et al. [2] distinguish between educational "inter-action" including direct encounters and exchanges with others and "interaction" based on indirect associations via persistent artifacts - both lead to individual and group-level learning. Based on some interactions in educational systems the meaningful uptakes appear during interaction of learners, teachers and resources when information is transformed to knowledge. In larger scale interactions in DLE generate learning flows and patterns within DLEs, which may be used for facilitating learning. In our learning analytics framework these learning flows are crucial.

We look at the concept of interaction from the following aspects:

(a) What actors interact in DLEs and how they appear to be mutually connected? What is characteristic to educational interaction in DLEs?
(b) What interactions/patterns of contingencies appear in DLEs?
(c) What kind of uptakes appear as a result of interaction in DLEs?

Distance education theorists have broken the interaction concept down to mainly based on the roles of the human and inanimate actors [17]. Moore's theory of Three Types of Interaction includes learner-content, learner-instructor, learner-content and is the first systematic approach to defining the typologies of interactions in distance education. Within the learning communities different types of interactions are crucial for the learning [3, 18]. Anderson has expanded Moore's three dyads of interaction - learner-content, learner-teacher and learner-learner to include content-teacher, content-content and teacher-teacher interactions [3]. Anderson's model is learning-centered and also takes into account material resources. For analytical purposes in DLEs we have to consider mainly those interaction actors and interaction dyads that can be automatically traced.

In education didactic interactions have several particularities – they happen be-tween actors with different level of knowledge and competences. Moore's Theory of Transactional distance [18] – describes the psychological and pedagogical separation that affects learning and has to be overcome by the dialogue (higher order interaction). Anderson and Garrison [3] proposed the Equivalency theorem assuming that in order the learning to take place, one of the interactions shall be at a high level. Other dyads of interaction can add value and increase the quality of learning but it must also estimate the costs of resources for these types of interactions.

The uptake framework [2] assumes that interaction is fundamentally relational, so the most important unit of analysis is not isolated acts, but rather relationships between acts. The uptake framework attempts to deal with on the following analytical challenges in distributed learning environments, which are also relevant in DLEs:

- Interaction may be distributed across actors, media, space, and time.
- There is a need to examine the sequential organization of interaction with-in learning episodes.
- It is not correct reducing the sequential history of interaction to the most recently occurring event category – it is needed capturing the aspects of the coherence of the mediated interaction that are not apparent in the threaded structures.
- There is a need to scale up analyses to more episodes and larger scale organization.
- Properties of distributed interaction place different demands on representations of data and analytic structures - analysis of interactional processes must reassemble interaction from the separate records of multiple media, but remain media aware to record how people make use of the specific affordances of media.
- An analytic program must be based on theoretical assumptions concerning what kinds of research questions are worthwhile - analytic representations should minimize assumptions concerning the answers to the research questions posed.

The uptake framework [2] attempts to provide a new methodological framework for the analysis of inter-subjective meaning making. The framework includes a media independent characterization of the most fundamental unit of interaction, which they call uptake. Uptake is present when a participant takes aspects of prior events as having relevance for ongoing activity. The concept of uptake supports diverse definitions of "interaction," including any association in which one actor's coordination builds upon that of another actor or actant. Uptake can be refined into interactional relationships of argumentation, information sharing, transactivity, and so forth. The contingency graphs serve as abstract transcripts that document relationships between events. They capture the potential ways in which one act can be contingent upon another. Contingencies provide evidence that uptake may exist, but do not automatically imply that there is uptake. For example the following contingencies may be found: media dependency, temporal proximity, spatial organization, semantic relatedness, inscriptional similarity. The analyst interprets sets or patterns of contingencies as evidence for interaction.

## 4 Dippler - a DLE with an Ecological Learning Analytics Approach

We have built a prototype of DLE called Dippler [19] which consists of three interconnected core components: a central learning flow management service, institutional course management environment and a personal blog-based e-portfolio for each learner. Learners can extend their personal learning space by integrating external social media tools, services and content to their e-portfolios through simple technologies such as RSS-feeds, embedding, linking and widgets.

While in LMS (e.g. Moodle) all learning interactions take place within a single closed Web information system and the data is stored in one centralised database, the situation changes radically in distributed DLEs. In order to add learning analytics functionalities to DLE like Dippler, two necessary steps must be taken: (1) harvesting, storing and monitoring interaction-related data with rich semantics from distributed systems that DLE consists of and (2) identifying methods and tools for analyzing and visualizing the data.

Most of the tools for gathering the learning analytics data [11, 20] are directed to the closed LMS systems, while the most of the learning happens outside the LMS. Cohere [21] is another analytic tool that deals with the discourse network analysis and break down the learning interaction analytics to a discourse unit. The GLASS tool suggested by [22] for learning analytics visualization captures data from different computer applications but does not provide the data recorded in a the form of interactional dyads and is restricted only to learner-content interaction. We argue that a holistic, automated and event oriented unit of analysis must be a focus in learning inter-action analytics.

Ferguson and Shum [23] propose a notion of SNLA - social learning analytics and after reviewing different types social learning analytics (social learning network analytics, social learning discourse analytics, social learning disposition analytics, social learning content analytics, social learning context analytics) offer visualizations and recommendations to support learning. They introduce a SocialLearn media space specially accustomed to learning. This environment is a good example of combining different social learning analytics and this way might seem like a good idea for improving learning, it cannot offer learning interaction analytics data for automated semantic learning analytics and especially for studying the depth and quality of interaction.

Lehman et al. [24] use two distinct approaches to study "off-topic" that is regarded as a part of a dialogue that has no pedagogical value. First they recorded tutoring and introduced coding schemes, that were later categorized into three pedagogically-relevant groups: Tutor Motivational Dialogue Moves, Tutor Pedagogical Dialogue Moves, and Student Dialogue Moves. The other approach deployed Linguistic Inquiry and Word Count Tool. The authors conclude that these methodologies seem to sup-port the initial casual observations that the "off topic" is not simply another category. That the "social exchange" cannot be categorized as simply "other" and this type of exchange also serves a pedagogical value. Although this research combines different approaches and tries to analyze to the depth and quality of one particular type of interaction, it is clear that the question on automated interaction analysis as well as scaling up the results remains.

Krüger et al. [25] give a similar unit of analysis and architecture of a tool for structuring and exporting data, relevant to our work, what they call a Schema i.e. data model that captures the essence of the event - Actor, Verb, Object, Timestamp. But this work is mainly based on the traditional LMS data (view/submit frequencies and quiz scores) and uses association rules instead of exploratory sequential data analysis. Just like many other experimental products, this tool might be interesting for researchers, but it would be a challenge to make it meaningful and usable for an average teacher in a domain other than computer science.

In the open DLEs the activities happen in the user environment and the interaction patterns can be traced only based on the logs retrieved from those environments, therefore the monitoring of the interactions and logging data needs to be designed having a predefined theoretical foundation. The ecosystem approach in Dippler considers an upside down roles where the "species" or "organisms" (i.e. users, content, tools) interact with each other and the broader technological landscape and socio-cultural contexts make up the environment. In this sense there must be an analytical system for learning interaction, a system where the interaction can be analyzed within the ecosystem approach of distributed learning.

Common analytical practices of coding and counting interaction types for statistical analysis that are prevalent in TEL literature obscure the sequential structure and situated methods of the interaction [2]. In order to analyze the learning interactions in DLE, it is necessary to model the patterns of interactions and record the related data in real time in a way it could be easily used for learning analytics.

Harvesting, storing and monitoring the data on learning interactions poses challenges due to the very nature of DLE concept – it's a distributed learning environment where different social tools are selected, used, added and removed from the learner side. Four types of learning interactions take place in such settings: learner-teacher, learner-learner, learner-content and content-content (e.g. aggregators). The current version of Dippler documents these interactions in the form of Activity Stream, which is based on the pedagogically enhanced Activity Base Schema (activitystrea.ms). Dippler's Activity Stream displays the main types of interactions in the form of a proposition, containing the Actor (a user), the Action (a verb from restricted vocabulary), the Object (a target of the Activity) and timestamp. The approach resembles to one proposed by TinCan API or xAPI, which makes two activity stream technologies easily interoperable.

The Experience API is a service that allows for statements of experience (typically learning experiences, but could be any experience) to be delivered to and stored securely in a Learning Record Store. The Experience API is dependent on Learning Activity Providers to create and track learning. Learning ActivityProvider is a soft-ware object that communicates with the LRS to record information about the learning experience. Learning activity is a unit of instruction, experience or performance that has to be tracked. A Statement consists of <Actor (learner)> <verb> <object>, with <result>, in <context> to track an aspect of a learning experience. Several statements can be used to track the whole experience. The statements are recorded in the LRS - Learning Record Store [12].

As most of the Objects and Activities in Dippler are annotated with the domain-related categories (keywords structured as taxonomy), it opens the potential for a different kind of learning analytics not currently supported in the traditional LMS. In order to support multi-level, multi-theoretical analysis of learning interactions in Dippler, we decided to adapt its interaction-monitoring component to make it compliant with the uptake framework introduced by [2].

The uptake framework examines the interaction in the distributed learning setting. It views the analytics of the interaction in the hierarchical structure. The hierarchies start with traces and domains – the unit already readily recorded in forms of events through the Learning Activity Streams using adapted version of xAPI.

With the help of recorded dyadic interactions in the forms of events it will be easier to create an automated analytic system that will scale up the interaction analytics. Also, it will solve the problem with identifiers that is brought up in the uptake framework [2]: '*A key concern is persistence of identity across tools and sites: some work may be required to ensure that each given actor is represented by the same identifier in the event model, and likewise for the identity of digital objects shared across tools (ideally persistence of identity should be addressed in mash-ups for the learners' sake. Once this has been accomplished, the event and domain models taken together provide an abstract transcript of the data that re-assembles in one analytic artifact the diverse events that were for their actors a single activity*'.

So the uptake framework combined with adapted Activity Streams can offer the following advantages:

- Recording interactions in dyadic events will encompass the processes, traces, domains.
- The relations with a domain will be already identified through annotation, entities and their relationships established and recorded.
- Enable recording the activities happening outside the LMS, so it will support the concept of distributed interactions [2].
- It will make the learning interaction analytics automated.

## 5 Sample Scenario: Collaborative Concept Mapping

Let us illustrate the discussion above with a fictional scenario, involving a service-species based on a didactical method called collaborative concept mapping. This method involves engaging students in a small group work, where a concept mapping tool is used for identifying the core set of concepts for a given domain along with and their relations with each other. This scenario belongs to a set of design artifacts, which were created to conceptualise and guide the process of development of the learning analytics module for Dippler.

In our sample scenario, teacher gives an assignment to the students in Dippler platform, while connecting the assignment explicitly with a specific learning outcome. As each learning outcome is previously annotated with 2–3 keywords from domain ontology, the Dippler connects all related learner interactions also with these keywords. In the given case, the assignment is: "Form the groups of 2–3 and identify core concepts related with digital competence and their relations, so that it would be compatible with three digital competence standards. Read the Chap. X from the course textbook and compare three given digital competence standards. Output of your group work should be submitted in the form of a concept map that includes initial set of concepts".

Student groups start working on the assignment in their personal learning spaces, the blogs that communicate to the BOS service of Dippler all interactions. Each student separately identifies the set of concepts and reports about them in his blog, students can monitor each other's blog posts and comment each other's work – the goal is to come to the common ground about which concepts should be used in the concept map. In this phase some teachers like to comment students blogs, whereas others don't intervene to the process and wait only for the final assignment result. Next, students start working with the shared concept map in a Web-based tool Bubbl.us, using this set of concepts, and they use Skype for discussing while they work. Final concept maps are submitted as assignments by each student group. Extended xAPI record for such interactions are documented in the following format:

In <Context>, <User> performs <Action> on <Object> with <Tool> producing <Result> at <Time>. For instance, a specific line in the record might look like this:

In **Assignment 3**, **John adds** a **comment** to **blog postX** with **toolX** at **12:30 12-07-13**. All the xAPI records related to this assignment are then passed to the learning analytics module of the Dippler, which returns an overview of interactions, recommendations and feedback in the form of diagrams.

The success of this assignment in different groups may be monitored and analyzed using the ecosystem principles and fed back to the groups:

- How many learning services of support are available at different time moments of the activity and is there a variability – are some support comments more effective and more fit than others; is there a competition between them on user attention or do they complement each other, for example, when student comments appear seldom, teacher's comments become more frequent and vice versa; How well are different learning services of support interconnected into network (for example by push and pull and mash services between student blogs and Dippler), and how does this affect the network permeability, keep the learner attention and enable the formation of coherent group understandings;
- How do different support service "organisms" enable the feedback loop to and from the ecosystem – what is the impact of support comments with different life-span on the formation of coherent group understandings – those that are stored in blogs, and the same comments when they appear mashed way on Dippler wall for monitoring the group work or the comments shared via Skype;
- How well do different support services send signals to each other of their presence, abundance in the current time moment in the ecosystem – this may enable synergy between them, and for the group members and teacher it gives the feedback whether the team is active or it would need prompting for creating a coherent understanding.

## 6 Conclusions

This paper proposed a new approach to learner interaction analysis, especially through new methods of data collection and analysis inspired by connecting multi-level, multi-theoretical uptake framework with key principles of digital learning eco-systems and capabilities of Experience API. The next steps of our research will implement and validate empirically our learner interaction analytics framework and related technological solution as an integral part of Dippler DLE.

**Acknowledgments.** This study was partly funded by the targeted research grant No. 0130159s08 issued by the Ministry of Education and Research of the Republic of Estonia.

## References

1. Laanpere, M., Põldoja, H., Normak, P.: Designing Dippler – a next-generation TEL system. In: Ley, T., Ruohonen, M., Laanpere, M., Tatnall, A. (eds.) OST 2012. IFIP AICT, vol. 395, pp. 91–100. Springer, Heidelberg (2013)
2. Suthers, D.D., Rosen, D.: A unified framework for multi-level analysis of distributed learning. In: Proceedings of the First International Conference on Learning Analytics & Knowledge, Banff, Alberta, pp. 64–74. ACM, New York (2010)
3. Anderson, T., Garrison, D.R.: Learning in a networked world: new roles and responsibilities. In: Gibson, C. (ed.) Distance Learners in Higher Education, pp. 97–112. Atwood Publishing, Madison (1998)
4. Anderson, T.: Getting the mix right again: an updated and theoretical rationale for interaction. Int. Rev. Res. Open Distance Learn. **4**(2), 111–124 (2003)
5. Garrison, D.R., Anderson, T., Archer, W.: Critical inquiry in a text-based environment: computer conferencing in higher education. Internet High. Educ. **2**(2–3), 87–105 (2000)
6. Tang, T., McCalla, G.: Smart recommendation for an evolving elearning system: architecture and experiment. Int. J. E-Learn. **4**(1) (2005). ISSN 1537-2456. Association for the Advancement of Computing in Education (AACE), Chesapeake, VA
7. Garrison, R.D.: Facilitating cognitive presence in online learning: interaction is not enough. Am. J. Distance Educ. **19**(3), 133–148 (2005)
8. Zaiane, O.: Building a recommender agent for e-learning systems. In: Proceedings of the International Conference on Computers in Education, pp. 55–59 (2002)
9. Tang, T., McCalla, G.: Smart recommendation for an evolving elearning system: architecture and experiment. Int. J. E-Learn. **4**(1), 105–129 (2005). ISSN 1537-2456
10. Muirhead, B.: Enhancing social interaction in computer-mediated distance education. Educ. Technol. Soc. **3**(4) (2000). ISSN 1436-4522
11. Dawson, S., Bakharia, A., Lockyer, L., Heathcote, E.: 'Seeing' networks: visualising and evaluating student learning networks (2011). http://www.olt.gov.au/system/files/resources/CG9_994_Lockyer_Report_2011.pdf. Accessed 31 January 2013
12. ExperienceAPI Specification. http://tincanapi.wikispaces.com/file/view/Experience+API+Release+v0.95.pdf. Accessed 31 January 2013
13. Reyna, J.: Digital teaching and learning ecosystem (DTLE): a theoretical approach for online learning environments. In: Williams, G., Statham, P., Brown, N., Cleland, B. (eds.) Changing Demands, Changing Directions. Proceedings of Ascilite 2011, pp. 1083–1088. University of Tasmania, Hobart (2011)
14. Odling-Smee, F.J., Laland, K.N., Feldman, M.W.: Niche Construction: The Neglected Process in Evolution. Princeton University Press, Princeton (2003)
15. Young, M.F.: An ecological psychology of instructional design: learning and thinking by perceiving-acting systems. In: Jonassen, D.H. (ed.) Handbook of Research for Educational Communications and Technology, 2nd edn. Lawrence Erlbaum Associates, Mahwah (2004)

16. Wagner, E.D.: In support of a functional definition of interaction. Am. J. Distance Educ. **8**(2), 6–26 (1994)
17. Anderson, T.: Modes of interaction in distance education: recent developments and research questions. In: Moore, M. (ed.) Handbook of Distance Education, pp. 129–144. Erlbaum, Mahwah (2003)
18. Moore, M.G.: Three types of interaction. Am. J. Distance Educ. **3**(2), 1–6 (1998)
19. Laanpere, M., Pata, K., Normak, P., Põldoja, H.: Pedagogy-driven design of digital learning ecosystems: the case study of dippler. In: Klamma, R., Specht, M., Leung, H. (eds.) Advances in Web-Based Learning, pp. 307–317. Springer LNCS, Berlin (2012)
20. Graf, S., Ives, C., Rahman, N., Ferri, A.: AAT: a tool for accessing and analysing students' behaviour data in learning systems. In: LAK 2011 Proceedings of the 1st International Conference on Learning Analytics and Knowledge, pp. 174–179 (2011)
21. De Liddo, A.; Buckingham Shum, S.; Quinto, I.; Bachler, M., Cannavacciuolo, L.: Discourse-centric learning analytics. In: LAK 2011: 1st International Conference on Learning Analytics & Knowledge, Banff, Alberta. ACM Press: New York (2011)
22. Leony, D., Pardo, A, Valentín L., Castro, D.S., Kloos, C. D.: GLASS: a learning analytics visualization tool. In: Buckingham Shum, S., Gasevic, D., Ferguson, R. (eds.) Proceedings of the 2nd International Conference on Learning Analytics and Knowledge, pp. 162–163. ACM Press, New York (2012)
23. Ferguson, R., Buckingham Shum, S.: Social learning analytics: five approaches. In: Proceedings of the 2nd International Conference on Learning Analytics & Knowledge, 29 April–May, Vancouver, BC. ACM Press, New York (2012)
24. Lehman, B., Cade, W., Olney, A.: Off topic conversation in expert tutoring: waste of time or learning opportunity. In: Proceedings of the 3rd International Conference on Educational Data Mining, 11–13 June 2010, Pittsburgh PA (2010)
25. Krüger, A., Merceron, A., Wolf, B.: A data model to ease analysis and mining of educational data. In: Proceedings of the 3rd International Conference on Educational Data Mining, 11–13 June 2010, Pittsburgh PA (2010)

# Research Trends of Language Learning in Virtual Reality from 2003 to 2012: A Content Analysis

Tsun-Ju Lin[1], Yu-Ju Lan[2(✉)], and Yu-Hsuan Kan[2]

[1] Kainan University, Taoyuan, Taiwan
[2] National Taiwan Normal University, Taipei, Taiwan
yujulan@gmail.com

**Abstract.** This paper conducted a content analysis of studies in language learning in three dimensional multi-user virtual environments (MUVEs) that were published in four journals from 2003 to 2012. A total of 23 articles were cross-analyzed by categories including research topics, target languages, technology usage, and research methodology to identify some of the research issues and limitations in the research area. It was found that research in communication was the most explored topic in MUVEs, and the 3D virtual world tool Second Life was the most widely used in language learning. However, the list of research topics and studying languages were rather limited. Thus, there are definitely needed more studies to enrich the research area. We hope that this paper can involve more language researchers in 3D MUVEs to provide students input- and output-rich and immersive environment where learning can be appealing, meaningful, and fun.

**Keywords:** MUVEs · Virtual reality · Virtual worlds · Content analysis · Research trends

## 1 Introduction

Owing to the rapid advance and popularity of wireless communication and multimedia environments, virtual reality/world, so called multi-user virtual environments (MUVEs), has received considerable attention in the recent five years [4]. Virtual reality is generally defined as small representations of content area or domains designed to "bridge the gap between reality and abstract knowledge by the discovery method" [5] (p. 72). In order to create such environments, the systems commonly are theme-based and comprise full integration of artificial intelligence products and a wide variety of social communication tools. Because of its unique combination of features, virtual reality has been quickly introduced for educational purposes to promote authentic and immersive learning environments.

Virtual reality tools in nowadays are a far cry from the early two-dimensional (2D) text-based online virtual reality, such as multi-user domains (MUDs) and MUD-object oriented (MOOs), to which multiple users can be connected at the same time. Current virtual reality environments evolve more sophisticated interactive systems and a high degree of visual appeal, such as massively multiplayer online role-playing game


D.K.W. Chiu et al. (Eds.): ICWL 2013 Workshops, LNCS 8390, pp. 73–81, 2015.
DOI: 10.1007/978-3-662-46315-4_8

(MMORPGs), to allow a wide range of interlocutors to communicate, cooperate, and compete through their customized three-dimensional (3D) virtual spaces and avatars (called residents). Furthermore, virtual reality utilized in computer-assisted language learning (CALL) area usually provides multiple communication channels (i.e., instant messaging and voice chat) and data-recording features, to which additional sources of input, output, and feedback can be offered for language learners. Accordingly, several evidences have proved that such virtual learning environments can effectively increase learning involvement and motivation [8, 17], reduce learner anxiety [9], support the development of learner autonomy [10], and promote interactive and creative ways of teaching and learning [7].

Comparing to other Web 2.0 tools, however, virtual worlds have been less frequently explored [2, 15]. As a consequence of this, virtual reality in language learning has been claimed to be the least published research topic in the CALL area [4], and thus what virtual reality (or virtual world) actually means today remains controversial. Thus, the purpose of this study is to conduct a content analytic approach systematically to review and synthesize the literature of language learning in virtual reality from 2003 to 2012 (ten years). Reviewing the research trend of MUVEs may help practitioners, educators, and researchers identify research interests and gaps, and further provide them with a reference to make plans in the future. For the research purpose, this leads us to ask questions such as, "How important is MUVEs in learning languages?", "Are there particular software which can better meet the needs of certain types of language programs?", and "Is there a reason why virtual reality is claimed to be the least published research topic in the CALL area?" In order to answer these questions, the four "best" English language journals in the field of CALL were examined, including Language Learning & Technology (LLT), CALICO Journal, Computer Assisted Language Learning (CALL), and ReCALL [12]. This study further extends the previous studies' frameworks to analyze virtual reality research trends according to four categories, namely the research topics, the used technology programs, the target languages, and the research methodology [4, 13]. Four research questions addressed by this paper include:

1. What topics related to language learning in virtual reality were published in these journals from 2003 to 2012?
2. Which languages have been targeted to study language via virtual reality tools?
3. What technologies have been used in the studies on virtual reality?
4. What methodology (i.e., research types, methods, and sample groups) were applied in the studies on virtual reality from 2003 to 2012?

## 2 Methodology

To find studies for the content analysis, computer searches of journal databases were carried out. Top four CALL-specific and education technology-related journals [12] were selected, including Language Learning & Technology (LLT), CALICO Journal, Computer Assisted Language Learning (CALL), and ReCALL. There were a total of 1160 documents published by these four journals from 2003 to 2012. For the purpose of this study, the analysis included journal articles that went through a process of peer review, but columns, commentaries, editorial materials, and letters were excluded. After further comprehensive reviews through three researchers, a total of 41 document items from 2003 to 2012 were located through the researchers with the keywords as follows: simulation, virtual reality, 3D social virtual worlds (SVWs), 3D MUVEs, MOOs, MUDs, virtual learning environments, and MMORPGs. After coding the data, only 23 articles were considered as MUVEs (see Fig. 1 for the distribution of articles over time). These articles have to fit the definitions of MUVEs as follows: (1) A shared space which is multi-user domain, (2) Persistence of the in-world environment, (3) Aim for bringing simulated real life experiences, such as topography, movement, and physics that offer the illusion of being there, and (4) Optional: Non-player characters (NPCs), data-recording features, 2D, or 3D [11].

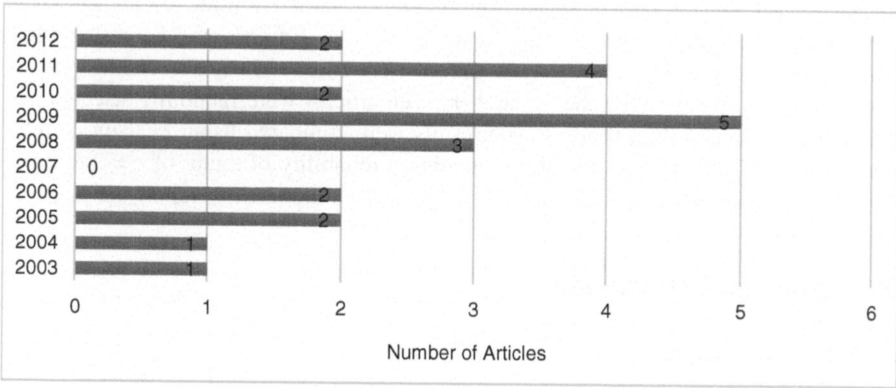


**Fig. 1.** Distribution of articles over time

## 2.1 Selection of Research Topics, Languages and Technologies

One of the major purposes of this paper was to indicate research topics in MUVEs from 2003-2012. All articles were categorizing according to focus of target topics, technologies, and target learning languages.

## 2.2 Choice of Research Types, Methodological Approaches and Sample Groups

After the three researchers' discussion and consensus, three categories of research types were identified: research article and review article. The methodological approaches were identified, including quantitative research approach, qualitative research approach, and mixed-method approach. Seven categories modified from Hue et al.'s (2012) study were utilized to identify the research sample groups as follows: 1. Elementary school, 2. Junior and Senior high school, 3. Higher education, 4. Pre-service or in-service teacher training program, 5. Adults, 6. Others, and 7. Non-specified.

### 2.3 Lesson Design

This study used all of the articles relevant to virtual reality published in *LLT*, *CALICO*, *CALL*, and *ReCALL* from 2003 to 2012 to investigate the research trends. Since "content analysis is a summarizing, quantitative analysis of messages that relies on the scientific method" [6] (p. 10), descriptive statistics was utilized to categorize the research topics, technology usage, target languages, sample groups, research types, and methodological approaches. It is important to note that some of the category analysis would not include the review papers, such as sample groups, target learning languages, and technology used for virtual reality since this type of articles did not provide empirical evidences.

To obtain more reliable outcomes from coding, three researchers (a professor, a post-doctoral researcher, and one assistant researcher) in educational technology helped to code these studies based on the aforementioned categories. Their number of years of language teaching experience ranged from five to 15 years. All three researchers knew more than one foreign language (e.g., Spanish, Chinese, English, and Italian) and had taught online courses in more than two different countries before. The coding process was carried out manually by the researchers. Ten articles were randomly selected and followed the same coding process. The results were compared using Pearson correlation coefficient measures of reliability, yielding a reliability of figure of $r = .88$. After the initial coding process, a descriptive analysis was conducted to report the data.

## 3 Results and Discussion

### 3.1 Research Topics

There were 16 target topics found in the aforementioned 23 articles. These topics can be further grouped in broader categories: learning behavior, attitude, and perception (i.e., learner engagement, self-efficacy, motivation, oral participation, and learner autonomy), communication skills (i.e., interaction, argumentation and critical thinking, negotiation of meaning, and vocabulary knowledge), instructional design (i.e., task design), type of online language course delivery (i.e., online tandem language learning), and review of the literature in general.

In particular, student communication skills have received considerable attention due to the special nature of its virtual reality (i.e., providing multiple communication channels and allowing multiple social interactions) (11/23). However, most of these studies seemed to sole utilize one medium, usually text-chat function, which "can restrict the development of cooperative interpersonal relationships necessary for effective communication" [8] (p. 70). Some studies have remained largely exploratory in learner behavior, perception and emotional investment in the learning environments (5/23). It deserves to be mentioned that these articles consistently agreed that virtual reality learning environments promoted positive attitudes and enhanced learner engagement and motivation. However, a number of negative attitudes and potential problems were mentioned from both client-side and server-side issues. For user-related issues, for example, novice Second Life users seemed to consistently suffer from problems with complicated interfaces and hardware requirements (e.g., good graphic cards and high-speed Internet connection) [8]. Server-side issues included down time, frequent updates, lag, etc. These barriers seemed to be the reasons to hinder educators and teachers to implement the relevant tools in their classrooms. It was suggested that user-related issues can be solved through the long-term training [2] and financial support from the institutes or government.

Furthermore, two studies emphasized on task design both selected pre-service teachers as their major participants to gain a better understanding of how to effectively utilize the strength of virtual reality and then integrate pedagogical activities into the environments. These articles have provided us with knowledge from teacher's perspectives of how to foster student creativity and design authentic learning conditions in MUVEs. Unfortunately, these articles represented only a small portion of articles among all the selected articles. This finding reflects that little has known from empirical research about teachers' perspectives and decision making in MUVEs. The gap existing between students' and teachers' perspectives to be engaged in these environments have yet to be studied and illustrated. Meanwhile, four studies from 2003 to 2006 seemed eager to implement virtual reality tools to promote bilingual tandem language exchanges. Surprisingly, this type of language learning format did not receive much attention after 2006. Due to these evidences, there is a need to focus more on any creative task design and innovative language teaching formats in such environments (e.g., role-playing, information gap, and jigsaw), so teachers and practitioners will have better understanding of how to implement virtual reality in their classrooms. Also, a broader range of topics are needed to explore, such as personal identity and behaviors of avatars in-world, the development of non-verbal communication (i.e., physical gestures, poses, and animations), isolating experience in such environments, etc. Consequently, the research development of the virtual reality in language learning can be increased.

## 3.2 Technology Used for Language Learning

Through the selected empirical studies, Second Life (N = 7, 37 %) were the most used virtual reality technology for language learning. The second and third most used technology was text-based MOO (N = 4, 21 %) tools and Active World (N = 3, 16 %). Other technologies also included Quest Atlantis, The SIMs, Sim Theme Park, Utility, and Autodesk 3ds MAX (formerly called 3D Studio Max). It is important to note here that three quarters of the studies using MOO as the language learning platform was published before 2006. These findings indicate that text-based virtual reality can no more satisfy practitioner' needs. Rather, 3D virtual reality tools with the feature of multiple communication channels, such as Second Life and Active Worlds, might better suited for teachers' needs to create more interactive and collaborative tasks and thus to provide multiple ways of input, output, and feedback [8]. Since Second Life and Active Worlds were mostly used among the selected studies, we can also imply that these two platforms might more popular and mature tools dedicated in language learning [16]. Among the selected studies, we also found that five of them combined virtual reality tools with other asynchronous technologies in their studies, such blog, e-mail, Microsoft Power Point, Moodle, etc. to balance the disadvantages and advantages of both asynchronous (i.e., allowing students more time to reflect on the class materials and to organize their thoughts) and synchronous technologies (i.e., promoting real-time activities).

### 3.3 Target Learning Languages

According to the result, most empirical studies emphasized on English (15 articles) as a foreign language, a second language, a lingua franca, a bilingual tandem language learning, or for special purposes. Obviously, English learning has been widely implemented in different purposes and types of language teaching comparing to other languages. The next most frequently target languages in the selected studies were German and Spanish, found in four and three respectfully. It is important to note that three studies involved teaching two languages particularly in these enhancing tandem language learning based on mutual language exchange between partners who are native speakers of the target languages. The finding indicates that none of the East Asian languages (e.g., Mandarin Chinese, Japanese, and Korean) and Arabic languages, and only few languages of Europe, were investigated in virtual reality learning environments. This implies the pioneer stage of virtual reality in language learning research. As researchers, we definitely need more inquiry into this research area by involving diverse learner groups within various methods of language teaching.

### 3.4 Target Sample Groups

As seen in Fig. 2, Out of 23 studies selected for this paper, 11 articles involved language learners in higher education. The same number of studies followed in junior and senior high schools (N = 3), and in pre- and in-service teacher training programs (N = 3). Only one involved language learners in an elementary school, and none of the studies were focused on adults and others. Five articles were not specified since all of these articles were identified as review papers. It is worth to be mentioned that K-12 settings were using the software, such as Autodesk 3ds MAX or Quest Atlantics, rather than Second Life (even though Second Life was rated as the most used technology in the previous section).

As most researchers will agree, Second Life contains complicated interfaces [8] and requires frequent updates [3]. Since it is an open source with various kinds of features and virtual spaces, instructors does not much control over who will communicate with their students outside of class time, what locations they will visit in the virtual environments, etc. Safety remains concern for using such software in education settings. To solve the barriers, Second Life has divided its regions into general, moderate, and adult regions to avoid residents under 18 receiving adult content. Additionally, several software were developed and advocate its educational objectives by carefully incorporating pedagogy into the immersive spaces (e.g., Active World Educational Universe, Croquelandia and Zon) [14].

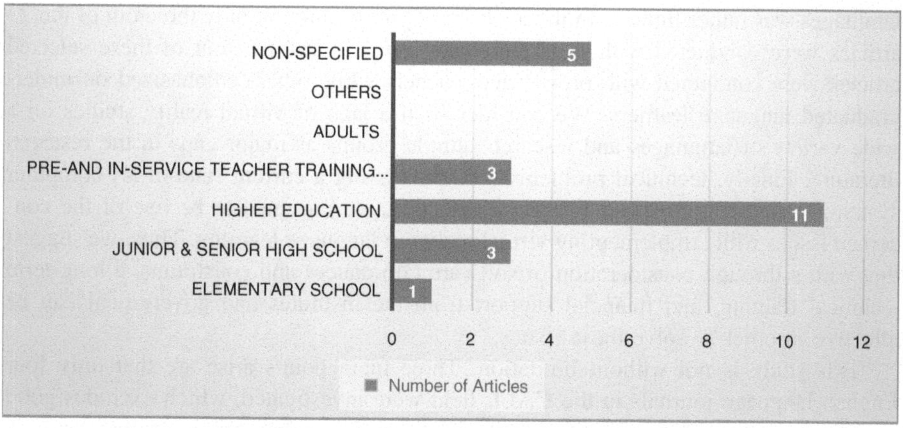


**Fig. 2.** Distribution of sample group selections from 2003 to 2012

### 3.5 Research Types and Methodological Approaches

The research types were distinguished research articles (N = 19, 78 %) and review articles (N = 5, 22 %). Among the research articles, most of them conducted qualitative research (N = 12, 52 %) which involve case study, discourse analysis, and action research approaches through the analysis of chat recordings, field notes, interviews, participant self-refection reports, essays, floor spaces, turn lengths, turn taking patterns, etc. The same number of studies followed quantitative research (N = 3, 13 %) and mixed-methods (N = 3, 13 %). While quantitative research involved objective measurement and statistical analysis to answer the research questions, mixed-methods applied both qualitative and quantitative research approaches. Although these articles conducted different research approaches, authors consistently advocated that MUVEs as promising arenas for language learners by offering significant opportunities for engaged student-centered collaborative and social interaction, for the development of engaging tasks (i.e., increasing motivation, self-efficacy and autonomy, and reducing student anxiety), and then enhancing learners' communicative skills [1, 7, 8, 14]. Furthermore, pedagogical implementation and technical problems seemed to mention throughout most of the articles.

## 4 Conclusion and Future Prospects

These selected studies definitely shed light on what educators can do to make their language teaching virtual reality more effective. However, there are several issues needed to be further explored. The analysis of the topics of the selected articles showed that these articles primarily emphasized on learner's learning behavior, attitude and perception, and their communication skills. Due to the result, a broader range of research topics are needed, such as task design, student personal identity, the usage of the non-verbal communication tools in MUVEs, etc. We also found that English, German, and Spanish were most frequently researched; however, the list of the languages was rather limited. In the analysis of group samples, only three out of the 23 articles were conducted with K-12 language learners; and two out of these selected articles were conducted with pre-service teachers while others emphasized on under-graduated language learners. We consider such a lack of virtual reality studies on a wide variety of languages and research sample groups as major gaps in the research literature. Finally, technical problems (i.e., possessing a current state-of-art computer system, having a high speed Internet connection, etc.) seemed to be one of the concerned issues while implementing virtual reality in language learning. Thus, we suggest that with a through consideration of software affordances and constraints, a long-term technical training, and financial support from the institutes and government can be effective in order to solve these issues.

This study is not without limitation. Three main points arise are that only four English language journals in the CALL field were investigated, which excludes good work in other languages and relevant publications. It is suggested that future research should conduct similar studies with more research data to develop more deliberate analysis.

**Acknowledgment.** The authors would like to thank the Ministry of Science and Technology, Taiwan, R.O.C., for financially supporting this research under Grant Nos. NSC 101-2511-S-003-031-MY3 and MOST 103-2628-S-003-002-MY3. They are also thankful that this research is partially supported by the Aim for the Top University Project and Center of Learning Technology for Chinese of National Taiwan Normal University (NTNU), sponsored by the Ministry of Education, Taiwan, R.O.C., the International Research-Intensive Center of Excellence Program of NTNU and the Ministry of Science and Technology, Taiwan, R.O.C. under Grant No. NSC 103-2911-I-003-301.

## References

1. Cooke-Plagwitz, J.: New directions in CALL: an objective introduction to second life. CALICO J. **25**(3), 547–557 (2008)
2. Deutschmann, M., Panichi, L., Molka-Danielsen, J.: Designing oral participation in second life: a comparative study of two language proficiency courses. ReCALL **21**(2), 206–226 (2009)
3. Ho, C.M.L., Rappa, N.A., Chee, Y.S.: Designing and implementing virtual enactive role-play and structured argumentation: promises and pitfalls. Comput. Assist. Lang. Learn. **22**(5), 381–408 (2009)
4. Hsu, Y.C., Ho, S.N., Tsai, C.C., Hwang, G.J., Chu, H.C., Wang, C.Y.: Research trends in technology-based learning from 2000 to 2009: a content analysis of publications in selected journals. Educ. Technol. Soc. **15**(2), 354–370 (2012)
5. Lee, J.: Effectiveness of computer-based instructional simulation: a meta-analysis. Int. J. Instr. Media **26**(1), 71–85 (1999)
6. Neuendorf, K.A.: The Content Analysis Guidebook. Sage, Thousand Oaks (2002)
7. Peterson, M.: Learner participation patterns and strategy use in second life: an exploratory case study. ReCALL **22**(3), 273–292 (2010)
8. Peterson, M.: Towards a research agenda for the use of three-dimensional virtual worlds in language learning. CALICO J. **29**(1), 67–80 (2011)

9. Roed, J.: Language learning behaviour in a virtual environment. Comput. Assist. Lang. Learn. **16**(2–3), 155–172 (2003)
10. Schwienhorst, K., Borgia, A.: Monitoring bilingualism: pedagogical implications of the bilingual tandem analyser. CALICO J. **23**(2), 349–362 (2006)
11. Smart, J., Cascio, J., Paffendof, J.: Metaverse Roadmap: Pathway to the 3D web. (2007)
12. Smith, B., Lafford, B.: The evaluation of scholarly activity in computer-assisted language learning [focus issue]. Mod. Lang. J. **93**, 868–883 (2009)
13. Stockwell, G.: A review of technology choice for teaching language skills and areas in the CALL literature. ReCALL **19**(2), 105–120 (2007)
14. Sykes, J.M., Oskoz, A., Thorne, S.L.: Web 2.0, synthetic immersive environments and mobile resources for language education. CALICO J. **25**(3), 528–546 (2008)
15. Wang, S., Vásquez, C.: Web 2.0 and second language learning: what does the research tell us? CALICO J. **29**(3), 412–430 (2012)
16. Warburton, S.: Second life in higher education: assessing the potential for and the barriers to deploying virtual worlds in learning and teaching. Br. J. Educ. Technol. **40**(3), 414–426 (2009)
17. Wehner, A.K., Gump, A.W., Downey, S.: The effects of second life on the motivation of undergraduate students learning a foreign language. Comput. Assist. Lang. Learn. **24**(3), 277–289 (2011)

# International Workshop on Ubiquitous Social Learning

# An Interactive 3D Social Graphs for Social Learning

Noorkholis Luthfil Hakim(✉), Shun-Kai Wang, Timothy K. Shih, Wu-Yuin Hwang, Yu-Ren Chen, and Ankhtuya Ochirbat

Department of Computer Science and Information Engineering, National Central University, Jhongli, Taiwan
{koliskol, timothykshih}@gmail.com

**Abstract.** In the past time, Social Learning has been the most natural way for people to learn. However, traditional e-learning system only plays a role of teaching assistant, and seldom has functionalities to enhance interaction that can support social learning, like problem discussing and idea brainstorming. Therefore, we try to use the power of social networks to build a social learning environment. In this paper, we use Facebook as the social networks platform and integrate with an e-learning system. Using the social functionalities provided by Facebook, we can enhance discussion and interaction between users. Moreover, we use the social information and learning information to design a recommendation system, providing friend or course recommendation to user, and build a social tool called Interactive 3D Social Graph, providing the features of information 3D visualization and navigation with kinematic gestures. These idea and features can fully support social learning, and enhance more discussion and interaction on learning between users in learning environment.

**Keywords:** Social learning · Information visualization · 3D graphics · Web technology

## 1 Introduction

From then until now, Social Learning has always been the most nature way to learn new things. Via the discussion, interaction or collaboration between students and teachers or student groups, student can construct related knowledge or experience in the process of social interaction. However, traditional E-Learning system usually has less communication functionalities to support social learning. It mainly plays a role of teaching assistant, which enables teachers to share learning content and manage classes, and enables students to receive learning content in the system. The ways in traditional e-learning system to discuss problems or enhance other interaction are only e-mail, short message, or chat room, forum in some advanced system. The interaction usually shows up between teacher and students for questions and answers, seldom between students for problem discussing or idea brainstorming. It can't offer an environment to fully support social learning. To enhance more interaction and make the learning experience more different, we try to use the power of social networks.


D.K.W. Chiu et al. (Eds.): ICWL 2013 Workshops, LNCS 8390, pp. 85–95, 2015.
DOI: 10.1007/978-3-662-46315-4_9

As an extension of traditional communication network, social networks sites enable users to share and discuss their interest and idea in the network. It makes the users become closer to their friends, and have more interaction in their daily life. To use the power of social networks, we design the integration of e-learning system and social networks, to create a new learning environment, learning in social networks.

In the view of learning, in our system, student and teacher can have learning activities as usual, and share learning related information to the social network sites, through the social functionalities integrated into our system. In the view of social networks, user can see other's learning information and enhance interaction and discussion on learning topic, which achieves the goal of social learning. For some advanced functionalities, first we collect user's social and learning information and build a recommendation system based on those information. Second, we use some 3D technologist and kinematic technologies to build a tool, *Interactive 3D Social Graph*, for the purpose of information visualization, which can make complex data more readable and clear, and kinematic operations, which provides an intuitional way to control the tool.

The following sections will explain our system design in a more specific way. Section 2 is some related work about social learning and information visualization. Section 3 is the design and architecture of our system. Section 4 is the conclusion of our research and future work.

## 2 Related Works

### 2.1 Social Learning

Social Learning Theory [1] states that social behavior(any type of behavior that we display socially) is learned primarily by observing and imitating the actions of others. In the process of learning social behavior, we may construct corresponding knowledge. Also, Social Constructivism [2], proposed by L. Vygotsky, says that knowledge is constructed while learner interacts or cooperates with other social members in the society, instead of one-way instruction. In light of this, while we have social behavior, we are forming some knowledge at the same time.

Distributed Constructionism [3], proposed by M. Resnick, puts emphasis on the idea that, in the activities of design and construction, there needs to have multi-participant to construct sharing and discussion, especially in the online learning environment, which takes knowledge and cognition as the result of the interaction between individual and elements in the online learning environment. Besides, Resnick thinks that, to learn effectively in social environment, it is necessary to have collaboration to design and construct meaningful knowledge and products. According to the theories, the core concept of social learning is having collaboration and interaction with others, and constructing related knowledge at the process of those social behaviors. The concept makes individual to absorb knowledge, and learning experience in social behaviors, and, different from traditional e-learning, learner can receive complete learning participating experience from course constructing to after-school assessment, especially in individual learning scenery.

Previous studies indicated that, the early issue [4] in social learning was the collaboration and interaction in social networks, and the related research [5] studied users' motivation and satisfaction [6, 7] received from distant learning system in social networks. Other research [8] showed that interactive learning and collaborative learning can give user higher learning motivation and better learning efficiency than individual learning.

### 2.2 Information Visualization

Information visualization is the study of visual representations of abstract data to reinforce human cognition. The visualization of social network data as a graph has a long tradition in the social networks studies in social science. Linton Freeman [9] gives the example of using shape, color, position, and the size of nodes to be the main features for presenting distinct view on the data. Many social networks visualizations researches applied for researcher analysis tool instead of provide it for end-users.

In recent years, with the growth of social network sites, projects about social networks visualization for the end-users showed up. Heer and Boyd came out with their tool called Vizter tool [10]. Vizter tool does the visualization of one of the famous social network website, Friendster. They provided exploration tool for the users to play around their social network. The features such as connectivity highlighting, linkage views for viewing network content, X-ray mode and profile search for exploring member profile data and visualization makes this tool is more explore-based play than analysis. The other project came from matter and Pfeiffer [11]. They proposed social networks visualization tool for Facebook. In their research they studied the comparison between 3D visualization of social network and 2D visualization. The result showed that the visualizations of social networks can be more effectively if 3D is utilized. We present tool for 3D visualization of integrated e-learning system and social network.

## 3 Proposed System Architecture

In this paper, we plan to design an e-learning platform that is integrated with social networks and social media. Figure 1 shows the architecture of our system:

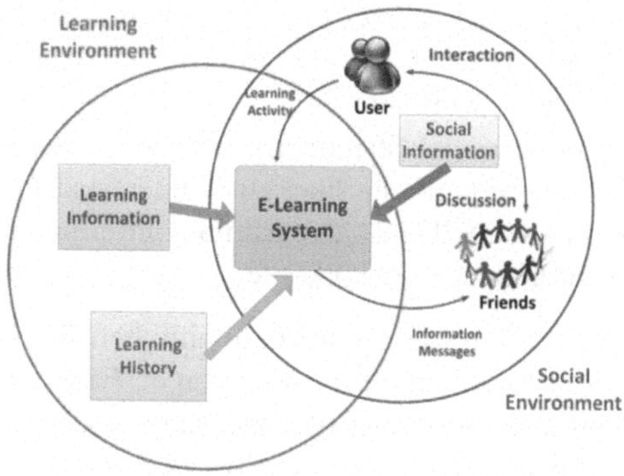


**Fig. 1.** System architecture of our system

Our system can be separate into three parts. First part is the integration of e-learning environment and social environment. We adjust traditional e-learning platform, which provides only learning functionalities, according to the features of social networks and social media. In the learning environment, by using the information sharing and notification functionalities, user can not only do learning activities, but also share learning information and their own learning experience to social network sites, which can enhance interaction and discussion on learning topic. This idea can achieve the main goal of social learning, sharing and collaboration.

The second part is the recommendation system based on the social learning environment. We acquire user's social information from social network site, and analyze with learning information. The final part is the *Interactive 3D Social graph,* which provides 3D information visualization and kinematic gestures to control the tool.

## 3.1 E-Learning System on Facebook

The social network site we choose to integrate with e-learning system is Facebook. The reasons are the following:

1. Facebook provides social functionalities such as information sharing and information respond. Moreover, it provides instant messenger, group chatting room and club. These social functionalities provide a good foundation for social learning.
2. Web application developers can register an application under Facebook, and display their web application in Facebook's frame. Users can use the e-learning services within social networks environment, instead of leaving social environment, which makes the learning experience complete harmony.
3. The Application Programming Interface, API, provided by Facebook is more completed than other social network sites. Web application developers can use the social functionalities provided by Facebook and acquire social information via those API.

Through the web application registration in Facebook, we integrate the e-learning system with social network site and, via the APIs provided by Facebook, use the social functionalities and acquire social information from social network site. We use the following social functionalities in our e-learning system:

1. Comment post: While in the learning process, user can share his learning experience and what he has learned in the courses to social network site by using the comment post functionality. Friends who see the information can have discussion and interaction on the social network site.
2. Like: "Like" is a special social feature in Facebook. User can click the "Like" button to show his opinion while he likes or is interested in some information or topics. In our system, we will post the learning information, which user clicks "Like", to user's wall on social network site.

Moreover, user can login the web application with their Facebook account and get the authorization from user to acquire his information on Facebook. Our system can be accessed at anytime and anywhere, just like the game applications on Facebook. It makes the integration of e-learning system and social networks more close.

### 3.2 Recommendation System

After obtaining the user's information and social information from social networks, we analyze the data with user's learning information in our e-learning system to build this recommendation system. We use the following information:

1. User information
2. User's current learning progress
3. User's learning history
4. User's friend list

We use learning information as a base, and design the friend/course recommendation system with social information.

Figure 2 is the workflow of recommendation:

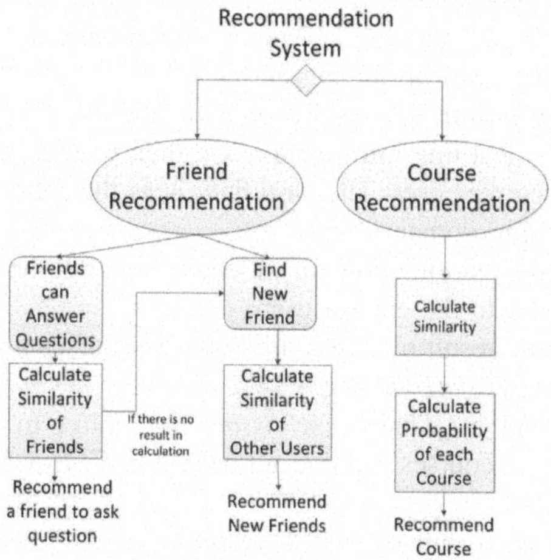


**Fig. 2.** Workflow of recommendation system

The recommendation system is based on the analysis of learning history similarity. We use *Mutual Information* to calculate the similarity of two data sets X and Y, and the result is *I(X, Y)*, the intersection of the two data sets.

Here are the mathematic equations of mutual information:

$$H(C) = -\sum_{n=1}^{N} f(c) log f(c) \tag{1}$$

$$\begin{aligned} I(X,Y) &= H(X) + H(Y) - H(X,Y) \\ &= \sum_{y \in Y} \sum_{x \in X} p(x,y) \log\left(\frac{p(x,y)}{p(x)p(y)}\right) \end{aligned} \tag{2}$$

H(C) is the information entropy of data set C and the definition is shown in Eq. (1). It can represent the distribution of the data set. We can use Eq. (2) to calculate the intersection of the two data sets, and retrieve the result I(X, Y), the joint distribution of the two data sets, which means the similar part of the two data sets.

There are two main functionalities in recommendation system:

1. **Friend Recommendation:** Friend Recommendation mainly finds out other users and recommends to the current user to enhance discussion and interaction. There are two modes, *Find New Friends* and *Friends can Answer Questions*, in the Friend Recommendation. The workflow is as the following:
   (1) Choose a course or learning domain
   (2) According to the mode we use, find out users whose learning history is similar to the current user.
      i. *Find New Friends*: focus on the users who are not in the friend list of the current user.
      ii. *Friends can Answer Questions*: focus on the users who are in the friend list of the current user. If it is fail to find a friend to answer question, our system will change to *Find New Friends* mode.
   (3) Recommend the result to the current user.
2. **Course Recommendation:** Course Recommendation mainly analyzes the current user and his friends' learning information, and then predicts the possible course to recommend to the current user. The workflow is as the following:
   (1) Choose a learning domain
   (2) According to the learning domain we chose, find out the users whose learning history is similar to the current user.
   (3) According to the result of step 2, find out the courses that they took together, noted as *CoursesTakeTogether, CTT*.
   (4) Taking *CTT* and as a base, use *Association Rules* to calculate the tasking probability of the courses that doesn't belong to *CTT* and be taken by the users found in step 2.
   (5) According to the result of step 4, recommend the courses that have higher taking probability.

Here we put a Friend Weight Value to increase the taking probability if the target user is a friend of the current user. This idea is to increase the impact of friends to the current user. By doing this, the current user can get the recommendation of what his friends are reading recently and make the learning history more similar to his friend. This way can make the current user and his friends become closer, and enhance more discussion and interaction on learning, achieving the main goal of social learning.

### 3.3 Interactive 3D Social Graph

One goal of information visualization is to visualize information, like social information in our system, from textual form description to visual representation, facilitating the perception and handling of hidden structures from underlying datasets [12]. We choose graph-based layout to visualize the information because it widely used to depict data in which information is comprised of objects and relationship between those objects such as relation between users. In our system we choose to use 3D based graph layout because literally it give more space for future growing graph, and human is more familiar with 3D in real world than 2D, which makes them easy to explore.

Drawing graph is another challenge in information visualization. We used Spring-Embedding (force-directed) Algorithm to draw the graph. This algorithm calculates the layout of a graph using only information contained within the structure of the graph itself, rather than relying on domain-specific knowledge [13]. Graph drawn by this algorithm tends to be aesthetically pleasing, and exhibits symmetries and crossing free. Though this algorithm is for 2D graph, it still can be used for 3D graph layout by some modification.

**Navigation and Interaction.** In this system, we design two kinds of interaction and navigation features, mouse keyboard interaction and Kinect interaction to explore the graph. For both interactions, we use common actions that used to explore in 3D space such as zooming, and rotating. In the Mouse-Keyboard interaction, we use a common way to control such as scroll button for zooming, right-click-hold for rotate, left-click-hold for panning action and W, A, S, D for keyboard action. We use Kinect because, by using own body movement as controller, user can easy to control, and feel more immersive and realistic while using our system.

The other reason we use Kinect interaction is, in the future, we want to combine this system and virtual smart classroom with Holodeck technology. We design several gestures to explore and interact with the 3D graph. The actions are as following:

1. **Zooming Action:** The Kinect Gesture of this action performs in two handed mode, where both hands left and right place in front of body and move both hands far apart each other on X-axis to perform zoom out and move both hand close to each other on X-axis will trigger the zoom in action.
2. **Rotating Action:** The Kinect Gesture of this action performs in two handed mode by holding the right hand higher than waist and left hand moving on the X-axis to control the rotation. Moving to left causes graph rotate clockwise and moving it to the right causes graph to rotate counterclockwise.
3. **Panning Action:** To do this action on Kinect interaction part, first user must be in one handed mode, placing left hand in front of user's body and holding it for few seconds to enter panning mode. After enter panning mode you can move your left hand up, down, right and left to perform the panning action.
4. **Select Object Action:** To do this action on Kinect interaction part, user can use the Object Picking action by moving one hand to the object and changing the moving axis from X-Y axis to Z-axis. When an object is selected, the content of the object will be shown on screen.

Figure 3 shows the example of Kinect interaction gesture:

There are other Kinect gestures to control 2D UI such as drag window, enlarge, and full screen mode. The drag action simply uses the same gesture as panning action on the selected window. Enlarge action, same gesture with zooming action, moves on the Y-axis to enlarge up and down, instead of moving on the X-axis. To change the screen mode, user needs to move both hands above the head and far apart for full-screen mode, and close to each other for the normal screen mode.

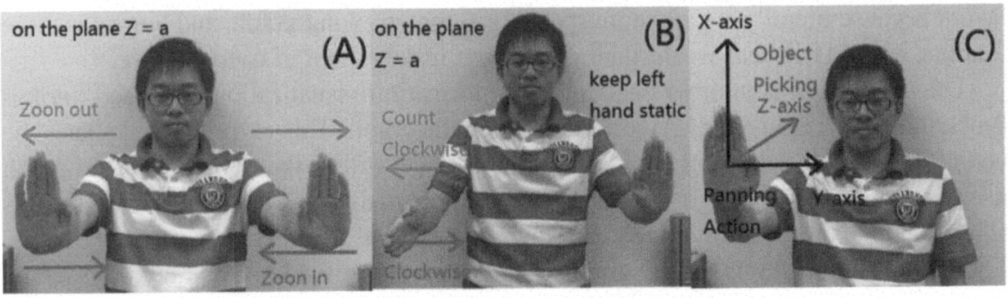


**Fig. 3.** Example of Kinect interaction gesture

**Operations and Features.** Our system provides several features. One of the features is called Social Graph, shown in Fig. 4 This feature contains the graph of the current user and his social relationship. The current user node presents in blue sphere, normal friend presents in green sphere shape with blue line, acquaintance presents in box shape with yellow line, and best friend represents in star shape with red line. The node information, including user ID, name, and taken course list, will show and highlight when we select the node. Another feature is called Course Graph, which provides course tree that contains learning history and score for each lesson. This feature can help student to track their course record and history.

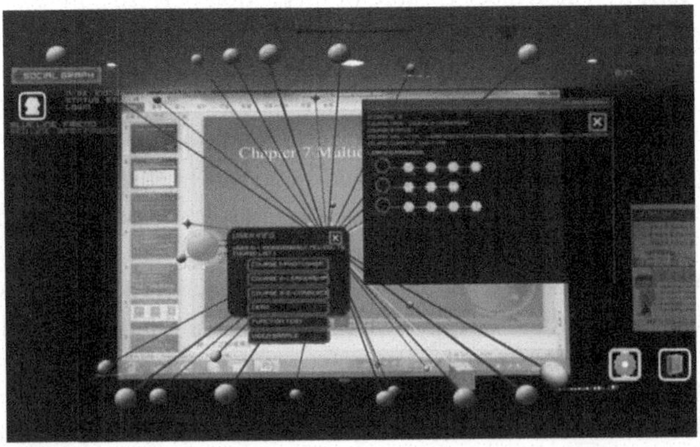

**Fig. 4.** Social graph

We also provide Focus operation and Recommendation features. Focus operation shown in Fig. 5, basically is the graph filter feature which can change the graph lay-out according to user's keywords. It makes the graph clearer to see and help users to find what they want. We design three filter attribute on this feature as following:

1. *Friend Similarity Operation* is feature to find the similarity of user and user's friends on some learning domain according to the keyword. The system will change the graph node's position, and the more similarity the more it closer to the user. Node with no similarity will be removed. To make it clear for user, the line edge color of the user and their friends also changes, according to the similarity.

2. *Same Course Operation.* In this feature, user can get the friend that learning progress is similar to him in specific course. Nodes will be presented in different distance and color, according to the learning progress. Friends that have same current lesson with the user will be placed closer to the user, and for other friends will be placed in the same distance and give it same color of line according to the lesson they took.

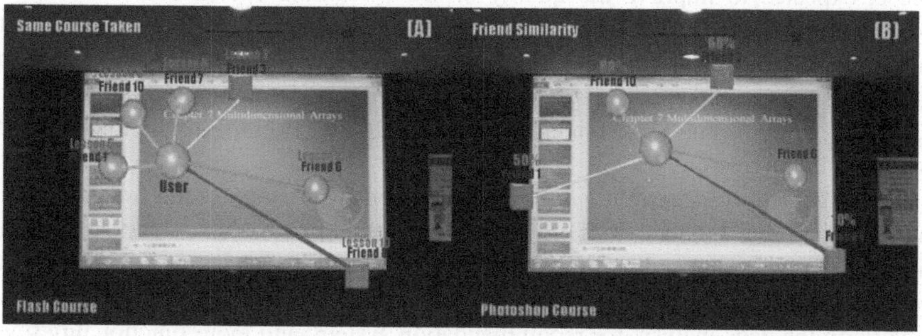


**Fig. 5.** Example of (A) Same course operation (B) Friend similarity

Recommendation feature is based on the analysis result of recommendation system we mentioned in Sect. 3.2, and Fig. 6 is the example of recommendation feature. It can be divided into two sub operation system, *Friend Recommendation* and *Course Recommendation.*

1. *Friend Recommendation* is a feature to help user find new friends based on similarity on learning (course taken, major, and current learning progress). If people have same or close similarity with the current user and are not friend of the current user, they will show up in the list of friend recommendation interface.
2. The goal of *Course Recommendation* is to give user suggestion about the next course that they can take, according to their learning progress. In this feature the user can get the recommendation course from the system and also from their friends. The list of the course recommendation will be shown on the list.

**Fig. 6.** Example of recommendation operation

## 4 Conclusion

In this paper, we present our e-learning environment with Interactive 3D Social Graph. Our e-learning system is integrated into social network site Facebook and provides social functionalities such as information sharing and comment post. These features can enhance more discussion and interaction on learning between users and their friends. For advanced functionalities, first our system provides recommendation for friend or course, expected to improve the quality of social learning environment. Second we provide Interactive 3D Social Graph, using information visualization technologies to make complex information more readable, and Focus operations, which can change the social graph according to user's needed information and make information clearer. Finally, we design some Kinect interaction gesture to give user the ability to control the tool in an intuitive way.

We have deployed basic e-learning environment with some social functionalities, and built the basic Interactive 3D Social Graph with some basic navigation functionalities such as zooming and rotation on both mouse-keyboard and Kinect interaction, to show the social relationship and learning information of the current user. We continue to work on the data analysis for recommendation system, and more functionalities and Kinect interaction gestures in Interactive 3D Social Graph.

## References


1. Bandura, A.: Social Learning Theory. http://www.alleydog.com/glossary/definition.php?term=Social%20Learning%20Theory. Accessed 25 Feb 2013
2. Vygotsky, L.S.: Thought and language. Bull. Orton Soc. **14**, 97–98 (1964)
3. Resnick, M.: Distributed constructionism. In: Proceedings of the 1996 International Conference on Learning Sciences, Evanston, Illinois (1996)
4. Rienties, B., Tempelaar, D., Van den Bossche, P., Gijselaers, W., Segers, M.: The role of academic motivation in computer-supported collaborative learning. Comput. Hum. Behav. **25**, 1195–1206 (2009)
5. So, H.-J., Brush, T.A.: Student perceptions of collaborative learning, social presence and satisfaction in a blended learning environment: relationships and critical factors. Comput. Educ. **51**, 318–336 (2008)
6. Evans, J.R.: Education creative thinking and innovative education in the decision sciences. Decis. Sci. **17**, 250–262 (1986)
7. Alavi, M., Leidner, D.E.: Research commentary: technology-mediated learning—a call for greater depth and breadth of research. Inf. Syst. Res. **12**, 1–10 (2001)
8. Stafford, T.F.: Understanding motivations for internet use in distance education. IEEE Trans. Educ. **48**, 301–306 (2005)
9. Freeman, L.C.: Visualizing social networks. J. Soc. Struct. (2000)
10. Heer, J., Boyd, D.: Vizster: visualizing online social networks. In: 2005 IEEE Symposium on Information Visualization, INFOVIS 2005, pp. 32–39 (2005)
11. Matta, N., Pfeiffer, T.: Relationships in social networks revealed: a facebook app for social graphs in 3D based on X3DOM and WebGL. In: Proceedings of the IADIS International Conference Web Virtual Reality and Three-Dimensional Worlds 2010 (2010)

12. Tarawaneh, R.M., Keller, P., Ebert, A.: A general introduction to graph visualization techniques. In: Visualization of Large and Unstructured Data Sets: Applications in Geospatial Planning, Modeling and Engineering - Proceedings of IRTG 1131 Workshop 2011, vol. 27, pp. 151–164. Schloss Dagstuhl–Leibniz-Zentrum fuer Informatik (2012)
13. Kobourov, S.G.: Spring embedders and force directed graph drawing algorithms. CoRR abs/1201.3011 (2012)

# Improving KeyNote Trust Management Model Based on User Behavior for Social Learning

Rui Xu, Guangquan Xu(✉), Dazhi Sun, Xiaohong Li, and Zhiyong Feng

Tianjin Key Laboratory of Cognitive Computing and Application School of Computer Science and Technology, Tianjin University, Tianjin, China
xuguangquan@tju.edu.cn

**Abstract.** Trust in social learning environment is influenced greatly by rapid-changing social elements. Therefore it is necessary for us to improve the KeyNote trust model to adapt the dynamic user behavior in social learning. In this paper, we mainly devote ourselves to the work of building a dynamic trust model based on indirect trust relationship. We take advantage of KeyNote to build the dynamic trust model, in which we use an indirect trust algorithm to calculate the trust value of indirect trust relationship. In this way, we can get the trust values of entities in the social learning network by indirect link. Finally our experimental results prove that this dynamic trust management model can deal with the dynamically changing relationship, and calculate user trust value by monitoring user behavior to realize the function of dynamically managing user access.

**Keywords:** KeyNote · Comentropy · Dynamic trust management · User behavior

## 1 Introduction

Social learning is a web-based learning which is different with traditional e-learning paradigm. As an abstract model of a social environment, a social network includes a set of nodes, which could be a set of individuals or a set of groups of individuals, and a set of relationships among these nodes [1]. Social learning focuses on the rapid-changing context, and so is the trust relationship. In the social network, trust value is dynamically changing during the change process of the context environment, and as time goes by, the behaviors of entities will be also changing. Therefore, trust research for social learning should be based on a dynamic management model because of the rapid-changing feature of social learning.

There have been many management systems and models, one of which is KeyNote trust management system, which has been used into IPsec [2] protocol and off-line payment of e-commerce [3]. However, the realized trust management systems just solved the defects of traditional access control methods in a certain degree, and many of them described the complex and dynamic trust relationship by an accurate and static solution without considering the complicacy and dynamics in the social relationship. Consequently, there is a very important realistic meaning to propose a trust management model which can satisfy the space-time dynamic demand [4].


D.K.W. Chiu et al. (Eds.): ICWL 2013 Workshops, LNCS 8390, pp. 96–103, 2015.
DOI: 10.1007/978-3-662-46315-4_10

As for the multiple attributes evaluation, there are some representative methods like Standard Deviation, entropy weight method, DIDF. These methods calculate trust value based on the dynamic data ignoring the relationship between indexes. Entropy is more general than variance for volatility measurement. And the entropy weight is really certain and objective, though the index is subjective [5].

It is normal that two nodes interact by the response of other entities, and we can calculate the trust value by the trust degree of entities at the mid of two nodes. Some research just consider a few indirect trust chains or even just one chain [6]. The general methods that calculate indirect trust value based on the chain of trust or broadcast start calculating from root node to goal node. There would be a lot of entity nodes on the chain, and it would be a big challenge to the convergence of calculating methods. The general network systems control the research to feedback information by Time to Live [7]. But this method is not suit for the distribute system which is highly dynamically changing, and the end time cannot be changed until the end of the TTL cycle.

The paper is organized as follows. Section 2 introduces the related work and the knowledge of Keynote. Section 3 proposes an algorithm which calculates the indirect trust between two nodes in the network. Section 4 proposes the dynamic trust management model based on KeyNote and describes the specific design of the dynamic trust management system. Section 5 shows the effectiveness and applicability tests of this system. Section 6 presents our conclusion and future work.

## 2 Related Work

Trust evaluation is a more and more important issue for online social network users [8]. And dynamic trust management is determining and applying the best operational settings at runtime in response to dynamically changing network conditions [9]. M. Blaze also proposed dynamic trust management does not rely on fixed boundaries between trusted and untrusted components [10]. KeyNote trust management system has been applied to access control field, especially in the Distributed Access Control System (DACS). However, KeyNote is just a prototype system and it has many inadequacies in implement system [11] for dynamic trust management.

### 2.1 Operating Mechanism of KeyNote

KeyNote is the second trust management model proposed by M. Blaze [12]. It proposes a uniform way to describe security policy. KeyNote includes seven features and definitions: (1) Application; (2) Action; (3) Principal; (4) Request; (5) Policy; (6) Credential; (7) Policy Compliance Checking.

The policies and trust certifications in KeyNote consist of a set of statements. A statement is a basic unit that KeyNote uses to definite policies and authorizations. And a statement includes KeyNote-Version, Authorizer, Licensees, Comment, Condition, Signature, etc. [13].

### 2.2 Definitions of KeyNote Statements

The trust relationship and delegation authorization of KeyNote are expressed by policy and trust certification. Policy and certification both consist of statements. A statement is a highly structured unit, and is always expressed in the format of the head of email by KeyNote. A statement is divided into several parts, such as version field, authorizer field, licensor field, local constant field, condition field, note field and signature field.

KeyNote is based on the basic of consistency verification algorithm, which is a depth-first search method trying to find out at least one policy that can be satisfied with requirement by recursion. KeyNote will automatically check the Condition field and Licensees field concurrently. We will improve KeyNote to satisfy the requirements of dynamic trust management.

## 3 Indirect Trust Calculating Algorithm

In the society communication, we'd love to trust people who have close relationship with us. And it can be seen in the network as that, the fewer mid nodes are, the higher trust value of target node is.

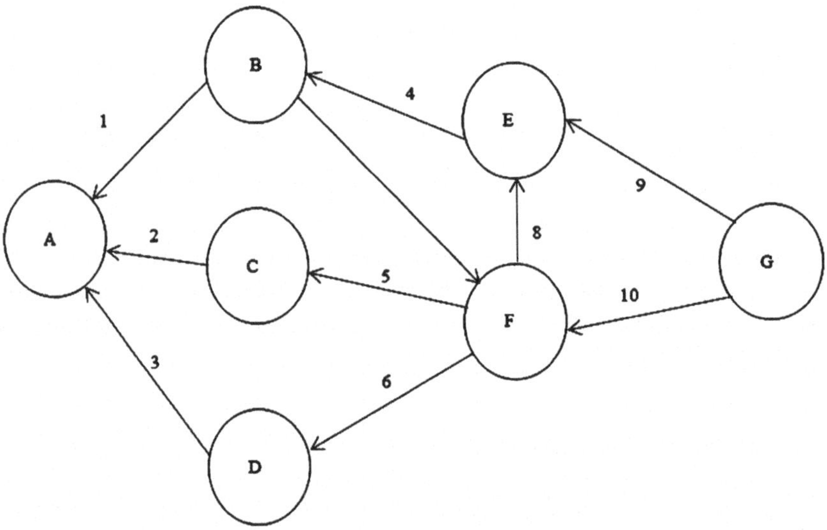


**Fig. 1.** Feedback Trust Path in Social learning environment

What shown in Fig. 1 is trust path of nodes from A to G. It is a directed graph, and B->A means entity B can provide feedback trust to entity A. And it also shows that A get the trust value of entity G by the trust value of the mid nodes B, C, D, E, F. This directed graph can be seen as a simple network with seven nodes.

Therefore, the indirect trust value in this paper cannot be calculated by the method of weighted average because of the different distance from feedback entity to initial entity and different trust weight. The trust degree of feedback entity can be calculated based on the number of mid entities. $w_{AN}$ is defined as trust degree from initial entity to a feedback entity, and it is calculated as followed:

$$w_{AN} = \frac{T_{AB} * 1 + T_{BC} * \frac{1}{2} + T_{CD} * \frac{1}{3} + \cdots + T_{(N-1)N} * \frac{1}{L}}{1 + \frac{1}{2} + \frac{1}{3} + \cdots + \frac{1}{L}} \quad (1)$$

$T_{AB}$ is directed trust value from A to B, L is the length of path from node N to root node A.

If there are several simple paths, we should calculate the total feedback trust value by the formula 2.

$$T = \sum_{q=1}^{s} (F_i(q) * {}^1/_l) \Big/ \sum_{q=1}^{s} {}^1/_l \quad q = 1, 2, \ldots, s \quad (2)$$

$F_i(q) = w_{AN} * T_{N(N+1)}$ is the indirect trust value from node A to node (N + 1) calculated by the trust value from node N to node N + 1, q is the name of path from A to N + 1. S is the number of simple feedback path, l is the hop count from initial node to target node.

For example, there are three simple feedback paths in Fig. 1: GEBA, GFCA, GFDA. The trust degree of each path can be calculated based on formula 1, then we also can get F(q) of each simple feedback path. And by formula 2, we finally get the total trust value T with the hop count from G to A.

## 4 Dynamic Trust Management Model Based on KeyNote

In our model, we assess user's trust value based on the used resource, and adjust the trust level dynamically. This model can record the historical behavior when user accesses system resources, and then calculate the trust level by using the user behavior value according to the evaluation methods defined previously. The trust level calculated before can be used as the data influencing user's access next time to realize the user's access control.

The framework of the dynamic trust management model based on KeyNote is shown as Fig. 2.

From the framework shown above, it is obvious that this model consists of six parts.

- Application: programs in a system.
- System Monitor: the module which is responsible for collecting and recording the user behavior while accessing system.
- DTM: the dynamic trust value calculating module. This module can calculate the direct trust value by the behavior value from system monitor module. It can also calculate the indirect trust value according to certifications from the Local Policy Base. And then calculate the total trust value combining direct with indirect trust values.

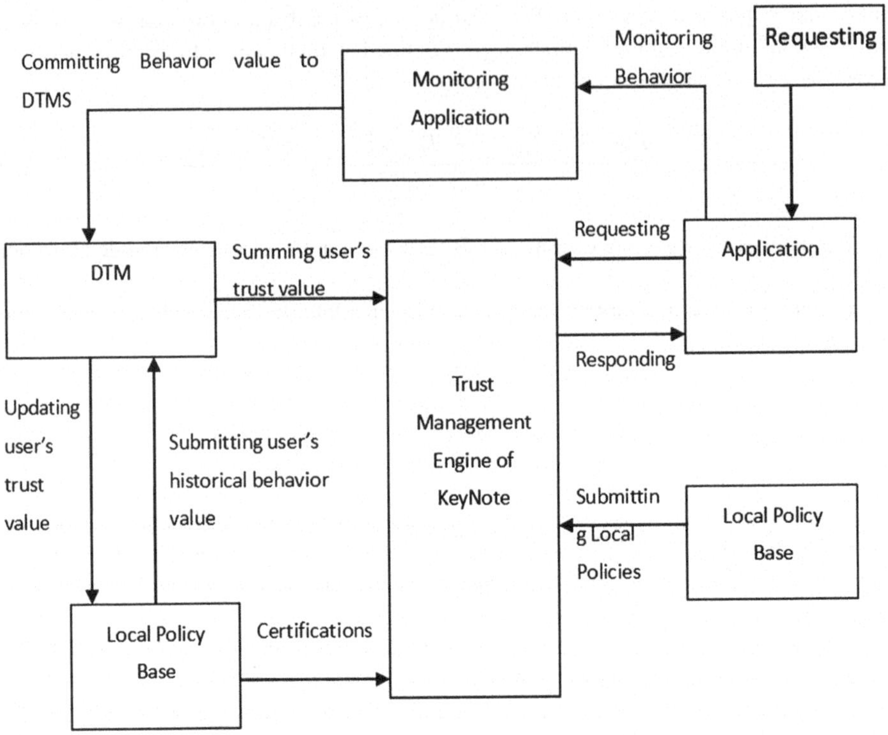


**Fig. 2.** Dynamic trust management model based on KeyNote

- Local Certification Base: this module stores certifications, and provides query function for DTM module.
- KeyNote Trust Management Engine: this module estimates whether users' request and the total trust value is suitable for a policy, and outputs whether the user's request is permitted.
- Local Policy Base: this module makes user behaviors match up with policies, each policy is an item.

# 5 Experiment and Analysis

## 5.1 User Behavior Normalization

User behavior proposed in this paper is a request that can be detected by software and can be used for estimating an entity's behavior. This paper chooses the system information and data in the Log system to analyze.

## 5.2 User Access Relationships

This experiment designed different kinds of scenes to verify the rationality, validity, and integrity of the dynamic trust management model based on the prototype system.

The relationship showed in Fig. 3 is user access relationship, and each node can be seen as an entity. Each number on the line between two nodes identifies the trust value.

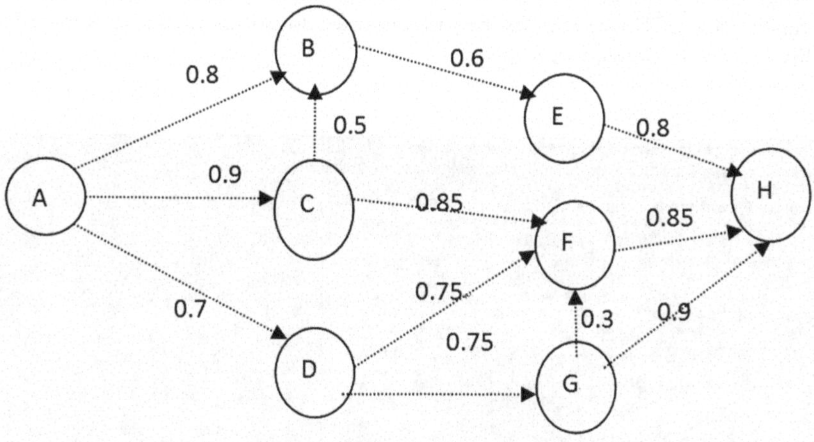


**Fig. 3.** User access relationships

### 5.3 Design of Authorization Certificate

We define "Trust Value" in the certification to show the trust degree between entities. And trust value of each entity in this experiment is initialized between 0 and 1.

As shown in Fig. 3, user A is the authorization entity. The direct trust values to the user B, C and D are respectively 0.8, 0.9 and 0.7, the certification of user A is shown as Fig. 4, and the other entities' certifications are designed in the same way.

```
"Authorizer: \"POLICY\"\n" \
"Licensees: A\n" \
"Local-Constants: \n" \
"    A = \"rsa-base64:MEgCQQCzxWCi619s3Bqf8QOZTREBFelqVWljw\\\n" \
"          vCwktO7/5zufcz+P0UBRBFNtasWgkP6/tAIK8MnLMUnejGsye\\\n" \
"          DS2EVzAgMBAAE=\"\n" \
"Conditions: app_domain == \"kn_application\" && \n" \
"         (name == \"B\" || \n" \
"         name == \"C\" || \n" \
"          name == \"D\") -> \"true\" \
" TrustValue: B == 0.8 " \
" TrustValue: C == 0.9 " \
" TrustValue: D == 0.7 " \";
```

**Fig. 4.** Certification design of A

### 5.4 Indirect Access Experiment

From Fig. 3, user H and Server A is indirect relationship, so there is no trust value in certification of A. A calculates the feedback trust value by the direct trust value and trust relationship of H stored in its trust tree in order to get the final trust value of user H. This process is shown in Fig. 5.

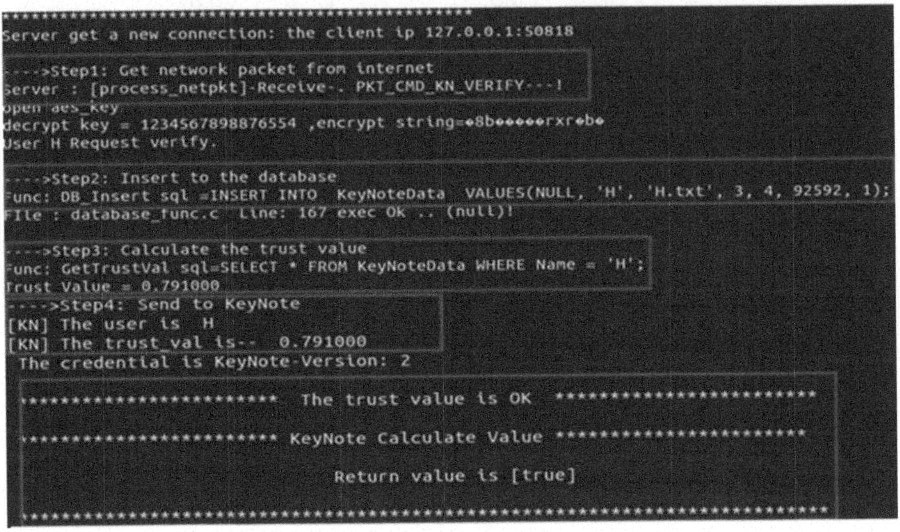


**Fig. 5.** Process of Server A verifying user H

## 6 Conclusion and Future Work

This paper proposed a dynamic trust management model based on user behavior in the rapid-changing social learning environment. We also proposed an indirect trust algorithm to get user's trust value, which can be used to manage access right of each user to realize the dynamic management of user behavior for social learning.

Obviously there are still some problems to be improved for our proposed trust management system. In the system, all certifications have been stored in the server-side, so the burden of the servers is increased too much. Therefore, the saving mechanism of trust certifications is to be solved in our near future work.

**Acknowledgment.** This work is partly supported by National Program on Key Basic Research Project (973 Program) under Grant 2013CB329304, National Natural Science Foundation of China (No. 61003080), and the Opening Project of Shanghai Key Laboratory of Integrate Administration Technologies for Information Security (No. AGK2012007).

## References


1. Wang, T., Krim, H., Viniotis, Y.: A generalized Markov graph model: application to social network analysis. IEEE J. Sel. Top. Sig. Proces. **7**, 318–332 (2013)
2. Blaze, M., Ioannidis, J., Keromytis, A.: Trust management for IPSec. In: Proceedings of the Internet Society Symposium on Network and Distributed System (SNDSS 2001), vol. 5, pp. 139–151 (2001)
3. Blaze, M., Ioannidis, J., Keromytis, A.D.: Offline micropayments without trusted hardware. In: Syverson, P. (ed.) FC 2001. LNCS, vol. 2339, pp. 21–40. Springer, Heidelberg (2002)
4. Samarati, P., Reiter, M.X., Jajodia, S.: An authorization model for a public key management service. ACM Trans. Inf. Syst. Secur. **4**, 453–482 (2001)
5. Li, W., Shang, Y., Ji, Y.: Analysis of multiple objective decision methods based on entropy weight. Comput. Intell. Industr. Appl. **1**, 953–956 (2008)
6. Guha, R., Kumar, R., Raghavan, P.: Propagation of trust and distrust. In: WWW 2004, pp. 403–412 (2004)
7. de Mello, E.R., van Moorsel, A., da Silva Fraga, J.: Evaluation of P2P search algorithms for discovering trust paths. In: Wolter, K. (ed.) EPEW 2007. LNCS, vol. 4748, pp. 112–124. Springer, Heidelberg (2007)
8. Li, M., Bonti, A.: T-OSN: a trust evaluation model in online social networks. In: 2011 IFIP 9th International Conference on Embedded and Ubiquitous Computing, pp. 469–473 (2011)
9. Chen, I.-R., Bao, F., Chang, M., Cho, J.-H.: Dynamic trust management for delay tolerant networks and its application to secure routing. IEEE Trans. Parallel Distrib. Syst. **99**, 1 (2013)
10. Blaze, M., Kannan, S., Lee, I., Sokolsky, O., Smith, J.M., Keromytis, A.D., Lee, W.: Dynamic trust management. Computer **42**, 44–52 (2009)
11. Meng, L., Xu, R., Li, X., Xu, G.: The improvements of KeyNote trust management system. Adv. Inst. Convergence Inform. Technol. **6**, 177–185 (2012)
12. Blaze, M., Ioannidis, J., Keromytis, A.D.: Experience with the KeyNote trust management system: applications and future directions. In: Nixon, P., Terzis, S. (eds.) iTrust 2003. LNCS, vol. 2692, pp. 284–300. Springer, Heidelberg (2003)

# International Workshop on E-Book and Education Cloud

# Enhancing Teamwork Performance in Mobile Cloud-Based Learning

Geng Sun(✉) and Jun Shen

School of Information Systems and Technology, University of Wollongong, Wollongong, NSW 2522, Australia
gs147@uowmail.edu.au, jshen@uow.edu.au

**Abstract.** Mobile cloud-based learning is a novel trend that allows collaborative learning to happen among distributed learners, but it still lacks of mechanisms to enhance teamwork performance. Combining the features of the cloud, we have identified a learning flow based on Kolb team learning experience, executed by cloud-hosting learning management systems in conjunction with our newly designed system, 'Teamwork as a Service (TaaS)'. Each of TaaS's five web services aims to organize a certain type of learning activities, providing learners with an introduction, a 'jigsaw classroom', schedule planning, and mutual supervision during the whole collaborative learning process. In particular, enabling a rational group mechanism realized by the simulated annealing method, TaaS is able to allocate learners to their appropriate tasks in order to give their best performance. We also introduce details of the implementation of TaaS over the Amazon cloud.

**Keywords:** Mobile learning · Cloud computing · Collaborative learning · Teamwork performance enhancement

## 1 Introduction

Mobile learning (m-learning) is an evolved type of electronic learning (e-learning), which is very useful for learners, enabling them to learn wherever they are and whenever they want. It is obvious, however, that mobile devices are limited by insufficient computing speeds, lower storage space and narrower screen size. To make up for such shortcomings, linking m-learning to cloud computing in order to borrow powers supported by the cloud is a novel solution in which mobile devices are only used for input and output of data. Cloud computing provides massive data-handling capability, elastic storage, on-demand service and faster processing speed in order to facilitate m-learning, and, in addition, prompt and large-scale deployments of learning management systems (LMSs) is also easily enabled [21]. Hence, the application of mobile cloud-based learning is gaining wide acceptance [13].

Many system developers and researchers are interested in drawing support from cloud computing to build virtual learning environments (VLE) for m-learning, adopting the concept of service-oriented architecture (SOA) [5]. In addition, making use of Web 2.0 technologies, several of the latest LMSs are able to offer collaborative learning tools [22]. Because they are hosted over the cloud and available for mobile access, it is


D.K.W. Chiu et al. (Eds.): ICWL 2013 Workshops, LNCS 8390, pp. 107–117, 2015.
DOI: 10.1007/978-3-662-46315-4_11

possible for multiple learners to work together towards a common target by using mobile cloud-based learning.

On the other hand, to our knowledge, although collaborative learning happens more and more frequently in the mobile cloud-based learning environment, there are still comparatively few studies focusing on enhancing teamwork performance in this novel environment. In this paper, we introduce a novel approach to fill this gap in research, by offering a service-oriented system, 'Teamwork as a Service' (TaaS), which works as a third-party system by adding teamwork-focused functions to current cloud-hosting LMSs.

## 2 Motivation and Methodology

The context of mobile cloud-based learning is more specific than traditional learning, where learners are distributed over large geographical areas, even in countries all around the world. These virtual teams are more focused on task-related outcomes and time constraints [6]. Thus, once a teamwork assignment is given in an m-learning course, because of geographical separation and even time differences, learners are faced with many unpredictable difficulties for which they are not prepared and perhaps the biggest of these is insufficient communication [15].

In addition, there are problems which also occur in traditional team learning which can negatively affect mobile team learning. The literature shows that learners belonging to the same team often have differing learning styles and therefore require diverse learning approaches [7]. Each learner's expectations and preferences also influence their motivation to work to the limit of their abilities [18]. Current assessment criteria also lack the mechanism to track the entire learning experience, and are generally based on learners' final outcomes. This means that problems can be hard to diagnose and solve in a timely manner, while the team learning is actually in progress.

Another character of m-learning is that its learning activities normally consist of two sections: online learning and offline learning [20]. Because mobile learners are free to download material into their mobile devices for viewing offline and being introduced and guided into their practices, they do not always stay online to access LMSs and attend tutorials [2]. A new concept, 'online to offline' (O2O), can help organize mobile cloud-based learning [24]. Using this, the process logic of mobile team learning can be clearly defined by online systems, including the transaction details and deliverable resources. So while learners are able to accomplish many of their teamwork tasks offline, for some necessary procedures, such as data entry and work submission, they need to go back online to finish.

To utilize the O2O concept to facilitate collaborative learning in the mobile cloud environment, we need to consider several aspects in order to exploit the merits of online systems:

- The system should be service-oriented to support flexible interoperation, especially with current LMSs.
- The interfaces of the system should be user-friendly when accessed through mobile devices.

- The Learners' strengths and weakness with regard to their learning styles should be identified [19].
- The learning process should be concise with indispensable activities, and more importantly, enable rational grouping within [16].

A feasible way to realize this teamwork-enhanced learning process is to orchestrate a learning flow [4], by compositing several web services. Generally, the traditional collaborative learning flow in mobile cloud-based learning can be abstracted as "receiving team assignments", "accessing team learning resources", "proceeding team learning" "submitting team outcomes" and "getting evaluations". By using Kolb's 'team learning experience' (KTLE) as the main concept [8], we implemented a teamwork-enhanced learning flow by automatically interoperating cloud-hosting LMSs and our newly designed service-oriented system, TaaS, that emphasizes building a better context for team learning. In the novel learning flow, which is shown as Fig. 1, the "proceeding learning content activities" is subdivided into the seven modules of KTLE, one or more of which are taken by each of the five web services of TaaS to organize a certain type of learning activity, working in parallel with the activity of "accessing learning resource".

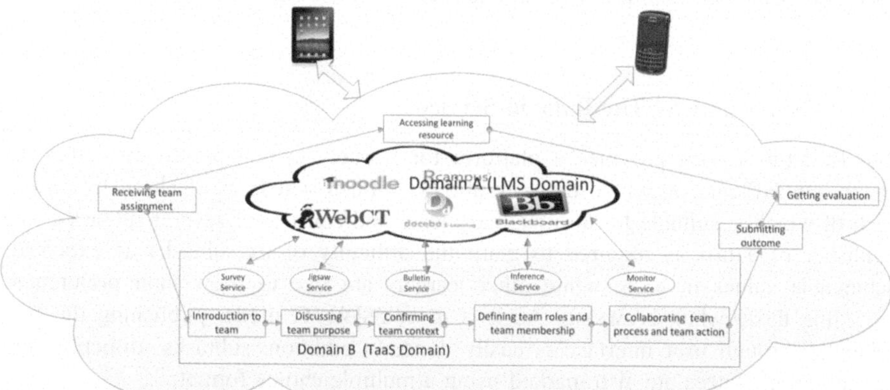


**Fig. 1.** Teamwork-enhanced learning flow for mobile cloud-based learning

# 3 System Framework

## 3.1 "Introduction to Teams" The Survey Service

The Survey Service is used for gathering data of learner information [19], which is about the Kolb's Learning Style (KLS) and their comprehensive teamwork skills. It offers interfaces to learners for answering questions to investigate their capabilities. Considering the limitation of screen sizes and typing method of the mobile devices, the survey is single-choice based. The survey can be operated as self-assessment or peer-assessment, which means the respondents of the surveys, can evaluate themselves or the other group members working with them by giving appropriate marks.

There are five sets of questions being pre-installed in the Survey Service, four of which are for the four aspects of KLS [9, 10], and the last is for comprehensive teamwork skills. These questionnaires come from [11, 23], and can be extended or reduced by teachers manually.

### 3.2 "Team Purpose" The Jigsaw Service

The jigsaw method introduced in [1] is classic for organizing efficient discussion about "team purpose" among learners, the three stages of which can be imitated by the Jigsaw Service:

1. For "initial discussion in original team", the Jigsaw Service groups learners into four-person original teams, keeping the total comprehensive teamwork skills of each equal with the others'. In each original team, the four KLS team roles are separately assigned to members [3].
2. For "joining expert team to refine cognition", it rebuilds four expert teams, within each of which learners who played the same roles in the original teams are involved.
3. For "backing to original group to teach others what was gained in expert group", it redirects learners into the original teams from which they have come.

### 3.3 "Team Context" The Bulletin Service

The Bulletin Service provides a platform for learners to collaboratively define the "team context" and on which they are able to publish schedules of alternative tasks, each of which is suitable for an imaginary team and consists of several subtasks. The publisher of a task is required to mark the difficulty of its subtasks as expected-achievable values in KLS, while other learners are free to show their preferences regarding those when browsing. As it is in WYSIWYG mode, publishing the task schedule through user interface is easily done. In addition, subtasks' difficulty and learners' preferences are also marked using a multiple-choice format.

### 3.4 "Team Membership" and "Team Roles" The Inference Service

For "team role" and "team membership", the Inference Service works like a team leader. Referring the capabilities and the preferences of learners, and the expected-achievable values of subtasks, it assigns each learner a subtask, and also groups learners who take subtasks belonging to the same task into a team. This is the core of TaaS because it makes rational decisions to cover the uncertainty of the mobile environment, concentrating on outlining learners' responsibilities clearly and bringing their strengths into full play. We suppose two ways of forming a team, with different focus:

- "Keeping the balance between each team", which means the upcoming teams will have approximate comprehensive teamwork skills. In addition, the learners' preferences and capability levels are diverse in confined shapes, meaning that if we regard each team as an independent unit, its integrated preferences and capability values are highly close to those of other units. Therefore, we can say that the inter-team competition between the upcoming teams starts from the same scratch line and is assured fair.

- "Letting the learners show their capabilities mostly", which means each of them is able to put their superiorities to use as much as possible, so that whether the team members are "good at" and "happy to" their upcoming subtasks will be the main indexes that direct the reasoning processing of task allocation.

The mathematical model of the task allocation is shown in Table 1. In [17], we introduce a simulated annealing (SA) method to solve the problem of task allocation.

**Table 1.** Problem setting and definition for computing in the inference service

| Element | Definition | Notation |
|---|---|---|
| $L^k$ | The k<sup>th</sup> Learner | Learner ID |
| $Task^i$ | The i<sup>th</sup> Task | Task ID |
| $Suntask^{ij}$ | The j<sup>th</sup> Subtask of the i<sup>th</sup> Task | Subtask ID |
| $KLS^k$ | $L^k$'s survey results of KLS capability | $KLS^k = \{AC^k, AS^k, C^k, D^k\}$, each value is a real between 1 and 10. $AC^k$, $AS^k$, $C^k$, $D^k$ and $CT^k$ represent the capability values of accommodating, assimilating, converging, diverging and comprehensive teamwork skills, respectively. Note the first four values are according to KLS. |
| $CT^k$ | $L^k$'s survey results of comprehensive teamwork capability | $CT^k$ is a real between 1 and 10 |
| $P_k^{ij}$ | $L^k$'s preference to the $Suntask^{ij}$ | $P_k^{ij}$ is an integer between 1 and 5 |
| $ST^{ij}$ | $Suntask^{ij}$'s expected-achievable degree in KLS | $ST^{ij} = \{AC^{ij}, AS^{ij}, C^{ij}, D^{ij}\}$, each value is a real between 1 and 10 |
| $N^i$ | The number of subtask in the i<sup>th</sup> Task | $N^i$ is a integer greater than 0 |
| $DeP_k^{ij}$ | The preference gap between $L^k$'s ideal and reality. | $DeP_k^{ij} = 5 - P_k^{ij}$ |
| $DeK_k^{ij}$ | The deviation of $L^k$'s KLS capability values versus $Suntask^{ij}$'s KLS expected-achievable degree. (Note the deviation is defined by the expression of Euclidean distance. It is the lower the better.) | $DeK_k^{ij} = -\{sign[\sum(KLS^k - ST^{ij})]\} \cdot \lVert KLS^k - ST^{ij}\rVert$ subject to: $KLS^k - ST^{ij} = \{AC^k - AC^{ij}, AS^k - AS^{ij}, C^k - C^{ij}, D^k - D^{ij}\}$ $\lVert KLS^k - ST^{ij}\rVert = \sqrt{(AC^k - AC^{ij})^2 + (AS^k - AS^{ij})^2 + (C^k - C^{ij})^2 + (D^k - D^{ij})^2}$ |

The operation of SA is to use simulated annealing regulation to optimize a set of initial solutions, iteration by iteration, towards an ultimate purpose for each, which is described by an objective function. The initial solution is a random array of *k* learner/subtask pairs, where *k* is the number of learners. A new solution is generated by swapping the positions of learners of two learner/subtask pairs in a previous solution.

Solutions in the two scenarios should be measured by (1) or (2), respectively. The ultimate solution will not be reached until achieving the lowest value of $R_m$:

$$\mathrm{R_m} = \mathrm{Min}\,(\alpha VarCT + \beta VarDeP + \gamma VarDeK + \varepsilon \overline{DeP} + \eta \overline{DeK}) \tag{1}$$

$$\mathrm{R_m} = \mathrm{Min}\,(\alpha VarCT + \beta \mathrm{SumDeP} + \gamma \mathrm{SumDeK}) \tag{2}$$

### 3.5 "Team Process" and "Team Action" The Monitor Service

The Monitor Service aims to provide mutual supervision for "team process" and "team action". In each team, it appoints one learner as the coordinator for each subtask, who is different from the task completer [14]. Each pair of them is linked by a file transmission channel, through which the completer is asked to submit their periodical outcome to be reviewed. The coordinator takes responsibilities to judge whether his corresponding completer has reached the rate of progress and are capable to continue or not, by grading him "satisfactory" or "unsatisfactory". A penalty mechanism is embedded in this service. It automatically deducts the completer's marks if he gets any "unsatisfactory" grade on a stage of his work in progress. All lost marks are accumulated and fed back to teachers at the end of team learning.

## 4 System Implementation

To implement TaaS, we have launched a Linux instance, of the Amazon Elastic Cloud Computing (EC2). We have configured the server environment as Apache + PHP + Mysql, and hosted our TaaS package on it. We have uploaded an open-source LMS, MOODLE, into the Amazon EC2, hosted on the same instance.

As shown in Fig. 2, these services are integrated in a system, and we have added a user-management module for controlling accounts. Abbreviations in this class diagram can be referred to the Table 1, and the web methods provided by each service are also listed. The single-sign-on (SSO) technique is realized to enable users (teachers and learners) to log in to TaaS if they have valid MOODLE accounts. We created a new database of TaaS for storing teamwork-related data, such as learners' KLS capabilities, preferences, etc., meanwhile basic learning information, such as learner name, course name, etc., are invoked from MOODLE through its web service APIs, namely, core_user and core_course. In addition, the new database exposes a web service API for remotely invoking from LMSs other than MOODLE. After any change of team information, TaaS automatically updates it to MOODLE by invoking the core_group API.

The screenshots of UI are caught from a Samsung Tablet. Users are free to access TaaS and cloud-hosting LMSs by simple operation (e.g. finger actions on the touch

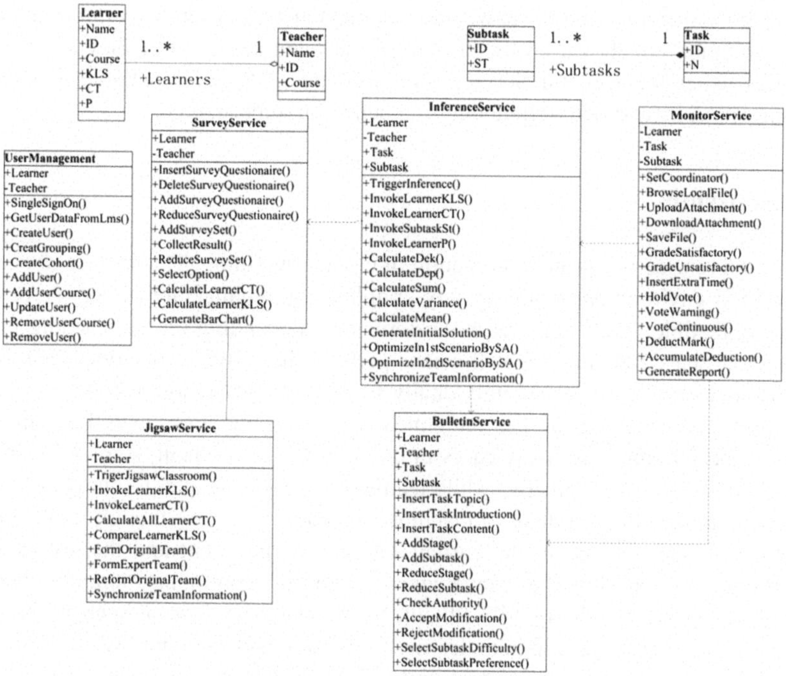


**Fig. 2.** UML class diagram of TaaS

screen) through their mobile devices, while the whole computing process is handled over the cloud. The UI of teachers' main page of TaaS is shown as Fig. 3. Teachers can click buttons to launch several events, such as starting each stage of the Jigsaw classroom and activating grouping by triggering the Inference Service. They also have authority to change the structure of surveys, pre-set the deduction for the learner's each "unsatisfactory" outcome, the number of subtasks in a task and so on.

The UI of learners' main page is shown as Fig. 4. Learners' capabilities in five areas are summarized in a bar chart, and can be checked by their teammates. They can click buttons to participate in learning activities by entering new pages. The status of the

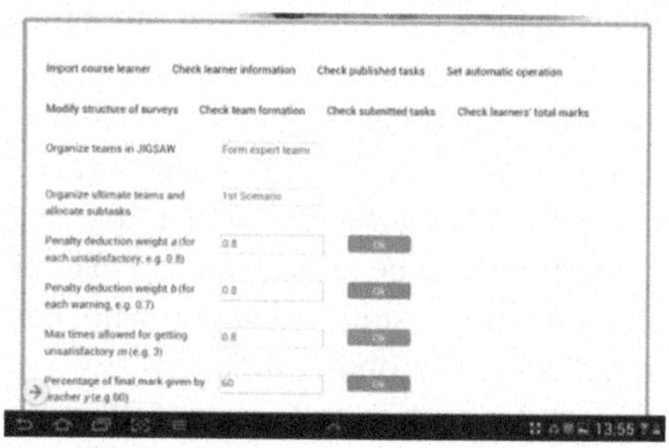

**Fig. 3.** Main page of the teacher user

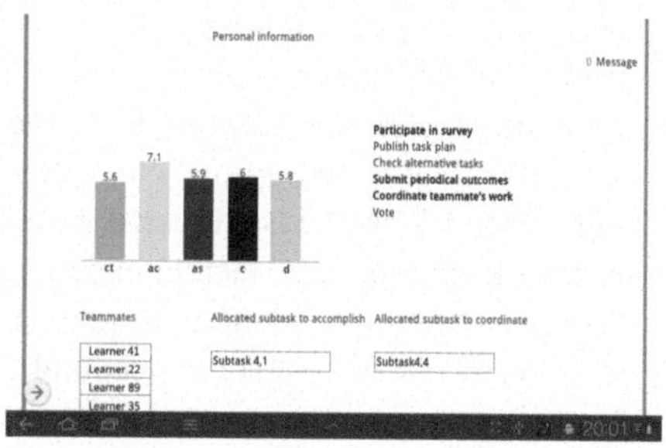

**Fig. 4.** Main page of the learner user

message box changes when the new announcement arrives. Their team information and task information are shown on the bottom of the main page. While they are planning schedules using the Bulletin Service, the structure of tasks is scalable, by adding/reducing subtasks and adding/reducing the stages of subtasks.

## 5 Discussion

On-demand service is a prominent feature of cloud computing. Thanks to web services in the cloud environment being loosely coupled, the architecture of service-oriented systems is flexible. TaaS is therefore customizable depending on the teaching plan in mobile cloud-based learning, which means parts of these five web services can be de-coupled or re-coupled to work individually to meet special requirements.

In any case, the use of the integrated system is recommended for enhancing teamwork performance. In many cases in the mobile environment, learners' behaviors and mental abilities vary greatly, while teamwork is more related to human-to-human interaction rather than human-to-machine interaction. Even though collaborative learning tools are not rare in the current Internet environment and the use of social networking is improving the convenience of digital communication, the learning activities of virtual teams are still difficult to maintain, because of such problems as incompatibilities between different learners' abilities and learning styles. Thus, it is useful for an online system to contribute to the guidance and regulation of what learners do offline, so as to maintain progress towards their common goals. Additionally, as TaaS exposes standardized service-oriented APIs that allow dynamic integration over the web, they can be easily invoked by external services and are seamless to work in conjunction with LMSs for building a function-complete VLE.

Hosting TaaS over the cloud can enable the multiple accesses from education providers in different level by one large-scale deployment of TaaS, and let TaaS be protected by load balancers in the cloud to keep the robustness when suddenly increasing visit volumes occur. The needs for data and computation during the team learning process can be controlled by the cloud, thus the complexity of system will not be aggravated by the limitations of the mobile devices. TaaS has the ability to solve problems which could undermine the work of the whole team. Main enhancements of teamwork performance brought by TaaS are the following:

- The mature KTLE theory helps learners to structure the essential competencies necessary for team learning in a succinct way, which can be executed smoothly using mobile devices.
- Learning styles are identified by means of KLS, in order to explore learners' strengths. It aims to improve efficiency by ensuring that the completer is the 'expert' in the subtask she/he is entrusted with. For example, a learner who is better at active experimentation and concrete experience is appropriate to be allocated a subtask of "accommodating", whereas a subtask of "assimilating" suits a learner who has stronger skills of abstract conceptualization and reflective observation.
- Knowing one another is very useful to help teammates to prepare for their following work. However, in the mobile learning environment, learners find it difficult to

introduce themselves due to their limited interactions. TaaS does not focus on describing learners' social features, hobbies or resumes, but rather gathering necessary data about learners' individual capabilities. It directly introduces learners by a visual tool, bar chart, thereby establishing a culture of trust within the team.

- The cloud-based jigsaw classroom gives learners opportunities to discuss and understand the different dimensions of team purpose, with the principle that "a better way to learn something is to teach it to someone else". Similarly, they are encouraged to assimilate others' viewpoints.
- Learners participate in real practice to explore the nature of team context, and critically demonstrate how to solve problems. Learners plan for themselves based on their actual situations and skills, thus their tasks are achievable.
- Though challenging, it is essential for team members to pre-plan a way to achieve their target successfully. Detailed task schedules are necessary to avoid confusion and the waste of resources.
- Learners who see their work as habits rather than choices are more likely to perform better, and have more motivation when faced with difficulties. So we take their preferences into consideration in TaaS.
- Reference [12] suggests that a solution to facilitate collaboration and reduce conflict is that leadership of mobile virtual teams can be shared. We borrow the idea and mend it by abolishing the concentrated leadership and dispersing the duty of it to the both sides of the O2O. Herein, the kind of duty that picks the suited learner to form a capable team and defines the clear-cut role for each team member is in charge of the Inference Service, and the rest duty that monitors team members' work is replaced by mutual supervision among learners.
- We formalize the problem of team grouping into a mathematical task allocation, using SA to achieve the multi-objective optimization that lets learners exploit their talents fully and complement each other's talents. The arbitrariness of team formation is minimized, and some negative interpersonal factors in traditional team learning are avoided.
- Creatively importing peer-assessment in the progress of team learning means that mutual supervision is now available so that learners can keep pace with each other [14]. It promotes positive competition within the team, and decreases the chance that the whole team's outcome be delayed because of a few under-performing members. To some extent, TaaS is also able to detect and prevent a student from claiming another's work as their own.

## 6 Conclusion

In this paper, we introduce a service oriented system, TaaS, to enhance teamwork performance in mobile cloud-based learning. It can work in conjunction with the cloud-hosting LMSs to establish a collaborative learning flow. The five services of TaaS concentrate on covering the gaps caused by the characteristics of mobile environments, making it easy to organize the necessary learner information gathering, efficient discussion, schedule planning, mutual supervision, and rational task allocation. We have implemented TaaS on the Amazon EC2 cloud. In future research, we will bring in case studies to evaluate how much learners' teamwork performance has been enhanced through the use of TaaS.

## References


1. Aronson, E., Blaney, N., Steophan, C., Sikes, J., Snapp, M.: The Jigsaw Classroom. Sage Publications, Beverly Hills (1978)
2. Attewell, J.: A technology update and m-learning project summary. Mobile Technology and Learning, Learning and Skills Development Agency, UK (2005)
3. Belbin, R.: Team Roles at Work. Butterworth Heinemann, Oxford (1993)
4. Cao, X.M., Zhao, P., Wang, X.: Study on design and development e-learning system based on learning flow. In: World Congress on Software Engineering (WCSE) (2009)
5. Chua, F.F., Tay, E.S.: Developing virtual learning environment 2.0 using web services approach. In: 12th International Conference on Advanced Learning Technologies (2012)
6. Cramton, C.D.: The mutual knowledge problem and its consquences for dispeared collaboration. Organ. Sci. **12**, 346–372 (2001)
7. Feldmann, B.: Group types in e-learning environments-study team, working team and learning team. In: 7th International Conference on Information Technology Based on Higher Education and Trainning (ITHET), Australia (2006)
8. Kayes, A.B., Kayes, D.C., Kolb, D.A.: Developing teams using the Kolb team learning experience. Simul. Gaming **36**, 355–363 (2005)
9. Kolb, A.D.: Experiential Learning: Experience as a Source of Learning and Development. Prentice Hall, Upper Saddle River (1984)
10. Kolb, A.Y., Kolb, A.D.: Learning styles and learning spaces: enhancing experiential learning in higher education. Acad. Manage. Learn. Educ. **4**(2), 193–212 (2005)
11. Lingard, R: Teaching and assessing teamwork in engineering and computer science. In: Proceeding of International Symposium on Engineering Education and Educational Technologies (EEET) (2009)
12. Pinola, M.: Mobile collaboration and community tools for virtual teams. In: Woodill, G. (ed.) The Mobile Learning Edge. McGraw-Hill Companies, New York (2011)
13. Rao, N.M.: Cloud computing through mobile-learning. J. Comput. Inf. Technol. **16**(4), 235–246 (2008)
14. Sadler, P.M., Good, E.: The impact of self- and peer-grading on student learning. Educ. Assess. **11**(1), 1–31 (2006)
15. Saunders, C.S., Ahuja, M.K.: Are all distributed teams the same? Differentiating between temporary and ongoing distributed teams. Small Group Res. **37**(6), 662–700 (2006)
16. Schwabe, G., Goth, C., Frohberg, D.: Does team size matter in mobile learning. In: International Conference on Mobile Business (ICMB), Sydney, Australia (2005)
17. Sun, G., Shen, J.: Evaluations of heuristic alogrithms for teamwork-enhanced task allocation in mobile cloud-based learning. In: 17th IEEE International Conference on Computer Supported Cooperative Work in Design (CSCWD)
18. Thiele, J.E.: Learning patterns of online students. J. Nurs. Educ. **42**(8), 364–367 (2003)
19. Terrell, S.R., Dringus, L.: An investigation of the effect of learning style on student success in an online learning environment. J. Educ. Technol. Syst. **28**(3), 231–238 (2000)
20. Trifonova, A., Ronchetti, M.: Mobile learning: is anytime + anywhere = always online?. In: 6th IEEE International Conference on Advanced Learning Technologies, Netherlands (2006)

21. Vouk, M.A.: Cloud computing-issues, research and implementations. J. Comput. Inf. Technol. **16**(4), 235–246 (2008)
22. Wentling, T.L., Waight, C., Gallaher, J., Fleur, J., Wang, C., Kanfer, A.: e-learning - A Review of Literature. Knowledge and Learning Systems Group, University of Illinois at Urbana-Champaign, Illinois, USA (2000)
23. Wheelan, S.A.: Creating Effective Teams: A Guide for Members and Leaders. Sage Publications, Thousand Oaks (2005)
24. Wu, H., Hamdi, L., Mahe, N.: Tango: a flexible mobility-enabled architecture for online and offline mobile enterprise applications. In: 11th International Conference on Mobile Data Management, Kansas, USA (2010)

# An E-Book Based Competitive Learning System for Conducting Mobile Plants Learning Activities to Improving Student Learning Outcome

Hsueh-Liang Lin[1], Chen-Chien Fang[1], Yen-Ning Su[2(✉)], Chia-Cheng Hsu[2], Ming-Yi Shih[1], and Yueh-Min Huang[2]

[1] Department of Computer Science and Information Engineering, National Changhua University of Education, Changhua, Taiwan
x3290x@gmail.com, s12362384@hotmail.com, myshih@cc.ncue.edu.tw

[2] Department of Engineering Science, National Cheng Kung University, Tainan, Taiwan
yenning@mail.tn.edu.tw, chia.cheng.hsu.tw@gmail.com, huang@mail.ncku.edu.tw

**Abstract.** In recent years, mobile technologies have developed and applied in education fields, and some mobile emerging carriers with mobile technologies include a personal digital assistant (PDA), smart phone, and e-book. Some of the mobile carriers combines context-aware technologies or involve into wireless network environments to make effective use through the combination of learning scenarios and technologies, and then provide students new learning experiences differed from the past learning. In view of the application of mobile technology in education, some previous studies have addressed that mobile learning is a meaningful learning that can improve the interaction between students and the situations and reach the purposes of learning. In the main stream of mobile learning, using mobile carriers with suitable learning methods or strategies in mobile learning activities for different students to enhance learning have gradually become a important and concern issue. The purpose of this study is to investigate the learning achievement and learning attitude of elementary school students on a campus plant learning activity when they use mobile carriers and competitive learning strategies. The experimental results show that the competitive learning group of students have better learning performance than non-competitive learning group of students. After completing the learning activity, the two groups of students presented high positive attitudes towards learning.

**Keywords:** Competitive learning · Mobile learning · Campus plants · Elementary school · E-Book

## 1 Introduction

In the past decade, the maturity and popularity of mobile technology have inspired the emerging issues of mobile learning and ubiquitous learning in education. In mobile


D.K.W. Chiu et al. (Eds.): ICWL 2013 Workshops, LNCS 8390, pp. 118–127, 2015.
DOI: 10.1007/978-3-662-46315-4_12

learning environments, mobile carriers such as PDAs, smart phones, e-books, and other types of mobile carriers have attracted the attention of scholars that have attempted to adopt mobile technologies in related learning environments to assess its impact on students' learning motivation and learning effects [1–7]. Chen and Huang [8] used handheld devices, radio-frequency identification (RFID), and wireless network technologies to design a context-aware ubiquitous learning system in a museum guide. The experimental results show that the proposed system indeed helps improve the sixth grade students' learning achievement and enhance the students' willingness to the learning subjects. Wu et al. [9] developed a ubiquitous English Reading Learning System (UERLS) through combing PDA, RFID-based location-aware technology and portfolio-centric article reading guide, on an English learning activity for university students. In such the learning situation, the system can sense the location of the students via PDA, RFID reader and wireless network technology, and then recommend English text highly associated with the situation on the screens of mobile learning carriers for reading. The experimental results show that the English text recommended by the system can help the students improve English learning achievement. In order to train the abilities of museum volunteers, Chen et al. [10] built a scenario-based training system that present context-based virtual guiding screen by using the virtual reality technology with the microphone to simulate Museum Guided situations, and then provide museum volunteers a virtual practice environment. The study results showed that the museum volunteers participating in the experiment had positive feedback on the training function of museum guiding, and this training system was helpful for their skills of tour guiding and improved their quality of explaining ability. Huang, Lin, and Cheng [11] built a campus plant mobile learning system, and students can use handheld PDA with the learning system to conduct a series of learning on campus plants. The results presented that the students using the plant mobile learning system have better learning effect than the group using the guide book. In addition, the students using the plant mobile learning system have a higher willingness to continue to participate in learning activities. The above studies of mobile and ubiquitous learning demonstrated that the mobile carriers with context aware technology applied in suitable learning environments indeed help to improve students' learning outcomes. In addition, an appropriate learning strategy designed in mobile learning activities also a important issue to improve students' learning.

The competitive learning strategy is that students in learning process must compared with their peers and each student has a final learning outcome through the comparison with each other [12]. Julian and Perry [13], and Davis and Rimms [14] agreed to the competitive learning strategy that is an effective learning method to stimulate the students' motivation to learn and to improve their learning. Previous studies have attempted to import competitive learning strategies in learning activities and have obtained a positive effect on learning [15, 16]. Therefore, it is worthy to investigate the learning effect of using competitive learning strategies in mobile learning activities. The purpose of this study is to explore the impact of the competitive learning strategy in a mobile learning activity of campus plant on learning achievement and learning attitude of students. Compared with traditional mobile learning, the impact of the competitive learning strategy in a mobile learning on the learning performance of students can feedback to teachers as a reference for planning mobile learning activities in the future.

## 2 Methods

### 2.1 Participant

In this study, there were 19 participants that were elementary school high grade students in a remote area in southern Taiwan. The 19 students included 12 boys and 7 girls, and all of they had basic ability of information technology (IT). In order to avoid the analysis results were biased, the researchers had a consultation with the class teacher for removing students with learning disabilities. After screening, the number of students for analysis was reduced to 18, 11 boys and 7 girls. The information of the 18 students that included a pre-test, a post-test, and questionnaires, was used to analyze to assess the learning of students in a learning activity on campus plant learning.

### 2.2 Experimental Tools

In order to explore the impact of competitive learning strategies into mobile learning activities of campus plant on the learning achievement and learning attitude, this study implemented an experimental learning activity and adopted tests and questionnaires to measure the performance of students and the learning attitude.

In the study, the researchers built a campus plant mobile learning environment through tablet computers, network servers, QRcode, and wireless networks. The system structure was shown in Fig. 1.

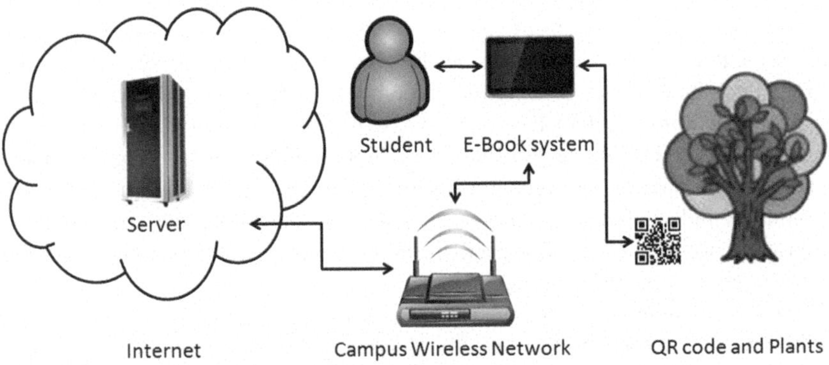


**Fig. 1.** The frame of a campus plant mobile learning environment

This learning system was developed with Eclipse 2.72 in Android environment. The main functions of this system included the scanning of QR code, and the presentation of plant learning data. In order to investigate the impact of learning strategy on learning achievement for campus plant learning activity, this study adopts two learning strategies that are competitive learning strategy and non-competitive learning strategy. The main difference between the two learning strategies is that the competitive learning strategy has immediate question function. When students arrive a plant learning point, the system with competitive learning strategy will ask questions and issues related to the location of plants on their mobile carriers, and the students need to observe the plants and read plant materials on the screen of mobile carrier, and then answer the questions. The question results of all students are used to compare with peers so that the students enter competitive learning strategies in the learning situation. The system with a non-competitive learning strategy does not provide the immediate question feature. This is that when students arrive a plant learning point, they read plant materials on the screen of a mobile carrier through the QR code scanning function, as well as botanical observation, and then go to next plant learning point. The functions of the campus plant mobile learning system are shown in Fig. 2a, b.

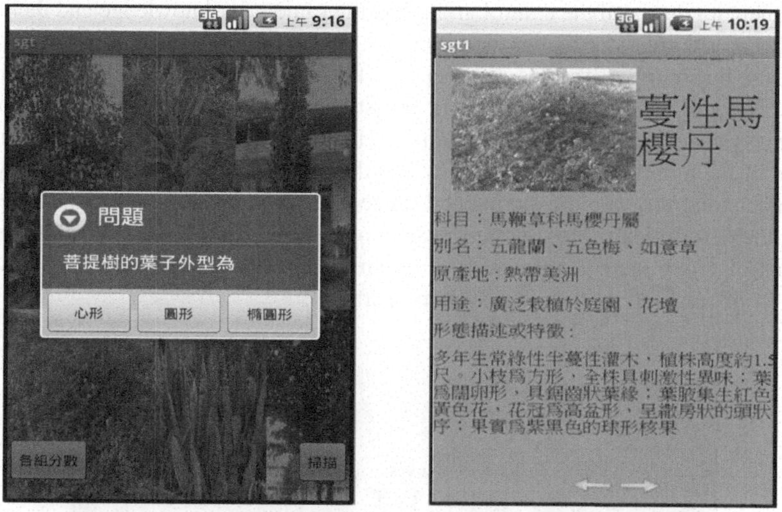


a. The immediate question function

b. The plant learning page

**Fig. 2.** The functions of the e-book system

In order to understand the learning effect of student participating in learning activities of campus plant, a teacher that has many years of teaching experience in elementary school was asked to make an examination paper that contains seven kinds of plants for the pre-test and post-test. The examination paper has 23 questions with one point per item, and the total score is 23 points. In order to eliminate the memory effect of students on questions, the items of questions are adjusted for the pre-test and post-test.

On the other hand, in order to understand learning attitude of students on the campus plant mobile learning activities, this study used a learning attitude questionnaire that was designed by Hwang and Chang [17]. The questionnaire contains seven questions with Likert five-point scale, in which one means strongly disagree and five means strongly agree, and the questionnaire score ranged from seven points to thirty-five points. The value of Cronbach's Alpha of this questionnaire was 0.79, indicating that the learning attitude questionnaire had good internal consistency.

## 2.3 Experimental Design and Procedure

The purpose of this study is to explore the learning effectiveness of students on plant learning when a competitive learning strategy is imported in a campus plant mobile learning activities. Therefore, in this study, nine students were assigned to the experimental group with competitive learning strategy, and the other nine students were the control group with a non-competitive learning strategy.

In order to ensure that the experimental group and the control group of students have the same ability before learning, this study compared their prior knowledge of two groups through the pre-test whether their knowledge is consistent. The result of pre-test shows that $t = -0.78$, $p > 0.05$, not statistically significant difference, indicating that the experimental group and the control group had the same prior knowledge and their prior knowledge was regarded as consistency.

At the beginning of this learning activity, the researcher conducted the description of this learning system operation, and the students received the knowledge of the learning system operation and were trained to understand the operation of this learning system of the mobile carrier so that they had the ability to operate the learning system and understood the whole experimental procedure. In order to avoid the John Henry effect, the description of this learning system operation for the experimental group and the control group were implemented at different learning places. Figure 3 shows the situation of teaching the learning system operation.

**Fig. 3.** The description of teaching system operation

After the researcher completed the description of this learning system operation, the students were assigned to eight learning teams. Each learning team had two or three students, and hold a tablet computer to run the learning system for the learning task of campus plant knowledge. There were seven plant learning points in this study, as shown in Fig. 4.

In this experimental procedure, the average residence time of each team at a learning point was about 5–6 min. At each learning plant point, the students used the

**Fig. 4.** A plant learning point

tablet computer to scan QR code to obtain the learning material of plant, and observed some features of the plant, such as the shape of the plant, the features of leaf and flower, and the growth environment, as shown in Fig. 5. The total learning time of completing the plant learning task was about forty-five minutes.

After the end of the plant learning task, the students took a test of learning achievement, called post-test, and then completed a learning attitude questionnaire for the plant learning activity.

**Fig. 5.** The learning situation of students using the e-book

## 3 Results and Discussion

The purpose of this study is to explore the effectiveness of learning achievement and learning attitude of students, when the competitive learning strategy was imported into mobile learning activities. In this study, eighteen high grade elementary school students were randomly assigned to two groups, the experimental group and the control group. The experimental group included nine students and conducted competitive learning strategy; the control group included nine students and conducted non-competitive learning strategy. Both the two groups of students completed the learning task by using this e-book system. Through the implementation of the learning achievement tests (pre-test, post-test) and the learning attitude questionnaire, the study analyzed the experimental data using the statistical methods that were descriptive statistic, independent sample t-test, and paired sample t test.

Table 1 presents the paired sample t test of learning achievement of all the eighteen students, $t = 2.447$ ($p < 0.05$), indicating that there was a statistically significant difference. The result shows that all the students (the experimental group and the control group) improved their learning achievement through the plant learning activity.

**Table 1.** The t-test of learning achievement between the pre-test and post-test of all students

| Group | Learning tasks | | | t | $\eta^2$ |
|---|---|---|---|---|---|
| | N | M | S.D. | | |
| Pre-test | 18 | 7.44 | 3.03 | 2.447* | 0.69 |
| Post-test | 18 | 9.17 | 1.82 | | |

*Note: *p < .05, "η2" means the effect size.*

Moreover, in order to explore the difference of learning achievement between competitive learning strategy and the non-competitive learning strategy, this study used independent sample t test to examine the post-test of two groups of students. The results is $t = 2.132$ ($p < 0.05$), presented a statistically significant difference, shown in Table 2. The results show that the learning achievement of the students with using the competitive learning strategy in a campus plant mobile learning activity is significantly higher than those of student with using non-competitive learning strategy.

**Table 2.** The t-test of learning achievement of post-test between the experimental group of students and the control group of students

| Group | Learning tasks | | | t | $\eta^2$ |
|---|---|---|---|---|---|
| | N | M | S.D. | | |
| Experimental group | 9 | 10.00 | 1.66 | 2.132* | 1.01 |
| Control group | 9 | 8.33 | 1.66 | | |

*Note: *p < .05, "η2" means the effect size.*

On the other hand, in order to understand the learning attitude of students after completing the learning activity, this study analyzed the learning attitude questionnaire through independent sample t test and the analyzed result was $t = 0$ ($p > 0.05$), indicated that it should accept the H0. The result shows that the two groups of students have same learning attitude on the campus plant learning activity. In addition, the score of learning attitude of two groups was 32.57, indicating that the learning attitude of the two groups of students was very positive (Table 3).

**Table 3.** The t-test of learning attitude between the experimental group of students and the control group of students

| Group | Learning tasks | | | t | $\eta^2$ |
|---|---|---|---|---|---|
| | N | M | S.D. | | |
| Experimental group | 9 | 32.67 | 4.95 | 0 | 0 |
| Control group | 9 | 32.67 | 4.80 | | |

*Note: "η2" means the effect size.*

As the above mentioned, this study found that the students had a positive trend on learning achievement in campus plant learning activities regardless of the competitive learning strategy. Moreover, through comparing the experimental group and the control group of students participating in learning activities on campus plant, the learning achievement of students using the competitive learning strategy was higher than those of the control group of students. The result of this study is the same as the previous study of Portilla-Figueras, Jimenez-Fernandes, and Salcedo-Sanz [18] that competitive learning contributes to students' learning outcomes. In the future teaching environment with the combination of mobile technology and campus plant learning activities, teachers can consider using competitive learning strategies to improve students' learning achievement. For the highly positive attitude of two groups of students towards learning, the reason may causes from the students' learning experience. The experimental school is located on remote area of southern Taiwan in which the student had fewer opportunities to use new technology into learning activities, although they had several years of basic information competence. In the research observation of this experiment, the researchers found the students had a high motivation and willingness to learning through the use of mobile carriers and course content. The learning phenomenon may reflect the results of learning attitude of students.

## 4 Conclusions

In recent years, with the advanced development of mobile technology, using mobile carriers as learning assistant tools have applied to a variety of learning issues, such as mobile learning and ubiquitous learning, in education. Besides the advantage of using mobile technology to improve learning, a worthy issue is how import different learning strategies in mobile learning to explore the learning achievement. In this study, the researcher consider that using the competitive learning strategy in campus plant learning activities to investigate whether the learning strategy can help elementary school students in remote areas improve their learning achievement and learning attitude. The results presented that the participated students in the learning activities increased their learning achievement. Moreover, the learning performance of the students using the competitive learning strategy is significant higher than those of the students using the non-competitive learning strategy. In the future learning activities, teacher can consider using competitive learning strategies to plan their learning activities with mobile technology. On the other hand, due to the current crisis facing

Taiwan's low birth rate, the number of students sharply drops so that the number of the participating students in some remote areas is inadequate. Although all the high grade students of the elementary school participated in this study, the number of experimental subjects still lack, which may affect the external validity of this study. In future research, we recommend to increase the number of subjects in compliance with the principle of sampling results so that the results can be inferred to other areas in Taiwan. We hope the results of this study could help to deepen the mobile technology application in education, and the evaluation of the specific benefits of using competitive learning strategies in mobile learning is able to use as a learning activity reference when the follow-up teachers plan and make the implementation of educational mobile learning activity.

**Acknowledgements.** This work was supported by the Tainan Municipal Guanmiao District Singuang Elementary School and National Science Council (NSC), Taiwan, ROC, under contracts No. NSC 100-2511-S-006-014-MY3, NSC 102-2811-S-006-002, NSC 101-2511-S-041-001-MY3, and NSC 101-3113-P-006-023-.

## References

1. Chin, K.Y., Chen, Y.L.: A mobile learning support system for ubiquitous learning environments. Procedia – Soc. Behav. Sci. **73**, 14–21 (2013)
2. Chiou, C.K., Tseng, J.C.R., Hwang, G.J., Heller, S.: An adaptive navigation support system for conducting context-aware ubiquitous learning in museums. Comput. Educ. **55**(2), 834–845 (2010)
3. Chu, H.C., Hwang, G.J., Tsai, C.C.: A knowledge engineering approach to developing mindtools for context-aware ubiquitous learning. Comput. Educ. **54**(1), 289–297 (2010)
4. Huang, Y.M., Huang, Y.M., Huang, S.H., Lin, Y.T.: A ubiquitous English vocabulary learning system: evidence of active/passive attitudes vs. usefulness/ease-of-use. Comput. Educ. **58**(1), 273–282 (2012)
5. Hwang, G.J., Yang, T.C., Tsai, C.C., Yang, S.J.H.: A context-aware ubiquitous learning environment for conducting complex science experiments. Comput. Educ. **53**(2), 402–413 (2009)
6. Hsu, C.C., Chen, H.C., Su, Y.N., Huang, K.K., Huang, Y.M.: Developing a reading concentration monitoring system by applying an artificial bee colony algorithm to e-books in an intelligent classroom. Sensors **12**(10), 14158–14178 (2012)
7. Huang, Y.M., Liang, T.H., Su, Y.N., Chen, N.S.: Empowering personalized learning with an interactive e-book learning system for elementary school students. Educ. Tech. Res. Dev. **60**(4), 703–722 (2012)
8. Chen, C.C., Huang, T.C.: Learning in a u-Museum: developing a context-aware ubiquitous learning environment. Comput. Educ. **59**(3), 873–883 (2012)
9. Wu, T.T., Huang, Y.M., Chao, H.C., Park, J.H.: Personalized English reading sequencing based on learning portfolio analysis. Inf. Sci. **257**, 248–263 (2011)
10. Chen, H.R., Yang, Y.S., Chen, K.W., Wu, T.T., Huang, Y.M.: Applying technology acceptance model to examine a context-simulated learning system for museum docents training. Int. J. Digit. Learn. Technol. **4**(1), 43–62 (2012)

11. Huang, Y.M., Lin, Y.T., Cheng, S.C.: Effectiveness of a mobile plant learning system in a science curriculum in Taiwanese elementary education. Comput. Educ. **54**(1), 47–58 (2010)
12. Kohn, A.: No Contest: The Case Against Competition. Houghton Mifflin, New York (1992)
13. Julian, J., Perry, F.: Cooperation contrasted with intra-group and inter-group competition. Sociometry **30**, 79–90 (1967)
14. Davis, G., Rimm, S.: Education of the Gifted and Talented. Prentice-Hall, Englewood Cliffs (1985)
15. Fu, F.L., Wu, Y.L., Ho, H.C.: An investigation of coopetitive pedagogic design for knowledge creation in web-based learning. Comput. Educ. **53**(3), 550–562 (2009)
16. Juan, C.B.: Using game theory and competition-based learning to stimulate student motivation and performance. Comput. Educ. **55**(2), 566–575 (2010)
17. Hwang, G.J., Chang, H.F.: A formative assessment-based mobile learning approach to improving the learning attitudes and achievements of students. Comput. Educ. **56**(1), 1023–1031 (2011)
18. Portilla-Figueras, A., Jimenez-Fernandez, S., Salcedo-Sanz, S.: A project-based competitive learning scheme to teach mobile communications. Int. J. Electr. Eng. Educ. **47**(4), 460–468 (2010)

# The E-Book Learning System with Problem-Based Learning in a Public Health Nursing Practice Course

Shu-Hsien Huang[1], Ting-Ting Wu[2(✉)], and Yueh-Min Huang[1]

[1] Department of Engineering Science, National Cheng Kung University, Tainan, Taiwan

[2] Department of Information Management, Chia-Nan University of Pharmacy and Science, Tainan, Taiwan

wutt0331@mail.chna.edu.tw

**Abstract.** Following the advance of technological innovations and the ensuing popularity of technological equipment, technology has become a crucial part of modern existence. Learning devices with technological advantages, like the PDA Tablet, E-book, etc., have become components of mainstream instruction. These devices have been applied to aid instruction in Medicine, Nursing and other fields. Problem-based learning (PBL) is a learner-centered instructional method which has its origins in medical education. Therefore, this study attempted to integrate the PBL strategy into the E-book learning system for a Public Health Nursing Practice Course. In their learning process, learners need to organize and prepare health education data before home visits, as well as related home visit data which was collected and arranged through case study and PBL question/answer sessions. Based on this data, the present study not only provided learning achievements in the public health nursing practicum, but also spread related public health knowledge (e.g. information on colorectal cancer, etc.) to each participant before their home visits.

**Keywords:** Problem-based learning · Public health nursing practice course · E-book

## 1 Introduction

Science and technology have seen rapid developments over the past decades. From the personal computer (PC) and notebook to tablet PCs and personal digital assistants (PDAs), mobile devices have gradually become more mainstream. Through these devices and the wireless network, many different functions can be implemented, like immediate search capabilities, data storage and data sharing. Consequently, people working in education have been highly anticipating the E-book, which was developed as a lightweight and portable tablet PC. Therefore, many recent studies have discussed the implications of the E-book on education [1–3]. Its application is relevant to all levels of education, from kindergarten to university. At the kindergarten level, preschoolers can be taught to read and write with the help of material on E-books [3]. Korat has demonstrated that primary school students learning with E-books experienced significant


D.K.W. Chiu et al. (Eds.): ICWL 2013 Workshops, LNCS 8390, pp. 128–135, 2015.
DOI: 10.1007/978-3-662-46315-4_13

gains in their reading and writing abilities [2]. On the other hand, Woody et al. investigated the impressions of university learners on using E-books and discovered that they favoured paper-based learning instead of the E-book [4]. The reason for this result was that the function of E-books cannot satisfy the users' learning requirements, e.g. annotation, highlight. In another study, Wu, Lee and Lin investigated the influence of using a device on a learner's reading experience [5]. The results from this study showed that device with smaller screen were associated with visual fatigue.

Problem-based learning (PBL) is a learner-centered instructional strategy and learning process that provides a method to a course [6]. It encourages learners to learn actively and to solve problems using high-level thinking [7]. In fact, it was first applied in school-based education in the 1960s [8]. Professor Barrows of McMaster University in Canada adopted it in medical education and achieved positive learning outcomes [8]. Other universities subsequently used the strategy in different fields [9], such as educational psychology [10], pre-school education [11], junior high and elementary school education [12], and physics [13] and social work as well as sociology.

As mentioned in the above discussion on E-books, a learner's perception of reading can depend on the course and associated equipment. Studies have indicated that E-book function may not conform to the users' requirements and that smaller devices can aggravate the users' visual fatigue. In view of this, the present study developed an E-book learning system that was designed for a public health nursing practicum. All of the participants used the E-book learning system on a tablet PC. Although previous studies have shown that the PBL strategy has been applied to the field of medicine, it has rarely been observed in nursing education, especially regarding the learners' perception. Thus, in this study, the E-book learning system was implemented with the PBL strategy. Health education data was collected before home visits by reading and annotation with an E-book through PBL question/answer sessions (Q/A). The expected outcome of this study was that using the PBL strategy would enhance the effectiveness of home visits. This effectiveness can be translated to better preparation prior to home visits as well as improved outcomes on subsequent home visits.

## 2 E-Book Learning System with Problem-Based Learning

PBL is an instructional method that is intended to organize the learning process using designed problems. With guidance, learners can develop a problem-solving strategy by defining the problems, assumptions, data searching approach and tests to perform until they find the best solution. With PBL, the learners can develop critical thinking, problem-solving abilities and cooperative skills [14]. Most PBL activities are based on the Barrow Model by Barrows and colleagues [15, 16]. The underlying steps include problem posing, problem analysis, problem solving, deriving results from group interaction and reflection and evaluation. In this study, these five steps were applied to fourth year students at a five-year technical college, who were taking public health courses during the semester. The learners could access the public health nursing practicum courseware by PBL from E-books or paper-based teaching in classroom activities.

**(1) Problem posing**

Before the start of instruction, the teacher set up learning objectives according to the materials used in the course. Then, the teacher presented problematic situations to elicit the learners' motivation to learn and to lead them to actively solve the problem presented.

**(2) Problem analysis and division of the learners into groups**

According to the questions posed by the teacher, the learners analyzed the situational problems using their prior knowledge and experience. The learners tried to share their ideas and develop multiple ways of thinking and problem-solving skills. For the purpose of this study, the "KND form" that was developed by Fogarty was slightly revised at this stage for the design of learning sheets that the learners would analyses [17]. They then planned the problem-solving approach and division of work according to their individual expertise among a group of four to five learners.

**(3) Problem solving**

This stage is the key to PBL. This study conducted experiments on the E-book learning system and paper-based teaching. At this stage, the learners acquired the knowledge needed to solve the problems posed at them using the available resources. The group members evaluated and integrated the resources they had obtained. They then shared the knowledge they had acquired and analyzed and discussed it in order to propose solutions, and the activity was repeated until they found a satisfactory solution (Fig. 1).

**Fig. 1.** Use of the E-Book learning system with problem-based learning in group activities.

**(4) Results from group interaction**

After the group discussion, the members presented and reported their results to all classmates in order to demonstrate the knowledge and skills that they had obtained through the problem-solving process. In this stage, the teacher invited the classmates to share their opinions. Through different group presentations and discussions, all learners were able to recognize the information and implications related to the health education data they needed before home visits and related home visit data.

**(5) Reflection and evaluation**

The last stage was not only an evaluation of the learners' performance, but also an attempt to reinforce the importance of the health education data before home visits to the learners. The purpose of the evaluation was to examine the learners' progress, to enhance the interest of both the individuals and the groups in learning and to improve their learning skills. The teacher shared opinions and facilitated the discussion among the groups, thus allowing learners to reconsider the problems according to the suggestions of both the teacher and other groups. Consequently, the learners were able to fully understand the health education data before home visits as well as related home visit data by PBL from the E-book or paper-based teaching, and were able to absorb and internalize the knowledge.

## 3 Research Design

### 3.1 Participants

The participants in this study were learners in two fourth year classes at a five-year technical college, who were taking public health courses during the semester. Both classes had 63 nursing school students who participated in this study voluntarily. The teacher responsible for practical training activities was the same for both classes, and had many years of instructional experience. The experiment used the class as the unit for random sampling to divide the sample into a control group (n = 32) and experimental group (n = 31). For the activities, learners in the experimental group used the E-book learning system. The E-book allowed learners not only to operate, use and save any function or information on the learning system, but also to annotate text to mark and highlight details. Learners in the control group used traditional methods, and the process of their learning activities was recorded on paper for exchange.

### 3.2 Experimental Procedure

The public health nursing practical training course lasted 4 weeks, with 7 h a day of instruction. In the first two weeks, the learners needed to organize and prepare the health education data before home visits and related home visit data. The two final weeks contained the home visit activities. This study focused on the first two weeks of preparation for experimentation and exploration. The overall research procedures are shown in Fig. 2.

During the instructional activity, the teacher explained the procedures and flow of the PBL strategy, and allowed the learners to practice how to use the E-book learning system. In this process, technicians were available to provide immediate assistance if there were any questions, so that learners could become familiar with the system operations and avoid problems due to unfamiliarity with it, which could result in disruption to or termination of the experimental activities.

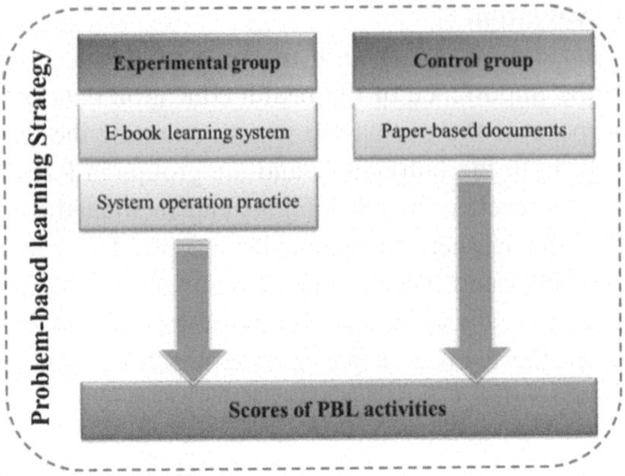


**Fig. 2.** Experimental process

## 3.3 Measuring Tools

### 3.3.1 Scores of PBL Activities

For both the experimental and control group, joint evaluations of the teacher and learners were held following the end of the PBL activity. Learners had a total score that was jointly given by the teacher and their peers. Analysis and comparison of scores showed whether or not learners had improved in their home visit preparation after using the E-book learning system. In addition, this study sought to understand whether or not the E-book learning system, when used for collaborative learning, could enhance learning effects.

### 3.3.2 Interview

After the whole instructional experiment was finished, qualitative in-depth interviews were conducted with teachers and learners in the experimental and control group. The purpose of the interview was to understand whether or not the incorporation of information technology in public health nursing courses could effectively enhance learning effects, and to determine how this would differ from traditional instructional methods. In addition, the interviews sought to understand how well the teacher and learners accepted the introduction of the E-book learning system to their activities. They also aimed to understand how teachers and learners viewed the incorporation of PBL into traditional instruction.

# 4 Results and Discussion

## 4.1 Evaluation of Learning Effectiveness

The joint evaluation grades of the experimental group and control group after PBL activity was explored in an analysis of learning accomplishment by using an independent sample t-test. The resulting p-value was $p = 0.003$ ($p < 0.05$), which indicates a significant difference between the two groups (Table 1). Furthermore, this study explored the means between the two groups and found that learners in the experimental group clearly had higher mean scores than those in the control group. This result suggests that learners in the experimental group, through the E-book learning system, achieved better learning outcomes than learners who used traditional PBL instruction. Moreover, an analysis of the standard deviations showed that the experimental group had a lower standard deviation than the control group. This means that learners in the experimental group had smaller learning gaps among them. Thus, the E-book learning system to conduct PBL can effectively enhance learning effects and lower differences among peers.

**Table 1.** The result of the independent sample t-test

| | N | Average | SD | F | *p* |
|---|---|---|---|---|---|
| Experimental | 31 | 88.74 | 6.31 | 8.76 | 0.003** |
| Control | 32 | 79.23 | 10.42 | | |

*$p < 0.05$, **$p < 0.01$, ***$p < 0.001$

## 4.2 Interview

Interview results showed that the introduction of the E-book learning system can decrease the burden on teachers. Furthermore, the functions of E-book can effectively help teachers to supervise the discussions of groups, and give assistance or feedback at suitable times. In addition, using E-books for exchange and discussion allows for more enthusiastic interaction, which can enhance the quality of exchange between teachers and learners. Conversely, for learners in the control group, the usage of traditional paper methods for team discussion and data collection made it difficult for them to control the amount of time used, and the report content was not as lively or interesting as the experimental group. Thus, the teacher also hoped that future courses would be conducted using the E-book learning system.

Learners in the experimental group liked the PBL learning strategy, as it enabled them to use their interests to select the cases they wanted to explore. Team members were responsible for sub-topic content, so that each member was able to use their own ability to contribute to the team, and learning was no longer boring but increased the interdependence among team members. In addition, most learners had a positive attitude towards the E-book learning system for conducting PBL learning activities, and thought that the system provided a convenient way to collect and arrange health education data. The absence of paper use enhanced the reusability and fluidity of information.

Learners in the control group liked using the PBL learning strategy for team collaboration. However, since discussions were conducted using paper and time was limited for the discussion process, most team members had to complete the presentation of information within a tight schedule. Thus, they hoped for more time in the learning activities or for the assistance of devices in the discussion process to improve their learning accomplishments.

## 5 Conclusion

In traditional practical training courses for nursing school, there is usually only one practical training teacher responsible for supervising and guiding all the learners. Even though the instructional environment is indoors, the large number of learners in practical training and the many unpredictable problems prevents the practical training teacher from taking care of everything simultaneously. Learners are unable to obtain real-time feedback and assistance from teachers, which results in interruptions to learning or poor learning effects. In addition, most nursing-related literature has focused on clinical practice or major hospitals for the introduction and application of information, and has rarely explored regional medical institutions. PBL is a learner-centered instructional method which was first applied to education in medicine. For this reason, the present study used the E-Book learning system with PBL in a public health nursing practicum. It was introduced to students in public health nursing practical training courses, and explored the home visit preparation process. The teams used autonomous planning, distribution and integration to enhance their subjective feelings about the value of tasks, and in turn cultivated their abilities in information exchange, interaction and problem-solving.

Experimental analyses showed that learners who used the E-book learning system to conduct PBL performed better than those who used paper to carry out PBL. The E-book learning system can be used by instructors to immediately grasp the learning conditions of their students so that they could offer assistance. Its high fluidity and interactivity can further improve the dynamics of exchange and interaction between teachers and learners.

This study only explored the preparation process before practical training. In the future, it is possible to apply the E-book learning system and platform to home visit activities, or introduce it to other related courses for exploration. In addition, questionnaires can be filled out to determine system satisfaction and system acceptance, in order to understand user problems associated with the system. Furthermore, learning history can be explored in-depth and can be used as a reference for instructional improvement. This study will be ongoing, and it is hoped that these research results can be used as a reference for scholars in related studies. It is also hoped that continuous research would provide learners and teachers in the nursing field with more comprehensive and convenient learning environments and strategies.

**Acknowledgment.** This work was supported in part by the National Science Council (NSC), Taiwan, and ROC, under Grant NSC 102-2511-S-041-002, NSC 101-3113-P-006 023 and NSC 100-2511-S-006-015-MY 3.

## References

1. Shamir, A., Shlafer, I.: E-books effectiveness in promoting phonological awareness and concept about print: a comparison between children at risk for learning disabilities and typically developing kindergarteners. Comput. Educ. **57**(3), 1989–1997 (2011)

2. Korat, O.: Reading electronic books as a support for vocabulary, story comprehension and word reading in kindergarten and first grade. Comput. Educ. **55**(1), 24–31 (2010)
3. Korat, O., Shamir, A.: The educational electronic book as a tool for supporting children's emergent literacy in low versus middle SES groups. Comput. Educ. **50**(1), 110–124 (2008)
4. Woody, W.D., Daniel, D.B., Baker, C.A.: E-books or textbooks: Students prefer textbooks. Comput. Educ. **55**(3), 945–948 (2010)
5. Wu, H.-C., Lee, C.-L., Lin, C.-T.: Ergonomic evaluation of three popular Chinese e-book displays for prolonged reading. Int. J. Ind. Ergon. **37**(9-10), 761–770 (2007)
6. Barrows, H., Kelson, A.: Problem-Based Learning: A Total Approach to Education. SIU School of Medicine, Department of Medical Education Springfield, Springfield (1998)
7. Jonassen, D.H.: Toward a design theory of problem solving. Educ. Tech. Res. Dev. **48**(4), 63–85 (2000)
8. Barrows, H.S., Tamblyn, R.M.: Problem-based learning: An approach to medical education. Springer, New York (1980)
9. Andrew, W., Brett, E.S.: Problem-based educational games: connections, prescriptions, and assessment. J. Interact. Learn. Res. **19**(4), 663–684 (2008)
10. Steinkuehler, C.A., Derry, S.J., Hmelo-Silver, C.E., Delmarcelle, M.: Cracking the resource nut with distributed problem-based learning in secondary teacher education. Distance Educ. **23**(1), 23–39 (2002)
11. Zhang, M.L., Parker, J., Eberhardt, J., Passalacqua, S.: "What's So Terrible About Swallowing an Apple Seed?" problem-based learning in kindergarten. J. Sci. Educ. Technol. **20**(5), 468–481 (2011)
12. Huang, T.C., Huang, Y.M., Yu, F.Y.: Cooperative weblog learning in higher education: its facilitating effects on social interaction, time lag, and cognitive load. Educ. Technol. Soc. **14** (1), 95–106 (2011)
13. Mestre, J., Dufrense, R.J., Gerace, W.J., Hardiman, P.T.: Promoting skilled problem solving behavior among beginning physics students. J. Res. Sci. Teach. **30**(3), 303–317 (1993)
14. Albanese, M.A., Mitchell, S.: Problem-based: a review of literature on its outcomes and implementation issues. Acad. Med. **68**, 52–81 (1993)
15. Barrows, H.S., Tamblyn, R.M.: Problem-based learning: An approach to medical education. Springer, New York (1980)
16. Barrows, H.S.: How to design a problem-based curriculum for the preclinical years. Springer, New York (1985)
17. Fogarty, R.: Problem-Based Learning and Other Curriculum Models for the Multiple Intelligences Classroom. Skylight, Arlington Heights (1997)

# Increasing Students' Vocabulary Size Through the Use of Latent Semantic Analysis in a Mobile Learning Environment

Yu-Fang Chiou, Bor-Chen Kuo(✉), and Chen-Huei Liao

National Taichung University of Education, Taichung, Taiwan
{yvonnechiou65, chenhueiliao}@gmail.com,
kbc@mail.ntcu.edu.tw

**Abstract.** Research studies have claimed that there is a positive correlation between vocabulary and extensive reading. Hence, this study intended to increase vocabulary by having extensive reading. Latent Semantic Analysis (LSA) technique was applied to help EFL teachers and learners best select reading materials. The effectiveness of mobile learning along with English Vocabulary Learning System and English Vocabulary Assessment System was recognized in the study.

**Keywords:** Vocabulary size · Latent Semantic Analysis (LSA) · EEL learning · Mobile learning

## 1 Introduction

### 1.1 Vocabulary and Extensive Reading

Research studies have indicated that vocabulary has a critical impact on children's oral language skills as well as has a causal relationship with later school success and reading comprehension [1, 2]. Collins [1] also points out that experiences of "story reading, involvement in conversations, and exposure to novel words" (p. 407) affect children's early vocabulary growth. Laufer's study [5] adds that reading could be considered as a fundamental source of acquired vocabulary at the initial stage of vocabulary acquisition. Through the process of reading, language learners can extend their knowledge of familiar words or strength their memory of unfamiliar words.

Hunt and Beglar [3] assert that EFL (English as a Foreign Language) reading should emphasize more on meaning-focused reading materials because this can "immerse students in a word-rich environment that can result in incremental increases in vocabulary size, the elaboration of lexical knowledge and the development of reading fluency" (p. 39). Further, research studies recognize extensive reading improves "motivation, reading, writing, spelling, vocabulary growth and reading fluency" (p. 39). Hence, it is crucial to implement extensive reading in EFL curriculums in order to increase vocabulary size and improve reading fluency.


D.K.W. Chiu et al. (Eds.): ICWL 2013 Workshops, LNCS 8390, pp. 136–144, 2015.
DOI: 10.1007/978-3-662-46315-4_14

### 1.2 English Learning Situation in Taiwan at the Elementary School Level

English is a foreign language and considered as a learning subject at the elementary school level in Taiwan. Starting from grade 3, children typically learn English for one to two class hours on average each week. According to the English content standards set by the Ministry of Education of Taiwan, 3rd to 6th graders are only required to be capable of using three hundred words for speaking and using one hundred and eighty words within these three hundred words for writing. Researchers question that this group of EFL (English as a Foreign Language) beginners has adequate time to learn English at school and argue that this low standard for EFL beginners will impede the progress of English learning [7].

Besides, English teachers might be facing a difficulty in a classroom because each class has about 30 children with different learning styles and at different English proficiency level but teachers teach only for one to two class hours every week on average. In order to keep students involved and engage in vocabulary learning activity, and prevent students with higher English proficiency to get bored in classes and students with lower proficiency not to be able to catch up with other classmates, how to effectively and efficiently increase vocabulary size based on each individual's needs has become a concern for language teachers.

Nevertheless, traditional EFL teachers does not have a reliable mechanism to tell their students which reading materials should be the most necessary for themselves if considering the most effective way to increase vocabulary size. That is how EFL learners know these reading materials are the ones they should read first for someone at a certain English proficiency level. In our study, we intended to create a mechanism that helps EFL teachers and learners select reading materials based on their individual needs in terms of English vocabulary acquisition by utilizing LSA techniques.

### 1.3 Latent Semantic Analysis (LSA)

Although reading materials for EFL (English as a Foreign Language) learners available on the market are abundant and English teachers and learners have many choices, it could not be saying that learners or English teachers are capable of selecting suitable reading materials for themselves or their students, respectively, in terms of increasing vocabulary size effectively and systematically. English reading materials typically would be classified by book companies for different school ages, and English teachers, parents, or children might select books based on that classification. However, it should not take it for granted that reading materials designed for a certain school age would be suitable for children of that age. Fortunately, Latent Semantic Analysis (LSA) techniques can help with EFL teachers to learners to best select reading materials that have closed correlation with vocabulary that learners are not familiar with.

Latent Semantic Analysis (LSA) is a completely automatic statistical-algebraic technique which assumes words that have more closed meaning will be more likely to appear together in text [4]. Typically, the construction of a LSA space requires four steps, including constructing a term-by-document occurrence matrix, giving a weighted value for each term, applying singular value decomposition (SVD) to the matrix, conducting dimension reduction, etc. After finishing the construction of a LSA space,

LSA provides concrete values (cosine value) to tell contextual meaning and latent relationships behind words.

## 1.4 Corpus

In line with the government's educational policy of improving English learning achievement at the elementary school level in Taiwan, researchers of this study have constructed an English corpus for Taiwanese EFL (English as a Foreign Language) beginners to systematically increase English vocabulary size as supplemental learning materials outside of classroom.

Although the concept of using English corpora as a language teaching and learning tool is not new and has been implemented for educational purposes for years, there is no such an English corpus that is constructed particularly for EFL elementary school students in Taiwan for educational purposes. Since these students only have to know about 300 English vocabulary on average based on the content standards designed by the Ministry of Education in Taiwan, it is then necessary to construct a corpus for such a group of language learners at the beginner level.

## 1.5 Corpus and LSA

In order to construct a corpus, this study first collected English learning materials that are designed particularly for EFL (English as a Foreign Language) beginners available on the market. After extracting all the contextual words from this set of documents and removing repeating words, the corpus contains 1509 English words of text. The corpus employed latent semantic analysis (LSA) techniques, including constructing a term-by-document occurrence matrix, giving a weighted value for each word, applying singular value decomposition (SVD) to the matrix, conducing dimension reduction, and so on. After these steps, a LSA space with 300 dimensions was made. The researchers then analyzed the data and produced concrete cosine values to represent semantic relationship between words in the corpus. For instance, in the corpus of this study, top three words with the strongest correlations to the word "bus" are showed to be by (cosine value 0.7674), wheels (0.6786), and round (0.6723) in order (Table 1). These three words might not be associated with bus by instinct; nevertheless, LSA has shown that they actually have the strongest latent semantic relationship with bus in corpus.

## 1.6 Semantic Space

Such a LSA semantic space can be implemented as an effective vocabulary learning tool for EFL learners. Instead of learning vocabulary by grabbing any written texts on hands, LSA tells learners which words are semantically closed together. For EFL beginners, it then systematically increases their vocabulary in an effective and efficient way.

On the other hand, this adaptive learning style empowers learners to learn English at his/her own pace. Once learners know how to use this tool, they can learn vocabulary systematically anytime and anywhere as long as they can access the Internet.

**Table 1.** Latent semantic relationship with bus in the corpus of this study.

詞彙: bus

語意空間：英文兒童語意空間(更新版)

Dimension：300

送出

| 詞彙 | 關聯性 |
|---|---|
| bus | 1 |
| by | 0.735 |
| wheels | 0.688 |
| round | 0.6573 |

Besides, this LSA space can be further implemented as an individual English reading tool based on personal needs. Because of its unique feature, it can not only tell learners semantic relationships between words but also link to a list of recommendation books (e.g. children's storybooks). Hence, this learning method could contribute to English reading as well. Typically, teachers might have to assign the same English supplemental reading materials for children at the same proficiency level or even for the whole class because they do not have a handy tool to facilitate with students' individual assignment. Nevertheless, by utilizing this learning tool, after entering key words, this online learning system directs learners to a book list where books contains these key words. Each learner can read a book that is more suitable for him/her. For instance, if an individual learner does not know one key word, he/she can enter that word and then select a book from the recommendation book list. In this way, reading a book with that certain word occurs most frequently might be more helpful for beginners to learn vocabulary.

### 1.7 Mobile Learning Model

As new mobile devices emerge and the increasing growth of broadband and wireless Internet, mobile learning (m-learning) has been widely discussed and applied to education settings. Peng, Chou, & Tsai [6] defined m-learning as "e-learning using mobile devices and wireless transmission" (p. 172), and m-learning has contributed to change the way people learning and read. It enables people to learn as long as they have a mobile device with Internet access at hand.

In the study, researchers have created an online English Vocabulary Learning System (EVLS) and English Vocabulary Assessment System (EVAS) utilizing LSA techniques that intended to help EFL learners increase vocabulary size eventually.

## 2 Methodology

This study recruited two classes of $5^{th}$ graders in Taiwan, 29 participants total to conduct the experiment. Subjects in the study was given a tablet PC as an e-schoolbag and engaged in a new EFL teaching and learning approach in order to achieve the learning goal of ubiquitous learning. Another two classes with 27 students were treated as a control group to compare the effectiveness of the treatment. All these four classes were taught by the same teacher. Students in the control group were given regular teaching materials and approaches. That is they learned extended vocabulary by flash cards, and did not have tablet PCs while learning and doing assessment tests. Teacher and students did not use any online EVSL and EVAS in classes, either (Fig. 1).

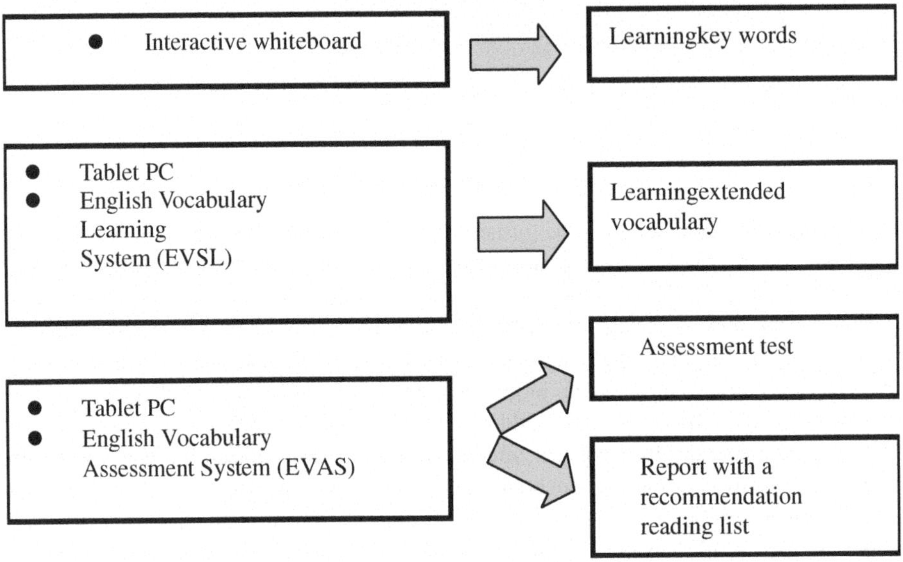


**Fig. 1.** English learning model

During the period of a seven-week experiment, the teacher used interactive whiteboard to teach basic key words in textbook and utilize English Vocabulary Learning System (EVLS) to teach extended words of key words. Each student was given an ID and password and they could assess EVLS anytime to learn vocabulary. System would record each student's learning history. Flower buds in Fig. 2 represent the words with the most closed meaning to the word "bus" in the corpus. After clicking flower buds to know meaning of words, the flower buds would open.

After finishing teaching vocabulary each week, students were required to take an online assessment test in English Vocabulary Assessment System (EVAS) by using their tablet PCs in order to trace the learning outcomes (Fig. 3).

Each student would get a test report right after finishing the online test. The report recorded vocabulary that student answered both correctly and incorrectly and listed a recommendation reading list generated by using LSA (latent semantic analysis) technique. Students were asked to read at least one book on the list. Each book title has been set up to link to an e-book, and they could choose to read online or download it to the e-schoolbag (tablet PC) and read after classes (Fig. 4).

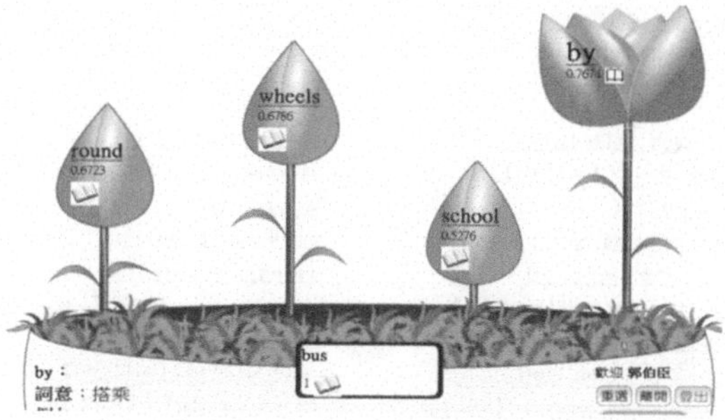


**Fig. 2.** English Vocabulary Learning System (EVLS) interface. Extended vocabulary of the word "bus"

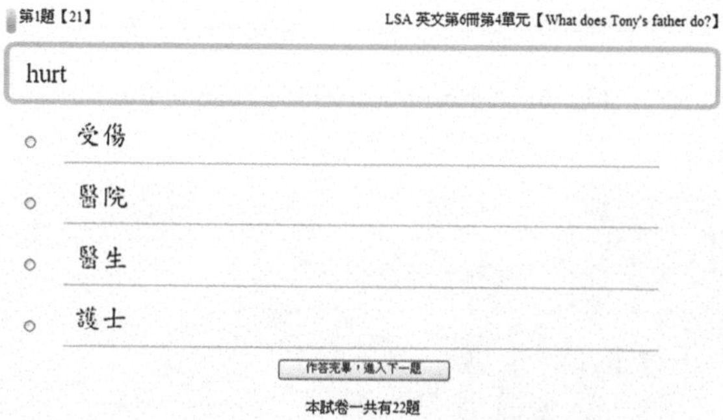


**Fig. 3.** English Vocabulary Assessment System (EVAS)

本次測驗作答情形（卷1）

| 題號 | 題目 | 對錯 | 學生作答 | 正確答案 |
|---|---|---|---|---|
| 1 | bank | o | 銀行 | 銀行 |
| 2 | bookstore | o | 書局 | 書局 |
| 3 | park | o | 公園 | 公園 |
| 4 | post office | o | 郵局 | 郵局 |
| 5 | supermarket | x | 郵局 | 超市 |
| 6 | town | o | 鎮 | 鎮 |
| 7 | behind | o | 在…後面 | 在…後面 |
| 8 | between | o | 在…之間 | 在…之間 |
| 9 | in front of | o | 在…前面 | 在…前面 |
| 10 | near | o | 在…附近 | 在…附近 |

**Fig. 4.** Test report

E-books with pictures and a narrator were selected by English practitioners and elementary EFL teachers and were suitable for EFL beginners in Taiwan. LSA technique was applied to generate a recommendation reading list that were most correlated with vocabulary that test takers did not answer correctly. By reading an e-book shown

推薦之課外閱讀本
【 LSA 英文 第6冊 第3單元 Mr. Frog Goes to Town】

| 推薦序號 | 推薦讀本書名【檔名】 | |
|---|---|---|
| | 卷1 | 卷2 |
| 1 | can I keep him【book11.swf】 | where is Tobi【book29.swf】 |
| 2 | Doris school day【book1.swf】 | my birthday story【book16.swf】 |
| 3 | where is Tobi【book29.swf】 | my vacation【book18.swf】 |
| 4 | a hungry rabbit【book5.swf】 | can I keep him【book11.swf】 |
| 5 | my overcoat【book17.swf】 | a greedy mouse【book4.swf】 |
| 6 | lets make a new friend【book15.swf】 | we will do everything together【book28.swf】 |
| 7 | my birthday story【book16.swf】 | a hungry rabbit【book5.swf】 |
| 8 | the skinny pig【book22.swf】 | the sun and the wind【book23.swf】 |
| 9 | we will do everything together【book28.swf】 | the teddy bear is the best【book24.swf】 |
| 10 | we are the best【book27.swf】 | bear, the great cook【book8.swf】 |
| 11 | the sun and the wind【book23.swf】 | Doris school day【book1.swf】 |
| 12 | rich Toto and poor Momo【book19.swf】 | we are the best【book27.swf】 |
| 13 | a greedy mouse【book4.swf】 | going to the zoo【book12.swf】 |
| 14 | I love my brother【book3.swf】 | a monkey and a turtle【book7.swf】 |
| 15 | bear, the great cook【book8.swf】 | the skinny pig【book22.swf】 |

**Fig. 5.** A Recommendation reading list

**Fig. 6.** Online English reading

on the list, students were expected to catch vocabulary and improve reading comprehension (Fig. 5).

In order to compare the learning outcomes between experimental and control group, students in these two groups all took a pre-test in the beginning of the experiment and post-test at the end of the whole experiment. This test was named as Web-based Vocabulary Pronunciation Test, which included all key words in textbook and sight words at the pre-primer level. Students had to log into the test system and it recorded students' pronunciation of each word. To ensure students did know the meaning of each word, they had to tell Chinese meaning as well. This test intended to assess whether participants had a better vocabulary learning outcome after having a treatment (Fig. 6).

## 3 Results and Discussion

In order to know the effectiveness of the treatment, data collected from the pre- and post-test were analyzed by conducting ANCOVA. To avoid drawing incorrect inferences about the prediction of the dependent variable from the independent variable, pre-test was measured and used as a covariate. After excluding missing data, a total number of 51 valid responses, 26 in experimental group and 25 in control group, were entered into the statistical software for analysis.

Table 2 presents the means for two groups on post-test of Web-based Vocabulary Pronunciation Test. Experimental group got an average score of 50.65 (equals to 76.74/100), and control group got 37.08 (equals to 56.18/100).

**Table 2.** Group mean scores

| Group | Mean | N |
|---|---|---|
| Experimental group | 50.65 | 26 |
| Control group | 37.08 | 25 |
| Total | 44.00 | 51 |

The ANCOVA table (Table 3) has showed that the model was significant. It indicates that there was a significant difference between experimental and control group on learning English. It can be inferred that students learned English by this model had better learning outcomes, and knew more vocabulary than the other group of students.

**Table 3.** Tests of between-subjects effects

| Source | Type III sum of squares | df | Mean square | F | Sig. |
|---|---|---|---|---|---|
| Corrected model | 16849.617 | 2 | 8424.809 | 74.551 | .000 |
| Intercept | 6480.802 | 1 | 6480.802 | 57.348 | .000 |
| Pre-test | 14501.342 | 1 | 14501.342 | 128.321 | .000 |
| Group | 1545.144 | 1 | 1545.144 | 13.673 | .001 |
| Error | 5424.383 | 48 | 113.008 | | |
| Total | 121010.000 | 51 | | | |
| Corrected total | 22274.000 | 50 | | | |

Besides, from teacher's observation, students in experimental group were interested in spending more time on learning vocabulary by using Vocabulary Learning System and reading e-books, which was concerned as an innovative way of learning vocabulary from both teacher and the students' perspectives. From students' feedbacks, they enjoyed using tablet PCs to learn English because they were able to learn anywhere and anytime as long as they could assess the Internet. For them, using tablet PCs was much fun than paper-based textbooks. They assessed EVLS after classes and were eager to know more vocabulary. From students' reports, "it is fun to see flower buds open, and see which words are related to the key words." They also shared e-books because each of them had individualized and adaptive recommendation reading lists. They would like to read more books. In short, mobile learning with online learning system empowers students in the learning process and gives them more freedom and control in terms of learning pace.

## 4 Conclusion

In this study, Latent Semantic Analysis (LSA) technique was applied to an online English Vocabulary Learning System (EVLS) and an English Vocabulary Assessment System (EVAS) that developed particularly for EFL beginners in Taiwan. After a seven-week experiment that engaging students in a mobile-learning environment with EVLS and EVAS, the results have shown a significant difference between experimental and control group. That is students could effectively increase vocabulary size by having these treatments.

## References


1. Collins, M.F.: ESL preschoolers' English vocabulary acquisition from storybook reading. Read. Res. Q. **40**(4), 406–408 (2005)
2. Dickinson, D.K., McCabe, A., Anastasopoulos, L., Peisner-Feinberg, E.S., Poe, M.D.: The comprehensive language approach to early literacy: the interrelationships among vocabulary, phonological sensitivity, and print knowledge among preschool-aged children. J. Educ. Psychol. **95**(3), 465–481 (2003). doi:10.1037/0022-0663.95.3.465
3. Hunt, A., Beglar, D.: A framework for developing EFL reading vocabulary. Read. Foreign Lang. **17**(1), 23–59 (2005)
4. Landauer, T.K., Foltz, P.W., Laham, D.: Introduction to latent semantic analysis. Discourse Proc. **25**, 259–284 (1998)
5. Laufer, B.: Vocabulary acquisition in a second language: do learners really acquire most vocabulary by reading? Some empirical evidence. Can. Mod. Lang. Rev. **59**(4), 567–587 (2003)
6. Peng, H., Chou, Y.S., Tsai, C.-C.: Ubiquitous knowledge construction: mobile learning re-defined and a conceptual framework. Innovations Educ. Teach. Int. **46**(2), 171–183 (2009)
7. Wu, H.-R.: The problem of English vocabulary size in the elementary school. Friends Nat. Educ. **59**(3), 47–53 (2008)

# Analyzing Immersion in Digital Game-Based E-Book Learning Through Learners' Facial Expressions

Hong-Ren Chen(✉), Qing-Fu Chen, and Yeng-Lin Lu

Department of Digital Content and Technology,
National Taichung University of Education, Taichung 403, Taiwan
hrchen.ntcu@gmail.com

**Abstract.** Research has demonstrated the positive educational benefits of digital game-based E-book learning (DGEL). Understanding student characteristics and factors involved in digital game participation can effectively enhance their effects on learning. The design of DGEL environments tends to view learner immersion in the game activity as an important factor. This indicates that DGEL should be based on an understanding of the learning process. This paper describes the implementation of a DGEL system that uses video capture technology for automatic detection of learner facial expressions to analyze the learner's immersed state. This learning system can also supplement learning and provide timely stimulation to enhance the learning effects of DGEL.

**Keywords:** Video capture technology · Immersion analysis · Digital-based E-book learning

## 1 Introduction

The rapid development of digital content combined with the animation and special effects of digital games make it easy for players to become immersed in the lifelike context of games. Digital games have many attractive characteristics such as entertainment, interactivity, and self-fulfillment [1] so that digital games have gradually become an essential part of many young people's lives [2]. Digital games play an important role in life as well as in learning and the education process [3]. The content of digital games can provide the learner with the chance to become immersed in the game experience, and this type of immersion is a state of learning knowledge while playing different roles [4]. When the learner engages in digital game-based E-book learning (DGEL), the learning activity is more challenging than the activities used in traditional school education [5, 6]. Digital game research has demonstrated many benefits; rather than simply providing entertainment, games have become powerful tools to guide learning [7].

The design of DGEL systems based on understanding the characteristics and factors related to student participation in games can effectively enhance learning motivation, learning participation, and learning effects [8–10]. DGEL is often fun and provides an attractive environment with easy immersion so that learners are willing to engage in it frequently; it thus provides a high degree of learning motivation [1, 11]. Immersion in


D.K.W. Chiu et al. (Eds.): ICWL 2013 Workshops, LNCS 8390, pp. 145–151, 2015.
DOI: 10.1007/978-3-662-46315-4_15

digital games is a dynamic and gradual process with different factors related to its various stages. The immersion experience increases as perception of these factors increases [12, 13]. The [14] suggested that when students interact with a game situation, they have a sense of control over the game environment, respond only to concrete objectives, and become less aware of outside stimuli, which means they have entered an immersed state. Digital games usually have storylines that entice the learner into becoming immersed in the game situation, making them willing to devote time to learning to enhance the learning effects [15]. DGEL can also promote active participation in learning to help students cultivate a habit of lifelong learning [16, 17]. Compared to traditional lecture-based instruction, DGEL has the advantages of provoking active learning by learners and promoting learning motivation [1, 18].

Research has revealed the factors in the immersive DGEL process that have a crucial influence on active learning and that increase learning effects. However, most studies have overlooked the measurement of immersive learning processes and states in digital games. If the learning system can provide timely stimulation in learning, it would help learners become immersed in the context of DGEL. This paper describes the implementation of a DGEL system that uses video capture technology for automatic detection of learner facial expressions to analyze the learner's immersed state. This learning system can also supplement learning and provide timely stimulation to enhance the learning effects of DGEL.

## 2 Literature Review

### 2.1 Digital Game-Based E-Book Learning

The interactive animation and special effects of digital games generally cause learners to be highly motivated in participating in game activities [19]. Integrating computer games into learning activities definitely enhances learning motivation [20]. The most important effect of games in learning is to elicit learning motivation, and studies have shown that DEGL has a positive effect on learning and can inspire student creativity [9, 18]. Thus, DGEL converts the motivation for participating in games into motivation for participating in learning activities to enhance student learning effects. DGEL has been the subject of study aimed at using game characteristics to elicit learner motivation and promote their learning experiences for better learning effects. The top design priority of current DGEL environments focuses on learner immersion in games [13]. It is clear that game learning should be based on an understanding of the learning process and conform to learning needs.

The [21] proposed a system design model for DGEL that has been widely applied to learning effects in physical therapy, military training, and medical prevention [22, 23]. The [24] found that educational computer games can enhance student learning motivation, interest, and concentration. There have been many recent studies on game-based learning systems. The [25] designed a board game using railway operations to help teach minimum spanning tree concepts. The [10] developed an adaptive DGEL system that provides specialized suitable learning content for different learners to enhance learning effects. The [26] explored the construction of an intelligent and adaptive DGEL system suitable for the learning styles and needs of different students. The [27] used constructive learning theory combined with world geography instructional materials from a junior high school social studies curriculum to create a DGEL system that inspires active attention, realization, personal experience, and individual learning to enhance learning motivation and independent learning ability

### 2.2 Immersion Theory

Immersion theory explains the state that humans enter when engaging in activities. In the immersed state, a person concentrates on the situation at hand and filters out external influences and unrelated perceptions. When learners engage in learning activities, they are in a state of learning immersion if they are completely engaged and ignore everything outside of the learning activity [13]. Being immersed can bring a feeling of joy and reward for intrinsic motivation. In other words, a person is motivated to continue an activity because the feeling of joy brought on by the activity itself is a reward, and this type of joy is the intrinsic motivation of the person involved in the activity [28]. The immersion model has two main dimensions: challenge and technique. Different situations lead to different immersed states. At first, the user perceives similar levels of challenge and technique, and they enter the immersed state. However, if the difficulty of the activity exceeds the user's capability, the user senses pressure that leads to anxiety. The user would then choose to reduce the challenge or learn new techniques. The user again enters the immersed state once this balance between challenge and technique is restored. If the user still finds the activity difficult despite a certain degree of ability, the user starts to worry. Conversely, if the level of challenge is too low, the user becomes bored and can increase the level of challenge to return to an immersed state [29, 30].

The number of studies related to immersion theory has increased as immersion theory is used in different fields. For instance, immersion theory has been incorporated into research on real instructional sites [31], online learning [32], blog learning [29], and online DGEL [33]. The [34] focused on Internet users to conduct usage experience surveys for online communication tools; they used a technology acceptance model to explore the extrinsic motivation for using online communication tools and combined it with immersion theory to explore intrinsic motivation factors. Interactivity and perceived ease of use significantly influence the immersion experiences of individuals while the effect of immersion theory on attitude is greater than perceived ease of use and perceived usefulness.

## 3 System Design and Immersion Analysis

Video capture and image recognition technology have been broadly used in fields as diverse as gate supervision, identity recognition, smart home imaging, and automobile security. Many image-processing studies have used facial features as the basis for recognition along with image preprocessing to enhance facial expressions to obtain the necessary feature information and enhance image quality. Facial detection usually uses two-level digitization to isolate the main features of the image quickly. Current image-processing methods include varimax [35], histogram [36], and color-conversion approaches [37]. Facial-recognition calculations include identifying the external profile and local features for facial profile extraction, and interpreting information derived from image analysis [38].

In technological research relating to facial detection, first it is necessary to know if a face exists in an image [39, 40]. If there is, its location, length, and width need to be marked. Facial detection methods can be divided into the following four strategies: (1) Knowledge-Based Method: these methods would observe the relationships between facial features and establish some corresponding rules, and use these principles to sear for whether there are faces on the screen; (2) Feature-Based Method: these methods would first find some features that do not change as much based on variability in angles and light sources, then use these verified unchanging features to find the location of faces; (3) Template-Matching Method: this method needs to first define patterns that represent faces, and contrast the input image and with the correlation value of the template to detect positions in which faces may appear; (4) Appearance-Based Method: these methods need to use machine learning from a set of known facial images and use statistical analysis to learn facial models.

In the present study, we used video capture of the learner's facial image to analyze and study immersion using the steps and procedures shown in Fig. 1 [41]. First, the learner enters the DGEL system to begin using the game scenarios. The DGEL site uses situational games and a simple operational interface with a context-based game design to help students learn Chinese poetry [42]. As the learner engages in DGEL, the video-conferencing system automatically captures continuous facial images as shown in step 1 of Fig. 1. In step 2, the system begins to analyze the stream of facial images, dividing them into external profile and internal features, and then uses color-space conversion rules to mark facial features with different colors. When the system completes recognition of facial features and interpretation of images, it proceeds to step 3 to start immersion analysis of the facial features. This analysis has two parts: concentration (observation of eye movement) and enjoyment (observation of mouth movement).

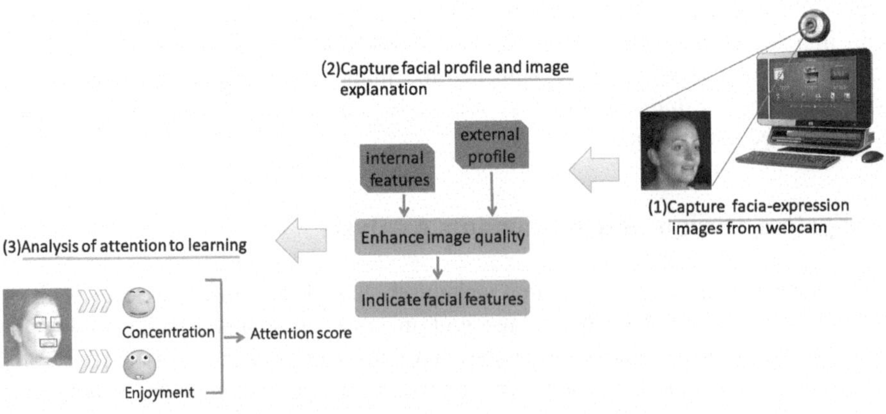


**Fig. 1.** The process of capturing facial-expression and evaluating learning attention.

The learner achieves a certain level of immersion upon reaching high levels of both concentration and enjoyment. The video capture setting of DGEL system and screenshot of DGEL demonstration are shown in Fig. 2.

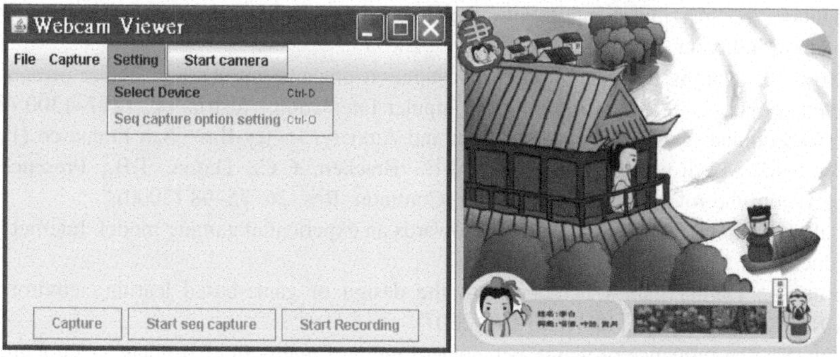


**Fig. 2.** Video capture setting and game-based learning

## 4 Conclusions

The digital game-based learning should understand the process of the learner's learning process. In digital game-based learning environment, this study uses video capture technology to automatically detect learner facial expressions to analyze their immersed state. The implemented learning system can also give learning supplement and stimulation timely to enhance the learning effects from digital game-based learning.

## References

1. Prensky, M.: Digital Game-Based Learning. McGraw-Hill, New York (2001)
2. Fromme, J.: Computer games as a part of children's culture. Games Stud. **3**(1) (2003). http://www.gamestudies.org/0301/fromme. Accessed 10 Feb 2011
3. Liu, E.Z.F., Lin, C.H.: Developing evaluative indicators for educational computer games. Br. J. Educ. Technol. **40**(1), 174–178 (2009)
4. Gee, J.P.: What video games have to teach us about learning and literacy?. Palgrave Macmillan, New York (2007)
5. Jenkins, H.: Game theory. Technol. Rev. **29**, 1–3 (2002)
6. Rosas, R., Nussbaum, M., Cumsille, P., Marianov, V., Correa, M., Flores, P., et al.: Beyond nintendo: design and assessment of educational video games for first and second grade students. Comput. Educ. **40**(1), 71–94 (2003)
7. Hsiao, H.-C.: A brief review of digital games and learning. Paper appears in The First IEEE International Workshop on Digital Game and Intelligent Toy Enhanced Learning (DIGITEL 2007), Jhongli, Taiwan (2007)
8. Asgari, M., Kaufman, D.: Relationships among computer games, fantasy, and learning. Paper presented at the Proceeding of the 2nd International Conference on Imagination and Education, Vancouver, Canada (2004)

9. Kirriemuir, J., McFarlane, A.: Literature review in games and learning. Nestafuturelab, Bristol (2004)
10. Tan, P.H., Ling, S.W., Ting, C.Y.: A review on game design and game-based learning models. In: DIMEA 2007: Second International Conference on Digital Interactive Media in Entertainment and Arts, Perth, Western Australia (2007)
11. Whitton, N.: An investigation into the potential of collaborative computer game-based learning in higher education. Ph.D. thesis (2007)
12. Brown, E., Cairns, P.: A grounded investigation of game immer-sion. Paper presented at International Conference for Human-Computer Interaction, Austria, pp. 1297–1300 (2004)
13. Csikszentmihalyi, M.: Beyond Boredom and Anxiety. Jossey-Bass, San Fransisco (1975)
14. Lombard, M., Reich, R.D., Grabe, M.E., Bracken, C.C., Ditton, T.B.: Presence and television: the role of screen size. Hum. Commun. Res. **26**, 75–98 (2000)
15. Kiili, K.: Digital game-based learning: towards an experiential gaming model. Internet High. Educ. **8**(1), 13–24 (2005)
16. Gros, B.: Digital games in education: the design of game-based learning environment. J. Res. Technol. Educ. **40**(1), 23–38 (2007)
17. Huh, S.: The influence of genre, perception, and personality on dependent video game use. In: Proceedings from International Communication Association, New York (2008)
18. Tennyson, R.D., Jorczak, R.L.: A conceptual framework for the empirical study of instructional game. In: O'Neil, H.F., Perez, R.S. (eds.) Computer Games and Team and Individual learning, pp. 3–20. Elsevier, Amsterdam (2008)
19. Wu, T.-K.: Development of a gamed-based learning system for enhancing learners' motivation and self-perception in energy education. Master thesis, National Central University, Taiwan (2006)
20. Ku, S.-C., Lin, H., Chou, C.: Constructivistic Gamelike MUD Learning Environment. Instr. Technol. Media **37**, 28–41 (1998)
21. Garris, R., Ahlers, R., Driskell, J.: Games, motivation, and learning: a researchand practice model. Simul. Gaming **33**(4), 441–467 (2002)
22. Krichevets, A.N., Sirotkina, E.B., Yevsevicheva, I.V., Zeldin, L.M.: Computergames as a means of movement rehabilitation. Disabil. Rehabil. **17**(2), 100–105 (1995)
23. Terrell, S., Rendulic, P.: Using computer-managed instructional software to increase motivation and achievement in elementary school children. J. Res. Comput. Educ. **26**(3), 403–414 (1996)
24. Kulik, J.: Meta-analytic studies of findings on computer-based instruction. In: Baker, E.L., O'Neil Jr., H.F. (eds.) Technology Assessment in Education and Training. Lawrence Erlbaum Associates, New York (1994)
25. Lim, D.: Taking students out for a ride: using a board game to teach graph theory. Paper presented at the 38th SIGCSE Technical Symposium on Computer Science Education, pp. 367–371 (2007)
26. Magerko, B., Heeter, C., Medler, B., and Fitzgerald, J.: Intelligent adaptation of digital game-based learning. FuturePlay, Toronto (2008)
27. Tuzun, H., Yilmaz Soylu, M., Karakus, T., Inal, Y., Kizilkaya, G.: The effects of computer games on primary school students' achievement and motivation in geography learning. Comput. Educ. **52**(1), 68–77 (2009)
28. Chou, S.-Y.: The influence of thinking style on flow experience in casual games. Master thesis, National Chian Tung University, Hsinchu, Taiwan (2008)
29. Lin, W.-H: The impact of flow factors on forming consumer loy-alty on website. Master thesis, Feng Chia University, Taichung, Taiwan (2006)

30. Chang, Y.-H.: Learning effectiveness of using the recommendation learning system based on multiple intelligences theory. Master thesis, National Taichung University of Education, Taichung, Taiwan (2010)
31. Yang, C.-C.: The research of the impacts of interpersonal interac-tion and flow experience on the effectiveness of adult on-line learning. Master thesis, National Kaohsiung Normal University, Taiwan (2004)
32. Huang, H.-Y.: The study on the relationship between the cogni-tion, the tolerance of problem behaviors of students and occupational burnout for the elementary school teacher. Master thesis, National Yunlin University of Science and Technology, Taiwan (2008)
33. Chen, L.-X.: The influence of playfulness on flow state through self-regulation: casual game as a platform. Master thesis, National Chian Tung University, Taiwan (2009)
34. Chang, H.-H., Wang, I.-C.: An investigation of user communication behavior in computer mediated environments. Comput. Hum. Behav. **24**(102), 2336–2356 (2008)
35. Chen, C.W., Huang, C.L.: Human face recognition from a single front view. Int. J. Pattern Recogn. Artif. Intell. **6**(4), 571–593 (1992)
36. Otsu, N.: A threshold selection method from gray-level histogram. IEEE Trans. Syst. Man Cybern. **9**(1), 62–66 (1979)
37. Alattar, A.M., Rajala, S.: A facial feature localization in front view head and shoulders images. Paper presented at Proceedings of IEEE International Conference on Acoustics Speech and Signal Processing, pp. 3557–3560 (1999)
38. Loh, M.P., Wong, Y.P., Wong, C.O.: Facial expression recognition for e-learning systems using gabor wavelet & neural network. Paper presented at Sixth IEEE International Conference on Advanced Learning Technologies (2006)
39. Li, C.-M.: Diagnosing learning difficulty with facial expression recognition. Master thesis, National Taiwan Normal University, Taiwan (2008)
40. Yang, M.H., Kriegman, D.J., Ahuja, N.: Detecting faces in im-ages: a survey. IEEE Trans. Pattern Anal. Mach. Intell. **24**(1), 34–58 (2002)
41. Chen, H.R.: Assessment of learners' attention to e-learning by monitoring facial expressions for computer network courses. J. Educ. Comput. Res. **47**(4), 371–385 (2012)
42. Chen, H.R., Lin, Y.S., Huang, S.Y., Shiau, S.Y.: Content design for situated game-based learning: an exploration of chinese language poetry learning. Paper presented at the IEEE International Conference Computational Intelligence and Software Engineering, Technology Education Section, China (2009)

# International Workshop on Cloud Computing for Web-Based Learning

# The Learning Effect of Students' Cognitive Styles in Using Cloud Technology

Ching-Hung Yeh[1] and Chia-Cheng Hsu[2,3](✉)

[1] Department of Computer Science and Information Engineering, Far East University, Tainan, Taiwan
chyeh@cc.feu.edu.tw

[2] Department of Engineering Science, National Cheng Kung University, Tainan, Taiwan

[3] Department and Graduate School of Visual Communication Design, Tainan University of Technology, Tainan, Taiwan
chia.cheng.hsu.tw@gmail.com

**Abstract.** Internet combines information technology into our daily life in which cloud technology is the popular application and the education and learning also be enhanced recently. Learning has been enriched by digital functions that abstract concepts be concreted to improve the effectiveness of learners. Many researches have carried out the study of electric learning, and has confirmed the association between e-learning and cognitive style, but less researches focus on the cloud technology introduces into e-learning. The purpose of this study is to explore the learning effect of students' cognitive styles in using cloud technology. We infer the important factors in cloud technology applied to learning that provide to design adaptive learning to achieve better learning outcomes.

**Keywords:** Cognitive style · Cloud technology · E-learning

## 1 Introduction

With the rapid growth of computer technology, some applications on computer networks have attracted attention of people in education, such as e-learning, mobile learning, and ubiquitous learning. In 1981, IBM launched the first personal computer that makes human life into a new information age that is called the first information technology revolution. People began to use computers to deal with trivial matters of life and help improve the efficiency of producing. After a decade, the 1990 s of the 20th century, the release of the web browser has brought tremendous change. For example, people can use web browsers to go shopping, make communication with each others, and search for information that they need. These browsing behaviors and consumption on computer network have been gradually changing the lifestyle and mindset of human. With the increase in data transmission speed of network, the Internet is becoming and indispensable tool in human life, and some multimedia contents can naturally appear in the web browser over a network [1, 2]. At the same time, the change of network speed has attracted attention of education scholars and experts, and they try


D.K.W. Chiu et al. (Eds.): ICWL 2013 Workshops, LNCS 8390, pp. 155–163, 2015.
DOI: 10.1007/978-3-662-46315-4_16

to design useful tools and teaching approaches to transfer knowledge for learners through a network.

E-learning is to use electronic media and information and communication technologies to improve the learning of learners in education. The e-learning covers a broad range that includes using the Internet, television, satellite broadcasting and compact disk read-only memory (CD-ROM) to process the teaching and learning. In order to assist learners that cannot acquire knowledge in a classroom at school, in traditional teaching, learning materials are made into compact disks (CDs), and learners can receive knowledge through borrowing CDs or television broadcasting (distance learning). The e-learning with information technology and network began to replace the traditional correspondence distance learning, and developed many efficient learning and teaching methods in a network, such as online teaching, cooperative learning, distributed learning, and Internet remedial instruction [1].

In a traditional classroom, instructors impart knowledge to students via using textbooks and lectures. From the aspect of instruction, an instructor would like to know whether the students in a classroom receive knowledge, and provide suitable learning materials according to the learning status of students [3]. The e-learning environment can help instructors to build a teaching and interactive environment to provide a variety of learning materials in which students can access materials according to their needs [4]. Therefore, the use of information technology has changed the model of teaching and learning, and has attracted attention of many educational experts resulting in superior research with computer network to meet the needs of individual learning, such as mobile learning, game-based learning, learning behavior analysis, online learning of cognitive style or learning style, computer-assisted learning, cooperative learning with information technology, and so on [5–8]. The model of teaching and learning has transformed the model of teacher-center into the model of student-center. In order to meet the individual learning needs and effective learning, instructors must understand the favorite way to deal with information and personal difference, such as learning style and cognitive style, and then provide different learning materials to effectively improve their learning.

Cloud technology raised another revolution of information technology [9]. The cloud technology known as cloud computing represents a change in the way information technology services. Cloud technology provides virtual services of hardware, platform, and software, and those resources of cloud technology are built on web-based network [10]. Users of cloud technology can use the resources of cloud without buying servers, storage equipment, and network hardware infrastructure, and only pay for the actual usage. Moreover, users of cloud technology do not need to pay the costs of software and maintenance manpower.

Cloud that appears in the traditional information technology is used to represent the telecommunication network in which users can access any useful information. Cloud computing means an Internet-based computing; some hardware and software resources and information can be shared with other computers and other devices through this way [9–12]. Therefore, users can use the smart mobile devices, such as laptop computers, smart phones and tablet computers, to conveniently enjoy the benefits of cloud technology. When cloud technology is applied in education, users can achieve the effectiveness of mobile learning and ubiquitous learning without the limitation of space and time [13, 14]. In such a learning environment by using cloud technology, the effectiveness of personalized learning is more prominent. The presentation of learning content of applications with cloud technology may have different impact on students based on their cognitive learning. Most of previous studies focused on the impact of learning achievement on different cognitive styles for cloud technology; a little study investigated the relationship between the preference of application tools using cloud technology and cognitive style. This study is to explore the relationship between the preference of learning materials of application tools using cloud technology and the cognitive style of learners. The study uses a cognitive questionnaire for students at a university in Taiwan, and provides some application tools for their learning activities, and analyzes their preference of learning. The study hopes to provide key factors for instructors to design suitable learning materials and select useful tools using cloud technology for students and improve their learning outcomes.

## 2 Related Work

### 2.1 Cognitive Style

Birch & Hayward addressed that cognitive style is related to human thinking, memory, perception and information processing methods that not only include memory, process information or problem solving, but also include how a person faces the surrounding environment [15]. Cognitive style has a great impact on the effectiveness of learners when they are in cognitive activities of the courses [16, 17], but it was not significantly related to or directly related to the intelligence level [18, 19]. Messick [19] defined cognitive style as an individuals' consistent approach to organizing and processing information during learning. Therefore, cognitive style is a way of information processing in which a person receives external message context, analyzes information in inner psychology, presents an external inertial properties, and affects the performance of cognitive behavior.

In some studies of cognitive style, the field dependence-independence theory is currently the most studied and most widely used in educational fields [20]. The difference of the field dependence and the field independence is shown as follows:

1. Cognitive activity: The field independent learners are good at the organization of information from the context of a complex environment, and reduce the impact of the surrounding space. The learning performance of the field independent learners is more than that of the field dependent learners, when the teaching is in the less structure sensitive method. The field dependent learners tend to view the surrounding context as a whole without analysis, to conduct perceptual discrimination with a whole method, and to like structured teaching methods.
2. Personality property: The field independent learners have a tendency within reference architecture in self-reference, usually referred to their own values and ethical standards. The field dependent learners refer to outside field as the reference architecture, and rely on others or the authority.
3. Emotional expression: Field independence is easier to control emotion, not impulsive, and presents rational and dull for the surrounding environment. The field

dependent learners are more vulnerable and more easily excited, but cannot control or adjust the expression of emotion and perform more forthright.

4. Learning activity: When the field independent learners are in a clear environment, they can organize learning without the assistance of others to achieve the learning performance. Conversely, the field dependent learners in high structure learning environment can achieve learning outcomes. When the field dependent learning in low structure learning environment, they need to rely on others to achieve the target of the effective learning.

As mentioned above, different cognitive styles of learners have presented the preference for learning materials. Therefore, suitable learning materials can be classified according the cognitive styles of learners. Many e-learning systems applied cloud technology to provide more flexibility for students. In such learning environments, some adaptive learning with cloud technology should be considered when instructors used the online tools as the assistant learning tools [21, 22]. Learning materials should match the students' cognitive style to achieve the quality of the effective teaching and learning.

## 2.2 Cloud Technology

Cloud technology is a concept term for network and means that cloud technology connects computers at the same time to run distributed computing over a network [23]. In general, cloud technology is cloud computing over a network and provides a variety of virtual services for the needs of users, such as hardware, software, storage space and other resources. The services of cloud technology can be divided into three parts that include infrastructure as a service (IaaS), platform as a service (PaaS), and software as a service (SaaS) [10, 11, 23]. IaaS means that some computers are connected together via a network to delivery information, such as virtual computers, servers, storage equipments. This mode has high flexibility, and users can rent equipments without the management of cloud computing. In the PaaS model, cloud providers offer users a computing platform that includes an operation system, programming language environment, database and so on. Users do not need to manage and control basic equipment, network, servers, operating system and related software license. In the SaaS, cloud providers offer a variety of application software over a network, and the use of the SaaS is priced on a pay-per-use basis. Users in the SaaS can access application software from cloud clients, and they do not need to install and run the application on their own computers.

National Institute of Standards and Technology addressed that there are five important characteristics for using cloud computing [10, 12]: (1) On-demand self-service, (2) Ubiquitous network access, (3) Resource pooling, (4) Rapid elasticity, and (5) Measured service.

1. On-demand self-service: Users can request, obtain, and configure cloud services and resources, such as servers or storage space, according to their individual needs without interacting with the resource providers.
2. Ubiquitous network access: Cloud providers offer services with standard mechanisms through a variety of online channels, and users can use thick and thin clients to access services on a network.

3. Resource pooling: The cloud computing resources are pooled to serve multiple users. Users do not need to know the exact location of resources used.
4. Rapid elasticity: Cloud providers have the ability to scale resources both up and down as needed. Users can purchase any number of services and resources at any time.
5. Measured service: Cloud computing resource usage can be measured, controlled, and reported. The information technology services of cloud computing are charged per usage metrics - pay per use. The more the user utilizes the higher the payment.

From the physical dimensions of the resource perspective, cloud technology includes a variety of resources that are computers, storage equipments, network components, and operation systems. Cloud storage is a mode of storage where data is stored in virtualized pools of storage, not in the user's computer. A public storage service has the main benefits that are availability, reliability, efficient retrieval, and data sharing [13]. Cloud technology applied to education is an inevitable trend which can bring the following benefits [14]:

1. Cost saving. Educational institutions need to find methods to offer affordable services and tools. Cloud computing provides fewer management overheads in school.
2. Flexible information technology management. Cloud computing technologies include everyday services, such as calendar and e-mail. System administrators can bring new services while managing costs as operational expenses. Cloud computing helps system administrators manage risks.
3. Accessible information technology resources and services. Cloud computing technologies move on-site resources and services to a network, and make them accessible anytime.

The students in the technology age are highly dependent on the network and technology products which from learning tools have becomes into necessities. The learning behavior, the learning attitudes, and the perceived value of young people in the technology age are very different from the past. Today's smart mobile devices, such as smart phones, tablet computers and other terminal equipment, are quite popular among people, especially young people are almost to have one. In instructional design, teachers can more easily import the cloud technology in the teaching environments. If the teaching design or content can extend to students' smart mobile devices that build discussion groups or learning communities through the applications (APPs), the teaching results will be able to produce a fresh and effective learning environment.

## 3 Research Method

### 3.1 Research Design

Based on the above discussion and analysis of cognitive style and cloud technology in the learning, if instructors provide appropriate learning situations according to students' cognitive styles that will enhance the willingness of students to learn and increase their learning outcomes. For example group learning, cognitive styles affect the thinking and behavior of students in the group discussion. Compared with the field dependent students, the field independent student actively to speak to discuss the issue, but they less speak in the subsequent discussion. Therefore, the appropriate adjustments can be configured so that the two types of students can decrease the difference of learning [8].

The subjects of this were the second years students in the department of information engineering at a technology university in Tainan. First, the students completed a group embedded figures test to distinguish between field-independent and field-dependent. The test was originally compiled and published by Messick of The Education Testing Service in 1962. The group embedded figure test in this study is based Witkin, Oltman, Raskin and Karpy (Embedded Figures Test, EFT). Next, an instructor used to cloud technology in teaching, and the students in learning activity used cloud technology. After completing a learning activity, the students were asked to test the questionnaire of the cloud technology preference that include "the type of preference", "the interface affinity" and "the interest in learning".

The reason using the three factors was that this study would like to obtain the relationship between the cognitive style and the preference of using cloud technology in teaching application. Moreover, this study would like to discuss the interface design of related apps that provide the interactive media for learner and a good friendly interface whether reduce the use disorder, shorten the adaptive time, and thus attract continued investment in the use of learning to increase the effectiveness of learning. This study is to clarify the relevant factors through this questionnaire analysis. In the future research, the questionnaire can be used as a reference to design more convenient and beneficial use of the interface, or design useful user interface that users can self-set manually. According to Triantafillou et al. [21], the design of interface for different cognitive style students can lead to higher interest in learning; therefore, in the third part, the interest in learning is used to detect whether the teaching cloud technology stimulate the interest of the learners.

In the dimension of "the type of preference", this study divided the teaching with cloud technology into four categories by teaching type:

1. Social networking sites: The Facebook (www.facebook.com) is an information sharing site to exchange messages between individuals and groups of digital tribes from one-to-one, one-to-many, many-to-many methods. Facebook can be used as group learning discussion in the teaching application.
2. Community desk: MyWebDestop (www.mywebdesktop.com/) applies to group learning, and team members can share the work space and collect common needs to reach the convenience in data access and sharing.
3. Group file management: Such as Google Docs (docs.google.com) and Pbworks (www.pbworks.com) provides a variety of formats to save the file and edit functions, and the user interface has co-written and co-modified features. Members of the learning group can write together and share information at the same time to reduce the problem of version checking.
4. Group Calendar: Google calendar (www.google.com/calendar) provides users to set personal work schedule. The major application of the tool is that each member of the group can view the calender, and co-set the schedule.

### 3.2 Research Analysis

This study is to investigate the preference of application types and interface for different cognitive style learners, when they are contacted with cloud technology for learning. The questionnaire with using the SPSS statistical software was used to analyze the relevance of cognitive style and three dimensions, and summarize the different cognitive style learners prefer those patterns and interface cloud technology in learning to achieve expected learning outcomes. The results are summarized in Tables 1, 2, and 3.

**Table 1.** The preference percentage of using the four computer-assisted tools with cloud technology for the different cognitive styles of students.

| | Social networking sites | Community desk | Group file management | Group calendar |
|---|---|---|---|---|
| Field independence | 84.23 % | 75.64 % | 83.46 % | 71.25 % |
| Field dependence | 85.67 % | 86.74 % | 85.37 % | 80.28 % |

**Table 2.** The affinity percentage of interface for the four computer-assisted tools with cloud technology.

| | Social networking sites | Community desk | Group file management | Group calendar |
|---|---|---|---|---|
| Field independence | 86.21 % | 71.58 % | 82.69 % | 72.32 % |
| Field dependence | 86.14 % | 84.16 % | 78.31 % | 82.46 % |

**Table 3.** The percentage of interest in learning about the four computer-assisted tools with cloud technology.

| | Social networking sites | Community desk | Group file management | Group calendar |
|---|---|---|---|---|
| Field independence | 88.24 % | 74.36 % | 80.24 % | 71.26 % |
| Field dependence | 86.32 % | 85.31 % | 80.39 % | 83.25 % |

Table 1 shows that the acceptance of social networking sites between the different cognitive style students is very close and reflects the acceptance situation of the social networking site in young students. Regardless of the cognitive style type, the acceptance of the social networking is very high, and the similar result is shown in the group file management. In the community desk and group calender, it is obvious that the preference of field dependent students is higher than the field independent students, and the result show that the field dependent students are associated with the highest structure learning activities. Evidently, the community desk and group calender provide a structured framework supporting so that the field dependent student has a higher acceptance.

Table 2 is the observed result of the preference of the interface affinity dimension for different types of cognitive style. In community desk and group calender, the field independent students feel interface affinity less than the field dependent students. In order to improve the interface affinity dimension, the functionality and interface must be modified to improve the use and preference of field independent students. In addition, in the interface language, the students reflected that the traditional Chinese interface for students is less obstacle to use. The results also show that cloud technology in learning in Taiwan still has plenty of space to develop, such as the community desk, and group file management. It is also found that the foreign language skill of the students is poor so that the interface of software with the non-national language increases their burden.

The results of the interest in learning for the students of different cognitive styles on learning with cloud technology are shown in Table 3. The two types of students felt that the cloud technology can stimulate their interest in learning, and it is a trend that young students have high acceptance of technology products and applications in the high popularity. However, for the field independent students, the social networking site causes the highest interest in learning, while the interests in learning for the three cloud technologies are slightly lower. Obviously, The features of interaction in this stage and the future are still the mainstream.

## 4 Future Work

This study investigated and analyzed the relevance of three dimensions, including "the type of preference", "the interface affinity" and "the interest in learning", with different cognitive styles of students, when the computer-assisted tools with cloud technologies were used in teaching. The future research will focus on the effect of cloud technology in teaching and learning, including the pre-test, teaching with cloud teaching, post-test, and the assessment of learning performance.

## References

1. Razzaq, L., Heffernan, N.: Towards designing a user-adaptive web-based E-learning system. Extended Abstracts Proceeding of the 2008 Conference on Human Factors in Computing Systems, pp. 3525–3530. ACM, Florence (2008)
2. Hsu, C.-C., Wang, K.-T., Huang, Y.-M.: Modeling personalized learning styles in a web-based learning system. In: Pan, Z., Cheok, A.D., Müller, W., Zhang, X., Wong, K. (eds.) Transactions on Edutainment IV. LNCS, vol. 6250, pp. 12–21. Springer, Heidelberg (2010)
3. Hsu, C.C., Chen, H.C., Su, Y.N., Huang, K.K., Huang, Y.M.: Developing a reading concentration monitoring system by applying an artificial bee colony algorithm to E-books in an intelligent classroom. Sensors **12**, 14158–14178 (2012)

4. Cloud Security Alliance: Security Guidance for Critical Areas of Focus in Cloud Computing V2.1, December 2009, http://www.cloudsecurityalliance.org/csaguide.pdf
5. Witkin, H.A., Goodenough, D.R.: Cognitive Styles: Essence and Origins: Field Dependence and Field Independence. International Universities Press, Boston (1981)
6. Hsu, C.C., Chen, H.C., Huang, K.K., Huang, Y.M.: A personalized auxiliary material recommendation system based on learning style on facebook applying an artificial bee colony algorithm. Comput. Math. Appl. **64**, 1506–1513 (2012)
7. Tinajero, C., Páramo, M.F.: Field dependence-independence cognitive style and academic achievement: a review of research and theory. Eur. J. Psychol. Educ. **13**, 227–251 (1998)
8. Lin, Y.L., Chuang, T.Y., Su, S.H., Liu, C.C.: The content analysis of cognitive style in digital game: a case of Machinarium. In: 15th Global Chinese Conference on Computers in Education (GCCCE 2011), Hangzhou, China, May 2011
9. Lasica, J.D.: Identity in the Age of Cloud Computing: The Next-generation Internet's Impact on Business, Governance and Social Interaction. The Aspen Institute, Washington, DC (2009)
10. Mell, P., Grance, T.: The NIST Definition of Cloud Computing. National Institute of Standards and Technology (2009)
11. Sultan, N.: Cloud computing for education: a new dawn? Int. J. Inf. Manage. **30**, 109–116 (2010)
12. Grobauer, B., Walloschek, T., Stöcker, E.: Understanding cloud-computing vulnerabilities. IEEE Secur. Priv. **99**, 50–57 (2011)
13. Kamara, S., Lauter, K.: Cryptographic cloud storage. In: Sion, R., Curtmola, R., Dietrich, S., Kiayias, A., Miret, J.M., Sako, K., Sebé, F. (eds.) FC 2010 Workshops. LNCS, vol. 6054, pp. 136–149. Springer, Heidelberg (2010)
14. Tan, X., Kim, Y.B.: Cloud computing for education: a case of using google docs in MBA group projects. In: 2011 International Conference on Business Computing and Global Informatization (BCGIn 2011), Shanghai, China (2011)
15. Birch, A., Hayward, S.: Individual Difference. Macmillan, Basingstoke (1994)
16. Riding, R.J., Pearson, R.: The relationship between cognitive style and intelligence. Educ. Psychol. **14**, 413–425 (1994)
17. Riding, R., Agrell, T.: The effect of cognitive style on school subject performance. Educ. Stud. **23**, 211–323 (1997)
18. Sternberg, R.J.: The Nature of Creativity: Contemporary Psychological Perspectives. Cambridge University Press, Cambridge (1988)
19. Messick, S.: The nature of cognitive styles: problems and promise in educational practice. Educ. Psychol. **19**, 59–74 (1984)
20. Witkin, H.A., Lewis, H.B., Hertzman, M., Machover, K., Meissner, P.B., Wapner, S.: Personality through Perception: An Experimental and Clinical Study. Harper, NY (1954)
21. Triantafillou, E., Pomportsis, A., Demetriadis, S.: The design and the formative evaluation of an adaptive educational system based on cognitive styles. Comput. Educ. **41**, 87–103 (2003)
22. Hsu, C.C., Chen, H.C., Huang, K.H., Huang, K.K., Huang, Y.M.: The development of an adaptive group composition system on facebook for collaborative learning using an artificial bee colony algorithm. Appl. Math. Inf. Sci. **8**, 1–8 (2014)
23. Talib, A.M., Atan, R., Abdullah, R., Azmi Murad, M.A.: Towards new data access control technique based on multi agent system architecture for cloud computing. In: Snasel, V., Platos, J., El-Qawasmeh, E. (eds.) ICDIPC 2011, Part II. CCIS, vol. 189, pp. 268–279. Springer, Heidelberg (2011)

# Framework of Supporting Structured Game Script Learning System

Feng-Jung Liu[1(✉)] and Chun-Wei Tseng[2]

[1] Department of Digital Multimedia Design,
Cheng-Shiu University, Kaohsiung, Taiwan, ROC
fjliu@csu.edu.tw

[2] Department of Information Management,
Cheng-Shiu University, Kaohsiung, Taiwan, ROC
cwtseng@csu.edu.tw

**Abstract.** Game-based learning applications have been getting much attention and it has been widely applied on teaching activities of modern teaching. However, Game-based learning is used as well as the common computer games, so in the design of game-based learning it needs to keep users in the flow effect to intrigue learners to continue learning. Many studies have also pointed out the importance of faithful appropriation for learners in game learning, so that people tend to pay much attention on the entertainment effect. As to the design of the game, i.e., how to achieve the purpose of teaching and how to conduct different teaching effect by playing learning activities in some domain, and so on, it seems be ignored. Besides, many issues in the applications of game-based learning showed that the effect of Game-based learning is merely like the one of playing computer game but difficult to achieve effective learning outcomes if lacking of proper guidance and assistance.

In this study, we intended to design a RPG-based script editing system to build a game-learning platform. Using the game script editing system, it can help designers or teachers to easily plan their learning activities without consideration of game design. In addition, as the game playing, the guides or teachers can observe and guide students to learn in order to achieve the goal of adaptive learning.

**Keywords:** Game-based learning · RPG-based · Structured script

## 1 Introduction

Game-based learning in educational applications has been getting much attention. One of the main reasons is the game-based learning can intrigue learners' interest and motivation to use learning, achieve to improve students' learning efficiency, stimulate students' higher-level cognitive thinking, and then become one of effective learning modes. However, the most important thing of above is that the game-based learning is better capable of combining with different areas of discipline and easier to be immersed into a variety of life situations.

Many reports revealed that the game-based learning if lacking of proper guidance and assistance is just like playing games and rather difficult to achieve effective


D.K.W. Chiu et al. (Eds.): ICWL 2013 Workshops, LNCS 8390, pp. 164–169, 2015.
DOI: 10.1007/978-3-662-46315-4_17

learning. Therefore, the project aims to plan a role-playing game based learning platform, which not only to help designers or teachers to plan learning activities, but also each student can choose their favorite roles to proceed the game learning according to personal characteristics. In addition, teachers/guides can observe, assist and guide students to learn in game situation to achieve adaptive game-based learning goals.

## 2 Related Works

Due to game-based learning as the use of general computer game, it needs to be designed to keep users be immersed in flow effects to cause learners to use and to continue using. Therefore, many studies on the game-based learning application [7, 8] pointed out the importance of faithful appropriation of users. And therefore, most of learning games' designs tends to focus on their entertainment effect. Regarding to how to adopt game learning to achieve the teaching goal? how to apply the learning activities to various fields with game learning to improve learning efficiency? etc., it seems less attractive. In fact, many research issues about game-importing to learning need to be explored and discussed.

In the game-learning script design, about the methods of combination of traditional games activities and learning content, Umetsu, Hirashima and Takeuchi proposed the most common simple simulation method, the combination method and the fusion method which is to combine more closely than the combination method on game-based learning [4]. Both methods are shown in Figs. 1 and 2 respectively.

In the design of system development, domestic and foreign literatures [1–3] are still not too many. Ok-Hue Cho and Won-Hyung Lee [1] proposed an interactive event design tools, Easy Design tool of Game Event for rapid game Development, named EDGE, to assist rapid game development. EDGE system is based on Unity 3D engine and its development progress contains five procedures, as shown in Fig. 3. By adopting the game design procedures, the game prototyping can be constructed rapidly.

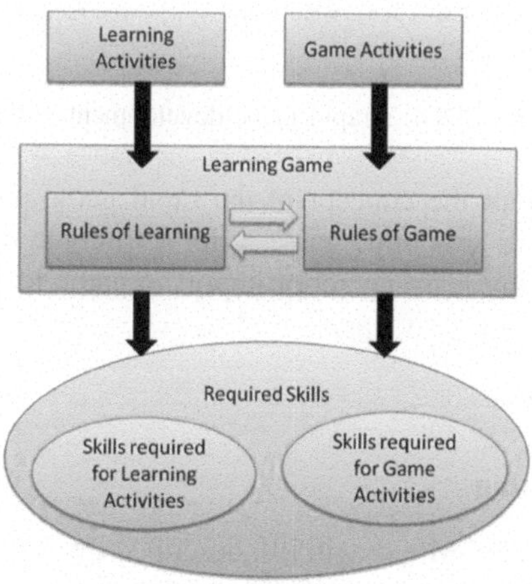


**Fig. 1.** Combination method.

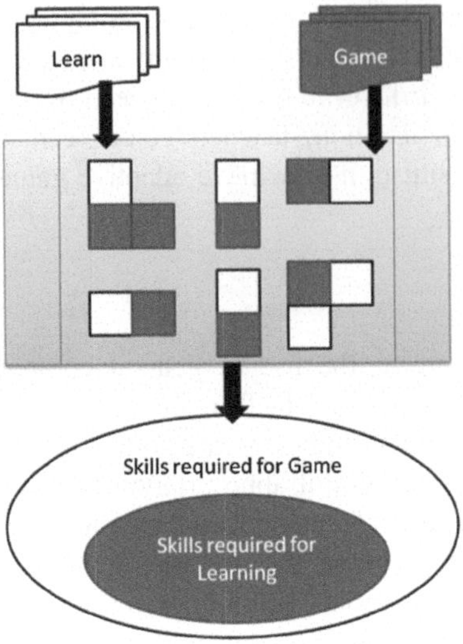


**Fig. 2.** Fusion method

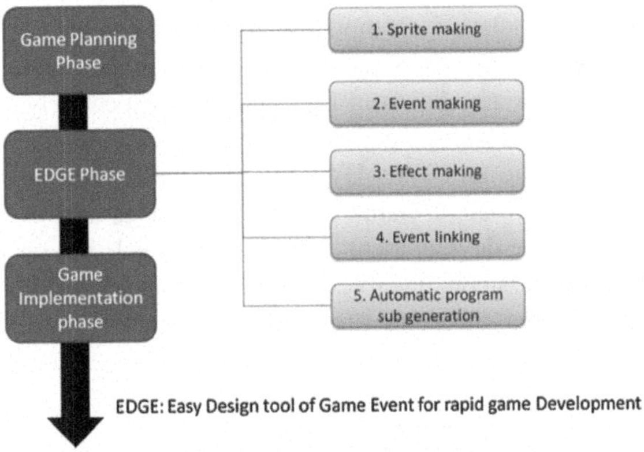


**Fig. 3.** EDGE's rapid game development process.

In this study, we adopt the concept of the rapid game prototyping to develop a supporting standardized or structured game script learning system platform to achieve the purposes of the quickly learning script import to game learning applications.

## 3 System Design

### 3.1 Game Story Writing

Campbell's 'Hero's Journey' Monomyth [9], described by Campbell in 1949, is a basic pattern to explain a classic sequence of actions that are found in many stories. The stages of the hero's journey are shown as Fig. 4.

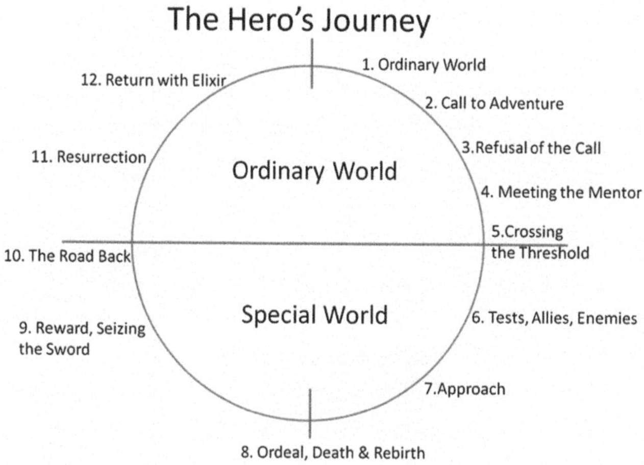


**Fig. 4.** Campbell's 'Hero's Journey'.

In the game script design process, it is divided into four steps and summarized as follows:

1. To setup the game script: According to traditional culture, the designer or teaching activity designers utilize and assign people, events, time, place and thing with real settings in order to act as a teaching guiding function.
2. To tell the story: Through experiences from teachers, to tell the space-time interleaving story. In this step, it doesn't focus on the reality of story, but the rationalization and harmony of the story development.
3. To write the script: Based on the Campbell hero's journey model, guide or instructional designer proceeded to write the script according the basic requirements of the rationalized concept of the story.
4. To design system: Based on the above planning and through structured system analysis, we progress to establish the template of standardized script design and activate the development of the structured game script editing system.

### 3.2 Game Script Editing System Design

As shown in Fig. 5, the design of game script editing learning system is based on the spirit of problem-based learning, PBL and constructed with the scaffolding and fading strategies [5]. In addition, we attempt to combine with SCORM-compliant digital teaching material to achieve learning objectives. Currently, the exchange of standard learning paths is mainly based on the Sequencing and Navigation specification of SCORM 2004 [6]. We intend to use the game script editor to assist guide/ teachers to combine the SCORM-compliant teaching materials to build an effective learning path.

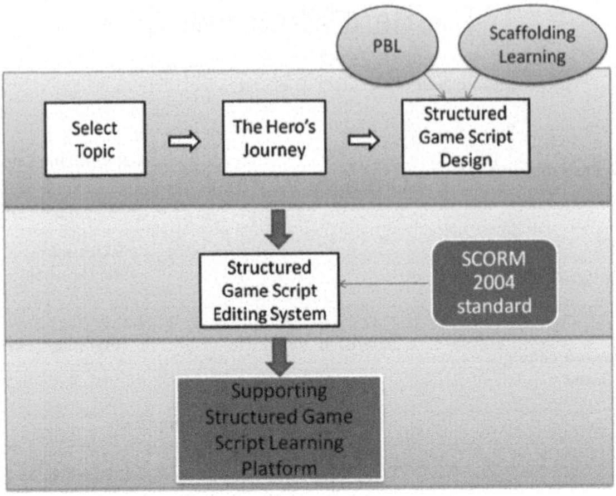


**Fig. 5.** System design of supporting structured game script learning system.

## 4 Conclusion and Future Works

In this study, we mainly proposed a RPG-based script editing system framework to help designers or teachers to easily plan their learning activities on game-based learning. In addition, we also attempt to follow the specifications of SCORM-compliant digital teaching material to provide an effective learning path in conjunction with game script design. Game design works, including the stories of game, characters, scenes, and so on, are the major part of the supporting structured game script editing system. But, the most important objective of the Game-based learning platform is to improve learning effectiveness.

In future work, we will refine the system architecture more clearly. We hope a teaching activity designers can design a learning game without the deep knowledge of a game and high ability of game design. We will construct the prototype of game-based script editing system that makes all designer can design a learning game easily.

## References

1. Cho, O.-H., Lee, W.-H.: An interactive event-design tool for rapid game development. In: 2011 IEEE 15th International Symposium on Computer Electronics, pp. 450–453 (2011)
2. Chen, H., Hou, H.T., Chou, Y.S., Lai, S.N., Wu, Y.S.: Perfect PAPA©: designing and evaluating digital instructional game combining situated learning and role-playing strategies for life skill training. Poster Presented at 2012 Fourth IEEE International Conference on Digital Game and Intelligent Toy Enhanced Learning (DIGITEL 2012), Takamatsu, Kagawa, Japan, 27–30 March 2012 (2012)
3. Garris, R., Ahlers, R., Driskell, J.E.: Games, motivation, and learning: a research and practice model. Simul. Gaming **33**(4), 441–467 (2002)

4. Umetsu, T., Hirashima, T., Takeuchi, A.: Fusion method for designing computer-based learning game. In: 2002 International Conference on Computers in Education (ICCE 2002), p. 124 (2002)
5. Linn, M.C.: Designing computer learning environments for engineering and computer science: the scaffolded knowledge integration framework. J. Sci. Educ. Technol. **4**(2), 103–126 (1995)
6. Advanced Distributed Learning (ADL). SCORM 2004, 4th edn. (2009). http://www.adlnet.gov/capabilities/scorm/scorm-2004-4th
7. Prensky, M.: Digital Game-Based Learning. McGraw-Hill, New York (2007)
8. Terrell, S., Rendulic, P.: Using computer managed instructional software to increase motivation and achievement in elementary school curriculum. J. Res. Comput. Educ. **28**(3), 403–414 (1996)
9. Campbell, J.: The Hero with a Thousand Faces. Bollingen Series XVII, Princeton University Press, Princeton (1949, 1968, 1973)
10. Schmidt, H.G., Rotgans, J.I., Yew, E.H.J.: The process of problem-based learning: what works and why. Medical Educ. **45**(8), 792–806 (2012). doi:10.1111/j.1365-2923.2011.04035.x. Accessed 16 Nov 2012

# Performance Analysis Using Petri Net Based MapReduce Model in Heterogeneous Clusters

Sheng-Tzong Cheng[1], Hsi-Chuan Wang[1], Yin-Jun Chen[1(✉)], and Chen-Fei Chen[2]

[1] Department of Computer Science and Information Engineering, National Cheng Kung University, Tainan, Taiwan
{stcheng,P76004651,p78981142}@mail.ncku.edu.tw
[2] Department of Information and Communications, Shih Hsin University, Taipei, Taiwan
cffchen@cc.shu.edu.tw

**Abstract.** Currently, big data and large-scale data processing techniques has become an important developing area. MapReduce is an enabling technology of cloud computing. Hadoop is one of the most popular MapReduce implementation, which is the target platform in this paper. When running a MapReduce job, programmers however cannot acquire the information about how to fine-tune the parameters of application. Moreover, programmers need much time on finding the most suitable parameters. This paper evaluates execution processes in MapReduce and form SPN-MR model with Stochastic Petri Net. In order to analyze the performance of SPN-MR, formulas of mean delay time in each time transition are defined. SPN-MR simulates the elapsed time of any MapReduce jobs with known input data sizes and then reduces time cost in performance tuning. SPN-MR carried out several actual test benchmarks. The results showed the average error rate is within 5 percent. Therefore, it can provide effective performance evaluation reports for MapReduce programmers.

**Keywords:** Cloud computing · MapReduce · Petri net · Performance analysis

## 1 Introduction

Cloud computing has been developed rapidly these years as the amounts of data created explosively growths in our life. In order to deal with these big data as fast as possible, parallel processing techniques have been focused all the time. MapReduce is one of the most important and well-known parallel processing technique, and it is widely used in cloud computing. It can be said that MapReduce is a programming model for large-scale parallel processing, or a software framework in Hadoop or other platforms such as GridGain, Phoenix and Mars. Each platform which implements the concept of MapReduce has different properties in the specific region. Nevertheless, Hadoop is the most popular open source implementation of MapReduce maintained by Apache Software Foundation and being improved by many software developers and researchers. Hadoop leads the big data world being focused by many companies and researchers these years in spite of some comments display that it still needs improvements.


D.K.W. Chiu et al. (Eds.): ICWL 2013 Workshops, LNCS 8390, pp. 170–179, 2015.
DOI: 10.1007/978-3-662-46315-4_18

As one of the users of Hadoop, building a MapReduce job is not that difficult as long as following the steps in tutorial documents. However, the performance usually cannot achieve the expected performance goal in many cases. In the cause of applying the full power of cluster, Hadoop users still need to look into several performance-related configurations such as the numbers of map and reduce tasks and many other adjustable parameters. Furthermore, when running a MapReduce job, users cannot get the information about how the performance of the application should be in their test environment. In the past, performance tuning need to run the loop of guessing suitable configurations by experience then waiting the actual MapReduce job completion for several times. Being a new MapReduce programmer, it is helpful if an estimated performance result about how this application will behave on a particular hardware specification and node configuration is provided. Consequently, it can save lots of time waiting the actual MapReduce job completion then reduce performance tuning time.

Performance bottlenecks of MapReduce are not easy to find. For instance, a MapReduce job can be separated to several stages, and it is hard to point out where the bottleneck happened. It may be caused by too much disk access time, some factors of heterogeneity cluster, different fault tolerance policy, or network delay. All the above are possible problems that may make the performance of a MapReduce job not in expectation.

In this paper, a Stochastic Petri Nets based MapReduce model which is shortly called as SPN-MR is proposed to make a full description about detailed operation of the MapReduce process. SPN-MR can afford Hadoop users to simulate the elapsed time of any MapReduce jobs with a known input data size in tens of milliseconds then reduce time cost of programmers in performance tuning. Moreover, a basic recommended configuration for customized jobs is provided to help Hadoop users achieve higher performance on running MapReduce jobs.

At first, MapReduce process is decomposed into seven stages and the cost time of each stage is well formulated. Meanwhile, an analytical method with time property is needed to describe MapReduce behaviors appropriately. Stochastic Petri Nets is considered to be agreed with our requirements. Petri Nets are a formal notation designed for modeling concurrency, causality and conflict and it has been widely used in performance evaluation of DEDS (Discrete Event Dynamic Systems) such as parallel distributed systems. MapReduce is also a kind of parallel distributed computation programming model. Furthermore, stochastic process, a collection of random variables can be used to represent dynamic delay time of each stage in MapReduce. After the SPN based MapReduce model constructed, many performance-related parameters is combined to compute the mean delay time of each timed transition in SPN-MR.

This is especially helpful in (1) Cluster Selection: what kind of hardware specifications that can achieve users' performance goals. (2) Performance Tuning: saving lots of time in testing different performance configurations and let users can estimate the job completion time. In simulation results, SPN-MR is compared with several actual test benchmarks and the error rate is within 5 percent; therefore, it can provide effect performance evaluation reports for MapReduce programmers.

The remainder of this paper is organized as followings. Section 2 introduces the related work about MapReduce, Petri nets and other existing work on MapReduce simulation. Section 3 discusses the analytical model about SPN-MR which is proposed in this paper in detail. Section 4 shows the performance evaluation as well as simulation results. Finally, we make a conclusion in Sect. 5, where the directions for future work are also outlined.

# 2 Related Work

## 2.1 MapReduce

A simple programming model for processing large data sets, and typically used to solve distributed computing on clusters of computers. Programmers can use a simple API with map and reduce function to split their jobs into parallel tasks and join the intermediate results to a final result. Programmers do not have to deal with issues of parallelization, remote execution, data distribution, load balancing, or fault tolerance.

In Hadoop, the homogeneity assumptions of MapReduce can cause worse performance in heterogeneous environments. Nevertheless, most cloud environments are heterogeneous, because it is hard to ensure that every server has the same hardware specifications. It had been proved that the default fair scheduler in MapReduce would bring out performance bottlenecks, which means that the fast node need to wait slow node until map tasks finished when running MapReduce jobs in heterogeneous clusters. Several better schedulers are proposed to solve this kind of problems [1]. The performance impact about MapReduce in heterogeneous clusters is also interested in this paper; therefore, the heterogeneity factors are added in SPN-MR model and integrated to our job execution time analysis.

Figure 1 displays a general structure about MapReduce process and demonstrate that the MapReduce process can be separated into six phases [2, 3]:

1. Fork: Fork user program to each worker node.
2. Assign map or reduce: Master node would decide the role of each worker node.
3. Read: Worker nodes in map phase would read the input splits which is assigned to processed by the node from local disk or through remote access.
4. Local write: After executing the map function, each worker node which act as a mapper would write the intermediate results on its local disk.
5. Remote read: Worker nodes in reduce phase would read the intermediate results as the input data of reduce function through remote access.
6. Write: After executing the reduce function, write the result into output files.

## 2.2 Petri Nets

Petri nets which is generally introduced in [4] are a graphical and mathematical modeling tool. It is one of the well-known formal methods for modeling and analyzing concurrent systems, parallel distributed systems and multiprocessor systems in earlier researches such as [5–13]. The basic elements of Petri Nets are shown in Table 1. A Petri net is a directed bipartite graph which is composed by places, transitions, tokens and arcs. A node or an action can be represented as a pair of place and transition which is connected with directed arcs. The rule for transition enabling and firing is revealed in Fig. 2.

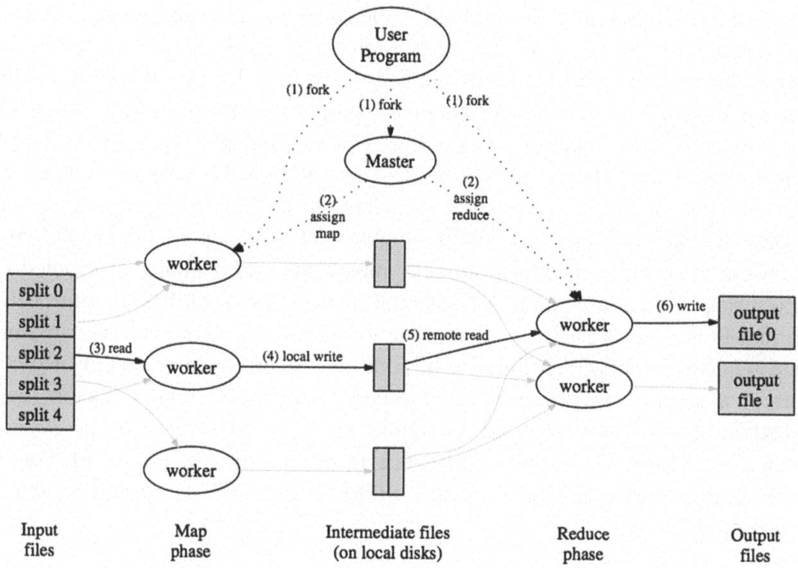


**Fig. 1.** MapReduce running system

**Table 1.** Basic elements of a Petri Net

| Elements | Notations | Meanings |
|---|---|---|
| Places | ○ a circle | Conditions, buffers or local system states. |
| Transitions | ▯ a rectangle | Actions, events, processors or computation steps. |
| Tokens | ● a dot | Data. It may move to the next places by executing "firing" actions. |
| Arcs | ⟶ an arc | Connect places and transitions which reflects the directions of the token flow. |

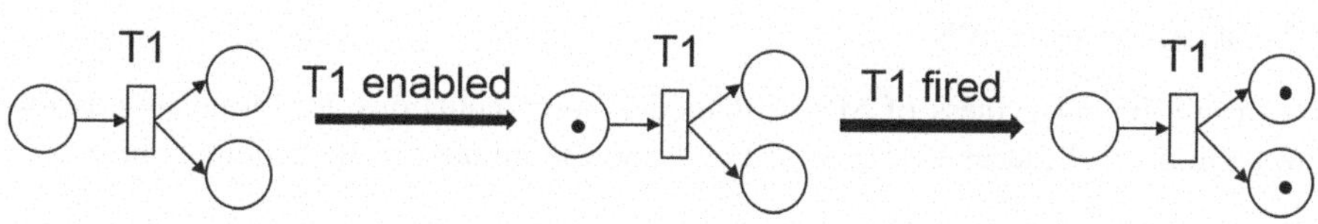


**Fig. 2.** Transition enabled and fired

A transition T1 is said to be enabled if the input place is marked with at least w tokens, where w is the weight of the arc from place to transition. If there are no labels on the arc, the default weight is 1. An enabled transition T1 may get fired immediately or after a period of time, which depends on the property of the transition. When T1 get fired, the token on each input place would be removed and added to each output place.

Timed Petri Net (TPN) and Stochastic Petri Net (SPN) are two extensions of classical Petri Nets. The time variables associated to the transition in petri net can be either deterministic variables or random variables. TPN means a fixed or random time delay on the firing of each transition. SPN means an exponentially distributed delay with the firing of each transition. Exponential distribution describes the time between events in a Poisson process. It is appropriate to think of the time interval as a random variable with exponential distribution. In addition, MapReduce is a kind of dynamic concurrent system. Network delay and other performance related factors can be described as a stochastic process. Therefore, SPN is considered to be a suitable modeling tool. However, in our MapReduce model, using few phases of fixed time delay is more accurate. Thus, a mixture of SPN and TPN is chosen as our final analytical model base.

# 3 Analytical Model

The stochastic petri net based analytical model for MapReduce which is called SPN-MR is described in this chapter. The analytical goals and detailed operation about the SPN-MR model are demonstrated in Sect. 3.1. Analytical methods with SPN are discussed in Sect. 3.2.

## 3.1 SPN-MR: Modeling MapReduce in SPN

Figure 3 illustrates the SPN-MR model designed to describe MapReduce process with two arguments M and R, where M is the number of map tasks and R is the number of reduce tasks. The graph of SPN-MR model differs according to different numbers of M and R. SPN-MR is combined with places, timed transitions, arcs and a token start from the initial place. SPN-MR is a dynamic system as the token get fired through each transition at different time then reach the next place and finally finish the MapReduce process.

## 3.2 Analysis with SPN

To ensure the correctness of SPN-MR model, some equations are formulated as follows. Number of places is shown in Eq. 1 and the number of transitions is in Eq. 2.

$$n_p = 3 * M + 3 * R + 2 \tag{1}$$

$$n_t = 3 * M + 2 * R + 2 \tag{2}$$

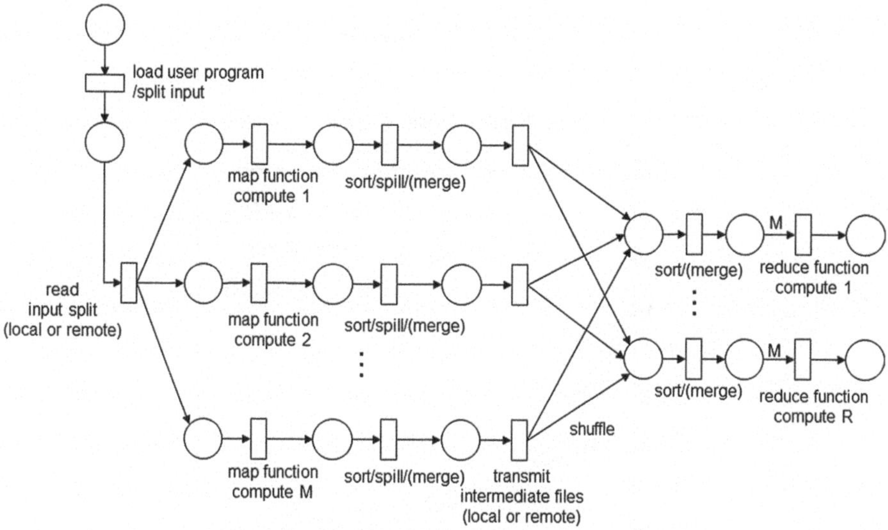


**Fig. 3.** SPN-MR model for general case

In Eqs. 1 and 2, *M* is the number of actual map tasks which is decided by split size in Hadoop and will be discussed at Sect. 4 in detail, and *R* is the number of reduce tasks that can be configured directly in user program. SPN-MR model can be defined by a marked stochastic petri net which is a 6-tuple (*P*, *T*, *I*, *O*, $M_0$, *L*), where

$P = \{p_1, p_2, \ldots, p_{n_p}\}$ is the set of $n_p$ places,

$T = \{t_1, t_2, \ldots, t_{n_t}\}$ is the set of $n_t$ transitions,

*I* is the transition input relation which is represented by arcs directed from places to transitions,

*O* is the transition output relation which is represented by arcs directed from transitions to places,

$M_0 = \{m_1, m_2, \ldots, m_{n_p}\}$ is the set of initial markings where the generic entry $m_i$ is the number of tokens in place $p_i$,

$L = \{\lambda_1, \lambda_2, \ldots, \lambda_{n_t}\}$ is the set of firing rates where $\lambda_j$ is the firing rate on transition $t_j$. In SPN, each transition is associated with an exponentially distributed random variable that expresses the delay from the enabling to the firing of the transition.

To evaluate the performance of a MapReduce job by SPN-MR model, firing rates is the most important factor that could affect the elapsed time on each stage. However, the time delay on timed transitions could be determined in several time specifications such as a value which means a fixed delay, an interval (min-max pair) which is a non-deterministic value in the interval or a probability distribution where the value is a random variable extracted from a distribution. In SPN-MR, an exponential distribution is selected to generate random variables as time delays on some timed transitions. Exponential distribution describes the time between events in a Poisson process. The exponential probability density function is defined as Eq. 3 where $\lambda$ is the rate parameter of the distribution (Fig. 4).

$$f_X(x) = \lambda e^{-\lambda x}, x \geq 0 \quad (3)$$

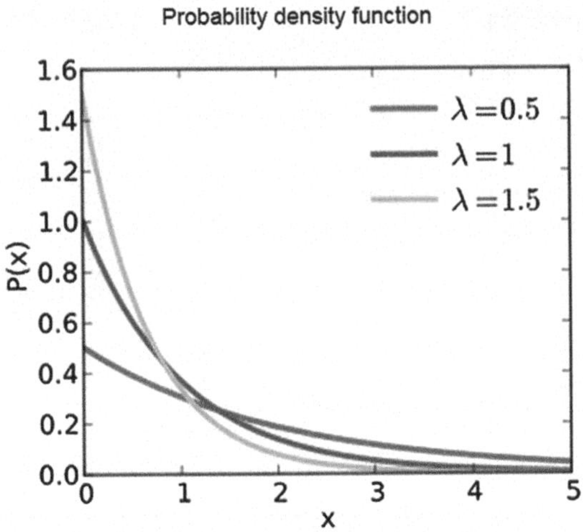


**Fig. 4.** Probability density function of exponential distribution

The mean or expected value of an exponentially distributed random variable *X* with rate parameter is given by Eq. 4.

$$E[X] = \frac{1}{\lambda} \quad (4)$$

Equation 4 can also be represented as the set of mean delay time *T* on each timed transition in Eq. 5.

$$T = \{T_1, T_2, \ldots, T_{n_t}\} \text{ where } T_i = \frac{1}{\lambda_i}, \text{i} = 1, 2, \ldots, n_t \quad (5)$$

By computing the mean delay time of each transition then get the inverse as the set of firing rates $L = \{\lambda_1, \lambda_2, \ldots, \lambda_{nt}\}$ where $\lambda_i = \frac{1}{T_i}$, i = 1, 2, …, $n_t$ the random time delay can be generated follow an exponential distribution. SPN-MR is divided into seven phases, so there are seven phases of mean delay time computation formulas. For limited page constraint, it will be discussed in future articles.

# 4 Performance Evaluation

## 4.1 Validation of the SPN-MR Model

PIPE2 [14] is the abbreviation of Platform Independent Petri net Editor 2 which is an open source and platform independent tool for creating and analyzing Petri nets including Generalized Stochastic Petri nets since 2002. PIPE2 use the "pnml" format which is similar to "xml" format that could describe the form of a petri net. SPN-MR simulator is constructed by Java and expected to release as a package in PIPE2.

SPN-MR model is validated through PIPE2. It is needed to confirm that our SPN-MR model conforms to the regulations of stochastic petri net. The SPN-MR model is drawn by the editor and verified by the animation mode which is shown in Fig. 5.

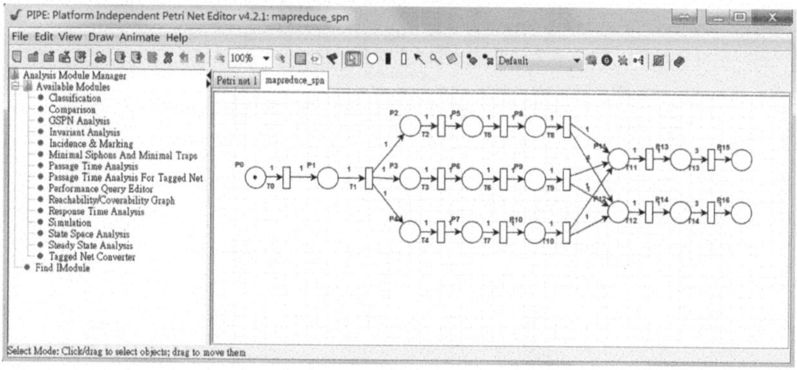


**Fig. 5.** SPN-MR model in PIPE2

## 4.2 Results and Evaluation

Figure 6 shows a job execution time simulation of a WordCount case on 2-node during 1 GB to 8 GB. The difference between "Sim" and "Actual" is quite approach which means the accuracy of job execution time estimation in this case is high.

Error rate is computed in Eq. 6(a). In Fig. 6(b), the error rates of the 2-node WordCount test on 1 GB to 8 GB input data are within 5 %. The fluctuation of error rate could be caused by the probability distribution properties on random variables.

$$\text{Error rate} = \frac{Sim - Actual}{Actual} * 100\,\% \tag{6}$$

Figure 7(a) displays job execution time estimation of WordCount on 3-node Hadoop cluster. Two Hadoop benchmarks were adopted to test the actual job execution time on a 3-node Hadoop cluster. Input data and Hadoop jar examples were downloaded from PUMA benchmarks (Purdue MapReduce Benchmarks Suite: http://web.ics.purdue.edu/~fahmad/benchmarks.htm) and used in this experiment. There are three lines which means actual, median simulated, and average simulated job execution time in the broke-line graph.

As Fig. 7(b) shows, Sim(Average) is more close to the actual job execution time than Sim(Median) under 5 GB input data size. However, the accuracy of Sim(Median) is obviously greater than Sim(Average) after 5 GB input data size.

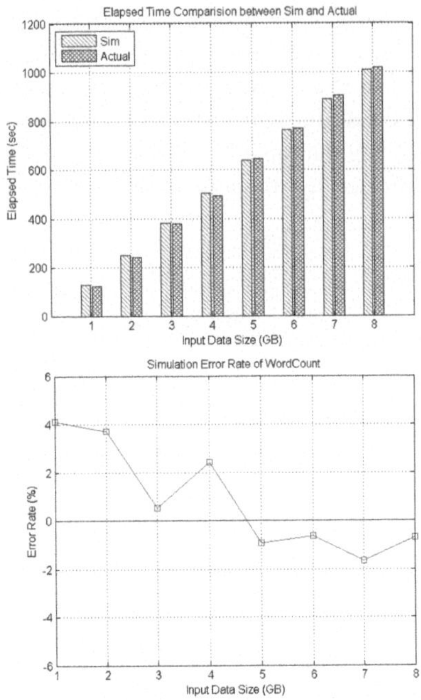


**Fig. 6.** (a) Job Execution Time Estimation of WordCount on 2-node (b) Error rate of the 2-node WordCount test

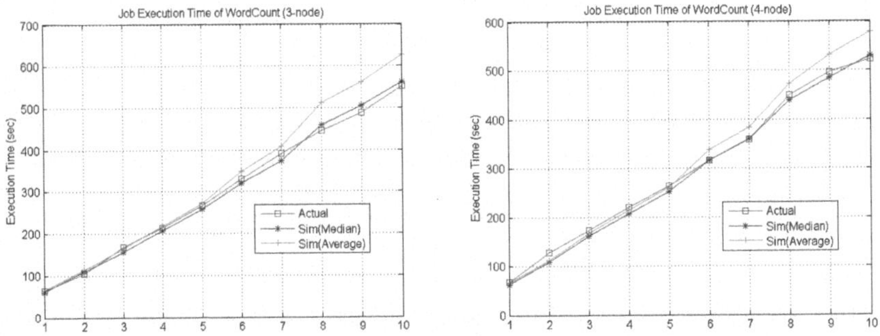


**Fig. 7.** (a) Job Execution Time Estimation of WordCount on 3-node (b) Job Execution Time Estimation of WordCount on 4-node

## 5 Conclusions and Future Work

In this paper, execution stages in MapReduce are modeled with Stochastic Petri Net, called SPN-MR model. In order to analyze the execution time of SPN-MR, each mean delay time is formulated among all transition stages. SPN-MR is able to simulate the elapsed time of MapReduce jobs with a known input data size with tens of milliseconds precision, and then reduce time cost of programmers in performance tuning.

In simulation results, SPN-MR is compared with several actual test benchmarks. The average error rate is within 5 percent. Therefore, it can provide effective performance evaluation reports for MapReduce programmers.

In our future work, another goal will be high accuracy execution time estimations on the variation of node configurations. Various existing MapReduce applications can be applied with our framework for further study.

## References


1. Zaharia, M., Konwinski, A., Joseph, A., Katz, R., Stoica, I.: Improving MapReduce performance in heterogeneous environments. In: OSDI 2008: 8th USENIX Symposium on Operating Systems Design and Implementation (2008)
2. Dean, J., Ghemawat, S.: MapReduce: simplified data processing on large clusters. In: OSDI 2004, pp. 137–150 (2004)
3. White, T., Cutting, D.: Hadoop: The Definitive Guide. O'REILLY Media, Sebastopol (2009). Chapter 6. How MapReduce Works
4. Murata, T.: Petri nets: properties, analysis and applications. Proc. IEEE **77**(4), 561–580 (1989)
5. Saavedra-Barrera, R.H., Culler, D.E., Eicken, T.V.: Analysis of multithreaded architectures for parallel computing. In: 2nd Annual ACM Symposium on Parallel Algorithms and Architectures (1990)
6. Marsan, M.A., Conte, G., Balbo, G.: A class of generalized stochastic petri nets for the performance evaluation of multiprocessor systems. ACM Trans. Comput. Syst. **2**(2), 93–122 (1984)
7. Ferscha, A.: A petri net approach for performance oriented parallel program design. J. Parallel Distrib. Comput. **15**(3), 188–206 (1992). Special Issue on Petri Net Modelling of Parallel Computers
8. Khazaei, H., Misic, J., Misic, V.B.: Performance analysis of cloud computing centers using M/G/m/m + r queuing systems. IEEE Trans. Parallel Distrib. Syst. **23**(5), 936–943 (2012)
9. Wang, G., Butt, A.R., Pandey, P., Gupta, K.: A Simulation Approach to Evaluating design decisions in MapReduce setups. In: IEEE International Symposium on Modeling, Analysis and Simulation of Computer and Telecommunication Systems (2009)
10. Liu, Y., Li, M., Alham, N.K., Hammoud, S.: HSim: A MapReduce simulator in enabling cloud computing. Future Gener. Comput. Syst. **29**, 300–308 (2013)
11. Tian, F., Chen, K.: Towards optimal resource provisioning for running MapReduce programs in public clouds. In: IEEE International Conference on Cloud Computing (CLOUD) (2011)
12. Ganapathi, A., Chen, Y., Fox, A., Katz, R., Patterson, D.: Statistics-driven workload modeling for the cloud. In: IEEE 26th International Conference on Data Engineering Workshops (ICDEW) (2010)
13. Yang, H., Luan, Z., Li, W., Qian, D.: MapReduce workload modeling with statistical approach. J. Grid Comput. **10**, 279–310 (2012)
14. Dingle, N.J., Knottenbelt, W.J., Suto, T.: PIPE2: A tool for the performance evaluation of generalised stochastic petri nets. ACM SIGMETRICS Perform. Eval. Rev. **36**(4), 34–39 (2009)

# Integration of MapReduce with an Interactive Boosting Mechanism for Image Background Subtraction in Cultural Sightseeing

Sheng-Tzong Cheng[1], Yin-Jun Chen[1(✉)], Yu-Ting Wang[1], and Chen-Fei Chen[2]

[1] Department of Computer Science and Information Engineering, National Cheng Kung University, Tainan, Taiwan
{stcheng, p78981142, P76004685}@mail.ncku.edu.tw

[2] Department of Information and Communications, Shih Hsin University, Taipei, Taiwan
cffchen@cc.shu.edu.tw

**Abstract.** Background subtraction is widely used in multimedia applications, such as traffic monitoring, video surveillance, and object tracking. Several methods with different advantages in different applications have been proposed. The advent of cloud computing also has made possible of the combination of various background subtraction techniques and the processing of large amounts of images. In this paper, an integrated algorithm for background subtraction is implemented and analyzed. The proposed AdaBoost algorithm combines weak classifiers: pixel-based background subtraction methods, block-based background subtraction methods, and graph-cut segmentation methods. After training, the program adjusts the weight of each weak classifier. The algorithm is accelerated using Hadoop cloud-computing architecture. By using a MapReduce framework, this system can parallel-processing on multiple servers in order to reduce computing time. When the system completes its task, the user can see the combined results on the screen and then choose the preferred result. The system can obtain user feedback and tune the combination mechanism.

**Keywords:** Cloud computing · Background subtraction · Boosting learning

## 1 Introduction

The foreground object detection and segmentation from videos are the most vital tasks of a video application; one common approach to these tasks is background subtraction. Background subtraction is widely used in multimedia applications, such as traffic monitoring, video surveillance, and object tracking.

Background subtraction methods have been researched for many years. The basic process consists of setting up a background model, comparing a new frame with the background model, and producing a binary mask. When the binary mask is overlapped on the original image, a foreground object can be obtained. Although numerous background subtraction methods have been proposed, certain challenges remain. Sometimes those methods work appropriately in stable environments. At other times,


D.K.W. Chiu et al. (Eds.): ICWL 2013 Workshops, LNCS 8390, pp. 180–191, 2015.
DOI: 10.1007/978-3-662-46315-4_19

however, they produce inadequate results because of sudden illumination changes, complicated background scenes, or moving background objects.

Several thresholds or parameters exist in image processing, which typically must be manually established and are difficult to adapt to different environments. Although different background subtraction methods must be considered to improve this situation, they remain a separate problem. To obtain superior results, allocating priority to different methods must be considered when combining background subtraction methods or methods with different parameters. Without a ground truth, evaluating the results in a specific environment becomes difficult. This paper proposes a unique mechanism for a system that helps determine the most effective combination by balancing the weights of image segmentation results.

Every method has different advantages and disadvantages. Certain pixel-based background subtraction methods [1] model the background independently at each pixel location by using statistical methods; although they are fast, they generate noise. Block-based background subtraction methods, such as [2], model the background using blocks instead of pixels. This approach can reflect the texture of the object and allow for slight shaking, but the edges of the foreground object might not be accurate. Other background subtraction methods use graph-cut [3] to obtain salient objects by calculating the similarities and gradients between pixels. Pixels are classified in multiple regions; pixels in the same region are similar, whereas pixels in different regions are dissimilar. When the color of the foreground object and the background scene is similar, the result might not be adequate.

Recently, the demand of image processing is higher than before because the amount of image and video is highly increased. In addition, the calculating time of image processing will be longer as image size is large. To solve this, one way is optimizing algorithms, and another way is parallelizing the program.

A traditional solution is using the message passing interface (MPI) to control parallel execution. When execution cross multiple computers, the program complexity and efficiency are hard to be satisfied.

MapReduce is a programming model for processing large data sets, introduced by Google. MapReduce is typically used to process parallelizable problems on clusters of computers and simplifies the design of parallel programs by two steps: "Map" and "Reduce". In "Map" step, the master node takes the input, divides it into smaller sub-problems, and distributes them to worker nodes. In "Reduce" step, the master node collects the outputs of sub-problems and combines them for original request. All maps can be performed in parallel on work nodes.

The Apache Hadoop project develops open-source software for reliable, scalable, distributed computing and was derived from Google's MapReduce and Google File System papers. It allows the distributed processing of large data sets across clusters of computers, and easy to scale up from single machine to thousands. It supplies local computation and storage instead of hardware. Hadoop Distributed File System (HDFS) is a distributed file system that provides high-throughput access to application data. The Apache Hadoop is an available and convenient framework for accelerate program by cloud computing. We will use Hadoop MapReduce and HDFS to optimize our work.

We have not seen many researches talking about image processing with cloud computing, especially on background subtraction fields. With Hadoop MapReduce and

HDFS, image process should work faster and more flexible with large amounts of high quality images. Setting distributed file system provides large storage and calculation ability than one machine can do. Image processing programs can divide their work on such cloud system to save execution time, especially application with large input images. Nowadays, thinking about the distribute work of image processing program may generate novel architecture design.

The remainder of the paper is organized as follows. Section 2 discusses related research on background subtraction and image processing methods that use cloud computing. The system model, including the system architecture, the map-reduction model, and the combination method, are described in Sect. 3. Section 4 presents the experiments and the simulation results; finally, Sect. 5 outlines the conclusions of this work and its future directions.

## 2 Related Work

### 2.1 Background Subtraction

Background subtraction is a widely used approach and has been considered from various perspectives. In [4], the background subtraction algorithms used in the early years of computer imaging, including running the Gaussian average, temporal median filters, a mixture of Gaussians, kernel density estimations, sequential KD approximations, co-occurrence of image variations, and Eigen-backgrounds, have been reviewed and evaluated.

A single Gaussian provides an easy method to subtract backgrounds in simple and static environments. To improve the tolerance of a shaking object on a background, [10] discusses modeling each pixel as a mixture of Gaussians and using an on-line approximation to update the model. The Gaussian distributions of the adaptive mixture model are then evaluated to determine which are the most likely to result from a background process.

Kernel density estimation is another available method for background subtraction. In [11], Elgammal et al. present a novel non-parametric background model based on kernel density estimation. However, using the last frames increases the memory requirements and the processing time.

In the texture-based method, the image statistics use blocks instead of pixels. In [2], each pixel is modeled as a group of adaptive local binary pattern histograms that are calculated over a circular region around the pixel.

### 2.2 Graph Cut

Approaches to finding an object in a frame consist not only of a background subtraction from serial frames but also of a foreground extraction from a single frame. To find a salient object in an image, GraphCut [6] entails a technique for a general purpose interactive segmentation of N-dimensional images. The user marks certain pixels as an "object" and a "background" to provide hard constraints for executing the segmentation.

Additional soft constraints incorporate both boundary and region information. The graph cuts are used to determine the globally optimal segmentation of the N-dimensional image.

When the colors of an object and the background scenes become clearly differentiated, GraphCut can produce an appropriate segmentation. When the boundaries between them are difficult to separate or an object comprises complex components, the performance might be inadequate. Later research improved Graph-Cut by adjusting the EM model or combining it with background subtraction.

GrabCut [5] extends the graph-cut approach. Two novel approaches to "iterative estimation" and "incomplete labeling" optimize the graph-cut algorithm and simplify the user interaction regarding high quality segmentation. A background cut [4] combines background subtraction, color, and contrast cues to extract a foreground layer. The pivotal idea is the background contract attenuation, which adaptively attenuates the contrasts in the background while preserving the contracts across the foreground and background boundaries.

### 2.3 Image Processing in MapReduce

The MapReduce framework provides a new approach to parallel algorithms. The image processing algorithms in MapReduce display improved scalability and efficiency. White et al. [7] provided an overview of MapReduce and common design patterns. They discussed the implementation of the algorithms: classifier training, clustering… and background subtraction in a single Gaussian method. Wan et al. [8] used a kernel density estimation method based on Chebyshev's inequality (MDSBC) based on MapReduce, proving the utility of the algorithm. Almeer [9] proved that Hadoop can be successfully used for image processing and most remote sensing applications. It makes the TIFF image file type available for the Hadoop file format and shows that processing multiple high-volume images is scalable and efficient.

## 3 System Model

### 3.1 System Architecture

Figure 1 shows the proposed system architecture. A user interaction system for background subtraction was designed. The system comprised two parts: the client side and the server side. At the client side, a fixed camera and a computer with a screen, an interaction device such as mouse and a keyboard, and the network were prepared. The camera was connected to the computer, and the program developed for this research handled the video file and the user operation and transferred them to the server through the network. At the server side, a cluster connected to multiple computers was constructed using Apache Hadoop. The server received the video data from the client, saving them to data storage, the HDFS. The program developed for this research read the video data and executed parallel processing by the Hadoop MapReduce Scheme.

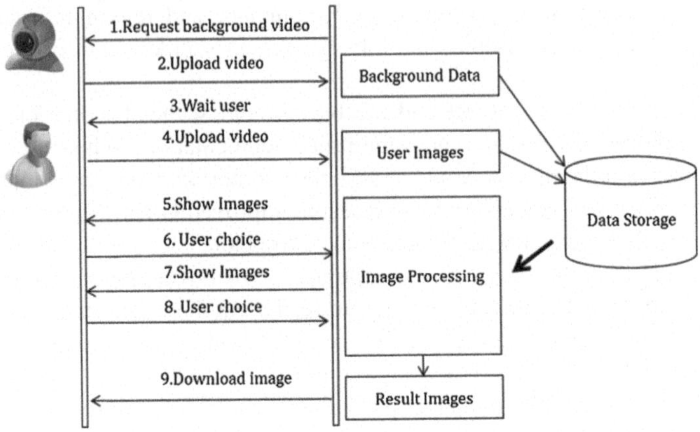


**Fig. 1.** System architecture

### 3.2 Image Processing in MapReduce

Figure 2 displays that the proposed method involves five processing steps:

1. Background subtraction methods execute parallel process by MapReduce framework. The result images will be saved to HDFS.
2. User chooses one of images from step 1. The best background subtraction result should be selected.
3. Do morphological operations on the image from step 2. The image will be slightly different.
4. User chooses one of images from step 3. We use this image as training sample data for AdaBoost.
5. Run AdaBoost with training sample from step 4. The detail is introduced at next section.

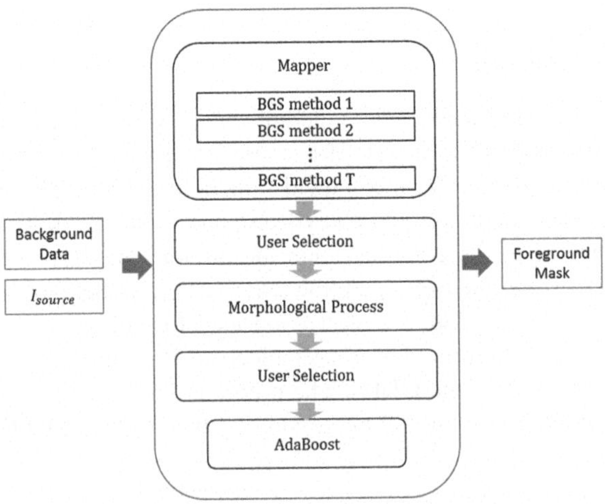


**Fig. 2.** Image processing flowchart

### 3.3 AdaBoost for Background Subtraction

In this section, the background subtraction methods are considered to be binary classifiers. Input an image, and classify pixels as foreground object or background scene. The AdaBoost algorithm can combine multiple classifiers to obtain one classifier. The AdaBoost algorithm was used to combine multiple background subtraction methods to obtain a superior performance (Fig. 3).

Machine learning algorithms learn by training data. In ideal conditions, the ground truth of a background subtraction algorithm can constitute training data. However, the ground truth images are typically produced using a manual human process. It is difficult to obtain ground truth while a program is running online. Therefore, a user feedback interaction function for this requirement was designed. The user can see the resulting images on a screen and choose the most appropriate. The system maintains a record of this preference and applies it to the next process. This preference is pivotal in the learning work of this study. AdaBoost learns from this preference rather than from ground truth. Using the learning process, the results of the background subtraction begin to fit the environment.

In the AdaBoost algorithm, the classifier to be combined is called a "weak classifier", whereas the combined classifier is called a "strong classifier". Each background subtraction method is a weak classifier of binary classification denoted by $h_t(x) : X \to \{-1, 1\}$, where $x$ is input data, $-1$ indicates the background and 1 indicates the foreground. The purpose of the algorithm is to train the weak classifiers to obtain robust background subtraction results. The strong classifier is denoted by $H(x) = \text{sign}(\sum_{t=1}^{T} \alpha_t h_t(x))$, where $\alpha_t$ is a weight of the weak classifier $h_t(x)$.

Let set $D_t = \{(\omega_1, x_1, y_1), \ldots, (\omega_m, x_m, y_m)\}, x_i \in X, y_i \in \{-1, 1\}, \sum_{t=1}^{m} \omega_i = 1$ denote a set of image samples for the training of AdaBoost, and $x_i$ denote a pixel in the image where the total number of pixels $m$, $y_i$ is the result of the classifier $h_t(x)$ indicated by the pixel belonging to the foreground object or where the background image, $\omega_i$ is weight of the sample.

The following lines are pseudo code of basic AdaBoost algorithm.

Step 1: Initialize weights of sample data = $1/m$

Step 2: For $t$ = 1… T:-

(1) Choose the weak classifier $h_t$ that minimizes the sum of the weighted classification

$$h_t = \arg\min_{h_j \in H} \varepsilon_j$$

$$\varepsilon_j = \sum_{i=1}^{m} \omega_{t(i)} [y_i \neq h_j(x_i)]$$

(2) Get the weight of the weak classifier

$$\alpha_t = \frac{1}{2} \log\left(\frac{1-\varepsilon_t}{\varepsilon_t}\right)$$

(3) Update weights of sample data

$$\omega_{t+1}(i) = \frac{\omega_{t(i)} \exp(-\alpha_t y_i h_t(x_i))}{Z_t}$$

Step 3: $H(x) = sign(\sum_{t=1}^{T} \alpha_t h_t(x))$

### 3.4 Morphological and Post Process

Morphological operations process binary images using set operator. There are two basic operations: erosion and dilation. Erosion shrinks the components of an image and dilation expands them.

Morphological opening operation is performed by an erosion operation followed by a dilation operation using the same structuring element. It smoothes the contour of an object, breaks the narrow part and eliminates thin protrusions. Morphological opening operation is performed by a dilation followed by an erosion operation. It smoothes the contour, but fuses narrow parts and eliminates small holes.

In this chapter, we introduce the methods of post image processing. Post processing for background subtraction is an important step and provides additional functions for repairing broken regions, smoothing boundaries and more accurate silhouette of human.

We use these morphological operations to remove holes and noisy parts of background subtraction mask, and provide help for generating trimap for Grabcut later introduced.

We add GrabCut to our post processing. GrabCut can not only segmentation in a rectangle region, but also manually use given "trimap" to help more accurate result. Our program automatically generates the trimap for GrabCut instead of manual labeling. GrabCut reads the trimap and classifies the undefined pixel to foreground part or background part. Trimap R sets every pixel x in three labels: foreground F, background B, undefined region U and is generated from background subtraction mask denoted *I*.

$$R_x = \begin{cases} T \\ U \\ B \end{cases}$$

$R_x$ is marked $T$ when $I_x$ belongs foreground pixel in proposed method mask. The undefined region is calculated from foreground regions. Using morphological dilation and opening operations, we get larger and smoother regions compared with the original foreground regions. For accurate human silhouette extraction, we add face detection function here, and add the face region to this region. If pixel $x$ belongs background region and this undefined region, $R_x$ is marked $U$. Otherwise, it is marked $B$.

## 4 Performance Evaluation

### 4.1 Experiment Settings

We implement our proposed method by OpenCV for C++/java and Hadoop framework. Each basic background subtraction methods have two versions by changing input image in different color space. RGB color space provides the basic view, and YCrCb color space could provides a different view. Background subtraction methods we used as weak classifier is in Table 1.

**Table 1.** Background subtraction method list

| ID | Background subtraction methods |
|---|---|
| 1 | Static Frame Difference (RGB) |
| 2 | Fuzzy Gaussian (RGB) |
| 3 | Fuzzy Sugeno Integral (RGB) |
| 4 | Simple Gaussian (RGB) |
| 5 | Mixture of Gaussian (RGB) |
| 6 | Texture-based Method (RGB) |
| 7 | Eigenbackground (RGB) |
| 8 | Non-Parametric Model (RGB) |
| 9 | Pixel Based Adaptive Segmenter (RGB) |
| 10 | AdaptiveSOM (RGB) |
| 11 | Static Frame Difference (YCrCb) |
| 12 | Fuzzy Gaussian (YCrCb) |
| 13 | Fuzzy Sugeno Integral (YCrCb) |
| 14 | Simple Gaussian (YCrCb) |
| 15 | Mixture of Gaussian (YCrCb) |
| 16 | Texture-based Method (YCrCb) |
| 17 | Eigenbackground (YCrCb) |
| 18 | Non-Parametric Model (YCrCb) |
| 19 | Pixel Based Adaptive Segmenter (YCrCb) |
| 20 | AdaptiveSOM (YCrCb) |
| 21 | Our method |

### 4.2 Results and Evaluation

We use two datasets for test our method. In each sub section, we show the training process and comparison of error rates.

**Sample 1.** Sample 1 is the National Cheng-kung University campus scene, with slightly dynamic tree waving and illumination change in the background. First, we use Sample 1-1 for training. We can see background subtraction result in Fig. 4, and we choose result of method 6. Figure 5 shows morphological process result, and we choose (iii) for training. Finally, (v) shows result of our method. Comparison of error rate between background methods is in Fig. 6.

Sample 1-2 use the weights of Sample 1-1 without training. Figure 9 shows the result. The improvement is shown in Fig. 10.

**Sample 2.** Sample 2 is a scenario of taking a photo for tourists in a culture sight spot (Figs. 7 and 8).

(i) (ii) (iii)

**Fig. 3.** Background and training frame of sample 1-1. from left to right: (i) Background image (ii) Training frame (iii) Ground truth

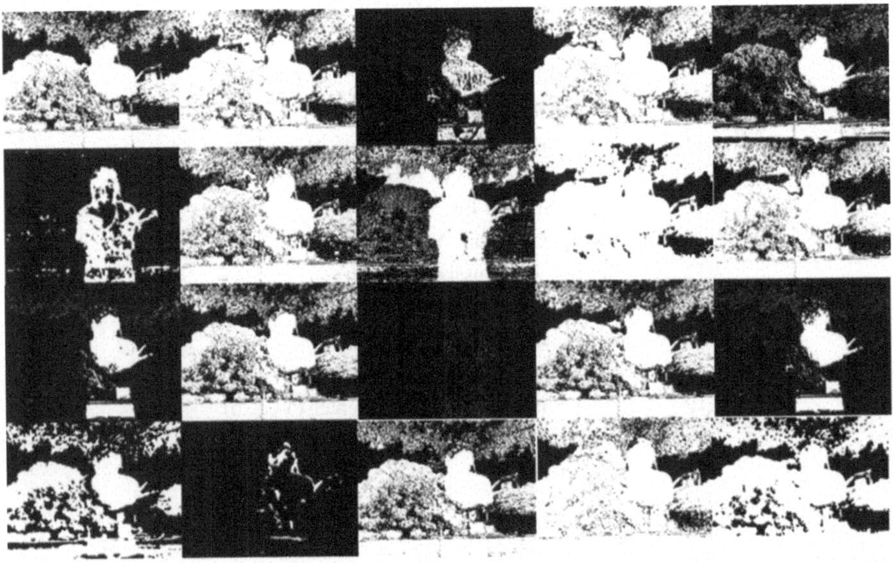

**Fig. 4.** Background subtraction result of sample 1-1. Reference medthod id on table above. First row: 1, 2, 3, 4, 5. Second row: 6, 7, 8, 9, 10. Third row: 11, 12, 13, 14, 15. Fourth row: 16, 17, 18, 19, 20

(i) (ii) (iii) (iv) (v)

**Fig. 5.** Morphological process result and boosting result of sample 1. (i) (ii) (iii) (iv) Morphological process (v) Result

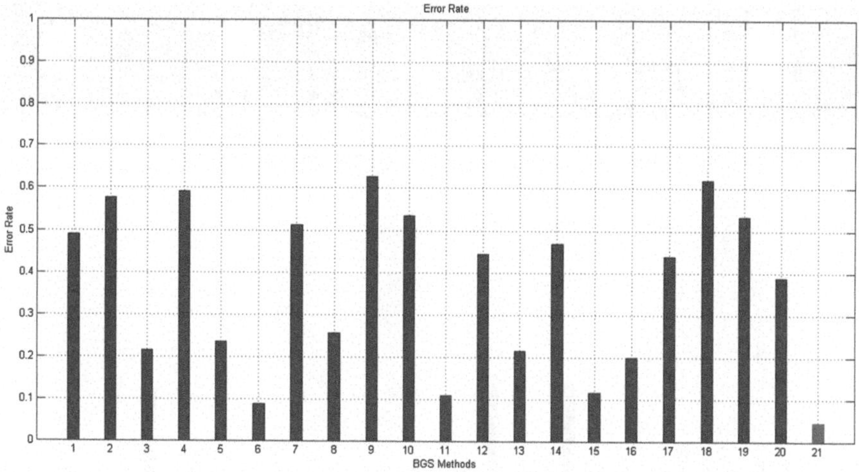


**Fig. 6.** Error rate of sample 1

**Fig. 7.** Background and training frame of sample 2

**Fig. 8.** Background subtraction result of sample 2

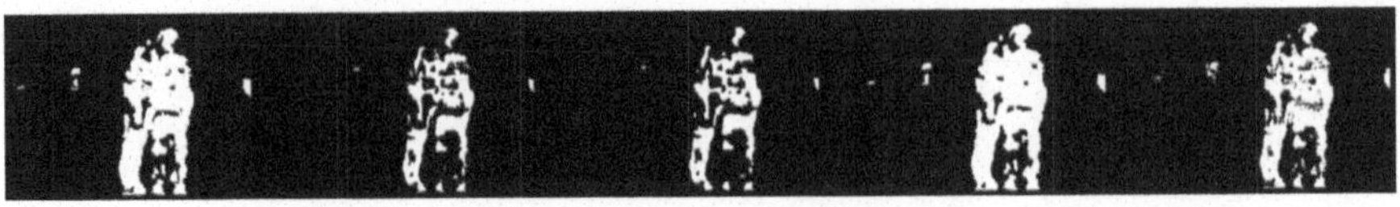

**Fig. 9.** Morphological process result and boosting result of sample 2

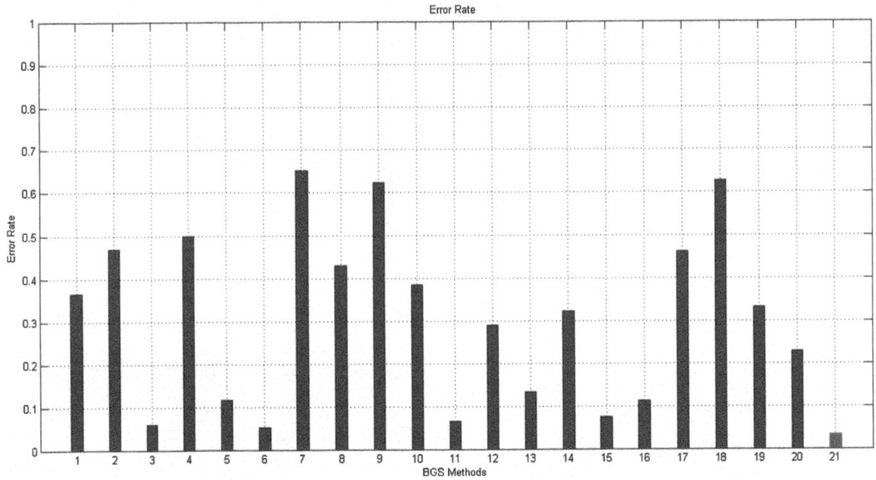


**Fig. 10.** Error rate of sample 2

## 5 Conclusions and Future Work

The experiment results show the improvement by our boosting method. First, when background subtraction methods are not good enough in some environment, we can make it better. User can tune the background subtraction system when device is set instantly. Second, the cloud computing can reduce many computing time of image processing program. In addition to improvement in computing time, the large data storage is also an advantage of cloud computing.

The proposed method is designed for general purposes. Image segmentations are still not perfect. In addition to combining background subtraction methods, it can add other mechanisms, like object tracking, human detection or combining by more robust machine learning algorithm.

## References


1. KaewTraKulPong, P., Bowden, R.: An improved adaptive background mixture model for real-time tracking with shadow detection. In: Proceedings of European Workshop Advanced Video Based Surveillance Systems (2001)
2. Heikkila, M., Pietikainen, M.: A texture-based method for modeling the background and detecting moving objects. IEEE Trans. Pattern Anal. Mach. Intell. **28**, 657–662 (2006)

3. Piccardi, M.: Background subtraction techniques: a review. In: 2004 IEEE International Conference on Systems, Man and Cybernetics, vol. 4, pp. 3099–3104 (2004)
4. Sun, J., Zhang, W., Tang, X., Shum, H.-Y.: Background cut. In: Leonardis, A., Bischof, H., Pinz, A. (eds.) ECCV 2006. LNCS, vol. 3952, pp. 628–641. Springer, Heidelberg (2006)
5. Rother, C., Kolmogorov, V., Blake, A.: GrabCut: interactive foreground extraction using iterated graph cuts. ACM Trans. Graph. **23**, 309–314 (2004)
6. Boykov, Y.Y., Jolly, M.P.: Interactive graph cuts for optimal boundary & region segmentation of objects in N-D images. In: Proceedings of Eighth IEEE International Conference on Computer Vision, ICCV 2001, vol. 1, pp. 105–112 (2001)
7. White, B., Yeh, T., Lin, J., Davis, L.: Web-scale computer vision using MapReduce for multimedia data mining. In: Proceedings of the Tenth International Workshop on Multimedia Data Mining, pp. 1–10 (2010)
8. Wan, C., Wang, C., Zhang, K.: MRKDSBC: a distributed background modeling algorithm based on MapReduce. In: Wang, J., Yen, G.G., Polycarpou, M.M. (eds.) ISNN 2012, Part I. LNCS, vol. 7367, pp. 668–677. Springer, Heidelberg (2012)
9. Almeer, H.M.: Cloud hadoop map reduce for remote sensing image analysis. J. Emerg. Trends Comput. Inf. Sci. **13**(4), 637–644 (2012)
10. Stauffer, C., Grimson, W. E.L.: Adaptive background mixture models for real-time tracking. In: Proceedings of IEEE International Conference on Computer Vision Pattern Recognition, pp. 246–252, Jun 1999
11. Elgammal, A., Harwood, D., Davis, L.: Non-parametric model for background subtraction. In: Vernon, D. (ed.) ECCV 2000. LNCS, vol. 1843, pp. 751–767. Springer, Heidelberg (2000)

# An Weighted-Content Strategy for Integrating Heterogeneous Itembanks

Shih-Pang Tseng[1(✉)], Wen-Hsiang Fu[2], and Chu-Sing Yang[2]

[1] Department of Computer Science and Information Engineering, Tajen University, Pingtung, Taiwan
tsp@tajen.edu.tw

[2] Department of Electrical Engineering, National Cheng Kung University, Tainan, Taiwan
winters421@gmail.com, csyang@ee.ncku.edu.tw

**Abstract.** The assessment is the most effectively tool for the teachers to realized the learning status of the learners. The effectiveness of e-assessment is exceedingly related to the content richness of the itembank. This paper proposed an improved method to integrated various itembanks into an unified itembank. These integrated itembanks can be with heterogeneous schemas. The experimental result shows that the proposed method is more effective than the previous work.

**Keywords:** E-learning · E-assessment · Itembank integration

## 1 Introduction

In the past twenty years, the great development of information and communication technologies facilitate the learning activities of human beings from the traditional classroom to the cyberspace. In this time, the various kinds of e-learning are widely applied on various types of educations, such as primary education and continuing education. The e-learning can aid the traditional learning to enhance the efficiency of learning, even the e-learning can be the main body of education due to the time and space restriction of the traditional learning in some cases.

Because the e-learning can provide more interactions among the teacher and the students and more flexible learning plan. The individualization [1] of learning tries to provide more suitable learning programs for each learners. For the individualization, it is necessary to realize the learning status of the learners. The most effective tool to realize the learning status is the assessment process [2]. Computer-based test (CBT), or e-assessment, [3–5] can provide more performance and lower cost than traditional paper-pencil test (PPT). The effectiveness of e-assessment is principally dependent on two factors: the quality of the itembank and the method of test sheet assembling. In addition, the requirements to the itembank for e-assessment are well-organized and content-rich. The paper focuses on upgrading the content richness of the itembank by integration the contents from the different and heterogeneous sources.


D.K.W. Chiu et al. (Eds.): ICWL 2013 Workshops, LNCS 8390, pp. 192–200, 2015.
DOI: 10.1007/978-3-662-46315-4_20

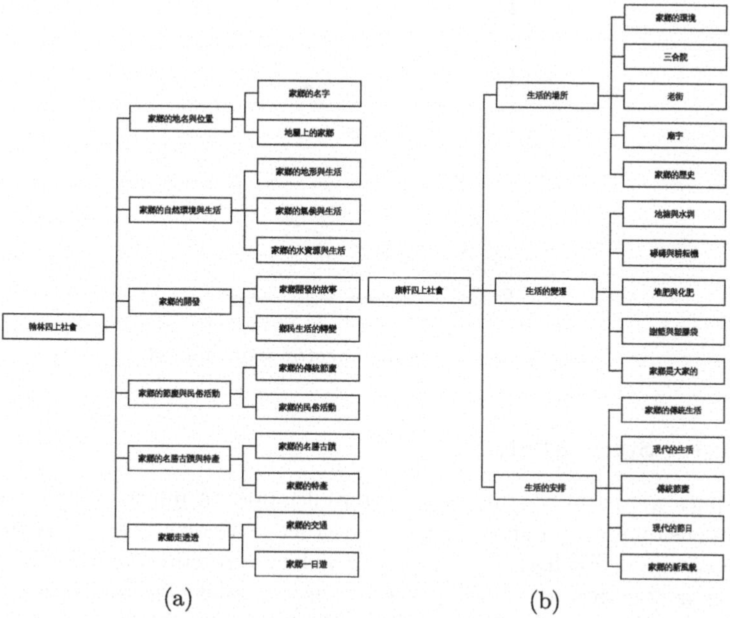


**Fig. 1.** (a) The course content from Han Lin Publishing. (b) The course content from Kang Hsuan Publishing.

Because of the various knowledge backgrounds or different philosophies of education, the instructors or the editors of the textbook may use the heterogeneous schema to organize the same group of learning contents. For example, Fig. 1 shows the schema of two textbooks which are from two different sources but edited according to the identical textbook standard.

The remainder of the paper is organized as follows. The related works are in Sect. 2. Section 3 introduced the proposed method. The experimental results are in Sect. 4. Conclusion is given in Sect. 6.

## 2 Related Works

### 2.1 Integrating Itembanks

Tseng et al. [6] proposed a method, heterogeneous itembank integrator (HIBI), based on classical vector space model to integrate a collection of itembanks with heterogeneous schemas to an unified itembank. The flat and tree structure classifying techniques were proposed in HIBI. The HIBI was shown that it is efficient and effective enough, but there is still the improved space in the accuracy of integration. Tseng et al. [7] proposed an extended version of HIBI based on ontology and fuzzy c-means to incorporate more types of Internet resources, like wikis and blogs, into the unified schema of the itembank for content sharing and test feedback.

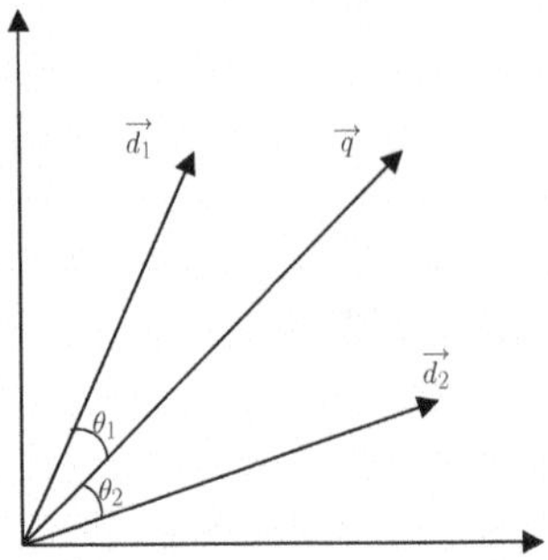


**Fig. 2.** An example of vector space model

## 2.2 Vector Space Model

Vector space model (VSM) [8] is an essential model in information retrieval. A multi-dimensional vector space can be constructed according to the terms in the set of documents. Each text document can be represented as a vector in this space. Figure 2 shows a examle of vector space model. The similarity between two documents can be evaluated by the consine of the angle between the two vectors which represent the two documents, shown as Eq.(1).

$$sim(d_1, q) = \cos(\theta_1) = \frac{\vec{d_1} \cdot \vec{q}}{\|\vec{d_1}\| \times \|\vec{q}\|} \tag{1}$$

The document is represented by a vector with the weights of terms in the classical vector space model, like Eq.(2).

$$\vec{d_i} = [w_{1i}, w_{2i}, \ldots, w_{Ti}] \tag{2}$$

In Eq.(2), there are $T$ terms in the set of documents. In general, the term weight is the product of the term frequency (TF) and the inverse document frequency (IDF), shown as Eq.(3).

$$w_{ti} = tf_{ti} \times idf_t \tag{3}$$

In Eq.(3), the $tf_{ti}$ is the term frequency of term $t$ in the document $i$. The $idf_t$ is the inverse document frequency of term $t$. It can be calculated by Eq.(4),

$$idf_t = \log \frac{D}{D_t} \tag{4}$$

The $D$ is the number of documents, and the $D_t$ is the number of documents which contains the term $t$.

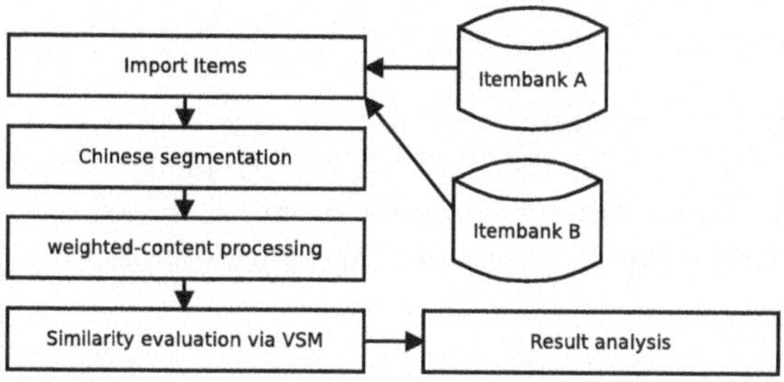


**Fig. 3.** Processing of integrating itembanks

# 3 Proposed Method

In this section, we proposed the *integrating itembanks with weighted-contents technique* (IIWC) to improve the integration result. Figure 3 shows the process of the IIWC. The weighted contents technique is based on the type and structure of the items. The terms in different parts of the item can be with additional weight. In addition, we try to post-process the result of Chinese segmentation to improve the accuracy.

According to the observation to the true/false and multiple choice items for e-learning assessment, not all terms in the items are suitable for classification. For example, the wrong option of one multiple choice item may contains some irrelevant or error terms. The influence of these irrelevant terms can be reduced by enhance the weight of the other terms.

## 3.1 Chinese Segmentation Post-processing

In our observation, many compound nouns would be segmented into two independent words in the CKIP Chinese segmentation service. For example, the "人口分布" (population distribution) would be segmented into "人口" (population) and "分布" (distribution). And we find that using the compound nouns can more precisely represent the concept in the item.

There are two rules proposed to repair the compound nouns problem.

- **Rule 1:** if one adjective directly followed by one noun, the adjective and the noun would be composed into a compound noun.
- **Rule 2:** if one noun directly followed by one noun, the two nouns would be composed into a compound noun.

## 3.2 True/false Items

The true/false item is with one direct stem and the learner can label the two alternatives "true" or "false." The true/false items can be divided into *true*-type or "*false*-type.

- **True-type:** all the item are with normal weights because the stem contains no irrelevant terms.
- **False-type:** Because the answer is false, it means that there are some irrelevant or error terms in the stem. But it is extremely difficult to identify the wrong terms automatically by computer program. The detail of answer would be involved into the classifying process and with double weight relative to the stem.

### 3.3 Multiple Choice Items

The multiple choice item consists of a stem and a set of options. The stem can be a question to be answered, or an incomplete statement to be completed, as well as any other relevant description. The options are the possible answers that the learner can choose from. The correct option is called as the key and the others are distractors. Only one option can be keyed as correct. If there can be more than one correct options, this item is called as *multiple response items.*

The multiple choice item can be divided into *positive*-type or *negative*-type. The positive-type multiple choice item means that the learner should chose the true/correct option. On the other hand, the learner should chose the false/wrong option from the other true/correct options in the negative-type multiple choice item. In this work, the negative-type multiple choice item is identified by seven Chinese keywords, "錯"(wrong),"非"(false),"不"(not),"誤"(error),"無"(no),"沒"(no), and"否"(not). If there is no one of the seven keywords in the stem, the item is considered as positive-type.

In general, the terms of the stem are relevant to the concept of this item. The terms in the stem are with double weight. The terms in the options are described in detail as following:

- **Positive-type:**
  - **Key:** since this option is true/correct, the terms in the key are with double weight.
  - **Distractors:** since this option can contain some error or irrelevant terms, the terms in the distractors are with normal weight.
- **Negative-type:**
  - **Key:** since this option can contain some really error or irrelevant terms, the terms in the key are with normal weight.
  - **Distractors:** since these options are really true/correct, the terms in the key option are with double weight.

## 4 Experimental Result

To evaluate the performance of the integrating methods, we use eight item-banks which are from three different sources, the Kang Hsuan Publishing [9], the Han Lin Publishing [10], and the Nani Publishing [11]. The eight item-banks are for the 4th grade of the elementary schools in Taiwan. There are two

**Table 1.** Itembanks

| | Socity | | Nature |
|---|---|---|---|
| | 1st semester | 2nd semester | 2nd semester |
| Nani | NA | 1529 | 270 |
| Han Lin | 697 | 950 | 699 |
| Kang Hsuan | 464 | 1106 | 461 |

courses,"Society"and"Nature". In the first semester, there are only the itembanks of the"Society"course from the Kang Hsuan Publishing and the Han Lin Publishing. In the second semester, there are total six itembanks, two courses and three publishings. Table 1 shows the number of items in theses itembanks. These eight itembanks are from the corresponding textbooks from the three sources. The textbooks for the same course are edited according to the same standard. There the textbooks for the same course can be considered with the same learning contents. Nevertheless, the text books are organized by the different schemas.

All the empirical analysis was conducted on an IBM x3200 M2 Server, with four CPU cores and 5 GB main memory running CentOS Linux. The all the programs are written by the PHP-5.1.6 in the Apache-2.2.3 and MySQL-5.0.45 environment. In this paper, we use HGLS [12], an e-Learning system we built, as a testbed of the proposed methods. HGLS has been put into use by Educational Network Center and several elementary schools in the city of Tainan, Taiwan. Currently, HGLS is running on Linux and supports IPv6. The Educational Network Center of Tainan City, Taiwan uses HGLS to support the learning activities of schools in the city of Tainan.

For illustrating the effect of integrating different heterogeneous itembanks, the *distinguishability* is defined as the measure. The distinguishability is based on the distribution of results of the integrating process. For each item from the source itembank, the leaf-node with the maximum similarity is considered as which should contain the item after the integrating process. To verify the confidence of integrating process, we can compare the difference of similarities between the twp most similar leaf-nodes. If the difference is relatively large enough, the integrating process is with more confidence for this item.

The distinguishability $\delta$ between a given item $t$ and leaf-nodes in the integrated itembank is defined as Eq.(5).

$$\delta = \frac{|sim(t, node_a) - sim(t, node_b)|}{\max(sim(t, node_a), sim(t, node_b))} \tag{5}$$

In the Eq.(5), the two most similar nodes are represented as $node_a$ and $node_b$, and the similarities computed by using VSM are $sim(t, node_a)$ and $sim(t, node_b)$ respectively. The $\delta$ $(0 \leq \delta \leq 1)$ indicates the confidence of integration. In this thesis, the threshold for the confidence of integration is set to 0.2. Thus, if $\delta < 0.2$, the item $t$ is assumed to be *indistinguishable*. Otherwise, it is *distinguishable*.

Figure 4 shows a example of distinguishable item. In this example, there are four leaf-nodes, sections $A$ to $D$. The similarity between item $t$ and sections $A$ to $D$ are 0.8, 0.5, 0.2 and 0.05 respectively. We can find that the section $A$ and $B$ are with the most two similarities. Thus, the distinguishability of item $t$ can be calculated as following:

$$\delta = \frac{|0.8 - 0.5|}{\max(0.8, 0.5)} = \frac{0.3}{0.8} = 0.375 > 0.2 \tag{6}$$

Therefore, the item $t$ is distinguishable and will be inserted into section $A$ in the integrated itembank.

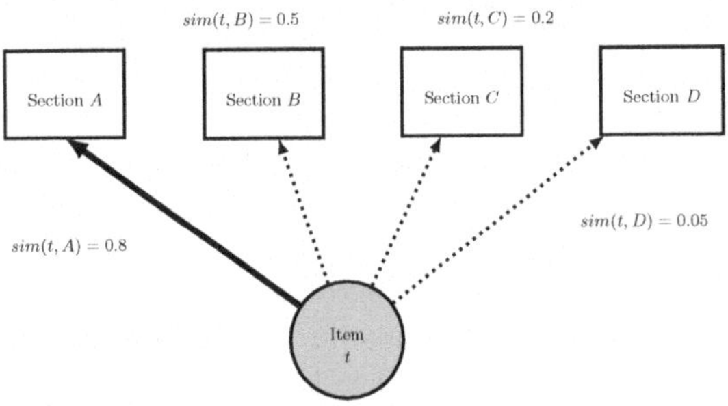


**Fig. 4.** A example of distinguishable item

The overall confidence of integrating process can be indicated by the *distinguishable ratio* (DR). The DR is defined as Eq.(7).

$$DR = \frac{N_d}{N_d + N_i} \times 100\,\% \tag{7}$$

The $N_d$ is the number of distinguishable items from the source itembank, and the $N_i$ is the number of indistinguishable items.

Table 2 shows the experimental result of IIWC and HIBI on the eight itembanks. Only the itembanks belong to the same course and semester would be integrated. The experiments include the flat and tree-structure classification. We can find that the weighted content strategy can effectively improve the distinguishability ratio in the flat and tree-structure classification.

## 5 Comparisons of Accuracy

For more precisely illustrating the performance of integrating itembanks, the *accuracy* is used as the measure. the accuracy AC can be evaluated as Eq.(8).

$$AC = \frac{N_{dc}}{N_d} \times 100\,\% \tag{8}$$

**Table 2.** The distinguishability ratio

| Semester | Course | Source | Destination | $HIBI_{flat}$(%) | $HIBI_{tree}$(%) | $IIWC_{flat}$(%) | $IIWC_{tree}$(%) |
|---|---|---|---|---|---|---|---|
| 1 | Society | Kang Hsuan | Han Lin | 79.10 | 93.53 | 96.12 | 96.34 |
| 1 | Society | Han Lin | Kang Hsuan | 78.80 | 87.37 | 91.39 | 90.96 |
| 2 | Society | Kang Hsuan | Han Lin | 72.60 | 89.33 | 92.50 | 93.22 |
| 2 | Society | Nani | Han Lin | 75.93 | 89.99 | 92.61 | 92.94 |
| 2 | Society | Han Lin | Kang Hsuan | 72.21 | 85.16 | 89.89 | 89.89 |
| 2 | Society | Nani | Kang Hsuan | 72.99 | 83.52 | 86.52 | 86.07 |
| 2 | Society | Han Lin | Nani | 71.52 | 89.96 | 91.23 | 91.23 |
| 2 | Society | Kang Hsuan | Nani | 76.11 | 88.74 | 92.11 | 91.16 |
| 2 | Nature | Kang Hsuan | Han Lin | 76.36 | 89.37 | 90.89 | 90.67 |
| 2 | Nature | Nani | Han Lin | 77.78 | 90.00 | 92.59 | 92.59 |
| 2 | Nature | Han Lin | Kang Hsuan | 71.53 | 82.55 | 85.98 | 85.98 |
| 2 | Nature | Nani | Kang Hsuan | 74.81 | 83.33 | 86.30 | 84.07 |
| 2 | Nature | Han Lin | Nani | 78.97 | 83.69 | 86.27 | 87.70 |
| 2 | Nature | Kang Hsuan | Nani | 78.09 | 84.82 | 89.80 | 89.15 |

**Table 3.** The accuracy rate

| Semester | Course | Source/Destination | $HIBI_{flat}$(%) | $HIBI_{tree}$(%) | $IIWC_{flat}$(%) | $IIWC_{tree}$(%) |
|---|---|---|---|---|---|---|
| 1 | Society | Han Lin | 97.40 | 98.09 | 99.14 | 99.73 |
| 1 | Society | Kang Hsuan | 97.60 | 97.33 | 97.60 | 97.62 |
| 2 | Society | Han Lin | 97.39 | 94.46 | 97.55 | 98.08 |
| 2 | Society | Kang Hsuan | 94.99 | 94.71 | 96.20 | 96.48 |
| 2 | Society | Nani | 96.06 | 94.91 | 96.13 | 96.60 |
| 2 | Nature | Han Lin | 98.48 | 99.57 | 99.71 | 99.71 |
| 2 | Nature | Kang Hsuan | 94.06 | 98.19 | 97.07 | 97.29 |
| 2 | Nature | Nani | 99.60 | 99.99 | 99.25 | 99.25 |

The $N_d$ is the number of distinguishable items and the $N_{dc}$ is the number of distinguishable items which is correctly integrated to the appropriate leaf-node in the integrated itembank. The evaluation of accuracy only takes the distinguishable items into account. It is reasonable because the indistinguishable would not be insert into the final integrated itembank. For the integrating different itembanks, it must be done by the professional expert to verify the integrating result of each items. It is a very hard and time-consuming work due to the several thousands of items in some different tries. Consequently, we design an alternative to measure the accuracy. In the experiments, the destination and source itembank is the same. Therefore it is easy to verify whether the item is inseted into the correct (original) leaf-node. The results are as shown in Table 3. As Table 3 shows, the HIBI and IIWC are not significantly different about the accuracy rate in the flat and tree-structured mechanisms It shows that the distinguishability can provide enough confidence for the itembank integration.

## 6 Conclusion

This paper presented an effective method, called by IIWC, to improve the performance of original HIBI. The weighted contents technique is based on the type and structure of the items. The experimental results showed that the weighted-content strategy is effective, especially in the distinguishability rate. In summary, the proposed method can be used to improve the content richness of the item-bank. In addition, the e-assessment can more really understand what the learners realize but not memorize.

The research is still suitable to the descriptive courses, like "Society" and "Nature". The concepts of one item should apparently in the terms of the item in the descriptive courses.

**Acknowledgment.** The authors would also like to thank Kang Hsuan Publishing and Han Lin Publishing for providing their itembanks and the Chinese Knowledge and Information Processing (CKIP) group, Institute of Information Science, Academia Sinica for providing their Chinese Word Segmentation System to support this research.

## References

1. Bork, A., Gunnarsdottir, S.: Tutorial Distance Learning. Innovations in Science Education and Technology. Individualization and interaction, pp. 47–62. Springer, Netherlands (2001)
2. Pellegrino, J.W., Chudowsky, N., Glaser, R.: Knowing What Students Know: The Science and Design of Educational Assessment. The National Academies Press, Washington, DC (2001)
3. Chua, Y.P.: Effects of computer-based testing on test performance and testing motivation. Comput. Hum. Behav. **28**(5), 1580–1586 (2012)
4. Llamas-Nistal, M., Fernndez-Iglesias, M.J., Gonzlez-Tato, J., Mikic-Fonte, F.A.: Blended e-assessment: migrating classical exams to the digital world. Comput. Educ. **62**, 72–87 (2013)
5. JISC: Effective practice with e-assessment: An overview of technologies, policies and practice in further and higher education (2007)
6. Tseng, S.P., Chiang, M.C., Yang, C.S., Tsai, C.W.: An efficient algorithm for integrating heterogeneous itembanks. Int. J. Innovative Comput. Inf. Control **6**(10), 4319–4334 (2010)
7. Tseng, S.P., Chiang, M.C., Yang, C.S., Tsai, C.W.: An ontology-based framework for itembank integration and knowledge sharing. Int. J. Fuzzy Syst. **12**(2), 116–124 (2010)
8. Salton, G., Wong, A., Yang, C.: A vector space model for automatic indexing. Commun. ACM **18**(11), 613–620 (1975)
9. Publishing, H.L.: (2013). http://www.hle.com.tw/
10. Publishing, K.H.: (2013). http://www.knsh.com.tw/
11. Publishing, N.: (2013). http://www.nani.com.tw/
12. HGLS: (2013). http://hgls.tn.edu.tw/hgls/

# Teaching Effectively with the Multi-screen Multimedia Integrated System

Tsung-Sheng Cheng(✉), Yu-Chun Lu, and Chu-Sing Yang

Department of Electrical Engineering, Institute of Computer and Communication Engineering, National Cheng Kung University, No. 1, University Rd., East Dist., Tainan City, Taiwan
{tsamcheng, lur.ncku}@gmail.com, csyang@ee.ncku.edu.tw

**Abstract.** Multimedia resources, such as images, sounds, videos and animations, aid for learning effectiveness when teachers utilize these elements to demonstrate concepts or conveying information. However, teachers often confronted with the limitations of showing more contents from multiple multimedia resources while preparing the teaching material. This research revealed that the multi-screen display could assist teachers to overcome the limitations and reduce the students' cognitive load. Moreover, a "multi-screen multimedia integrated system" was proposed to provide teachers a platform for designing and displaying the multimedia teaching materials in multi-screen. The system was developed with intuitive design interface and functional displaying objects. With practical experiments, the system was proved to increase the efficiency both in teaching and learning.

**Keywords:** Multi-screen · Integrated teaching system · Cognitive load · Multimedia

## 1 Introduction

Several factors affect the teaching efficiency including the teaching style, pedagogy, course content design, etc. Nowadays, teachers usually teach with computer and projecting devices to display the course materials in multiple multimedia formats such as text, picture, video, and animation. Combined with the highlighting function like teachers usually did on black board, this multimedia teaching model had been proved effective both in teaching and learning. However, this model could still confront with some limitations. For instance, the multi-citation that needs the context switching among different applications and the comparison among multi-documents might not only cause the interrupt in teaching but also incurred redundant cognitive load for learners. These imitations occurred due to the lack of hardware and software support when designing the course contents.

This paper revealed that the multi-screen display could provide the synchronous display of contents for citations or comparisons and solve the limitations in hardware. On the other hand, authors developed a "multi-screen multimedia integrated teaching system" as software to support the design and display of course contents in multiple screens. To achieve effective teaching and learning, this system provides teachers a


D.K.W. Chiu et al. (Eds.): ICWL 2013 Workshops, LNCS 8390, pp. 201–209, 2015.
DOI: 10.1007/978-3-662-46315-4_21

platform for better editing the teaching materials and displaying the multimedia materials. Furthermore, the system was tested by teachers and the students' learning effectiveness were measured based on a designed course contents. Results showed that the learning became more effective because the multi-screen multimedia teaching method helped reducing students' cognitive load.

## 2 Related Research

### 2.1 The Appliance of PowerPoint in Education and Its Limitations

Using PowerPoint to deliver a course with the auxiliary of images, videos, and animations is more interesting than the traditional method of using blackboard for students to learn. Along with some tips like arrangement of colors, outline of the information, size of character…, the use of PowerPoint is believed to increase students' learning curve [1].

PowerPoint is popular for its flexible edit, and it could be inserted with multimedia or hyper link freely. However, as mentioned in previous paragraph, citations from external resources require another window opened and that often caused the shelter of main slide as shown in Fig. 1. On the other hand, the highlighting function in PowerPoint does not support crossing the new opened windows. These are the limitations in the software.

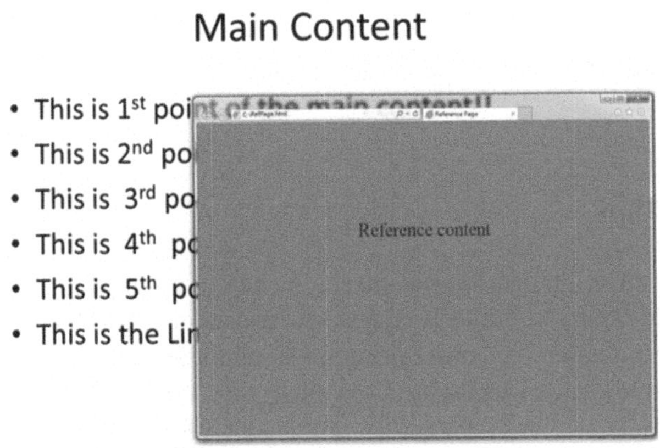


**Fig. 1.** The new opened reference file shelter the main content

### 2.2 The Multimedia Learning Theories

There are many multimedia and learning theories were derived from the Duel Code Theory proposed by Paivio [2]. The theory claimed that the cognitive system of human contains the verbal system and imagery system (mainly the sense of sight, but also including the sense of smell, touch, and emotion). Although there is upper limit of information processing in each system, the referential connection built through the cross-reference between these two systems can reinforce the cognition and raise the memory capacity. Mayer proposed a duel processing theory based on duel-code theory to discover how the combination among auditoria/verbal, visual/pictorial, and even the text information related to the learning process. That is to say, the multiple deliveries of related texts and images are beneficial for the learning process because it provides learners the space of options, systemization and integration to deal with the received information. Based on the Generative Learning Theory proposed [3] by Wittrock, Mayer also indicated that an efficient multimedia learning system should assist learners in building the verbal or imagery situational model through multiple stimulation in the sense system. Therefore, a well-designed multimedia material which combined different features from different resources would increase the multisensory stimulation of learner. It is proved to be effective in constructing the logic and raising the learning speed [4].

Based on the discussion above, Mayer suggested several principles about the presentation of a multimedia teaching material to satisfy the requirements for better cognitive learning:

- Spatial Contiguity Principle: The learning effectiveness would be better when two related figure and text were arranged closely. With this contiguity, the learner could decrease the loading of searching visual information for cognitive learning.
- Temporal Contiguity Principle: Although the composite cognitive ability is limit, different kinds of information that were processed in different channels simultaneously could be better accepted by learner. The learner would build the connections between the image and its accordant text.
- Segmentation Principle: When the multimedia teaching materials were segmented into pieces, it enables learners to choose and to organize/integrate the text or image in each segment. In traditional presentation format, user tempted to segment the material by pages in a temporal way. However, this might violate the temporal contiguity principle. If the space allows for parallel segmentation that the related contents could be displayed at the same time, it would be much more flexible in segmentation.
- Signaling Principle: If the main point were highlighted for learners during the teaching process, the learning effectiveness would be better. For example, using a colored arrow to indicate the learner to focus on a small piece of image or text would reinforce the impression. Most presentation software already facilitates the highlighting function (e.g. PowerPoint), however, this function could only be applied on its own application instead of crossing multi-applications.

### 2.3 The Techniques of Multi-screen Display

According to the theories discussed above, we expect that the teaching material could be delivered in multimedia format with plentiful display contents. Not sacrificing the learner's cognition and reading, the display space of the screen is the key point to achieve best arrangement of teaching contents. And upon the fix resolution of each screen, multi-screen display is the best solution for effective teaching.

We could insert all kinds of multimedia, such as animation, video, texts…etc., into the PowerPoint while editing the material. However, some references came from external applications. For example, the citations of a web page or a PDF file. We could only cut the image beforehand and then inserting it into the PowerPoint the teacher needs to interrupt for opening these external resources. Otherwise, if we embedded a video into the PowerPoint, the software only allow for demonstrated in single monitor. More videos are embedded in several pages would cause the load of cognition because of the shrink of visibility. Distribute related materials in multiple screens could solve the problem to broaden the visibility.

Multi-screen was initially used in stock market to provide investors for observing multi market at the same time. And while in security monitoring system, it helps to display more corners to be cared. People often expand their personal computer to more monitors to create a desktop which is big enough to contain large number of processes and windows [5, 6]. In education, multi-screen could be used to demonstrate more teaching contents at the same time and that enables learners to compare, verify and mapping the differences of contents. Although that frame distance among monitors caused the physical discontinuity in surface, related research indicated that it does not affect the visual effect. Teacher could also utilize this separation to divide the materials. Students could also organize these pieces of information and absorb it to form their own unique knowledge by themselves [7]. On the other hand, the multi-screen might cause the students in one side hard to see the screen on the other site clearly. Therefore, it needs that the multimedia teaching system support the content switching among screens.

Speaking of the hardware technology, AMD Company announced the ATI Eyefinity technique which enables the PC to expand to more than 6 display screens through one graphic card [8]. Also, notebook which is often used to project the slides in education supports usb interface to extend its graphical monitor. To this end, the multi-screen projection already exists for teaching but lack of an integrated system for editing and displaying.

In short summary, there are requirements of the functions depicted in Table 1 for designing an effective and practical teaching system.

**Table 1.** The requirement list of the system

| | Required functions | |
|---|---|---|
| The editorial part | 1. | Enable the extension from the most used PowerPoint file. Support simple insertion of script to transit the material from single-screen display into multi-screen display |
| | 2. | Enable the insertion of multi formats of multimedia files in the teaching material |
| The displaying part | 1. | Retain the same operation method as the current use of PowerPoint |
| | 2. | Support the integration of multiple displaying devices |
| | 3. | Support the display of multi formats of multimedia files |
| | 4. | Enable the highlighting function to cross multiple display devices and the content in multiple media formats |
| | 5. | Support the control of assigning the slide in specific display device |

# 3 The Design of Multi-screen Multimedia Integrated System

## 3.1 System Architecture

The system was developed based on Microsoft Visual C# +.Net Framework 3.5. The suggested operating system is higher than Windows 7 and the related viewer should be installed as well.

The most used file format of presentation slide is the “ppt”. Besides that, there are still other multimedia formats being used listed in Table 2. Some of these could be displayed based on the built-in software such as Windows Media Player (WMP) or plug-in packages in browser. The others require specific software pre-installed in the operating system. Therefore, the designed architecture of display objects as shown in Fig. 2 aims to support the preview and display of these multimedia files either in editorial process or in presentation.

**Table 2.** The various file format of multimedia

| Types | File name extension | Company | Viewer |
|---|---|---|---|
| Picture | .jpeg, .bmp, .png | | Picture Viewer |
| Documents | .pdf | Adobe | IE* add-ons |
| | .doc(x), .xls(x), .ppt, | Microsoft | Office Viewer |
| Video | .avi, .mpeg, .wmv, .mp3 | | Windows Media Player |
| | .swf | Adobe | IE add-ons /Flash player |

*IE: Internet Explore

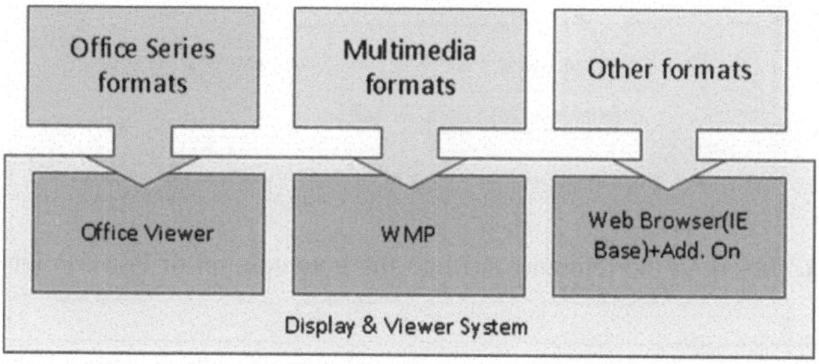


**Fig. 2.** The display objects in the proposed system

**– The editing part of the system**

In most merchandised educating system, it is often requested for using specific editorial or display tools. The additional installation of the specific tool or software might cause inconvenience. To avoid this condition, this system also supports any text editor to edit the teaching materials except for installing this system. User can just follow the designated format and save as the .fm file.

On the other hand, considering about the most used format in presentation tools is PowerPoint, the extension of multi-screen are developed with pre-defined scripts being attached to the comment column in PowerPoint. Editor could just follow the format of the scripts, write the referenced resources in scripts, and then attach it to the note column to extend the original PowerPoint file and thus to support multi-screen display. The pre-defined formats of script are list is Table 3. For example, the script "||2@http://icwl2013.tajen.edu.tw||" which means to display the referenced web page in the second screen was edit by user and inserted into the note column of slide as Fig. 3 shows.

**Table 3.** The pre-defined formats of script for supporting multi-monitors

| Format | Reference type |
|---|---|
| "\|\|" | Separate multiple scripts |
| No. of monitor + "@" | Assign the slide to show in which monitor |
| "@" + the referenced url or file path | Assign the referenced resources |

**Fig. 3.** Inserting the reference url into the note column of PowerPoint slide

Although this support does not require user to change their usage habit, sometimes the script editing could cost too much time as the amount of references increased. Therefore, we developed an editing system for user to produce the multi-screen display slides with drag and pull such simple intuitive way. As Fig. 4 shows, the upper slides in red frame are the core teaching materials which are to control the main switching of slides. The slides in blue frame are the referenced one to be arranged. If the referenced content is a web page or figure, user can click the position to be inserted and then enter the url or choose a file in the popped window. If the required references are files, user can open it in the black frame and drag the referenced page into the designated position. While there are many references exist in the same file, this drag and pull would spare a lot of time. The multi-screen display file can be chosen to store in .ppt format or .fm format.

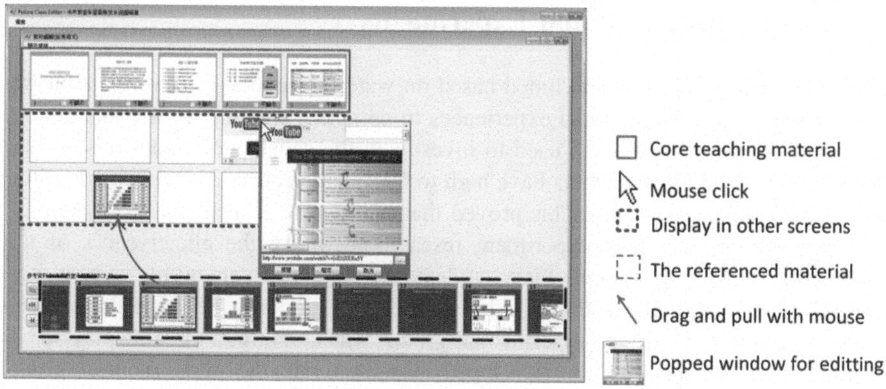


**Fig. 4.** The operation interface of the editing system

**– The display part of the system**

The display of multimedia materials in multi-screens was re-designed to fulfill the requirements mentioned in Table 1. First, we need to build a Main Form big enough to integrate display spaces of all the display devices. The system would retrieve the position and the resolution of each display screen. The Main Form is set up with the summation of the width and the maximum of the height among the display screens. As shown in Fig. 5, the system builds up a Main Form as its display space to cross all the display screens.

During the display, every switching of the slides would project the contents into the specific screen through using the display object mentioned above. Besides, the system would build a control panel which is responsible for the control commands such as page up/down, highlighting paint, the contents switching among screens. This control panel receives the click events of mouse and keyboard, and then display the operation according to the commands.

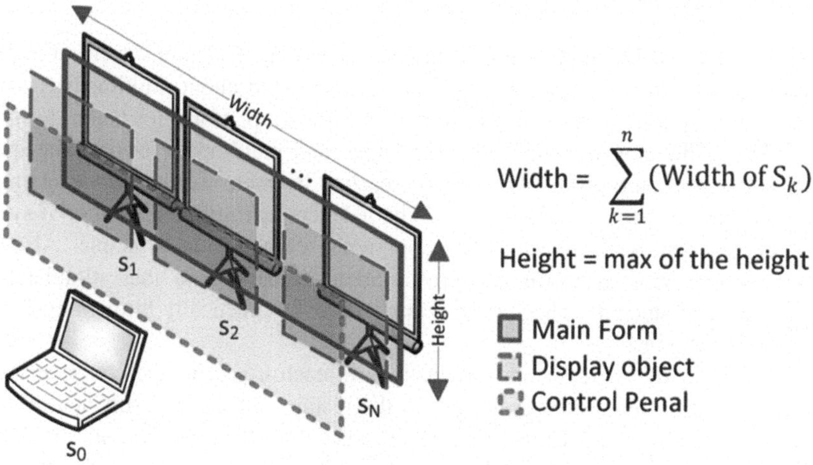


**Fig. 5.** The display system architecture

## 4 Design Verification and Experiments

The system was developed and tuned based on waterfall model. First verification was to provide ten teachers who had experiences in computer teaching to use this system. After that, a questionnaire was used to investigate the satisfaction about this system. The results revealed that teachers have high to 90 % satisfaction with either the editing system or the display system. This proved that our system is available in teaching.

Next, we use the quasi-experiment research to verify the effectiveness of this multimedia integrating system. Sixty students in computer networking course were selected to learn the course through the system. We randomly separate the students into two groups. One group (experimental group) was taught in a three-display-screen teaching environment with the developed system, while the other (control group) was taught in single-display-screen environment with the traditional slides show. The teaching contents were similar except for the arrangement. (The course design of the control group needs to reference other contents in hyperlink way or in new opened window while the one of the experimental group utilizes the display system to display the references in other screens.) The testers were asked to have the pre-evaluation and post-evaluation after the ninety minutes course. The results were first analyzed by SPSS analytic software and use the t-test to evaluate the differences between two groups. In case that the students' qualities affect the results, this research adopts the one-way analysis of covariance (ANCOVA) to remove the obscuring effects of pre-existing individual differences among students. We take the grades of pre-evaluation as control variable, the group as independent variable, and the grades of post-evaluation as dependent variable to analyze the results. The result p value is $.041 < .05$ which reached the level of significance and shows that the experimental group had better performance than the control group. It is proved that the system works well with those theories.

## 5 Conclusion and Future Work

This paper developed a multi-screen multimedia integrated teaching system to enhance the teaching effectiveness. Based on the detail discussion about multimedia learning theories, the proposed system aims to provide teachers a platform for better designing and displaying the course content in multi-screen and multimedia format. The spatial and temporal contiguity principle could be reached by more flexible arrangements of related contents in multi-display screens. The teachers can utilize the editorial system for better segmenting the teaching material with segmentation principle. Also, the system supports cross-platform and cross-screen signaling and that stimulates the learning curve of students. The system was also proved practically through evaluating it by actual teaching.

Nevertheless, there are several suggestions in each aspect of the course material, devices, and future researches according to the results and the experimental teaching feedback: in traditional education, teacher only needs to focus on editing one display screen without the need of caring about the referencing more materials. Therefore, the multi-screen multimedia teaching material definitely will cost teachers more effort in designing the course; on the other hand, most classrooms only facilitate one projector. Hardware support is an issue to promote the use of multi-screen multimedia teaching; moreover, the experiments were carried in a narrow amphitheater classroom and that incurred the students seated in the front sees unclear with the wide display of multi-screen. These are to be noticed when using this multi-screen multimedia display system.

## References


1. De Wet, C.F.: Beyond presentations: using PowerPoint as an effective instructional tool. Gift. Child Today **29**(4), 29–39 (2006)
2. Paivio, A.: Imagery and Verbal Processes. Holt, Rinehart & Winston, New York (1971)
3. Wittrock, M.C.: Generative processes of comprehension. Educ. Psychol. **24**, 345–376 (1989)
4. Greenlaw, R., Hepp, E.: In-Line/On-Line: Fundamentals of the Internet and the World Wide Web. McGraw-Hill, Boston (1999)
5. Robertson, G., Czerwinski, M., Baudisch, P., Meyers, B., Robbins, D., Smith, G., Tan, D.: The large-display user experience. J. IEEE Comput. Graph. Appl. **25**(4), 44–51 (2005)
6. Hutchings, D.R., Smith, G., Meyers, B., Czerwinski, M., Robertson, G.: Display space usage and window management operation comparisons between single monitor and multiple monitor users. In: Proceedings of Advanced Visual Interfaces, Gallipoli, Italy. ACM Press (2004)
7. Pobiner, S.: Collaborative multimedia learning environments. In: Human Factors in Computing Systems Montreal, Quebec, Canada. ACM Press (2006)
8. AMD Eyefinity FAQs. Global Provider of Innovative Graphics, Processors and Media Solutions. http://www.amd.com/us/products/technologies/amd-eyefinity-technology/how-to/Pages/faqs.aspx

# International Workshop on Smart Living and Learning

# Preliminary Investigation of Interactive Behaviors in Distant Collaborative Exergame

Wu-Yuin Hwang[1], Kanoksak Wattanachote[2(✉)], Timothy K. Shih[2], Shih-Ching Yeh[2], and Shi-Yi Zhan[1]

[1] Graduate Institute of Network Learning Technology, National Central University, No.300, Jhongda Road, Jhongli City, Taoyuan County 32001, Taiwan (R.O.C.)
wyhwang@cc.ncu.edu.tw, a832400la@yahoo.com.tw

[2] Department of Computer Science and Information Engineering, National Central University, No.300, Jhongda Road, Jhongli City, Taoyuan County 32001, Taiwan (R.O.C.)
{kanoksak.wattanachote, timothykshih}@gmail.com, shihchiy@csie.ncu.edu.tw

**Abstract.** This paper purposes to study the effect of three interaction models on team performance through a distant collaborative exergame. The distant collaborative interactions in game were designed and categorized into three scenarios namely, composite interaction, kinesthetic interaction and speech interaction. The kinesthetic interaction is emphasizing on the use of co-jump and push without speech, whereas only the use of speech is allowed for the speech interaction scenario. The composite interaction scenario combines the use of both kinesthetic and speech interaction. The experiment recruited thirty-three teams of sixty-six participants who whether have or not exergame play experience. The results show that the push and co-jump can effectively enhance team collaboration. The composite interaction is the best scenario for the enhancement of team collaboration, but the interesting effect is it did not affect to the tasks performance.

**Keywords:** Kinesthetic · Collaboration · Interactive behaviors · Distant collaboration

## 1 Introduction

The definitions of the collaboration given by the American Heritage Dictionary [1] described that (1) *To work together, especially in a joint intellectual effort*; (2) *To cooperate reasonably, as with an enemy occupation force*. The difference between collaboration and cooperation is that collaboration must allow all participants to set goals and assist in cooperation with each other to carry out the task, and with the completion of a common goal [9]. The collaboration has been described as a multi-player approach allows users to manipulate a task in a collaborative environment. Generally in collaborative game approach, the interactive cooperation between team members can enhance the achievement in game and encourage the interactive learning among team members. The players like to communicate and collaborate within their


D.K.W. Chiu et al. (Eds.): ICWL 2013 Workshops, LNCS 8390, pp. 213–222, 2015.
DOI: 10.1007/978-3-662-46315-4_22

teams as well as compete against the opposite teams. The collaboration between the players in team was explored that the interaction among team members helps team and individuals to attain flow [8]. The flow and team flow approaches have been studied and discovered by researchers aimed to explore the cooperative behaviors in various activities both in the individual and team. Understanding in the different perceptual learning styles in the collaboration can help the participants in a team to enhance the achievement of goal. According to the evolution of technology changes, researchers are increasingly interested in studying the perceptual learning styles which could be changed on the basis of those new technologies.

The concepts of learning style were found since the 1970 s in the different definitions and views. Leite et al. [10] classified learning styles into visual, auditory, kinesthetic or tactile. Perceptual learning style is individual approach because different people can have different learning style. Regard to the VAK model, perceptual learning styles consist of visual, auditory and kinesthetic learning conceptualized by Fleming [6] explains that (1) the *visual learners* have a preference for seeing as well as thinking in pictures including visual aids such as overhead slides, diagrams, handouts etc.; (2) *auditory learners* mostly learn through listening by lectures, discussions, tapes etc.; (3) *kinesthetic or tactile learners* prefer to learn via experienced moving, touching and doing. In this end, we modeled three interactive cooperation scenarios in accordance with VAK model to investigate the collaboration behaviors among team members. Besides, the study aimed to explore the effect of team collaboration on the tasks performance effectiveness. The rest of this paper is organized as follows. Section 2 devotes to related works. Section 3 describes the collaborative system and its functionalities, including the scenarios design. Results and analysis are demonstrated in Sect. 4. Finally, research findings, conclusions and suggestions for future development are drawn in Sect. 5.

## 2 Related Works

### 2.1 Collaborative System

Collaboration has been given various definitions according to collaborative ways, collaboration time and location. Maher et al. [11] divided collaboration into three models namely, mutual collaboration, exclusive collaboration and dictator collaboration. The *mutual collaboration* means the process of collaboration relevant to the online and real-time communication and mutual cooperation between participants. The *exclusive collaboration* means the task is divided into different work items and assigned to every participant, while the communication and coordination between the participants are allowed for the collaboration. The *dictator collaboration* means the collaboration is depended on a leader who is responsible for the management and coordination of any steps and decisions in the collaborative process. The collaboration based on time and location was categorized into four models [2] namely, face to face collaboration, synchronous distributed collaboration, asynchronous collaboration and asynchronous distributed collaboration. The *face to face collaboration* is the collaboration in same time same place, whereas the *synchronous distributed collaboration* means the collaboration in same time but in different places. Further, *asynchronous collaboration* means the collaboration in different time but in same place, and *asynchronous distributed collaboration* means the collaboration different both in time and place. Higgins et al. [7] proposed the multi-touch table which allows face to face discussion for children. The study showed that for the collaboration, learning to build on mutual response to solve the problems is easier than learning new concepts.

Based on mutual collaboration and synchronous distant collaboration, we developed a distant exergame by embedding the distant interactive cooperation in accordance with VAK model consists of push, co-jump and speech interactions. The players in team are located in different place and collaborate through the Kinect motion camera combining with the Skype's audio system by monitoring via the game screen. The data during play game was recorded for the interactive cooperation behavior evaluation.

## 2.2 Perceptual Learning Styles

The different perceptual learning styles of learners in games playing and learning based on VAK/VARK model can be explored as shown in Table 1. More specifically, the most frequently used learning styles are described in the following:

- *Visual learning style* is learning by seeing the pictures, images, graphics, diagrams and flowcharts for understanding and memorizing meanwhile creating the guidance images for remembering.
- *Auditory learning style* is learning by listening as the way to access the information. Learners need to hear the speech or discuss with other learners for easier understanding. The aural learners are always fast to absorbed and easy to understand with the speeches.
- *Kinesthetic learning style* is learning by physical movement, for example by using body movement through a story or tale to express the emotions. Learners are always learnt by activities like participating, playing sports, jobs training to gain the actual experiences.

**Table 1.** Perceptual learning styles based on Fleming VAK model and evaluation tools

| Researchers (year) | Evaluation tools | Learning styles |
|---|---|---|
| Barsch [3] (1980) | Barsch Learning Style Inventory | visual, auditory, kinesthetic |
| Reid [12] (1987) | Perceptual Learning Style Preference Questionnaire | visual, auditory, kinesthetic, tactile, alone, groups |
| Fleming and Mills [6] (1992) | VARK Questionnaire | visual, aural, read/write, kinesthetic |
| Dunn and Dunn [5] (1992) | Students' Learning 20 Style (Grades 3–12): Learning Style Inventory | auditory, visual, tactile, kinesthetic |
| Cohen and Weaver [4] (2006) | Sensory/perceptual learning style | visual, kinesthetic/tactile, auditory |

Aforementioned, this study decided to explore the effect of learning styles which players prefer for collaboration through the preferred media during play game. The learning styles embedded in our distant exergame consist of (1) *Visual learning* in accordance with push and co-jump notification on the game screen, learner must learn to interact with these graphical notification meaning to perform the mission as teammate needs. (2) *Auditory learning* in accordance with the speech to offer and request help, learner must learn to absorb and understand the speech to perform the mission as teammate needs. (3) Kinesthetic learning, learner must learn to express the action to offer and request including collaborate help in accordance with the coming mission on screen. For the evaluation, this study redesigned the Barsch Learning Style Inventory (BLSI) of self-assessment learning styles developed by Barsch [3] in 1980. The extended questionnaire was conducted to interview the players for finding out the collaborative behaviors through preferred media based on the individual and team perceptual learning styles.

# 3 Methodology

## 3.1 Research Strategy

A total of 66 participants were recruited to fully complete this study. The sample consists of 41 male (62.1 %) and 25 female (37.9 %) undergraduate and postgraduate students from a university in Taiwan with and without experience in exergame plays. Notably, around 30 % of the sample had never played exergame. The purpose of this research is to study the effect of three interactive cooperation behaviors based on three distant scenarios as illustrated in Fig. 1. The first scenario combines the use of speech, push and co-jump. The second scenario allows only the use of push and co-jump whereas the third scenario merely conducts the speech. The interactive cooperation information derived during game play was evaluated by an extended questionnaire.

This study used rotation experimental design. Each team had to play game completely three scenarios with the random order. At the beginning, researcher introduced about the system around ten minutes and then players were allowed to play a short practice session to work with system and team. After players got familiar with the system and the interactive cooperation scenarios, they were given forty minutes to complete three games in accordance with three scenarios in random order, including questionnaires. In addition, we used a voice recorder to record the player's interactive cooperation behaviors during game play. Besides, the system also recorded the data from students' tasks performance consist of lifetime and total number of coins. After the experiment, players individually needed to complete two questionnaires by rating several aspects of their collaboration. At the end, researchers conducted one-to-one semi structured interview regarding their perception toward mechanism and the functionalities for collaboration in a distant cooperation Kinect-based exergame. The system data including data derived from questionnaires and interviews were analyzed.

**Fig. 1.** The implementation of interactive cooperation models

### 3.2 Game Design and Implementation

The distant collaborative exergame was developed as a 3D virtual reality Kinect gesture-based game. The game development tools consist of Visual Studio 2010.NET, two motion cameras Kinect for Windows SDK Beta and XNA 3D game engine. The Kinect for Windows SDK beta which supports the features such as raw data streams accessed

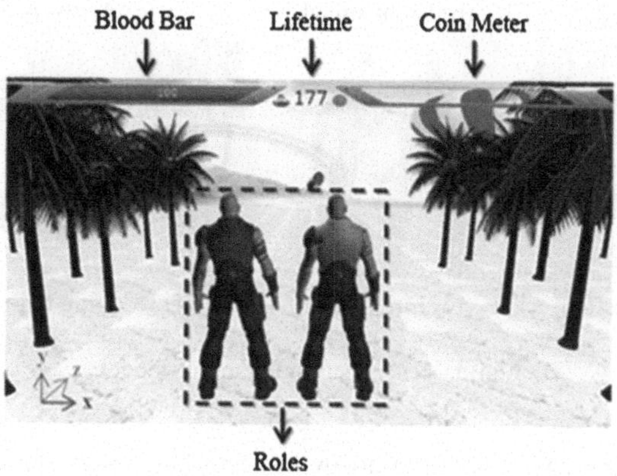


**Fig. 2.** Game interface

by the depth sensor, skeleton tracking for making easy to create gesture-driven applications, and advanced audio capabilities.

The game interface contains three parts that help players to keep track on the progress consists of blood bar, lifetime and coin meter as shown in Fig. 2. If blood value was decreased to zero then the game is over and the lifetime is stopped. Both players in a team have responsible for collecting the golden coin and avoid crashing against the bombs and mines to prevent the blood reducing. The collision objects in game consist of golden coins, bombs, mines, stars and golden boxes. The collision objects will randomly float to the front along z-axis. The participant roles are allowed to move along x-axis and jump along y-axis to dodge the bombs and mines or pick the golden coins. The collision objects characteristics are described below:

- *Golden coin:* pruning a coin will increase one point in the coin meter.
- *Star:* picking a star, life will be protected from encountering a bomb and can be inherited to teammate by overlapping the roles while encountering with a bomb.
- *Bomb:* crashing against a bomb will decrease 2 blood points.
- *Bomb king:* crashing against a bomb king will reduce 5 blood points.
- *Golden box:* contains 17 golden coins and allows players to collect as much as possible in accordance with the floating after breaking the box.
- *Mine:* crashing against the mines string will decrease 3 blood points.

The interactive cooperation behaviors in accordance with the three models are described how to effectively use as follows:

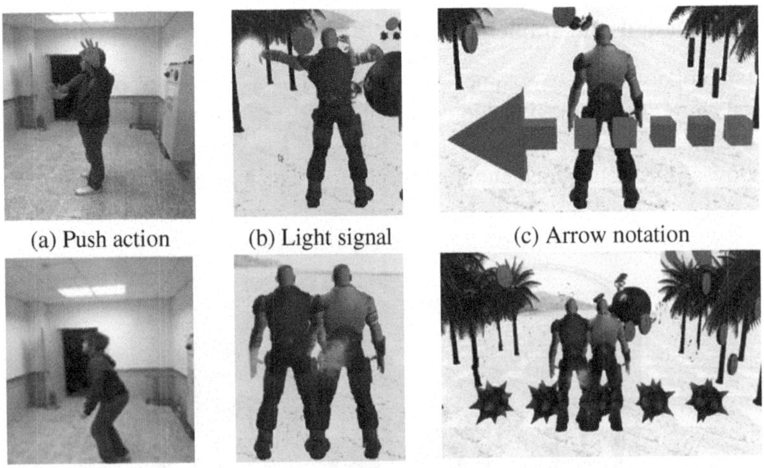

(a) Push action (b) Light signal (c) Arrow notation

(d) Jump action (e) Fire signal (f) Dodging bombs string

**Fig. 3.** Kinesthetic interaction model

- *push:* is used to create a notation arrow in accordance with pushing which will be appeared on the teammate's screen. The arrow will guide teammate or "helpee", for two purposes. On the one hand is to guide teammate move to the safe direction to dodge the floating bombs. On the other hand is to tell teammate the direction to prune the golden coin. The succeeded pushing notation on the helper screen is noticed by the lighting on the role's hands. Meanwhile the helpee can notice the pushing arrow signal on the screen as shown in Fig. 3(c). For example, student A in Fig. 3(a) is acting as helper by pushing left to send a left signal to helpee. In Fig. 3(b), helper can see his succeeded pushing by observing the light on his role's hands. In Fig. 3(c), helpee can get the notation arrow given by helper and decides to do a mission in accordance with helper needs.

- *co-jump:* only co-jump was designed to dodge the mines string. The co-jump can be activated by both roles have to move close to each other until the yellow fire appears on helper role's hands as a ready signal for co-jump. This action forces two players to jump together. For example, student A in Fig. 3(d) is acting as jumping in front of the Kinect after his role came close enough to his teammate's role by observing the yellow fire on the helper role's hands as in Fig. 3(e). Student A and his teammate must jump together to dodge the mines string as shown in Fig. 3(f).
- *speech:* using voice to communicate to teammates during game play which aims to offer and request help to complete the missions.

## 4 Experimental Results and Analysis

For the experimental results and analysis reports, we supposed S1, S2 and S3 to represent Scenario 1: the implementation of composite interaction model, Scenario 2: the implementation of kinesthetic interaction model and Scenario 3: the implementation of speech interaction model respectively. For each scenario we derived the different independent variables for the analysis as shown in Table 2. Suppose valid push in S1 and S2 means the pushing that can succeed in helping teammate to accomplish a mission, invalid push means in vice versa. Offer help and request help represents the use of speech to offer and request help respectively in S1 and S3. The dependent variables for each scenario in our experiment are lifetime and total coins, including the frequency of helps by using these collaborative interactions.

**Table 2.** Independent variables derived from each scenario

| Independent variables | S1 | S2 | S3 |
|---|---|---|---|
| valid push | ✓ | ✓ | |
| invalid push | ✓ | ✓ | |
| co-jump | ✓ | ✓ | |
| offer help | ✓ | | ✓ |
| request help | ✓ | | ✓ |

The averages of using the interactive cooperation through preferred media of each scenario are concluded in Tables 3 and 4. The *t*-test results shows that, the mean number of using push (sum of the average of valid and invalid push) in S2 is significantly higher than that in S1 ($t$-value = −8.554, p = .000). Due to only push and co-jump were allowed for collaboration in S2 during game play and the speech was not allowed to communicate through preferred media among team members. The mean number of valid push in S2 is significantly higher than that in S1 ($t$-value = −9.444, p = .000), since players were forced to use only the kinesthetic interaction designed in S2 without using speech. The number of invalid push, both in S1 and S2 are insignificantly different ($t$-value = −1.519, p = .139) means that invalid push done by players in S2 seldom occurred as normal. Besides, the mean number of co-jump in S2 is also significantly higher than that in S1 ($t$-value = −4.287, p = .000). The offer help in S3 is significantly increased and higher than that in S1 ($t$-value = −8.554, p = .000), on average, around 7 points, since the team was not allowed to use the kinesthetic interactions to offer help. On the contrary, whether push was allowed to offer help or not, the numbers of request help by speech in S1 and S3 are insignificantly different ($t$-value = −.459, p = .649). The study discovered that the team members liked to use speech to offer help more than to request help from partners during game play.

**Table 3.** Independent variables and $t$-test analysis on S1 and S2

| Kinesthetic interaction | S1 | | S2 | | $t$-value | Sig.(2-tailed) |
|---|---|---|---|---|---|---|
| | M | SD | M | SD | | |
| push | 7.85 | 4.590 | 18.67 | 7.114 | −8.554** | .000 |
| valid push | 5.79 | 4.241 | 15.94 | 5.841 | −9.444** | .000 |
| invalid push | 2.06 | 1.657 | 2.73 | 1.773 | −1.519 | .139 |
| co-jump | 2.00 | 1.768 | 3.97 | 2.172 | −4.287** | .000 |

**Table 4.** Independent variables and $t$-test analysis on S1 and S3

| Speech interaction | S1 | | S3 | | $t$-value | Sig.(2-tailed) |
|---|---|---|---|---|---|---|
| | M | SD | M | SD | | |
| offer help | 15.30 | 7.148 | 22.18 | 6.885 | −8.554** | .000 |
| request help | 1.82 | 1.211 | 1.94 | 1.560 | −0.459 | .649 |

The $F$-value ($F$ = 3.531, p = .042) of the frequency of helps shows that the frequency of using the collaborative interactions in S1 is significantly higher than that in S2 and S3 as shown in Table 5, since in S1 both kinesthetic and speech interactions are allowed to offer help. Additionally, the interview information shows that many participants used speech communication in S1 to overcome the mission rather than other behaviors. In Table 6, the $F$-value of lifetime ($F$ = 1.743, p = .192) shows that combining use of interactive cooperation including push, co-jump and speech could not increase the effective of the game play, since the mean of lifetime in S1, S2 and S3 are insignificantly different. Similarly, the mean of total coins in S1, S2 and S3 are insignificantly different ($F$ = 1.454, p = .249). In fact, according to the information recorded during game play including the interviews discovered that the inconsistent interactive behaviors of given direction by using speech and push in S1 often occurred and led the team member confuse in the delivered information to perform the missions in game. Consequently, the mean of tasks effectiveness both lifetime and total coins in S1 becomes lower than others with insignificance.

**Table 5.** The ANOVA *F*-test for frequency of helps

| Scenario | Mean | SD | *F* | Sig.(2-tailed) | Pos hoc |
|---|---|---|---|---|---|
| S1 | 26.970 | 1.390 | 3.531** | .042 | S1 > S2 |
| S2 | 22.636 | 1.441 | | | S1 > S3 |
| S3 | 24.121 | 1.287 | | | |

**Table 6.** The ANOVA *F*-test for tasks performance

| Scenario | Tasks performance | Mean | SD | *F* | Sig.(2-tailed) |
|---|---|---|---|---|---|
| S1 | Lifetime | 124.910 | 28.178 | 1.743 | .192 |
| S2 | | 131.910 | 28.980 | | |
| S3 | | 134.640 | 28.604 | | |
| S1 | Total coins | 95.485 | 29.371 | 1.454 | .249 |
| S2 | | 107.000 | 34.044 | | |
| S3 | | 106.909 | 36.462 | | |

In addition, the information recorded during game play including the interviews predicated that the main interactive cooperation behaviors used in S1 to help team for achieving the goal are speech to offer help and co-jump. In accordance with the Fleming's VAK model [6], suppose *VAK* represents visual, auditory and kinesthetic respectively. On the whole, for the combination of *VAK* type in S1, the interviews found that only *A* type was mostly preferred to use. The team preferred to use speech to help teammate rather than other types. Using *A* type in S1 could affect the interaction effectiveness as well. Additionally, based on *A* type, the players were agreed to inform each other about help by explaining the encountering situation early before asking for help. In S2, both co-jump and push of *K* type were effectively used. However, the players still wanted to participate in the combination environment of *AK* type. Because of less speech in S2, the interaction effectiveness was decreased. In S3, the players decided to have an agreement to divide the game screen into three parts of left, central and right for speech communication in accordance with *A* type. This strategy effectively led team to accomplish the goal. Further, according to the experimental recorded information and interviews found that the use of the combination of speech, valid push and co-jump could clearly offer teammates the right direction.

## 5 Conclusions

In this study, the game was developed based on Kinect gesture-based approach, which allows players to control and cooperate with team member through gestures and speeches. Since the kinesthetic learning encouraged learners to do something via their experienced moving or doing, hence, push and co-jump were designed to force the participants interact with teammate to overcome the obstacles. The actions done by push or co-jump were entered by Kinect camera to communicate with a distant learner by using image signals displayed on that distant learner's screen. In addition, the situations of with and without speech in the interactive cooperation were also studied in this experiment. We modeled three distant collaboration scenarios by combining the aforementioned interactive cooperation. The S1 combined push, co-jump and speech. S2 combined only push and co-jump and S3 designed for merely the use of speech. The experimental results showed that the collaboration in S1 is enhanced, but did not affect to the tasks performance. Conversely, the tasks performance output in S1 was decline. In accordance with the interviews information showed that many teams used speech interactions in S1 rather than other behaviors to accomplish the mission goal. However, the combination of interactive cooperation including push, co-jump and speech could not increase the effective of tasks performance. The interviews discovered that the inconsistent interactive behaviors of giving the direction by using speech and push in S1 model often occurred and led the team member faced with inconsistent interaction to perform the missions in game. The inconsistent interaction found in this research was planned to study in the future.

## References


1. American Heritage Dictionary. The American Heritage Dictionary of the English Language, 3 edn. Leather Bound (1992)
2. Anumba, C.J., Ugwu, O.O., Newnham, L., Thorpe, A.: Collaborative design of structures using intelligent agents. Autom. Constr. **11**(1), 89–103 (2002)
3. Barsch, J.: Barsch Learning Style Inventory. Academic Therapy Publications, Novato (1980)
4. Cohen, A.D., Weaver, S.J.: Styles-and Strategies-Based Instruction: A Teachers' Guide. Foreign Language Teaching and Research Press, Beijing (2006)
5. Dunn, R.S., Dunn, K.J.: Teaching Secondary Students Through their Individual Learning Styles. Allyn & Bacon, Needham Heights (1992)
6. Fleming, N., Mills, C.: Not another inventory, rather a catalyst for reflection. Improv. Acad. **11**(1992), 137 (1992)
7. Higgins, S., Mercier, E., Burd, L., Joyce-Gibbons, A.: Multi-touch tables and collaborative learning. Br. J. Educ. Technol. **43**(6), 1041–1054 (2012)
8. Jackson, S.A.: Toward a conceptual understanding of the flow experience in elite athletes. Phys. Educ. Recreation Dance **67**(1), 76–90 (1996)
9. Kvan, T.: Collaborative design: what is it? Autom. Constr. **9**(4), 409–415 (2000)
10. Leite, W.L., Svinicki, M., Shi, Y.: Attempted validation of the scores of the VARK: Learning styles inventory with multitrait–multimethod confirmatory factor analysis models. Educ. Psychol. Measur. **70**(2), 323–339 (2010)
11. Maher, M.L., Cicognani, A., Simoff, S.: An experimental study of computer mediated collaborative design. In: Enabling Technologies: Infrastructure for Collaborative Enterprises, pp. 268–273 (1996)
12. Reid, J.M.: The learning style preferences of ESL students. TESOL Q. **21**(1), 87–111 (1987)

# Second Heart Sound (S2) Decomposition by Hilbert Vibration Decomposition (HVD) for Affective Signal Modeling and Learning

Shovan Barma[1(✉)], Bo-Wei Chen[1], Hung-Ming Wang[1], Hung-Jui Wang[1], and Jhing-Fa Wang[1,2]

[1] Department of Electrical Engineering, National Cheng Kung University, Tainan, Taiwan
{shovan.barma, dennisbwc}@gmail.com
[2] Department of Digital Multimedia Design, Tajen University, Yanpu Township, Pingtung County, Taiwan

**Abstract.** This article presents a novel signal decomposition method, Hilbert vibration decomposition (HVD), for analyzing one of the major heart sound components second heart sound (S2) signal for affective signal modeling. In this proposed method, three kinds of simulated S2 signals are generated and the typical one is chosen for decomposition. For HVD method, a FIR filter is designed to separate each of the decomposed components. Finally, performance indicators, including the number of decomposed components, Hilbert spectrum, and spectral centroids, are measured.

To evaluate the performance of HVD, the decomposed components are compared with those generated by empirical mode decomposition (EMD) method. The experimental result shows that the number of meaningful decomposed components and frequency resolutions by using HVD method are better than those by using EMD. Such results also reveal the HVD method is superior to the normal EMD method, especially for low frequency narrow band bio-signals such second heart sound, thereby facilitating generating discriminant features for model learning.

**Keywords:** Hilbert vibration decomposition (HVD) · Empirical mode decomposition (EMD) · Second heart sound (S2) · Non-stationary signal decomposition

## 1 Introduction

The phonocardiogram (PCG) is a noninvasive, low cost, and easily repeatable technique for recording sounds produced by heart and great vessels, which provides valuable information about human cardiovascular systems. There are two dominant and normally audible components named S1 and S2 [1]. Both S1 (mixed with T1 and M1 components) and S2 (mixed with A2 and P2 components) do not function simultaneously. Even the subcomponents of S2, A2 and P2 come one after another within a very small time frame. It is quite difficult to distinguish A2 from P2 for human by using normal stethoscope. Heart sounds have very low frequency components like S1 with 10–150 Hz and S2 with 10–400 Hz, and the transient time is about 50–150 ms.


D.K.W. Chiu et al. (Eds.): ICWL 2013 Workshops, LNCS 8390, pp. 223–233, 2015.
DOI: 10.1007/978-3-662-46315-4_23

Proper signal processing tools are useful not only to identify these components but also to extract several features about the heart sound. Several techniques like time frequency, short time Fourier transform (STFT) [1, 2], Wigner-Ville distribution (WVD) [3], wavelet transform (WT) [3, 4], are applied to analyze the PCG signal. All these techniques are based on the classical Fourier analysis which considers the system/function stationary. However, the PCG signal is strictly non-stationary and nonlinear. Even the mentioned techniques have their own limitations. As a result, they are not suitable for PCG signal analysis. Other stationary signal processing approaches, like Hilbert-Huang transform (HHT), are also widely applied to heart sound analysis [5, 6]. The HHT technique is a comparatively proper tool for non-stationary signal analysis. It has an adaptive and iterative process named empirical mode decomposition (EMD) method, which considers the intrinsic mode function (IMF). Unfortunately, there are few limitations of EMD which limit us to apply this method to PCG signal analysis [7]. For instance, the EMD method is suitable for wide band signals and has low frequency resolutions, which only selects the frequency range of the next IMF range. Besides, such two IMF ranges differ by more than one octave.

Regarding feature extraction for nonlinear non-stationary signals, EMD is a powerful tool. Several works have been performed in this direction, like feature analysis of heart sound [8–12], emotion recognition from physiological signals [13], emotion recognition from ECG signal [14], accent extraction of emotional speech [15], and emotion recognition from brain signal [16]. After signal decomposition by EMD, several classifiers are used to extract appropriate meaningful features. Thus decomposed components carry a vital role in overall system performance. Zhang *et al.* [15] used EEMD-HHT method to recognize emotions from speech signal by considering marginal-spectrum parameters as features, and SVM was employed as a classifier.

This work is focused on to find appropriate decomposition method which can provide more meaningful features. A new method was introduced by M. Feldman named Hilbert vibration decomposition (HVD) [17] in 2006 to decompose a non-stationary signal into a sum of components with slowly varying instantaneous amplitude and instantaneous frequency. HDV is suitable for low frequency as well as high frequency signal decomposition and the frequency resolution is better than compared to EMD. For low frequency signals like heart sound, HVD is more applicable. In this work the S2 components is decomposed by HVD as well as EMD method, and several performance parameters, like the number of components, Hilbert spectrum, and spectral centroid are compared.

The rest of the paper is organized as follows. Section 2 introduces the theoretical background of EMD and HVD method. Section 3 describes the experimental methodology. Section 4 gives the experimental results, and finally Sect. 5 ends with conclusions and future work.

## 2 Theoretical Background of EMD and HVD

A non-stationary signal with slow varying amplitude and positive slow varying IF is referred as monocomponent signal. A measured signal can be represented by a composition (sum) of a finite number of monocomponent signals. $x(t) = \sum A_l(t) \cos(\int \omega_l(t)dt)$, where Al(t) is an instantaneous amplitude, and ωl(t) represents the IF for the l-th component. It has an ability to preserve the phase content of the signal by constructing every initial component in the time domain and preserving all of its actual phase relation.

### 2.1 Fundamental Concept of EMD

The idea of EMD decomposition is based on two certain condition proposed by Huang [8]. (1) In the whole dataset, the number of zero crossing must be either equal or differ at most by one. (2) At anytime the mean value of envelop of local maxima and envelop of the local minima must be zero. The IMFs are generated by the following steps:

(a) Identify all the local extrema for any signal $x(t)$. (b) upper envelop, $u(t)$, and lower envelop, $l(t)$ are created by separately connected all the maxima and minima with natural cubic splines. (c) Mean value of envelops is calculated by the formula $m(t) = [u(t) + l(t)]/2$. (d) A proto-IMF, $h(t) = x(t)–m(t)$ is generated. (e) Certain conditions like stoppage criteria and definition of IMF are verified against proto-IMF to determine final IMF, $c(t)$. (f) If the conditions are not satisfied by proto-IMF then repeat steps 2 to 5 many times as needed. (g) After getting the an IMF, a residue signal $r(t) = x(t)–c(t)$ is generated. (h) Operation continues until it meets the two basic conditions.

### 2.2 Fundamental Concept of HVD

A non-stationary multi-component signal can be decomposed by HVD into several mono-components. The fundamental method of HVD method considers iterative and based on Hilbert Transform but it does not involve spline fitting and empirical algorithm. By the HVD, the initial signal is decomposed the initial vibration signal into a sum of components with slow-varying instantaneous amplitude and frequencies. Every inherent synchronous component belongs to different time scale, which has estimated based on the global time analysis of IF of the initial signal. There is no doubt that each of the inherent synchronous components has physical and mathematical significance. The decomposition is based on two major assumptions:

1. The underlying signal is formed by a superposition involving at least one quasi-harmonic function with several full period lengths.
2. The envelope and frequency of each oscillating component differ.

The decomposition method performs in an iterative way having the following steps: (a) IF estimation: it considers the largest IF component of the signal; (b) detects the corresponding largest envelop by the synchronous detection and (c) the largest component is subtracted from the composition. On each iteration step the slow varying vibration components are separated by low pass filtering.

## 3 S2 Decomposition Methodology

Figure 1(a) is the overall system diagram for affective signal modeling and learning for physiological signal. The first step the signal acquisition and signal preprocessing. A proper low pass filter has to be designed and chosen an appropriate cut off frequency which suits for meaningful separation between two consecutive decomposed components. Finally this system chooses a classifier to extract meaningful features.

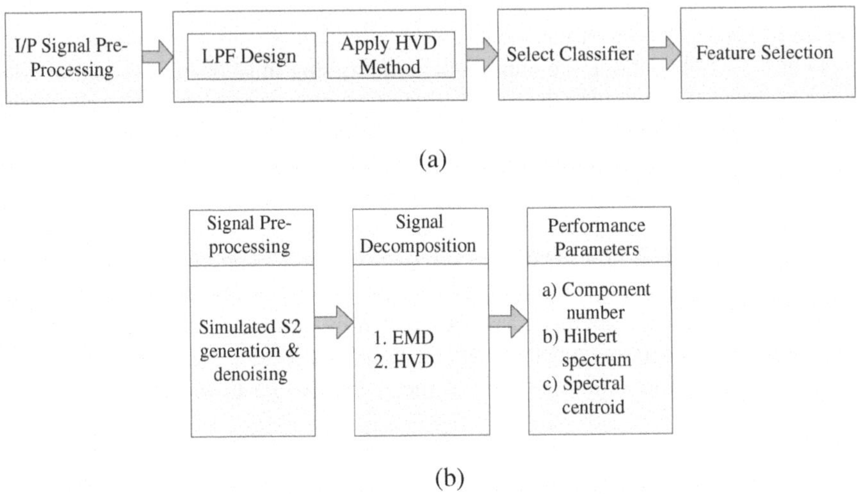


**Fig. 1.** (a) Overall system block (b) Block diagram of the proposed method

Figure 1(b) illustrates the proposed methodology to choose the appropriate decomposition method. This experiment is performed to justify decomposition by HVD over EMD for low-frequency physiological signals. Firstly, a simulated signal of S2 [18] is generated with noise and denoised by Daubechies-4 (DB-4) wavelet method. A low-pass FIR filter is designed according to Fig. 1(a) for proper separation between decomposed consecutive components by HVD. The denoised signal is then decomposed by EMD and HVD separately. Finally several performance parameters have been measured to compare the effectiveness of the decomposition techniques. The number of meaningful components, Hilbert spectrum, and spectral centroid are considered as comparative parameters.

First, the simulated S2 signal, which consists of two sub-components A2 and P2, is generated. A model of S2 by narrow band nonlinear transient chirp signal proposed by Jingping *et al.* [19] is adopted in this study. The parametric model of S2 (1) with decreasing instantaneous frequency (IF) is

$$S_2(t) = A_A(t)\sin(\varphi_A(t)) + A_P(t)\sin(\varphi_P(t - t_0)) + n(t) \tag{1}$$

Where $A(t)$ and $\varphi(t)$ are the amplitude and phase function of each component identified by the indices A for A2 and P for P2, respectively. Besides, $t_0$ is the splitting interval (time delay) between the onset and $n(t)$ is the additive Gaussian noise.

The amplitude functions are estimated by (2) and (3)

$$A_A(t) = 1.5(1 - \exp(\frac{-t}{8}) \exp(\frac{-t}{16}) \sin(\frac{\pi t}{60}) \tag{2}$$

$$A_P(t) = (1 - \exp(\frac{-t}{8}) \exp(\frac{-t}{16}) \sin(\frac{\pi t}{60}) \tag{3}$$

Furthermore, the phase functions are estimated by (4) and (5)

$$\varphi_A(t) = \int_{-\infty}^{t} IF_A(t)dt \tag{4}$$

$$\varphi_P(t) = \int_{-\infty}^{t} IF_P(t)dt \tag{5}$$

where IF functions are (6) and (7)

$$IF_A(t) = 24.3 + 225.7\frac{1}{\sqrt{(t+1)}} \tag{6}$$

$$IF_P(t) = 21.83 + 178.17\frac{1}{\sqrt{(t+1)}} \tag{7}$$

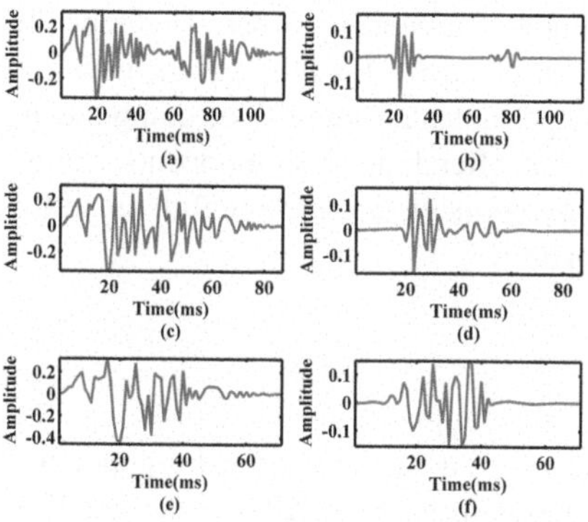


**Fig. 2.** (a), (c) and (e) simulated signal with noise for time delay ($t_0$) between A2 and P2 57 ms, 26 ms and 20 ms, respectively. (b), (d) and (f) are corresponding denoised signals.

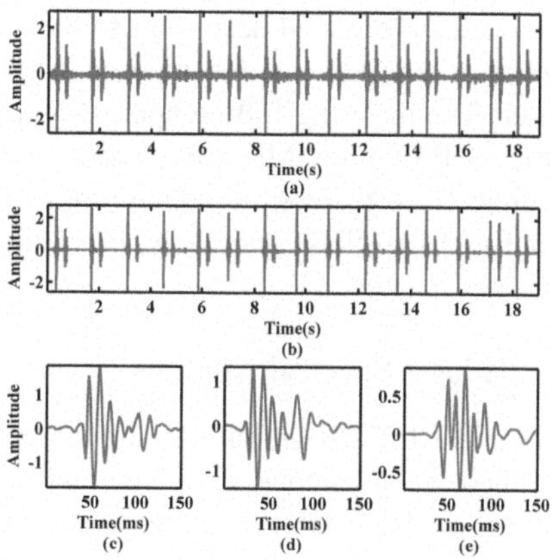


**Fig. 3.** (a) real life signal, (b) denoised signal (c) A2 and P2 clearly separated, (d) A2 and P2 partially merged, (e) A2 and P2 fully merged.

In most situations A2 comes first and is followed by the P2. Duration of each component is less the 80 ms. Two components can be separated from each other by 30 ms–80 ms and less than 15 ms during inspiration and expiration, respectively. However, the S2 often appears as single component [1]. Here the generated three different S2 signals are based on the various time delay, $t_O$, such as 57 ms (A2 and P2 are clearly separated), 26 ms (A2 and P2 are partially overlapped), and 20 ms (A2 and P2 are fully overlapped). The generated simulated signals are shown in Fig. 2. The mentioned three cares are observed in cases of real life [20], as shown in Fig. 3. From visual observation in real life signal, for $t_O = 26$ ms is suitable to consider as typical signal as compared to others. The further simulations are carried out considering the typical case. The each component is generated for 60 ms. ($0 \leq t \leq 60$). The decomposition methods have been performed on the signal shown in Fig. 2(d).

# 4 Experimental Results

According to Fig. 1(b) after decomposition of signal accomplished by EMD and HVD methods, distinct indicative measures have taken place which befits biological signal analysis. The IMFs and Ys are the outcomes by the EMD and HVD method respectively.

## 4.1 Number of Components

By the both method, the S2 signal is decomposed into several components. As both the method follows the iterative process so the number of iterations is equal to the number of components. The IMFs by EMD and Ys by HVD method are shown in Fig. 4. The components are sorted according to their frequency in ascending order. Theoretically number of components decomposed by EMD is six and by EMD is seven; which is greater. The meaning full component is more important than number of components. In Fig. 4 IMF-1 to IMF-3 has some meaning, but after that all components has no meaning. Nevertheless, in the case of Ys, more components are meaningful, as all the Ys are in same phase and show a meaningful pattern.

## 4.2 Hilbert Spectral Analysis

HVD and HHT [5] are simply a decomposition of a signal into several components with their instantaneous amplitude and instantaneous frequency. After obtaining IMF components from HHT and congruent components from HVD, further Hilbert transform can be carried out to each component to compute their IF in a successive way.

All the successive amplitudes and IFs are joined together to form a time-frequency distribution of the amplitude is called the Hilbert spectrum [21]. The time-frequency and correspond amplitude is plotted in Fig. 5. Here other than joint frequency components and corresponding their instantaneous amplitude and IF respect to time scale is shown to get a good rood resolution of meaningful components.

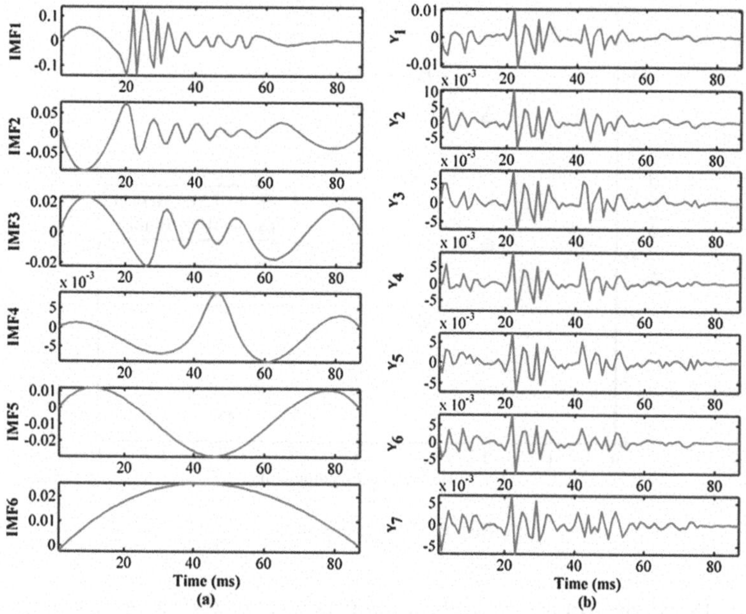


**Fig. 4.** Decomposed signals by (a) EMD and (b) HVD

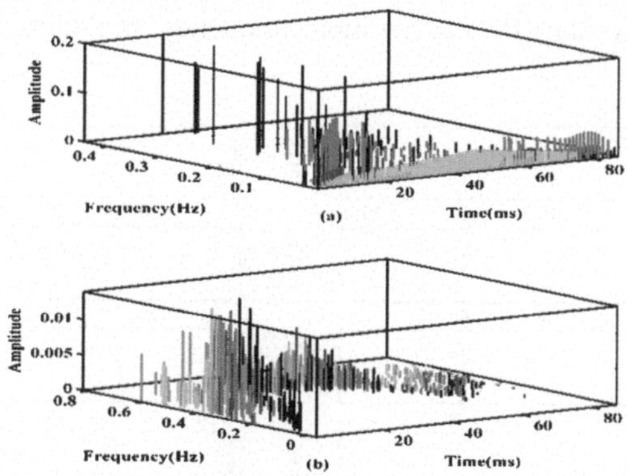


**Fig. 5.** Hilbert spectrum by (a) EMD and (b) HVD (see color version for details)

## 4.3 Spectral Centroid

Spectral centroid (SC) is one of the features commonly used in music timber, speech or speaker recognition system. It represents the brightness of a signal in frequency domain. Like the mass of gravity, here SC is relevant as the each component has very low frequency band.

Spectral Centroid (*SC*) is the average of entire frequency which is divided by several frequency bins. The frequency bins are based on window function where hann window generally is used. In our work hann window is applied. Mathematically it is

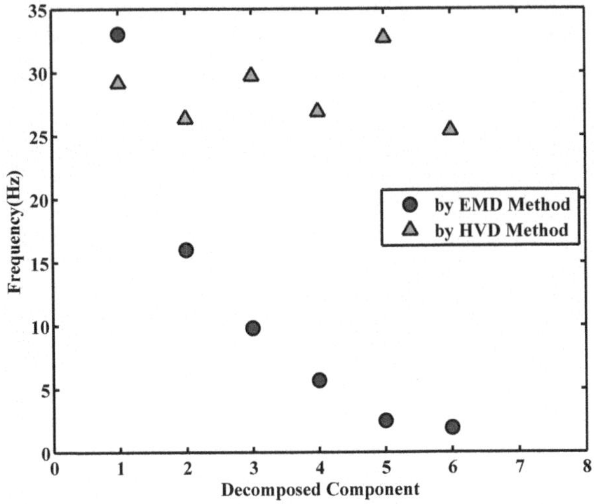


**Fig. 6.** Spectral centroid

defined by (8) where $x(n)$ is the weighted frequency value, $f(n)$ center frequency of each bin and $n$ is the number of bins. The generated components by both the method and corresponding to their spectral centroid are figured out in Fig. 6. The result shows the centroid in the case of HHT decays like exponentially compared to HVD decays linearly. It also shows the HVD keeps more frequency brightness.

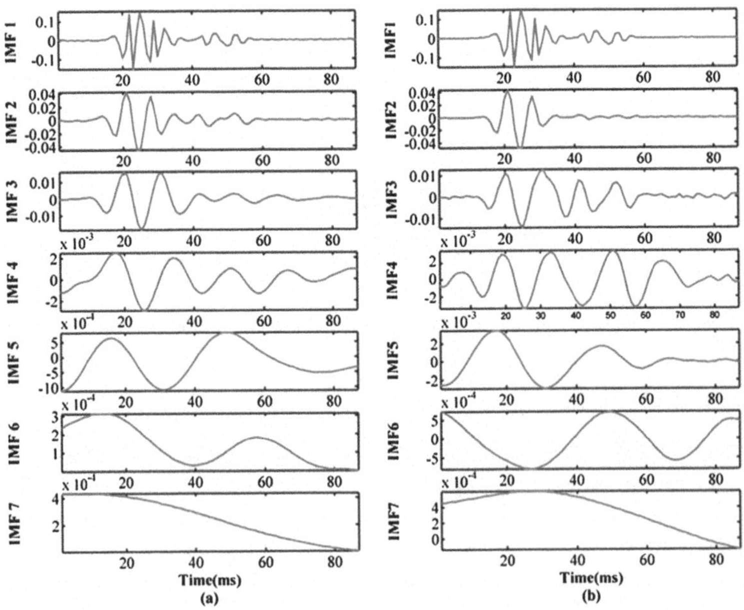


**Fig. 7.** Decomposed signals by (a) EEMD and (b) CEEMD

$$SC = \frac{\sum_{n=0}^{N-1} f(n)x(n)}{\sum_{n=0}^{N-1} f(n)} \tag{8}$$

The normal EMD method suffers from different problems like sifting, spline, etc. Advanced EMD like EEMD [22] and CEEMD [23] is also performed to decompose the S2 signal and the results are shown in Fig. 7. It shows the better IMFs compared to general EMD but not good like HVD.

## 5 Conclusions

This work presents a comparative study of EMD and HVD for signal decomposition of second heart sound (S2), which is nonlinear and non-stationary. Both of the methods have the same iterative and adaptive structure, but the decomposition principle is totally different. EMD method is suitable for wide band signals, whereas HVD is appropriate for wide band signals as well as narrow band signals. Furthermore, HVD is more efficient for bio-signals since which are generally narrow band. The frequency of one component to next component differs by one octave in the case of EMD method. On other size the frequency HVD one to next component differs based on the low pass filter coefficient and sampling frequency.

The results show that the number of decomposed components and frequency resolutions are better in the case of HVD method compared to EMD method. Even HVD provides more meaning full component than EMD. The main reason is behind in its fundamental decomposition technique. In the case of EMD, the frequency difference between one component to the next is one octave. However, the HVD is fully based on the low-pass filter so that the number of component and their frequency resolution depend on sampling frequencies and cutoff frequencies of the low-pass filter. The spectral centroid of IMFs decays faster compared spectral centroid of Ys become consistent.

Features, like entropy, cross entropy, and marginal spectrum, become more obscure in EMD than those in HVD. This implies that when HVD is applied to signal decomposition, more discriminant features can be generated for bio-signal modeling and learning. In future the work is further carried out by real life signal and other indicative measures are to be considered.

## References

1. Debbal, S.M., Bereksi, R.F.: Time-frequency analysis of the first and the second heartbeat sounds. Appl. Math. Comput. **184**(2), 1041–1052 (2007)
2. Chen, T.H., Han, L.Q., Xing, S.X., Wang, H.R., Wang, K.P.: STFT-based comparative studies of heart sound signals. In: 3rd International Conference on Bioinformatics and Biomedical Engineering, Beijing, China (2009)

3. Ergena, B., Tatara, Y., Gulcur, H.O.: Time-frequency analysis of phonocardiogram signals using wavelet transform: a comparative study. Comput. Meth. BioMech Biomed. Eng. **15**(4), 371–381 (2011)
4. Meziani, F., Debbal, S.M., Atbi, A.: Analysis of phonocardiogram signals using wavelet transform. J. Med. Eng. Tech. **36**(6), 283–302 (2012)
5. Zhao, Z., Zhao, Z., Chen, Y.: Time-frequency analysis of heart sound based on HHT. In: IEEE International Conference on Communications, Circuits and Systems, Hong Kong (2005)
6. Charleston, V.S., Aljama, C.A., Gonzalez, C.R.: Analysis of simulated heart sounds by intrinsic mode functions. In: 28th IEEE Annual International Conference on Engineering in Medicine and Biology Society, New York, pp. 2848–2851 (2006)
7. Huang, N.E., Shen, Z., Long, S.R., Wu, M.C., Shih, H.H., Zheng, Q., Yen, N.C., Tung, C.C., Liu, H.H.: The empirical mode decomposition and the Hilbert spectrum for nonlinear and non-stationary time series analysis. Proc. Roy. Soc. London Series A: Math. Phys. Eng. Sci. **454**, 903–995 (1998)
8. Tzu, H.H., Chia, C.C., Wai, C.F., Li, A.H.T., Yu, C.C., Bai, K.H., Yio, W.S.: Time-frequency analysis of heart sound signals based on Hilbert-Huang transformation. In: 16th IEEE International Symposium on Consumer Electronics Pennsylvania, pp. 1–3 (2012)
9. Ru, Z., Li, X., Chen, F., Yang, L., Li, X.: Research and simulation of speech enhancement algorithm based on HHT. Comput. Tech. Dev. **8**, 31 (2010)
10. Lihan, L., Haibin, W., Yan, W., Ting, T., Xiaochen, W.: Feature analysis of heart sound based on the improved Hilbert-Huang transform. In: 3rd IEEE International Conference on Computer Science and Information Technology, Beijing, China, pp. 378–381 (2010)
11. Charleston, V.S., Aljama, C.A.T., Gonzalez, C. R.: Analysis of simulated heart sounds by intrinsic mode functions. In: 28th IEEE Annual International Conference on Engineering in Medicine and Biology Society, New York, pp. 2848–2851 (2006)
12. Boutana, D., Benidir, M., Barkat, B.: On the selection of intrinsic mode function in EMD method: application on heart sound signal. In: 3rd International Symposium on Applied Sciences in Biomedical and Communication Technologies, Roma, Italy, pp. 1–5 (2010)
13. Cong, Z., Chetouani, M.: Hilbert-Huang transform based physiological signals analysis for emotion recognition. In: IEEE International Symposium on Signal Processing and Information Technology, Ajaman, UAE, pp. 334–339 (2009)
14. Zhiyuan, S., Qiang, W., Yi, S., Jing J., Yurong, L.: Accent extraction of emotional speech based on modified ensemble empirical mode decomposition. In: IEEE Instrumentation and Measurement Technology Conference, Austin, pp. 600–604 (2010)
15. Petrantonakis, P.C., Hadjileontiadis, L.J.: Emotion recognition from brain signals using hybrid adaptive filtering and higher order crossings analysis. IEEE Trans. Affectiv. Comput. **1**(2), 81–97 (2010)
16. Zhang, W., Zhang, X., Sun, Y.: Based on EEMD-HHT marginal spectrum of speech emotion recognition. In: IEEE International Conference on Computing, Measurement, Control and Sensor Network, Taiyuan, Chaina, pp. 91–94 (2012)
17. Feldman, M.: Time-varying vibration decomposition and analysis based on the Hilbert transform. J. Sound Vib. **295**, 518–530 (2006)
18. Xu, J., Durand, L.G., Pibarot, P.: Nonlinear transient chirp signal modeling of the aortic and pulmonary components of the second heart sound. IEEE Trans. Biomed. Eng. **47**(7), 1328–1335 (2000)
19. Xu, J., Durand, L.G., Pibarot, P.: Nonlinear transient chirp signal modeling of the aortic and pulmonary components of the second heart sound. IEEE Trans. Biomed. Eng. **47**(10), 1328–1335 (2000)
20. Rangayyan, R.M.: http://www2.enel.ucalgary.ca/People/Ranga/enel563/

21. Feldman, M.: Theoretical analysis and comparison of the Hilbert transform decomposition methods. Mech. Syst. Signal Process. **22**(3), 509–519 (2008)
22. Wu, Z., Huang, N.E.: Ensemble empirical mode decomposition: a noise-assisted data analysis method. Adv. Adpt. Data Anal. **1**, 1–41 (2009)
23. Yeh, J.R., Shieh, J.S., Huang, N.E.: Complementary ensemble empirical mode decomposition: a novel noise enhanced data analysis method. Adv. Adpt. Data Anal. **2**, 135–156 (2010)

# Clustering XML Documents for Web Based Learning

Ramanathan Periakaruppan(✉) and Rethinaswamy Nadarajan

PSG College of Technology, Coimbatore, India
rm_pk@yahoo.com

**Abstract.** The Web is increasingly used as a source of information for learning. Hence it is necessary that information on the web should be organized so that it can be used by the stakeholders efficiently. Most of the information in web is available in the form of XML documents. Grouping/clustering XML documents enhances the information retrieval process effectiveness. Computation of XML document similarity is a crucial task in clustering XML documents. In this paper we proposed a novel method to compute semantic structural similarity of an XML document by merging similar paths to address the above issues. In this method XML documents to be compared are represented by extracting all the paths from the root to the leaves and the comparison of paths is done based on a newly developed path matching algorithm. Similarity scores are given for exact, partial and contained in matches. In case of partial match merge operations are used namely the insertion of a new child (or descendants), parent (or ancestors) or both, and the creation of reference edges. More the number of merge operations more the dissimilarity of paths. Based on a similarity threshold the paths of XML documents are merged together and put in the same cluster and therefore avoiding pairwise similarity computations. Also, the matching process ensures the semantic structural similarity of the paths (i.e.) two XML paths may have a different order of hierarchy but semantically similar. Our proposed method shows an improved clustering accuracy.

**Keywords:** XML · Semantic structural similarity · Clustering · Web mining

## 1 Introduction

Due to the increasing usage of XML documents, efficient techniques are needed to manage high volume of XML data, so that it can be used in many web based applications. Hence grouping XML data in terms of structure and content gains much attention in research communities [1]. Since XML documents are hierarchical in nature clustering is a challenging task [2]. Challenges are mainly due to the heterogeneous nature of XML documents (i.e.) XML documents from different sources and they do not follow a common DTD/Schema. The key factor is to find an efficient technique for computing similarity between XML documents, considering the scalability of XML data.

XML document similarity, in general, can be classified as structure, content and semantics. The term semantic is applicable to structure, content and element name. In this paper our focus is on semantic structural similarity. By structural similarity we mean XML documents follow the same hierarchical order. However, in some cases


D.K.W. Chiu et al. (Eds.): ICWL 2013 Workshops, LNCS 8390, pp. 234–243, 2015.
DOI: 10.1007/978-3-662-46315-4_24

even if the hierarchical order changes the semantics will not be affected. For example consider the hierarchical orders

$$Movie \rightarrow Title \rightarrow Actor$$
$$Actor \rightarrow Movie \rightarrow Title$$

Even though they have a different structural order semantic meaning doesn't change and we call this as Semantic Structural Similarity. The difference between Structural Similarity and Semantic Structural Similarity is shown in Figs. 1 and 2 respectively.

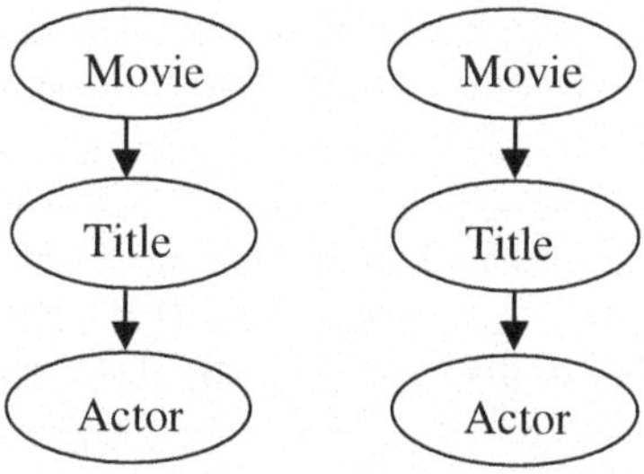


**Fig. 1.** Structural similarity of XML documents

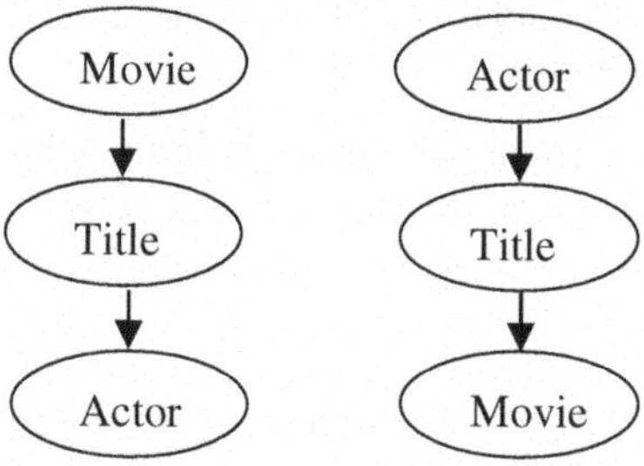


**Fig. 2.** Semantic structural similarity of XML documents

Earlier approaches for finding structural similarity between XML documents are based on tree edit distances. In this approach XML documents are represented as ordered labeled trees and they aim to compute cheapest edit sequence operations that can transform one tree to another. Tai [3] was first to introduce a non exponential algorithm for finding minimum edit distance between trees. Shasha et al. [5] provide an edit distance algorithm in which they allow insertion, deletion and relabeling of single nodes anywhere in the tree, however insertion and deletion of entire subtrees were not considered. Later Chawathe [4] frame an algorithm with time complexity $O(n^2)$ which considers the edit operations insertion and deletion at the leaf node levels and allows replacement of node anywhere in the tree but disallows the move operation.

Identification of subtree similarities was considered by Nierman et al. [6], however the overall complexity of the algorithm is $O(n^2)$. Combined methods of tree edit distance and semantic similarity based on information retrieval was proposed by Tekli et al. [7]. In general XML document similarity based on tree edit distance needs to compute pairwise similarity and hence there is huge computational complexity and has scalability issue.

Various algorithms were proposed to measure XML document based on path [8–10]. Buttler [9] shows that the similarity comparison can be reduced to constant time complexity by using the path Shingle technique. Rafiei et al. [8] shows that two XML documents are similar if they have more number of common paths in their path sets and they have a linear time complexity. Joshi et al. [10] use XPaths which captures the sibling information and the experimental results shows improved clustering results when compared with normal path based approaches. However in all these approaches semantic structural similarity is not considered. Vinson et al. [13] developed an algorithm PathSim which uses edit distance algorithm to compute similarity and doesn't consider the semantic structural similarity. Vacharaskunee et al. [11] improved this by considering semantic structural similarity however the clustering efficiency was not considered in their experiments. Choi et al. [12] proposed a clustering method called PSim based on path similarities of XML data. The clustering process was efficient and scalable than the previous approaches, however the semantic structural similarity is not considered.

Based on the above literature survey we observed that the factors to be considered for path similarity approaches are as follows:

- Computation of pairwise similarity and hence not scalable
- Semantic structural similarity

Table 1 provides details about path based algorithms based on these issues.

In this paper we proposed an algorithm which considers the semantic structural similarity and clustering efficiency thereby improving scalability.

**Table 1.** Comparison of path based similarity approaches

| Approach | Features | Semantic structural similarity | Scalable |
|---|---|---|---|
| Buttler [9] | Approximation algorithm Path Shingle technique | No | Yes |
| Rafiei [8] | Pairwise Similarity computation | No | No |
| Joshi [10] | Xpath technique | No | No |
| Vinson [13] | Edit distance | No | No |
| Vacharaskunee [11] | PathMatch cost matrix | Yes | No |
| Choi [12] | Combined clustering technique based on Path similarity | No | Yes |

The rest of the paper is organized as follows. Section 2 describes the XML document representation, Sect. 3 explains the Path-Merge algorithm, in Sect. 4 experimental results are shown and conclusion is discussed in Sect. 5.

## 2 XML Document Represenation

In order to capture the structural information, XML documents are generally represented as ordered labeled tree. For computation of similarity measure we introduce a definition Reference edge as follows.

**Definition 1: Reference Edge**
A reference edge is an edge between a node $n_k$ and any one of the nodes in the Root-to-leaf paths of XML document.

Examples for Root-to-leaf paths and Reference Edge are shown in Figs. 3 and 4 respectively.

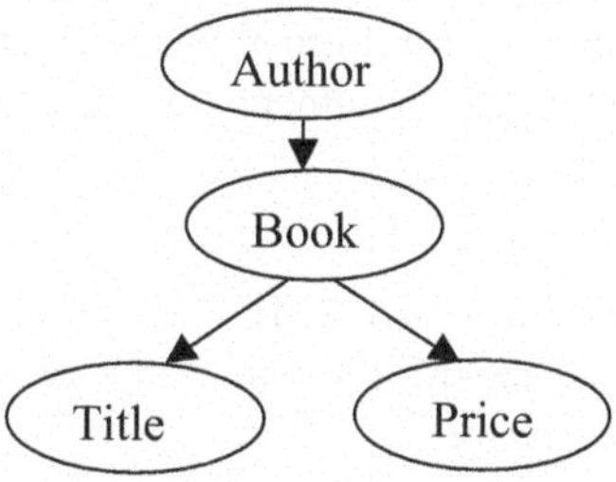


**Fig. 3.** Root-to –leaf paths

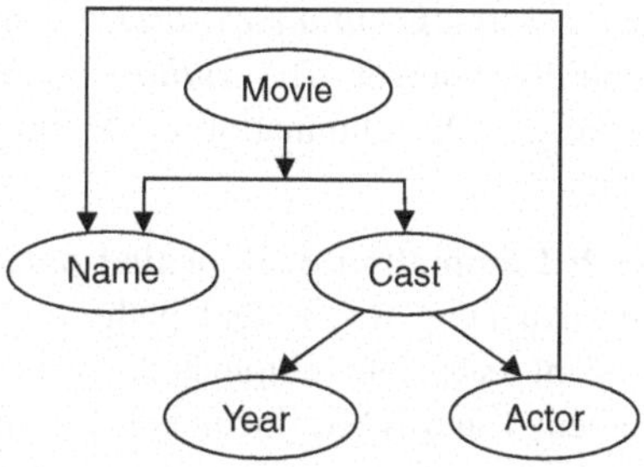


**Fig. 4.** Reference edge

The Root-to-leaf paths in Fig. 3 are
/Author/Book/Title
/Author/Book/Price

Reference Edge in Fig. 4 is shown in dashed line (i.e.) Actor - > Name. A Reference Edge is also included in path. The Root-to-leaf paths in Fig. 4 are

/Movie/Name
/Movie/Cast/Year
/Movie/Cast/Actor/Name

An XML document is represented by generating all Root-to-leaf paths including reference edges.

### 2.1 Pre-Processing of XML Document

Preprocessing of the XML document is done to simplify the computation of similarity. The identified cases for preprocessing are discussed as follows.

**Case 1: Redundant Information Node Filter**
Nodes which are redundant with information can be eliminated. As an example consider the XML documents in Figs. 5 and 6.

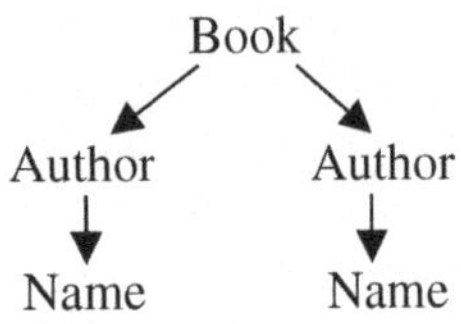


**Fig. 5.** XML document 1

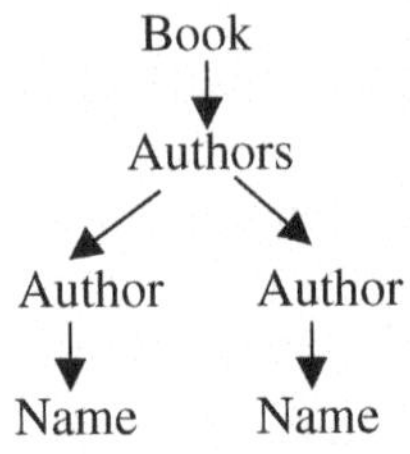


**Fig. 6.** XML document 2

The path in XML document 1 is ***Book/Author/Name*** and the path in XML document 2 is ***Book/Authors/Author/Name***. Both the paths are semantically similar but structurally different. The ***Authors*** Node is redundant with information which can be eliminated. After elimination of Authors node both XML documents are structurally similar.

**Case 2: Elimination of Repeated paths**
While extracting root-to-leaf paths of XML document 1 and XML document 2 the redundant paths are eliminated. After elimination, the root-to-leaf paths of XML document 1 and XML document 2 is /Book/Author/Name.

**Case 3: Element Name Preprocessing**
Element names are parsed to put into their basic forms, for example element name author1 is converted to author. Special symbols, punctuations and abbreviations are treated suitably (e.g. author_name is converted as authorname). Element names with short forms, for example initPage are converted as Page. Here a basic preprocessing is done with respect to syntactic and semantics are not considered.

## 3 Path-Merge Similarity Measure

XML documents are represented by generating root-to-leaf paths as explained in Sects. 2 and 3. To compute similarity between XML documents path edit operations are used and they are defined as follows.

**Definition 2: Node Set**
A Node Set N is the collection of all distinct nodes of an XML document.

**Definition 3: Insert child**
Given a path $P_1$ with a sequence of nodes $< n_1, n_2, \ldots n_p >$ and a path $P_2$ with a sequence of nodes $< m_1, m_2, .. m_q >$ then **InsertChild($\mathbf{n_i, m_{j+1}}$)** is an insert child operation applied to path $P_1$ at matching position i such that the following conditions holds good

i. $n_i = m_j$ (ii) $m_{j+1} \notin N$

**Definition 4: Insert parent**

Given a path $P_1$ with a sequence of nodes $< n_1, n_2, \ldots n_p >$ and a path $P_2$ with a sequence of nodes $< m_1, m_2, .. m_q >$ then **InsertParent($n_i$,$m_{j-1}$)** is an insert parent operation applied to path $P_1$ at matching position i such that the following conditions holds good

i. $n_i = m_j$ (ii) $m_{j-1} \notin N$

**Definition 5: Create ReferenceEdge**

Given a path $P_1$ with a sequence of nodes $< n_1, n_2 .. n_p >$ and a path $P_2$ with a sequence of nodes $< m_1, m_2, .. m_q >$ then **CreateReferenceEdge($n_i$,$m_{j+1}$)** is an creation of Reference Edge operation applied to path $P_1$ at matching position i such that the following conditions holds good

i. $n_i = m_j$ (ii) $m_{j+1} \in N$

**Example 1**

To illustrate the merge operations consider two path sequences

$P_1$ = ***/actor/filmography/movie/title***
$P_2$ = ***/movie/directedby/director***

In the mapping process of $P_2$ to $P_1$ the node ***movie*** is matched but the nodes ***directedby*** and ***director*** are not available in $P_1$ and hence they are inserted as child nodes through **InsertChild** operation. Paths $P_1$ and $P_2$ before mapping and after mapping are shown in Figs. 7 and 8 respectively.

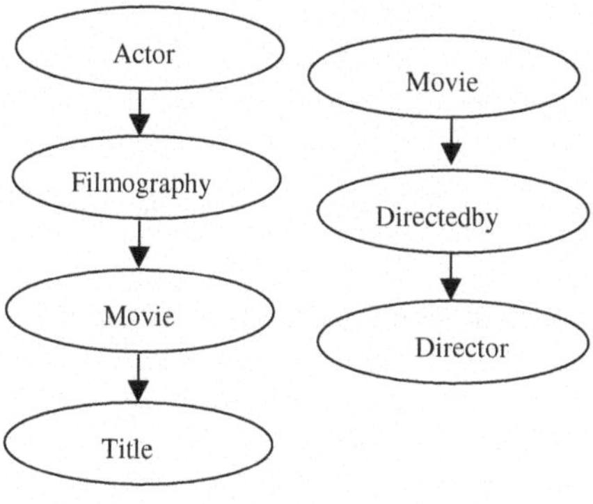


**Fig. 7.** Paths $P_1$ and $P_2$ before mapping

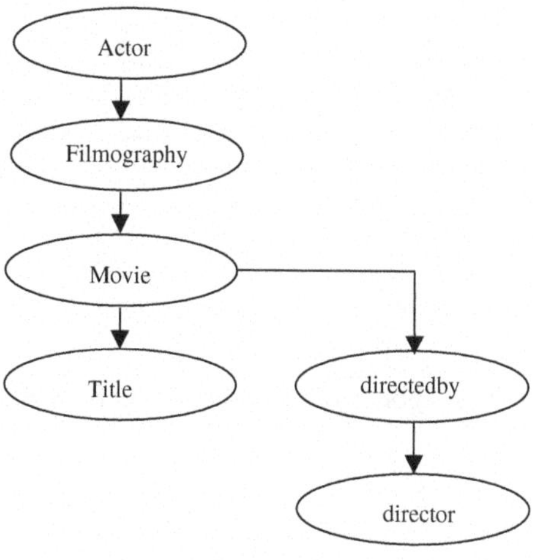


**Fig. 8.** Paths $P_1$ and $P_2$ after insertion

**Example 2** Consider two path sequences

$P_1$ = ***/book/author/title***
$P_2$ = ***/article/author/title***

The insert operations are shown in Figs. 9 and 10 respectively.

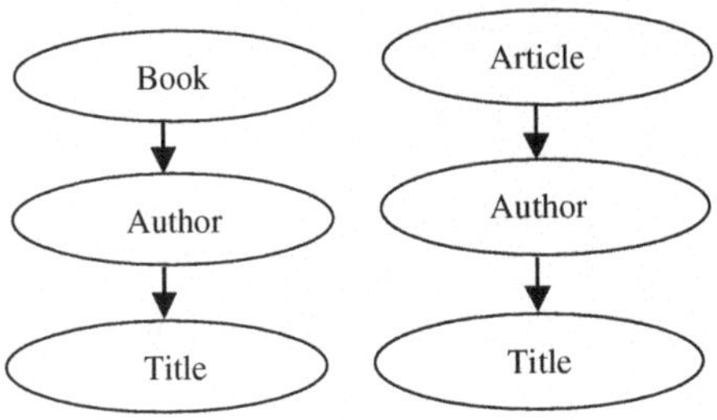


**Fig. 9.** Paths $p_1$ and $p_2$ before mapping

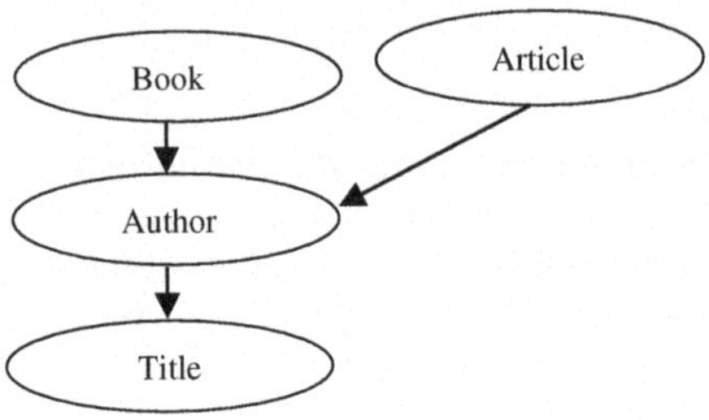


**Fig. 10.** Paths $p_1$ and $p_2$ after mapping

**Example 3**
$P_1$ = /actor/filmogrphy/movie/title
$P_2$ = /movie/title/actor

Figures 11 and 12 shows the creation of reference edge

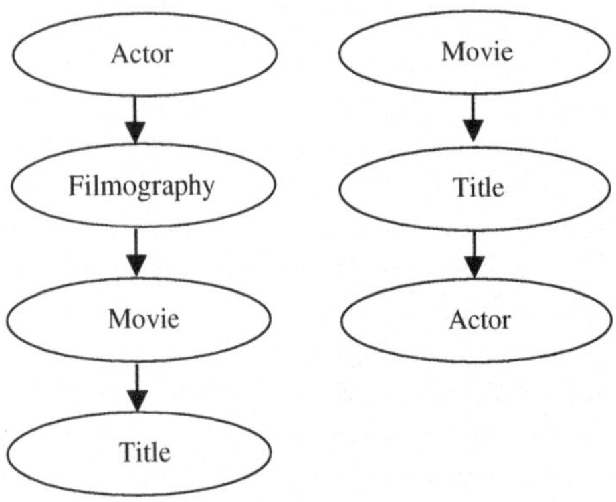


**Fig. 11.** Paths $P_1$ and $P_2$ before creation of reference

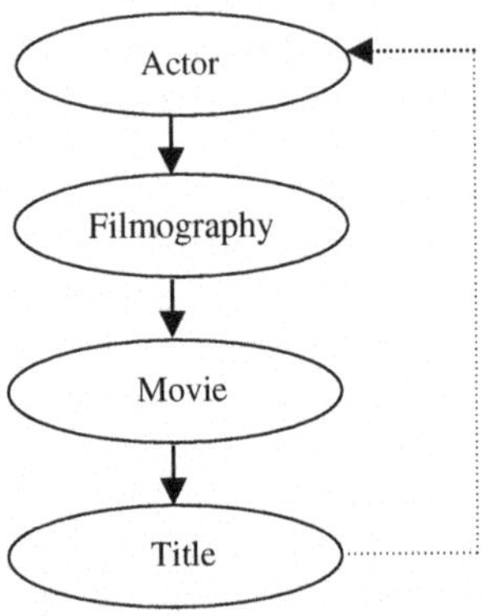


**Fig. 12.** Creation of reference edge

The algorithm for computation of XML document similarity is given as follows.

**Algorithm Path-Merge**

```
Input: P = {P1,P2,...Pn} and Q ={Q1,Q2...Qm}, the set of all root-to-leaf paths of
        XML documents D1, D2 generated based on pre-processing conditions.
Ouput: Similarity measure between P and Q
for each path Qi in Q , 1<= i <=m
        for each path Pj in P,  1<= j <=n
                L[j]=lcs(Qi,Pj)  /* lcs is longest common substring */
        end for
Sel_Path = Pj such that L[j] is maximum
if Qi = Sel_Path  /*exact match */
        Sim(Qi,Sel_Path)=1
else  /* partial match */
        k ← Number of nodes in Qi  /* q1,q2..qk*/
        l ← Number of nodes in Sel_Path /*s1,s2,...sl*/
        if q1 found in Sel_Path
                child_ins=true
        else
                parent_ins=true
        end if
        Sub_Path ← empty
        if child_ins
                call Insert_child(Sub_Path,sr)
            if parent_ins
                call Insert_parent(Sub_path,L[j])
            end if
        t ← Number of nodes in Sub_Path /* x1,x2...xt */
        M← Number of distinct nodes in Qi and Sub_path
        y[1,..M] ←0
        ctr ← 0
        Ref_wt ← 0
        if(ctr !=j)
                for k=ctr to j
                    if qk not found in any of the available nodes
                       y[k]=1
                    else /* creation of reference edge */
                      call Create_ReferenceEdge(Sub_path,qk)
                      Ref_wt ← Ref_wt + Node_Wt  /* Node_wt is the Reference
                                                               Edge Weight */
                      end if
                  end for
         end if
         Compute Similarity between paths
```

$$sim(Qi, Sub_{Path}) = \frac{\sum_{K=1}^{M} y[k] * W^{M-k} + Ref\_Wt}{\sum_{K=0}^{M-1} W^{k} + Ref\_Wt}$$

/* W – Weight assigned */

Compute Similarity between two documents

$$Sim(D1, D2) = \frac{\sum_{i=1}^{M} sim(Qi, Sel\_path)}{m}$$

**end for**
**end algorithm**

## 4 Experimental Results

We test the effectiveness of our algorithm by considering real time data set from InfoVis. InfoVis-2004 is a contest conducted in the field of information visualization the dataset contains complete metadata for all the papers of 8 years (1995–2002) of InfoVis Conference and their references. From this dataset we took 4240 XML documents for computing similarity. We have used an agglomerative clustering algorithm to cluster XML documents based on similarity threshold. We compare our algorithm with Choi et al. and the performance is shown in Fig. 13.

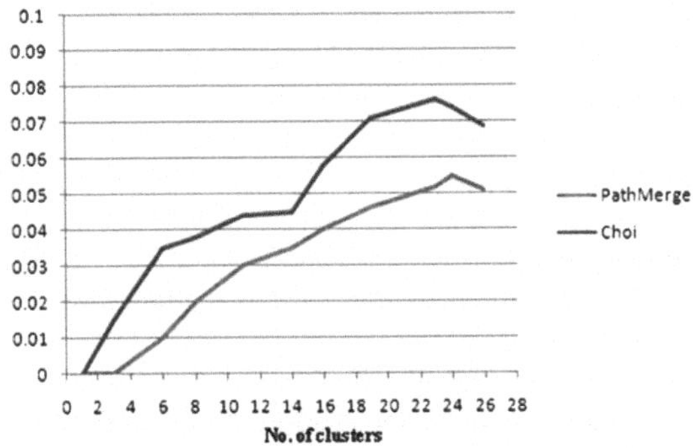


**Fig. 13.** Inter cluster similarity comparison

The graph depicts shows the inter cluster similarity and it is evident that our algorithm outperforms Choi's algorithm. The number of clusters varies from 1 to 26 depending on the similarity threshold value.

## 5 Conclusion

In this paper we have proposed an effective algorithm for computing structural similarity of XML documents using Path-Merge. This ensures effective clustering of XML documents and hence finds more application in web based learning. The main advantage of our algorithm is computing similarity by considering structural semantics. Through experiment we have demonstrated that our algorithm is effective in terms of clustering accuracy. In future we planned to extend our work by computing both structural and content semantic similarity.

## References


1. Tekli, J., Chbeir, R., Yetongnon, K.: An overview on XML similarity: background, current trends and future directions. Comput. Sci. Rev. **3**(3), 151–173 (2009)
2. Aggarwal, C.C., Ta, N., Wang, J., Feng, J., Zaki, M.: Xproj: a framework for projected structural clustering of xml documents. In: Proceedings of the 13th ACM SIGKDD International Conference on Knowledge Discovery and Data Mining, pp. 46–55 (2007)
3. Tai, K.C.: The tree-to-tree correction problem. J. ACM (JACM) **26**, 433 (1979)
4. Chawathe, S.S.: Comparing hierarchical data in external memory. In: Proceedings of the International Conference on Very Large Data Bases, pp. 90–101 (1999)
5. Shasha, D., Zhang, K.: Approximate tree pattern matching, Pattern Matching in Strings. Trees and Arrays. Oxford University Press, Oxford (1995)
6. Nierman, A., Jagadish, H.V.: Evaluating structural similarity in XML documents. In: Proceedings of ACM SIGMOD WebDB, pp. 61–66 (2002)
7. Tekli, J., Chbeir, R.: A novel XML document structure comparison framework based-on sub-tree commonalities and label semantics. J. Web Semant. **11**, 14–40 (2012)
8. Rafiei, D., Moise, D,, Sun, D.: Finding syntactic similarities between xml documents. In: Proceedings of the 17th International Conference on Database and Expert Systems Applications, pp. 512–516 (2006)
9. Buttler, D.: A short survey of document structure similarity algorithms. In: The 5th International Conference on Internet Computing, Las Vegas (2004)
10. Joshi, S., Agrawal, N., Krishnapuram, R., Negi, S.: A bag of paths model for measuring structural similarity in web documents. In: Proceedings of the ACM SIGKKD Conference on Knowledge Discovery and Data Mining, pp. 577–582, USA (2003)
11. Vacharaskunee, S., Sarun, I..: XML path matching for different hierarchy order of elements in XML documents. In: Proceedings of the 11th IEEE ACIS International Conference on Software Engineering Artificial Intelligence Networking and Parallel/Distributed Computing (SNPD) (2010)
12. Choi, I., Moon, B., Kim, H.-J.: A clustering method based on path similarities of XML data. Data Knowl. Eng **60**, 361–376 (2007)
13. Vinson, A.R., Heuser, C.A., da Silva, A.S., De Moura, E.S.: An approach to XML path matching. In: The 9th Annual ACM International Workshop on Web Information and Data Management, pp. 17–24 (2007)

# Cultural Sensitivity Training Task: An Avenue of Enhancing Students' Cultural Awareness and Its Perspectives of Web-Based Learning

Jaw-Shyang Wu[1(✉)], Tun-Whei Chuo[2], and Shu-Chin Yen[2]

[1] Tajen University, Yanpu Township, Taiwan (ROC)
jswu@mail.tajen.edu.tw

[2] Wenzao Ursuline University of International Studies, Kaohsiung City, Taiwan (ROC)
93005@mail.wtuc.edu.tw

**Abstract.** This paper proposes to discuss how teachers can enhance students' cultural awareness through cultural sensitivity training tasks (CSTT). Under the teaching philosophy of agency and epistemology, students experienced the stages of evaluating and re-evaluating their own cultures via classroom activities. Data were collected from two sources: first, Rew's et al. (2003) culture awareness questionnaire was revised and served as pre- and post-test. Second, a survey question was used to probe students' personal stages of change. Results of students' responses to the questionnaire showed that students' cultural awareness increased significantly after taking the course. These results strongly suggest that CSTT can effectively enhance students' cultural awareness.

**Keywords:** Cultural awareness · Culture sensitive · Cultural sensitivity training task · Web-based learning

## 1 Introduction

Gerchman and Weiss [1] suggested that language teachers teach culture "by direct experience [such as] meeting people from the country being studied, watching films or . . . using realia as tools" [2]. He claimed that to engage and provide students with "direct experience" is the best way to illuminate the relationship between language and culture. A network-based approach becomes very relevant to reach the goal of "direct experience" for intercultural exchange, which views language and culture to be interdependent [3]. E-mail exchange with students from different countries is one of the commonly used network-based applications in the language classroom [4]. Synchronous on-line communication enables learners of different cultural backgrounds to conduct direct intercultural exchanges [5].

To bridge the research gap of the current pedagogical applications in the course of Language and Culture, the study proposes to teach this course with a combination of direct experiences and a historic perspective with a view to enhancing students' cultural awareness. Cultural sensitivity training (CST) tasks is a utilized pedagogical application in the study. CST studies culture historically from the unconscious, cognitive


D.K.W. Chiu et al. (Eds.): ICWL 2013 Workshops, LNCS 8390, pp. 244–252, 2015.
DOI: 10.1007/978-3-662-46315-4_25

and socio-cultural perspectives. The teaching philosophy of CST tasks – agency and epistemology – enables students to experience and re-evaluate their own cultures and the target ones. CST realizes Magnan's language and culture instruction, which provides students avenues for direct experience of intercultural exchanges and examining culture from a historical perspective. Based on the research purpose, two research questions were target in the study:

1. Do the students enhance their cultural awareness after undergoing cultural sensitivity training tasks (CSTT)?
2. If yes, how was their cultural awareness enhanced? That is, how do they experience the stages of absolute conviction (my culture is good and correct) to that of transition (other cultures though different from mine can be interesting) and even to that of context (I am aware of my own culture and can accept other cultures as well)?

The answers derived from this research are beneficial to further development of web-based learning systems. If the cultural factors are considered in the design and implementation of learning web, better effectiveness and efficiency of that learning web are expected.

The rest of this paper is recognized as follows Literature reviews of cultural impact on teaching and learning, are presented in Sect. 2. Then a field study in a language college with two-year, four-year and five-year students is presented. The proposed methodology called as Cultural sensitivity training (CST) pedagogy is illustrated in Sect. 3. Statistical results are given in Sect. 4 to demonstrate the impact of the proposed methodology. Finally, this research is concluded in Sect. 5.

## 2 Literature Review

Hall [6–8] viewed culture from three main elements - cultural context, cultural space, and cultural time. Culture is experienced unconsciously as it is defined as "the system of shared beliefs, values, behaviors, and artifacts that the members of society use to cope with their world and with one another, and that we transmitted from generation to generation through learning" [9]. Also, friends and lovers who enter into a relationship may have been previously aware of their culture, long traditional values and expectations about dating and marriage. In contrast, very little is taken for granted in a low-context culture. Hence explanations are needed for almost everything. Western countries, such as the USA, are considered low-context. Business contracts are highly valued and considered imperative before any business can take place. Rules and expectations are often delineated in relationships, even romantic relationships.

From a cognitive perspective, Holland and Quinn [10] described culture as what people "must know in order to act as they do, make the things they make, and interpret their experiences in the distinctive way they do". The concept of superstition is derived from a universal human nature regardless of different races. It is "a man's yearning to know his fate and to have some hand in deciding it". Religion may also help cultures make sense of fate. The forms of superstitions and religion are presented distinctively in each culture. People can learn cognitively to be aware of the various forms of superstition and religion.

**A Socio-Cultural Perspective**

A socio-cultural perspective would include daily life and customs, human relationships, the youth world, mass media, and the presence of international relationships [11]. "Etiquette, expressions of politeness, and social dos and don'ts shape people's behavior through child rearing, behavioral upbringing, schooling, and professional training. ... People who identify themselves as members of a social group (family, neighborhood, professional or ethnic affiliation, nation) acquire common ways of viewing the world ... (which are) reinforced through institutions like the family, schools, workplace, church, and the government" [12].

**Agency and Epistemology**

To find a philosophy for teaching culture and language, we can look to Van Lier's concept of agency and to theories and studies on epistemology [15]. In order to learn meaningfully, Van Lier suggested that first students look honestly at their own beliefs and values, reevaluate those beliefs and values, and then be receptive to new cultures. Van Lier stressed that self-evaluation (i.e. re-examination) of one's own identity in the classroom is the key to effective learning as it indicates an on-going process- a transformation from one's original stage to another.

Epistemology suggests realms, or stages in an individual's reasoning that could help students be receptive to cultural understanding. In 1970, Perry theorized that college students' journey through nine positions of intellectual and moral development. Baxter-Magolda [13] used the term stages and claimed there were only four (Absolute, Transitional, Independent, and Contextual). Both the transitional stage (where the instructor provides an environment that rewards thinking and logic contrary to the teachers) and the contextual stage (which involves combining what we know with supporting evidence) are advantageous states for students to reevaluate their own cultural identities. To have a truly successful and rewarding language class, the higher stages of epistemology are necessary along with a high level of agency. Magnan offers excellent suggestions for the class time. For this study, number three (Maximize service learning) and number four (Re-orient study abroad toward new community building) are not practical. Although both of these would be highly desirable activities for language and culture learning, there are few opportunities for service learning (number three) when study for the target language is performed in the country of L1. Also, studying abroad (number four) is cost prohibitive for most of the students in this study. Interdisciplinary courses, is a curriculum design project requiring a faculty and administration effort. The remaining includes: (1) authentic documents, (2) virtual communities, (3) reflections on identity, and (4) students' portfolios appeared feasible in the actual classroom. However, due to the time limit in the study, only the first three approaches were utilized.

## 3 Methodology

**Research Site**

The site where the research was conducted is a college of foreign languages in southern Taiwan. There are multiple academic divisions including a two-year college section, a four-year college section and a five-year college section in this school. A sample of an intact class from the four-year college section with 60 students was selected as the research site. This study was implemented in the Language and Culture course, which aimed at enabling students to develop and express their own insights and experiences with respect to different aspects of the relationship between language and culture. To fulfill the goal, it was common for teachers to design relevant activities. In this study, the activities focused on inspiring students to self experience transformation and further re-evaluation of their own cultural identity.

**Participants**

Sixty senior English major students participated in the study. Among them, five participants had had short-term (two weeks to a month) overseas experiences. Additionally, there were two international students from South Korea. These participants' background indicated that some participants had had cross-cultural experiences.

**Cultural Sensitivity Training (CST) Pedagogy**

Magnan's [14] teaching avenues for language and culture framed the CST pedagogy, in which three approaches were adopted. They were (1) authentic documents, (2) virtual communities, and (3) reflections on identity. Based on Magnan's avenues, the instructional content and instructional strategy of CST were developed. For example, authentic documents and virtual communities constructed the CST instructional content. The CST instructional strategies mainly propose to encourage students' reflection on their identities.

**Instructional Content**

Authentic documents involved the materials of experiences (cognitive); beliefs, values and behaviors (cultural anthropology); and daily lives, customs (socio-cultural). A Few Kind Words of Superstition by Davies was a selected article to present the cognitive perspective of culture. The concept of superstition is derived from a universal human nature regardless of race. People should learn cognitively to be aware of the various forms of superstition to enhance their cultural awareness. In his article on the Anthropology of Manners, Hall views culture from the elements of cultural context, cultural space and cultural time. Thus, this article could be suitable material to interpret the unconscious aspect of culture. "Poverty" is a familiar daily-life issue; however, people' understanding of it may vary in accordance with different social contexts. Therefore, Parker's article of What is Poverty was included as the socio-cultural section of the teaching materials.

**Instructional Strategy**

Van Lier's concept of agency and studies on epistemology [15] were our teaching philosophy. The teaching philosophy suggests that students should, first of all, look honestly at their own beliefs and values, then re-evaluate them and finally, be receptive to new culture. In the light of the teaching philosophy,

**Data Collection Process**

The study began from the end of September, 2010, to the middle of January, 2011. Data were collected in two stages. In the first period of the Language and Culture course, the conceptualization of the cultural sensitivity training (CST) tasks was introduced to the participants as a course-oriented activity. Additionally, a cultural awareness questionnaire with the category of awareness of attitude was administered to the participants as a pre-test. This was the first stage of data collection. In the following sixteen weeks, all the participants underwent the CST tasks pedagogy. In the seventeenth week, the cultural awareness questionnaire with the three categories embedded was administered to the participants as a post-test. Furthermore, the answers to a survey question about students' opinions to the CST tasks pedagogy were collected. This was the second stage of data collection.

**Data Analysis**

A repeated measure design was employed to evaluate the pre- and post-test regarding the category of awareness of attitude. Additionally, it was used to estimate the impact of CST on both the students' cultural cognition and on their cultural experiences. Descriptive statistics was utilized to measure students' opinions of the CST from the aspects of the instructor's attitudes and classroom activities.

A constant comparison method was consulted to analyze the survey question. The data were analyzed under the following procedure: first, open coding and memos were two major initial analytical processes to generate concepts according to the properties and dimensions of the data. With the emergence of concepts, axial coding was used to link the relationships among concepts either horizontally or vertically. Thus, categories or mini-themes appeared. Integrative diagrams were used to show how sub-categories and concepts were related to the core category. After this, the data were revisited and reexamined for verification.

# 4 Results

A repeated measure design was utilized to measure whether students enhanced their cultural awareness after performing CST tasks. The result indicated that after students underwent the CST tasks ($M = 3.9093$), their cultural awareness was significantly enhanced ($t = -14.800$, $p < .05$). The mean scores on the pre-test of their cultural awareness were 3.2741.

As for the impact of CST tasks on students' cultural cognition and on their interactions with individuals from other cultural backgrounds, a repeated measure design was again used to estimate whether CST tasks had a significant impact on these factors. Results demonstrated that CST tasks did not significantly increase students' cultural cognition ($t = 1.461$, $p > .05$). However, the CST tasks did significantly promote students' reflection on how culture affected their beliefs, attitudes and behaviors ($p < .05$). The mean scores of the pre-test were 2.68 and those of the post-test were 4.56.

In view of the impact of CST tasks on students' cultural interactions with individuals from other cultural backgrounds, the results indicated that CST tasks significantly motivated students' interactions with these people. For example, results of the post-test indicated that these participants were willing to offer more assistance to individuals of certain cultural backgrounds, felt comfortable working with them and became more patient with them. CST significantly enhanced students' cultural awareness. Constant comparison was employed to analyze how students experienced the stages of absolute conviction, transition and context qualitatively. Two themes emerged from the data pool of the survey question, which helped to explain students' experiences from the absolute stage to the transitional stage and even to the contextual stage. They were1. students' tolerance of other cultures (n = 50); and2. students' acceptance of other cultures (n = 40).

Descriptive statistics was used to measure the participants' opinions of their instructor's attitudes in the classroom and the CST activities. Students highly confirmed their instructor's attitudes (M = 4.0750) and CST activities (M = 4.3056). In the category of the instructor's attitudes, students showed a very positive view to their instructor's respect for differences in individuals from diverse cultural backgrounds (M = 4.52, see Table 1). However, students did not seem to be very sure about whether their instructor's behaviors may have made students from certain cultural backgrounds feel excluded (M = 3.92). Additionally, students were not very sure about whether it was the instructor's responsibility to accommodate students' needs (M = 3.63). Students tended to hold different views on this issue; (the standard deviation was set at .863). That is, some students believed that the instructor was responsible to accommodate students' needs, while others thought otherwise.

In view of the CST activities, students made very positive comments. For instance, they felt comfortable discussing cultural issues in the classroom activities (M = 4.23), which helped them feel comfortable interacting with people from different cultural backgrounds (M = 4.37). To sum up, these experiences they believed greatly helped them to interact with others (M = 4.32).

## 5 Conclusions

The study probed the efficacy of CST tasks in the EFL language and culture class. The results suggested the following:

(1) CST tasks significantly enhanced students' cultural awareness, especially from the aspect of students' interactions with individuals from different cultural backgrounds.
(2) Students were motivated to interact with others through their instructor's attitudes and CST activities.
(3) Students were highly confirmed by their instructor's respectful attitudes toward other cultures; and
(4) The CST activities in the light of the students' personal reports accelerated them to transform. They transformed themselves from the absolute stage to the transitional stage and even to the contextual stage.

The results above also generate some issues for discussion. First, CST tasks ensure an effective pedagogical suggestion: transformation. Second, CST tasks have a potential for learner autonomy. Finally, teacher development in language and culture classroom is a necessity.

**CSTT Ensures an Effective Pedagogical Suggestion: Transformation**

The pedagogical design of cultural sensitivity training (CST) tasks emphasized the instructional strategies, encouraging students to reflect constantly. Results of the cultural awareness questionnaire indicated that CST successfully motivated students to reflect how culture affected their beliefs ($p < .05$). In addition, the results of the survey question indicated that the pedagogical design of CST transformed students to the transitional or even to the contextual stage. The findings are consistent with previous studies on effective learning philosophy. As Van Lier [15] claimed an on-going process – a transformation from one's original stage to another – is an effective way of learning. Students' transformation to the appreciation and acceptance of other cultures strongly suggested that CST can be an effective way to teach language and culture.

**CST Has a Potential for Learner Autonomy**

Three findings from the results suggest that CST has a potential for learner autonomy. First, results of the cultural awareness questionnaire indicated that CST tasks significantly promoted students to reflect how culture affects their beliefs, attitudes and behaviors. This finding suggests that CST has a potential to breed learning autonomy. Researches on learning autonomy hold that autonomous learners are "motivated learners" as they internalize the abilities of "reflection and analysis" (Little). Second, students tended to hold different views on the instructor's responsibility to accommodate students' needs (M = 3.63; standard deviation = .863). It seemed that some students believed that teachers should take the responsibility to fulfill students' needs; however, others thought otherwise. Some students might think that they, as learners, should take the responsibility of "independent learning" instead. This independent learning echoed the essence of learner autonomy, "the ability to take charge of one's own learning" [16].

Third, results of the significantly positive impact of CST tasks on students' interactions with individuals from other cultural backgrounds also support the fact that CST has a potential for learner autonomy. Holec [16] claimed that developing a learner autonomy approach will enable a person "to act more responsibly in running the affairs of the society in which he lives" (p. 1). Students' personal reports, after they had undergone CST, indicated that they may have the potential to run the affairs of society. For example, they were willing to offer more assistance to individuals of certain cultural backgrounds, became more patient with people from different cultural backgrounds and felt more comfortable working with these people.

**The Necessity of Teacher Development in the Language and Culture Class**

Results of the participants' opinions of their instructor's attitudes in the classroom indicated that the participants were approved of their instructor's attitudes (M = 4.0750). For example, the participants showed a very positive view of their instructor's respect for the differences in individuals from diverse cultural backgrounds (M = 4.52). However, these participants were not sure whether their instructor's attitudes may have made students from certain cultural backgrounds feel excluded (M = 3.92).

These findings suggest a necessity of teacher development for the course of Language and Culture. Byram and Kramsch [2] claimed that teacher development such as creating a forum can avoid teachers' "falling into historical revisionism or falling prey to stereotypes" (p. 32). In view of falling into historical revisionism, they recommended that teachers should make good use of diverse sources such as "newspapers, novels, pamphlets, essays . . . to gain an understanding of times and places different from their own" (p. 82). Teachers' development of historical cultural awareness may benefit them to treat stereotypes differently, from complete "rejection" to use with "caution" or use with "explicit reflection".

**Limitations and Future Implications**

Fruitful results are gained from the pedagogical design of CST tasks. This study, however, is not exhaustive. There are two major limitations in the study. First, the cultural awareness questionnaire needs to be enriched. That is, literature, which entails cultural awareness, cultural sensitivity, cultural knowledge and cultural skills, needs to be reviewed to develop a more rounded questionnaire. Second, to make the research method more complete, a triangulation for data collection and data analysis is necessary. In this study, a revised questionnaire and a survey question are the sources for data collection and analysis. Interviews should be included to access the validity and credibility of the study.

**Web-Based Application in Cultural Sensitive Learning**

As Magnan suggested virtual community is conducive to cultural sensitive learning. In other words, intercultural exchanges are the key elements of cultural sensitive learning because in the multicultural environment, the intercultural exchanges can be the "authentic documents." By means of the authentic document exchanges, students' identities can be sensitively reflected. In the future, we strongly suggest that cross culture exchanges can be attainable through web-based application such as cross cultural distance learning, where a virtual community will be created in future.

## References


1. Gerchman, Y., Weiss, R.: Teaching bacteria a new language. PNAS **101**(8), 2221–2222 (2004)
2. Byram, K., Kramsch, C.: Why is it so difficult to teach language as culture. Ger. Q. **81**(1), 20–34 (2008)
3. Belz, J.A., Thorne, S.L. (eds.): Internet-Mediated Intercultural Foreign Language Education. Heinle & Heinle, Boston (2005)
4. Belz, J.A., Müller-Hartmann, A.: Teachers as intercultural learners: negotiating German-American telecollaboration along the institutional fault line. Mod. Lang. J. **87**(1), 71–89 (2003)
5. Ware, P., Kramsch, C.: Toward an intercultural stance: teaching German and English through telecollaboration. Mod. Lang. J. **89**(2), 190–205 (2005)
6. Hall, E.T.: The Silent Language. Doubleday, New York (1959)
7. Hall, E.T.: The Hidden Dimension. Doubleday, New York (1966)
8. Hall, E.T.: Beyond Culture. Doubleday, New York (1976)
9. Bates, D.G., Plog, F.: Cultural Anthropology. McGraw-Hill, New York (1990)
10. Holland, D., Quinn, N.: Cultural Modes in Language & Thought. Cambridge Press, New York (1987)

11. De Castro, P., Sercu, L., Garcia, M.C.M.: Integrating language-and-culture teaching: an investigation of Spanish teachers' perceptions of the objectives of foreign language education. Intercult. Educ. **15**(1), 91–104 (2004)
12. Kramsch, C.: Language and Culture. Oxford University Press, Oxford (1998)
13. Baxter-Magolda, M.B.: Knowing and Reasoning in College: Gender Related Patterns in Students' Intellectual Development. Jossey-Bass Inc., San Francisco (1992)
14. Magnan, S.S.: The unfulfilled promise of teaching for communicative competence: insights from sociocultural theory. In: Lantolf, J., Poehner, M. (eds.) Sociocultural Theory and the Teaching of Second Language, pp. 351–379. Equinox, Sheffield (2008)
15. Walqui, A., Van Lier, L.: Scaffolding the Academic Success of Adolescent English Language Learner: A Pedagogy of Promise. WestEd, San Francisco (2008)
16. Holec, H.: Autonomy and Foreign Language Learning. Pergamon, Oxford (1981)

# Web-Based-Learning via Tajen Cloud

Wuu-Wen Lin[1(✉)] and Chiou-Mei Chen[2]

[1] Department of Computer Science and Information Engineering, Tajen University, Yanpu Township, Taiwan
wuuwen@mail.tajen.edu.tw

[2] Department of Information Applications and Management, Tajen University, Yanpu Township, Taiwan
chmach@mail.tajen.edu.tw

**Abstract.** According to the development project of Tajen University, we built a web based learning system for the faculty and students. The orientation of this project is highlighted in three major domains: cloud campus, mobile communication, and local content. The content of the cloud campus, we established a cloud environment as the platform for all services on the campus. The next one is the mobile communication which provides the usage of those intelligent mobile devices, such as smart phones and tablets, to access the cloud services. For the learning characteristics of TAJEN University, the proposed issues are course like mobile commerce and counseling resources to help students self-learning for pursuing his/her professional license/certificate. For the characteristics of local communities, the proposed local contents are the southern part of Taiwan area tourist guider's training. Right now, we finished to build a cloud-based computer classroom by using the desktop-cloud technology. We also provided a cloud-based Internet-of-Things (IOT) living laboratory for the special interesting students to do their ad hoc programs. We also extended the scope of the assessment and provided a new interactive assessment function in a future shop and a new Hakka culture-innovation platform.

**Keywords:** Cloud · Internet of Things · Web-based education

## 1 Introduction

During the last decade, we faced a tremendous rapid change in the knowledge domain, especially in the field of informatics. The concept of cloud computing [1–5] becomes one of the most important issues that everybody has to envisage. Traditionally, people gain their knowledge from well-prepared courses at schools [6]. Through specially designed textbooks, students learned some skills from their teachers by means of a blackboard. However, electronic devices change the situation. An overhead projector and slides replaced the blackboard. Further, when personal computers become popular, students' learning becomes more efficient through these computer-aided devices.

In fact, everybody enjoys the advantages which the electronic devices offered in learning. Therefore, almost in every classroom, there is a personal computer and an overhead projector provided. Relative to the traditional classroom, either the content of the teaching content or the quality is improved very much. The learning efficiency is


D.K.W. Chiu et al. (Eds.): ICWL 2013 Workshops, LNCS 8390, pp. 253–258, 2015.
DOI: 10.1007/978-3-662-46315-4_26

increased, accordingly. However, when you leaved out of the classroom, all the learning profits are stepped back to its original position. The prevalence of the webs soon overwhelmed all the fields of the education [7]. The popularity of mobile devices such as smart phone or tablet or personal digital assistance (PDA) has promoted a versatility of learning. Therefore, we knew that with the aid of the web networks, learning must be ubiquitous. The teaching material is not limited in a textbook. The studying place is not restrained in the classroom. The schemes in the web side are taken as topics of discussion in the meeting or debating cases. Hence, in the past three years, we proposed to found a Tajen Cloud as a learning aid for the faculty and students.

There are several problems following up. The first problem we envisaged is the capacity of the server provided on the campus is not qualified to support the requirement. The next one is the bandwidth of the campus intranet. Also, there is an urgent need for a ubiquitous campus. Obviously, all the dreams become reality when the Tajen Cloud is available.

## 2 The Content of the Cloud

The Tajen Cloud was founded within two years. In the first year, there are 12 servers constructed with 96 CPU cores, 96 GB random access memory (RAM) and 48 TB disk-array capacities at its initial stage. After that, we increased the amount of the RAM up to 288 GB at the end of the first year. During the next year, there are more 12 new servers added with 288 CPU cores and 480 GB RAM. Right now, the infrastructure of the whole system has total 24 servers with 384 CPU cores and 768 GB RAM. Consequently, the total capacity of storage is extended to 64 TB in the Tajen Cloud system.

There are several subprojects in this program. The first subproject is to construct an ad hoc cloud classroom for the faculty and students as a special purposed development center. By means of the computational power of these cloud servers, a virtualized learning laboratory was established. Mainly, a desktop cloud technique is developed and via the use of the technique, the task of configuring an information system becomes easier. Thus, the administrator can rapidly provide desktops for students on any device, anywhere, without the upfront costs and complexity of traditional desktop virtualization. Also, the university can deploy new services quicker. More important, such services can be used to improve the teaching qualities as they can be easily extended and shared as the cloud platform where they reside.

Through the cloud computing techniques, all the distributed personal computers in classrooms can be connected via networks. Surely, the security of the cloud is a key issue of deeply concern [8, 9]. The Tajen Cloud can store a vast teaching material and sources and can serve as a platform for sharing information among teachers and students. Right now, students can access the resources via mobile devices such as intelligent phones, tablets or notebooks anytime, anywhere. An ubiquitous learning system is constructed so that it can provide the students to do their learning without traditional restrictions. Such a scenario is an embodiment of "internet + virtual classroom + digital learning = integrated cloud digital learning."

This subproject also establish an experimental virtual teaching laboratory at the department of Computer Science and Information Engineering. This laboratory provides high speed network connections and personal cloud desktop services using cloud desktop techniques. This prototype laboratory will be extended to include all the PC classrooms in the c College of Smart Living at Tajen University as a local cloud service system. Also a prototype cloud management system that facilitates the management of the cloud services is developed.

In this subproject, we build an Intelligent Internet of Thing Cloud Laboratory (IIOTC Lab.). Based on the facilities built on the building of College of Smart Living at Tajen University is exploited as a living laboratory of part of the IIOTC Lab. Wireless communication facilities are implemented for environmental control of the living lab. which collects factors such as temperature, humility, light and air circulation etc. The lab supports for the data collection through CAN Bus, Zigbee, RFID, and/or GPIO based on a system build on an ARM/Android embedded development board.

A curriculum with credit points for the cloud IOT project is also proposed. The curriculum is opened for all the students of the college of management and informatics. Besides, the Department of Computer Science and Information Engineering (DCSIE) opened more then ten courses based on the IIOTC Lab. through this academic year. The instruments installed in IIOTC Lab. greatly provide advantages for the specific projects of the students in DCSIE Department.

This subproject is in order to construct continually the school Digital Learning Cloud of license counseling via cloud computing and mobile communications technology. It not only builds continually the certification examination range of cloud-mobile learning laboratory of the first plan phase but also improves the information system functionality of the previous phase. The used scope of professional certification examination learning is extended to that of the Department of Nursing, Tourism Management, and Marketing and Distribution Management. Each license can be used in the interfaces of PC, smart phones and Tablet of Android system. The learning formats are divided into the PDF file, browsing e-book, interactive e-book as well as the scoring system function which cannot be provided in e-book for each interface. The above results promote the completeness of scope and system function of license tutoring learning cloud.

This subproject under the original planning program is to build a Cloud Business and Cultural Marketing Lab. named as: “Intelligent Future Store” and “Hakka Cultural Navigation Platform”. The former includes remodeling an ordinary classroom, installing the RFID reader and automatic control system, touch Checkout processing system and etc.. In addition, the software installed in the “cloud” server system includes mobile payment system and the cultural fields’ navigation platform. Acrylic teaching billboards were also set up in the laboratory settings. These software and hardware has been used in the fall semester of 2012: E-commerce (3 credits), Retail Management (2 credits), Division of Continuing Education E-commerce (3 credits), Introduction to tourism (2 credits), Division of Continuing Education tourism training (2 credits). These programs enable students to learn theory from practicing, and to experience and understand how enterprises and cultural tourism deploy innovative business models. Enhancing students’ learning is the major step to reach the goal of technical and vocational education. Seminars and conferences were also held for faculty members and students to learn so as to enhance their professional competence (Fig. 1).

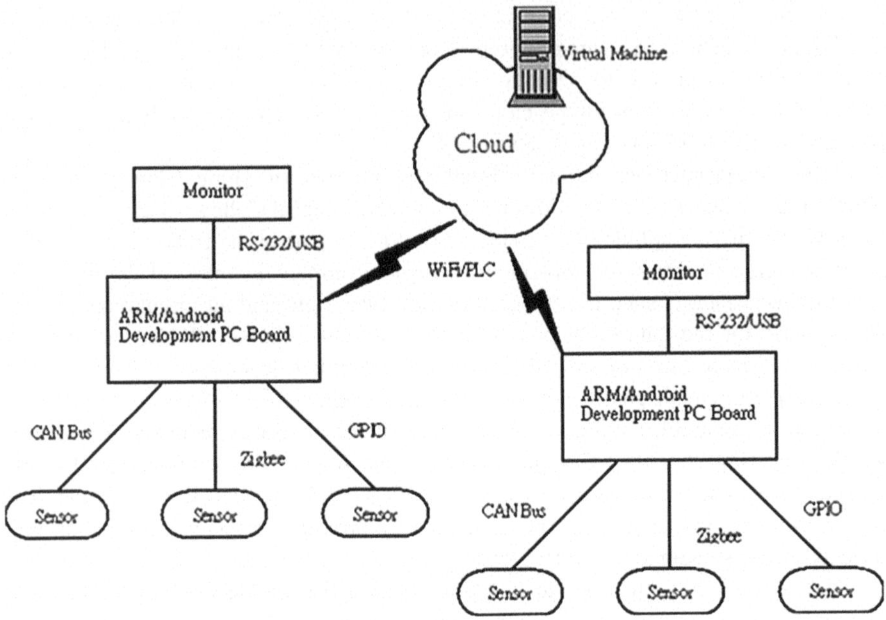


**Fig. 1.** The architecture of the Internet of Things

## 3 Web-Based Education on Campus

Except the hardware provided, we offered some software operation system. The Ubuntu 12.04 is used as the host operation system (OS) for the system. The KVM is associated with this OS for the reality of the virtuality. Hence, it served as an infrastructure as a service system for the faculty and students. Right now, we have 110 virtual machines operated on the system (2012/11/28). The usages of those virtual machines are listed on Table 1. Among them, there are 12 machines are used to support the operation of the subprojects. Most of them are used to support the teaching programs and the students' projects. The amount of them is 78.

There is several achievements worth to be mentioned here. In this Tajen Cloud, we offered a "Virtual classroom of the cloud." In this classroom, the students can access the operational environment of the virtual machine of the Tajen Cloud via a remote wire connection or wireless access protocol. The Laboratory of the Internet of Things (IOT) offered the students to submit all of their experimental data to the Tajen Cloud server. Also, the students used the databank of the Tajen Cloud to study. The feedback evaluation system helps the student by giving them a real time response for their performance. By the way, a mobile electronically smart business system and an automatically platform for the tourist guider are provided in the server of the Tajen Cloud (Fig. 2).

**Table 1.** The virtual machine used on campus (2012/11/28)

| Usage | Quantity |
|---|---|
| Support teaching | 67 |
| Students' project | 11 |
| Faculty research | 18 |
| Support subprojects | 12 |
| otherwise | 2 |
| Total | 110 |

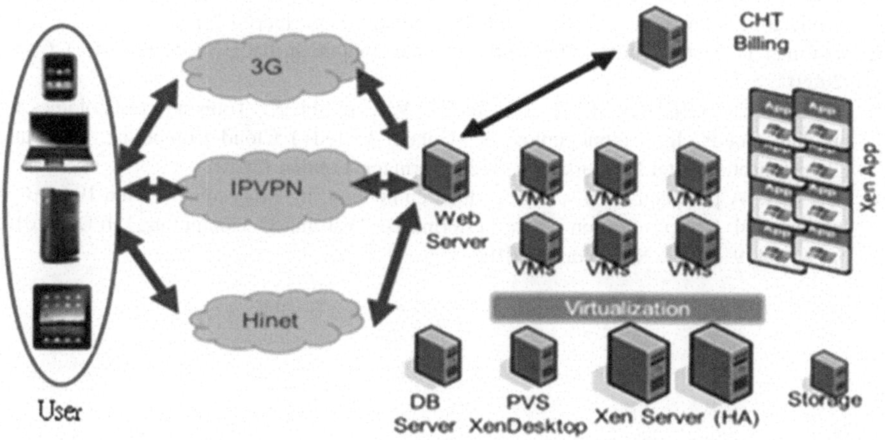


**Fig. 2.** The architecture of the special cloud classroom

## 4 Conclusion and Future Perspectives

In this paper, we study the requirement of the web based system on Tajen campus and set up the infrastructure of the Tajen Cloud to satisfy it. The TAJEN Cloud system had provides 24 servers, 384 CPU cores, 768 GB RAM and a total capacity of storage of 64 TB. It replaces the traditional teaching and learning style on campus. In the future, we expect that it can offer a ubiquitous learning environment for the faculty and students.

**Acknowledgement.** The authors acknowledge the financial support of this study from Ministry of Education.

## References

1. Dikaiakos, M., Katsaros, D., Mehra, P., Pallis, G., Vakali, A.: Cloud computing: distributed internet computing for it and scientific research. IEEE Internet Comput. **13**(5), 10–13 (2009)
2. Wikipedia (2011). http://en.wikipedia.org/wiki/cloudcomputing

3. Vaquero, L.M., Rodero-Merino, L., Caceres, J., Lindner, M.: A break in the clouds: towards a cloud definition. SIGCOMM Comput. Commun. Rev. **39**(1), 50–55 (2009)
4. Sun Microsystems, Introduction to cloud computing architecture (2009). http://www.bitpipe.com/detail/RES/1245442513540.html
5. Jin, H., Ibrahim, S., Bell, T., Gao, W., Huang, D., Wu, S.: Cloud types and services. In: Furht, B., Escalante, A. (eds.) Handbook of Cloud Computing, pp. 335–355. Springer, US (2010)
6. Kovachev, D., Cao, Y., Klamma, R., Jarke, M.: Learn-as-you-go: new ways of cloud-based micro-learning for the mobile web. In: Leung, H., Popescu, E., Cao, Y., Lau, R.W., Nejdl, W. (eds.) ICWL 2011. LNCS, vol. 7048, pp. 51–61. Springer, Heidelberg (2011)
7. Chan, C.-T., Chiu, D.K.: Web 2.0 with alert support for busy parents in suzuki method of children music teaching. In: Leung, H., Popescu, E., Cao, Y., Lau, R.W., Nejdl, W. (eds.) ICWL 2011. LNCS, vol. 7048, pp. 62–71. Springer, Heidelberg (2011)
8. Kaufman, L.: Data security in the world of cloud computing. IEEE Secur. Priv. **7**(4), 61–64 (2009)
9. Jin, H., Ibrahim, S., Bell, T., Qi, L., Cao, H., Wu, S., Shi, X.: Tools and technologies for building clouds. In: Antonopoulos, N., Gillam, L. (eds.) Cloud Computing. Computer Communications and Networks, pp. 3–20. Springer, London (2010)
10. Lee, C.A.: A perspective on scientific cloud computing. In: Proceedings of the 19th ACM International Symposium on High Performance Distributed Computing, HPDC 2010, pp. 451–459. ACM, New York (2010)

# Complementary to Web-Based Education on Summer Camp of Marine Energy

Chung-Liang Chen and Wuu-Wen Lin(✉)

Department of Computer Science and Information Engineering,
Tajen University, Pingtung County, Taiwan
clchen@mail.tajen.edu.tw, wuuwen@tajen.edu.tw

**Abstract.** While network become one of the major sources of student access to knowledge, on which also build community relations? Students can search the Web for scholarly information, or use the Internet to discuss the issues already published or make friends. But from this questionnaire, found on educational activities, teachers on students' development of knowledge, now continues to be act an important influence and function role. The major motivation is primarily due to teacher recommendation, announcement on school web and peer to peer influence are second motivated choice for participate.

The web setup for energy education may be not time-consuming and do not need huge money supported. The web-based system of marine energy education spread the knowledge but it did not realize the concepts about renewable Energy. In the promotion of students' renewable energy knowledge activities are well complementary to web-based education.

**Keywords:** Green energy · Marine energy · Web-based education

## 1 Preliminary

Energy is the driving force behind economic development and enhance the quality of human life an indispensable basic elements. In recent years, the energy crisis has been the lingering worry, power generation and petrochemical materials on the ecological and environmental impacts of nuclear power generation, driven by desire of the human quest for green energy, and in a variety of green energy, one of the most attractive for the development of marine energy.

Taiwan itself is a state surrounded by the ocean. Sea is a treasure trove of huge renewable energy potential; only kinetic energy of ocean waves, tides, currents, and sea temperature difference, salinity difference can amount up to astronomical figures. Non-renewable energy sources such as coal, oil, limited reserves, mining is less. Thus, the growing problem of energy supply, alternative energy, clean energy, green energy important research directions of the development of mankind, cannot be ignored.

Many of our patterns of learning involve some form of face to face communication between learners and teachers. The World Wide Web has become a medium of education in recent years. A number of models of web-based learning have been used.

In recent year, as the Government and civil society's focus on energy-related research and investment, the webs setup for energy education has established.


D.K.W. Chiu et al. (Eds.): ICWL 2013 Workshops, LNCS 8390, pp. 259–264, 2015.
DOI: 10.1007/978-3-662-46315-4_27

For general purpose, for example, the webs of ENERGY EDUCATION [1] and Renewable Energy [2], for specific topics, such as marine energy [3]. Internet is an open platform, youth have a strong need for self-expression, and the need to be accepted by the public attention, and the Internet offers many also provide a platform for young people to play themselves. Vocational high school students in this study to explore the objects and activities through student participation in marine energy knowledge, explore current learning of higher vocational students ' energy knowledge accepted attitudes of high school in order to better understand youth's internet behavior about access of energy education.

## 2 Result

Through three days and two nights with a careful arrangement of marine energy experience camp, organizing energy expert lectures, visits and other activities, High school students in higher vocational colleges Preliminary comprehensive experience of the marine energy technology development. After of the camp, conducted a questionnaire survey to understand the participative motivation are due to traditional suggestion by teachers, or on internet bulletin due to peer's invitation.

High school students are totally 71 students, including high school 27 People (38 %) and higher vocational education 44 people (62 %). They are 60 boys (85 %) and 11girls (15 %). Region distribution of students is shown in the Fig. 1.

The reason of this biased phenomenon can be attribute to the location of the activities mainly hold at south part of Taiwan. From Fig. 1, the students living at south region including Tainan, Kaohsiung, and Pingtung County is 93 %, in Central accounted for 4.2 %. It clearly shows that the energy campaign heavily affected by the region where the students are living. Marine energy educational outreach is just getting started; bet a great deal of effort is still required at the current stage, enhancing energy education. Experience camp further ways to attract students in different regions to participate in, is the positive direction in which to work.

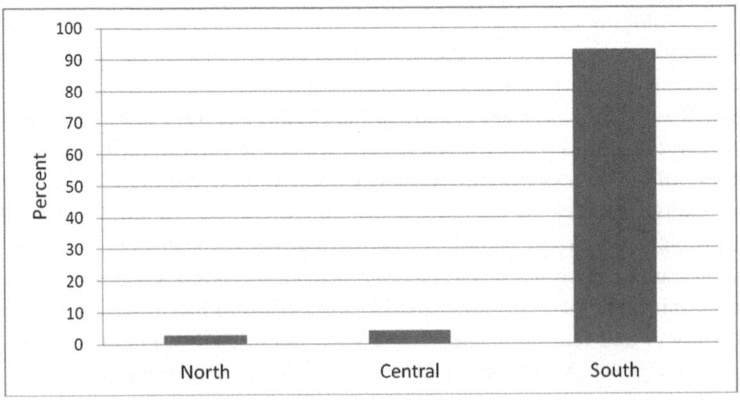


**Fig. 1.** Region distribution of students

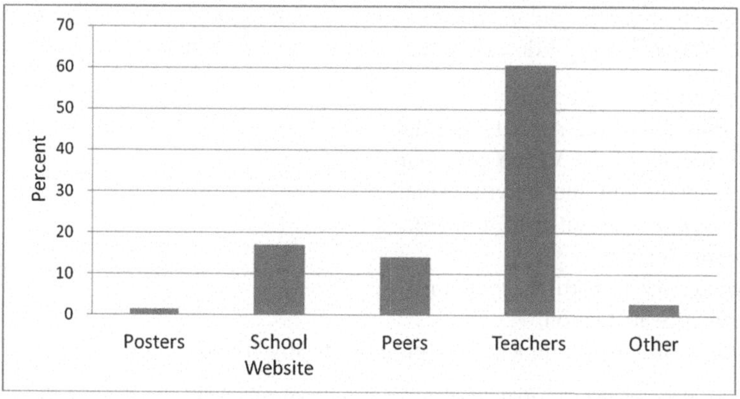


**Fig. 2.** Information source distribution

Wu [4] concluded that the marine energy education in current status have five strategies, three of which including, to set up the nationwide marine education center, to put marine education in the teacher education curriculum, to construct the marine education network for nonadjacent-sea schools. The camp can be used as partial materials of school teaching, arranged to attend the students to visit green energy research units, listen to lectures given by energy experts.

Figure 2 shows participation Motivation of students. It displays that teachers are the major source, about 61 %. School website and student peers are about 31 %. A group of youth with similar age will make the formation of peer groups. In traditional societies, they often depend on the geographic or situational constraints, such as the same schools or near neighbors, could gather in a particular geographical environment. Because of the limited environment such as geographical factors, or institutional factors such as school education, the teenager peer group for identity, not necessarily meet the real desire. Now, the prevalence of Internet, for this time is in the pursuit of self-identity, independent teenagers, they are very curious and willing to try a variety of new communication technologies, thus making the Internet continue to influence the role in which gradually spread into all aspects of daily life in adolescents. Network features, in which the young people to get a lot of satisfaction, such as experience, emotional sharing, exchange of views, lifestyle information obtained, but also to make a wide range of users. The network has become one of the major sources of students' access to knowledge, on which to build community relations. Even some of them got Internet addiction; they lived in the virtual world. But from this questionnaire on knowledge camp activity, although the web-based education has become the major source of the new generation of students to obtain new knowledge, but the traditional role of teachers is still the mainstay. "Youth is not as ignorant as we think their thoughts than we often imagine. Direct to the effect sometimes did not receive advice or guidance, companionship, to listen, to clarify their ideas, or to allow them in the face of e in the deluge of information, equip yourself stronger, more competence and judgment for network world" [5].

The questionnaire's goal intended to know student's satisfaction degree on Summer Camp of Marine Energy Education; there are 9 items as follows:

(1) Effect of the propaganda,
(2) Appropriate of the Activity schedule,
(3) Appropriate of the Venue arrangements,
(4) Satisfaction with the activities offered,
(5) The lecture's overall performance,
(6) Benefits for me,
(7) I would like to participate again,
(8) Means of satisfaction,
(9) I would like to recommend this program to my friends.

The average scores of satisfaction degree is shown in Table 1 (score 1 to 5, 1 means very disagree, 2 disagree, 3 no opinion, 4 agree, 5 strongly agree).

**Table 1.** Average of satisfaction degree

| Items | Mean | Standard deviation |
|---|---|---|
| 1. Effect of the propaganda | 3.92 | 0.84 |
| 2. Activity schedule is appropriate | 4.11 | 0.85 |
| 3. Venue arrangement is appropriate | 4.3 | 0.73 |
| 4. Satisfaction with the activities offered | 4.2 | 0.78 |
| 5. The lecture's overall performance | 4.24 | 0.86 |
| 6. Benefits for me | 4.54 | 0.53 |
| 7. I would like to participate again, | 4.47 | 0.63 |
| 8. Means of satisfaction | 4.49 | 0.63 |
| 9. I would like to recommend this camp to my friends | 4.51 | 0.69 |

Review item (1) to (9), in addition to the average of item (1) Propaganda is 3.92; item (2) to item (9) are greater than 4.1. But compared with the result shown in Fig. 2, the source of information for participants is the teachers 61 %, school Web sites 17 % and peers 14 %. The item (1) satisfaction degree of Propaganda is lower than the others due to the teachers are the major motivation for students.

Item (6) about benefit for students has the average score 4.54, shows that the camp, in the promotion of high school students' energy education is positive. Guide students to reflect on the energy crisis. Exploring the way, where is or what is human energy and alternative energy sources. In the human quest for clean and sustainable energy, marine energy, one of green energy, can promote more energy knowledge through learning activities to enhance students understanding of marine energy.

By items (7), (8), and (9) satisfaction degree average near 4.5, it shows positive on the camp. "one of the typical psychological characteristics of adolescents is active thinking, quick-agile, with a spirit of adventure, anything new, they are bold pursuit of new knowledge, the reception of new technologies faster, with strong creativity. So many adolescents of the N generation retained solipsistic consciousness on "I play, therefore

I am.", that they are really longing for" [6]. Therefore, from Table 1, marine energy education activities for Senior and Vocational High School Students, in addition to setting the web-based education, experience camp held are in favor of a positive meaning.

## 3 Conclusion

The result, boys are about 85 % and girls are 15 % is close to the conclusion made by Ku and Tseng. The most commonly engaged leisure activities for senior and vocational high school students involved static leisure activities, whereas male students of senior and vocational high schools prefer outdoor leisure activities and female students of senior and vocational high schools prefer indoor leisure activities [7].

Many educators point out the importance of interaction in high quality online education. The keys to the learning process are the interactions among students themselves, the interactions between faculty and students, and the collaboration in learning that results from these interactions [8]. Social networking services is a very hot topic, Network has become an important social choice to participate for student groups. Due to network and get to know their peers to carry out a diverse, coupled with its less restrictive, more selective, so the formation of peer networks, have the opportunity to replace the traditional peer support cannot be given the power. This is a traditional society that never ever a major change occurred.

Due to the camp could be taken as leisure activities. In the study of situation of the participation in leisure activities of teenage students in turn were "entertainment", "recreation", "social contact", "art", "sports", and "skills" [9]. The blocking factors of leisure activities in order were: "constructional", "interpersonal", and "individuals" factors [8]. It means that schools should consider reinforcing students' leisure education. Holding variety leisure programs in school are an important strategy. But participation motivation reveals that the motivation is primarily the teachers, then school website notice, student peers following behind. According Net Value survey report shows that Taiwan's largest user groups were age between 15 to 24 years among adolescents [10]. But from this questionnaire on education purpose activity, although the network has become the main type of activity of the new generation of students to obtain new knowledge, but teachers' influence on the knowledge formation of students is still the mainstay. For teenagers, there is most of the time is in the school environment; they get long time along with the teachers. Therefore teachers' role to guide students to learning knowledge on web is very important.

This experience camp in the improvement of vocational senior middle school students 'understanding of marine energy, is of positive interest. Ocean energy knowledge promotion through activities, such as well-organized camp, can enhance students' awareness and understanding of ocean energy. More able to understand humanity's quest one of the pollution-free and sustainable energy ocean energy significance.

The findings suggest that the significances associated with student learning and satisfaction in web-based education courses, the education program needs to include a significant element of interactions among students themselves, the interactions between teachers and students.

## References

1. Energy education. http://en-energy.ie.ntnu.edu.tw/
2. Renewable energy. http://re.org.tw/
3. http://meterec.ntou.edu.tw/Sea-energy.html/
4. Wu, C.K.: A review on the policy of school marine education in Taiwan (in Chinese). In: 2009 International Symposium on Promotion of Marine Education, pp. 111–132 (2009)
5. http://web.tiec.tp.edu.tw/otiec/teacherland/catalog/upload_file/15602.pdf (in Chinese), vol. 156, pp. 76–79 (2008)
6. Chen, Y.L.: The formation of cyberpeer and its impacts on youth socialization (in Chinese). J. Cyber Cult. Inf. Soc. **3**, 149–181 (2002)
7. Ku, C.T., Tseng, Y.C.: A study of current leisure activity participation and leisure constraint factors in senior and vocational high school students from miaoli county (in Chinese). Yu Da Acad. J. **30**, 75–102 (2012)
8. Palloff, R.M., Pratt, K.: Building Learning Communities in Cyberspace. Jossey-Bass, San Francisco (1999)
9. Chen, J.H.: A study of barriers and status quo for the teenagers' in cities and countries participating in leisure activities. Master's Thesis of National Taiwan Normal University (2009)
10. Foreseeing Innovative New Digi-services. http://www.find.org.tw/0105/news/0105_news_disp.asp?news_id=1234,2001/08/17

# Web-Based Ubiquitous Learning

Chiou-Mei Chen[1] and Wuu-Wen Lin[2(✉)]

[1] Department of Information Applications and Management, Tajen University, Taiwan, Taiwan
chmach@mail.tajen.edu.tw

[2] Department of Computer Science and Information Engineering, Tajen University, Taiwan, Taiwan
wuuwen@mail.tajen.edu.tw

**Abstract.** Certificates are very important to the students of professional and Technician University. Hence, it is a key issue to create a ubiquitous environment which students can learn in anywhere and anytime. Therefore, the purpose of this study is to construct a web-based learning system on campus through some mobile devices. We integrate several homogeneous or heterogeneous learning management systems (LMS) into this system. The users can login the system from a single sign on portal. He/She can choose different contents of learning material from this system. There will be a corresponding LMS to provide the needed content for each user.

By means the network, the user only needs to concern what he/she really wants to learn. He/She does not need to concern which LMS serves as his/her counterpart and what it can provide. In this study, we design some electronic books which can be used on a personal computer or any mobile device. The evaluation mechanism is also provided to serve the user a variety of learning way. An advanced learning evaluation scheme is designed to enhance the user some extra trial and error trainings. An intelligent methodology is adopted in this evaluation system. We expected that this system can do some favor to the learner through this web-based platform and enjoy the ubiquitous learning.

**Keywords:** Web-based learning · Ubiquitous learning · Learning management system

## 1 Introduction

Because of the prevalence of the colleges, there is a strong competence among job markets. In order to get a better opportunity, all job finders do their best to enrich their ability. Except the diploma, certificates become key issues among all potential candidates. Therefore, it is important to have a learning-aid platform to favor the students getting some professional certificates. Meanwhile, the availability of smart phones and mobile devices like tablets or personal digital assistors (PDA) promote the trend of web-based learning. The infrastructure of the Tajen Cloud was built under such an environment to match the requirement of the ubiquitous learning. The follow out project is to design an electronic learning aid facility to provide the students a trial and errors recursive tool. Obviously, an evaluation modeling scheme and performance


D.K.W. Chiu et al. (Eds.): ICWL 2013 Workshops, LNCS 8390, pp. 265–271, 2015.
DOI: 10.1007/978-3-662-46315-4_28

recording mechanism should be included to increase the learning efficiency. The final goal is to enhance the students' rates of certificates holder.

## 2 Research Objectives

This research is aimed to create a platform for students to do some simulation test for the certificates examination. Hence, the content of the platform is design to match each domain in professional field. The format of the program is modified to fit the ad hoc requirement of these mobile devices. The friendly design is considered not only the limited storage but also its convenience of learning of these mobile devices. The format of the learning package provided some electronic book for simulation test. There are a lot of varied interfaces provided for the choice of the students. On the option of the evaluation schemes, we adopted the artificial intelligence methodology. That is, the degree of toughness of the questionnaires is adjusted automatically by a regressive system according to the performance record of the students. Hence, the learning progress of the students is smoothly enhanced. Further, the learning record is also provided as a portfolio for the students. We expected that the students can earn the joyfulness in person through the variety of the interfaces of the system and formats of the package.

## 3 Research Design

This research employed the following components to design the information system of this research: Windows Server 2008 Operating System [1], Microsoft SQL Server 2008 Database System [2, 3], Eclipse [4, 5], Jsp [4, 5] and Java Script [6, 7] Programming Language…etc.

### 3.1 System Scope

This research employed certification requirements that a university of technology of Taiwan suggested; certification question database include information certification (including 7 kinds of certification question database: Level C technician for computer hardware fabrication, Level B of technician for computer software application, Level C technician for web page design, Level C technician for network installation and Information Technology Expert…etc.), nursing certification (including 12 kinds of certification question database: nursing administration, pathology, obstetrics & gynecology, psychiatry, pharmacology, Community Health Nursing, anatomical physiology, medical-surgical nursing, nursing and nursing techniques, microbiology and immunology, pediatric nursing and other related certification question database that is unclassified…etc.), tourist certification(including two kinds of certification question database: tour guide and tour leader practice) and marketing and distribution certification(including two kinds of certification question database: Corporation assistant E-planner and Level C technician for Chain Store Service).

This system has three available interfaces: the students may use it on smart phone, Tablet PC and PC. Each interface has four available learning formats: PDF, browse type e-book, interactive e-book and function of analogue scoring that e-book system couldn't provide.

Learning port's screens of this system are shown as follows:

(1) **Main screen of the system:**

(2) **Member registration screen:** If you are a new member, you have to register first before entering.

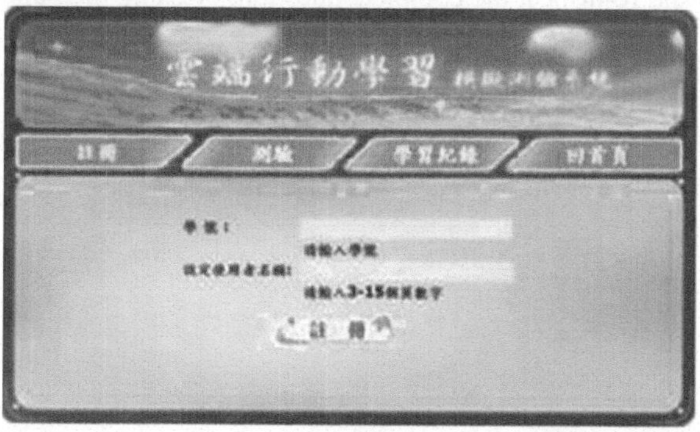


(3) **Test selection:** You may enter the test after selecting the academic category, subject, question amount and difficulty.

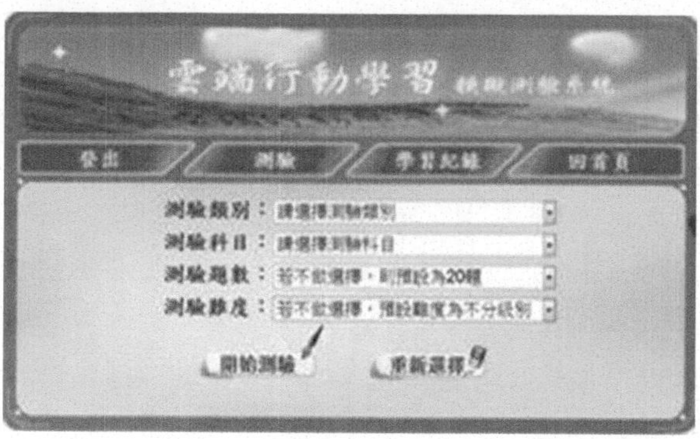

(4) **The screen during the test:** To switch between questions, please press the button of "Previous Question" and "Next Question" to answer; if you are not sure about the answers of the questions, you may press the button of "Mark", it would show red caution at the upper right corner so that you could recheck or answer it again subsequently; pressing the button of "End" to end your test.

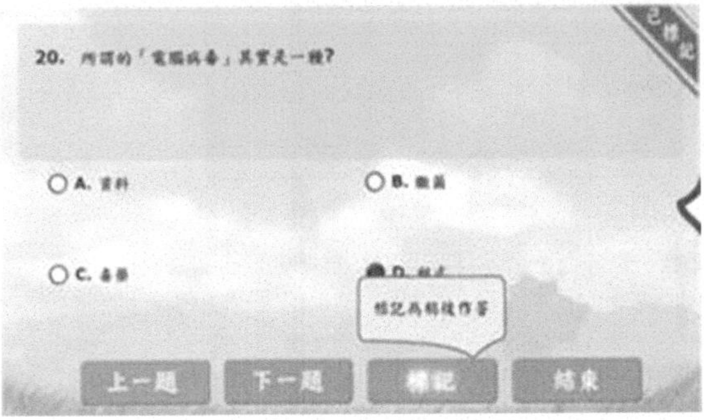


(5) **Browsing the questions screen before submitting the test:** You may browse all the questions of this test before submitting; you may press "Return to Inspect" to return to the question and re-inspect the complete question; pressing the button of "Score" to conduct the scoring.

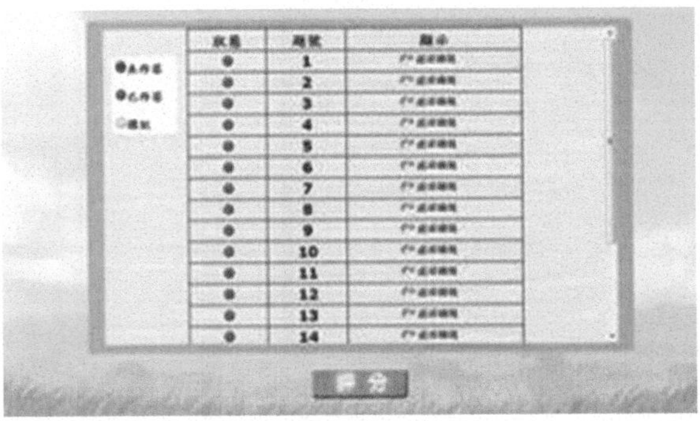


(6) **The score screen after submitted:**

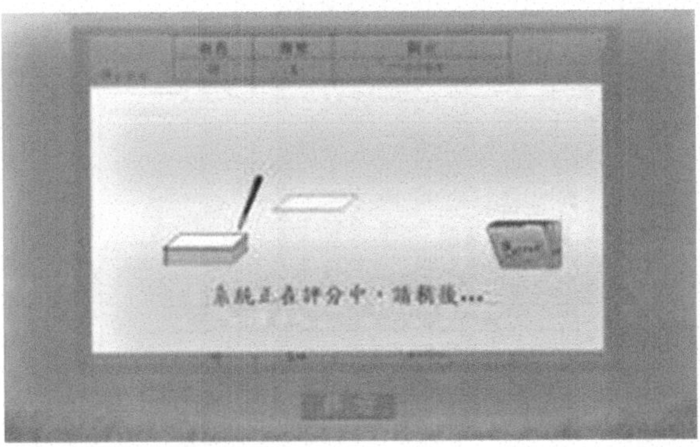

(7) **The screen of learning record:** Showing your personal learning record of past time and this time, this record includes the column of test date, time, subject, question amount that correctly answered and the rate of right answer. You may press "Inspect" to view all the questions of each test. Learners could strengthen themselves through the exercise of trial and error.

(8) **The screen of e-book system:**

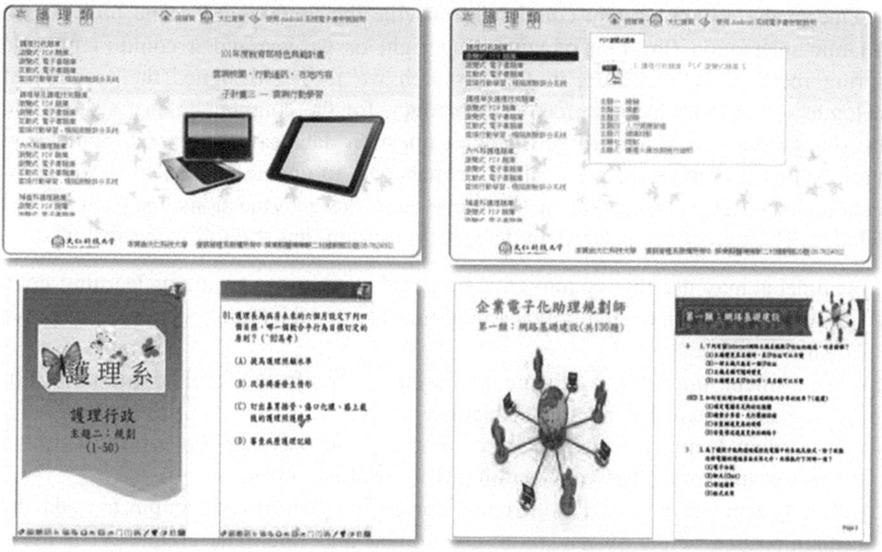

## 3.2 System Features

This system could use on the PC and portable device (Android Tablet PC and Android cell phone). The functions of this system could divide into two main parts, the first part is e-book system, this system could use on a smart phone, Tablet PC and PC. Each using interface has four available learning formats: PDF, browse type e-book, interactive e-book, and the frameworks are shown as Fig. 1.

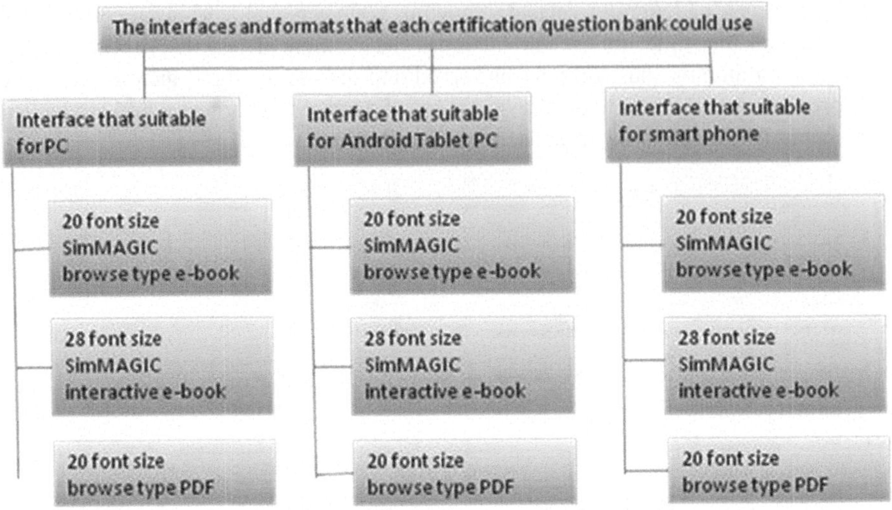


**Fig. 1.** The interfaces and formats that e-book certification question database could use

Due to the e-book system could only provide the functions of static browse and dynamic interaction (the hint of answering right or wrong) and it couldn't provide scoring mechanism, therefore, in this research we further designed the systems of analogue scoring and learning record. Moreover, for the completeness of system, we also designed a sub system of certification question database and used a humanized interface that is convenient for teachers or managers to update and establish the certification categories, subjects that each category includes and questions that each subject includes. Through above subsystem design, this system has the following features:

(1) Students may use this system anywhere and reach to a ubiquitous learning goal.
(2) The users could have multiple learning interfaces and learning formats to improve learning efficiency.
(3) An artificial intelligence scheme was used to classify the level of question difficulty, the system has intelligent feature.
(4) Recording learning record of every learner, you may see the historic learning records and strengthen your learning from trial and error.
(5) The system was uplinked to the cloud computing platform on campus to make the maintenance of the system more convenient and safe. The efficiency of using users' feedback is also improved.
(6) We not only design a user port system of multiple learning, but also further design a humanized background management system to make system's completeness feature prominent.

## 4 Conclusion

In this research, we have already finished the system design by now. In the future, we would further promote users to use, and follow-up to conduct system's use evaluation by Technology Acceptance Model [8], collect data by employing quantitative questionnaire method and conduct the analysis of data using SPSS and structural equation modeling (SEM) implemented in partial least squares (PLS) [9]. Hoping the learners could improve their learning efficiency through this learning system and promote the passing rate of professional certification test.

**Acknowledgement.** The authors acknowledge the financial support of this study from Ministry of Education.

## References

1. Dai, Y.W.: Windows Server 2008 Network Management and IIS Web Sites Setting up, GOTOP Books, Taipei
2. Zeng, Z.Z.: Theory & Practice of Database System 3/e (SQL Server 2008). Hwatai Cultural Publishing House, Taiwan
3. Chen, S.X.: Easy to Get Google Cloud Technology done: Maps.Android.App Engine.Cloud Instance Analysis of SQL and E-commerce. Chuan Hwa Book Co., Ltd, Taiwan
4. Dong, S.W., Wang, W.X., Hong, C.T., Lin, M.Z.: Android 2 SDK Development Introduction & Application. Sung Gang Asset Management Corp.Limited, Taiwan
5. Lin, G.S.: Google! Android 3 Introduction of Cell Phone Application Design (the fourth edition). Sung Gang Asset Management Corp.Limited, Taiwan
6. Duan, W.H.: Java Standard Edition 6 Programmer Certified Professional Exam:Latest Professional Accreditation of OCP Java SE 6 Programmer. GOTOP Books, Taipei
7. Chen, H.A.: New idea Java 7 Program Design Sample Textbook. Flag Publishing Co., Ltd, Taipei
8. Davis, F.D.: Perceived usefulness, perceived ease of use and user acceptance of information technology. MIS Q. **13**, 318–340 (1989)
9. Chin, W.W.: PLS-Graph Manual. University of Calgary (1994) (unpublished)

# A Virtual Reality Based Training System for Cultural Tourism

Shih-Pang Tseng[1], Mei-Wen Huang[2], Hsu-Jung Liu[3](✉), Chao-Cheng Chung[4], and Chun-Mei Chiu[4,5]

[1] Department of Computer Science and Entertainment Technology, Tajen University, Pingtung, Taiwan
tsp@tajen.edu.tw

[2] Department of Management Information Systems, Tajen University, Pingtung, Taiwan
mwhuang@mail.tajen.edu.tw

[3] Department of Digital Arts and Multimedia Design, Tajen University, Pingtung, Taiwan
hjliug@mail.tajen.edu.tw

[4] Department of Tourism Management, Tajen University, Pingtung, Taiwan
{ccchung,cmchiou}@mail.tajen.edu.tw

[5] Institute of Cultural and Creative Industries, Tajen University, Pingtung, Taiwan

**Abstract.** In the 21st century, the application of computer in the learning has been transferred from the computer assisted instruction to the e-learning. In the e-learning age, how to provide more practical training is an important research issue. The web-based VR technology can be used to construct a more practical training environment. This paper proposed an application of the VR 3D-panorama technology on the training of tour guiding. The web-based 3D-panorama training system can be applied in both the classroom and the scenic spot. This study shows that the 3D-panaroma training system can improve the study effectiveness of students of the tour guiding course.

**Keywords:** Virtual reality · E-learning · 3D-panorama

## 1 Introduction

From the past till now, learning is the most important human activity to change behaviors, enhance knowledges and enrich knowledges. In the 21st century, due to the changes of the society and environment, the learning efficiency becomes more and more important. On the other hand, the development of information and communication technologies, especially Internet, provides the facilities to enhance the efficiency of learning. It is one very important research issue to apply the information and communication technologies on learning in modern education.


D.K.W. Chiu et al. (Eds.): ICWL 2013 Workshops, LNCS 8390, pp. 272–277, 2015.
DOI: 10.1007/978-3-662-46315-4_29

In the earlier period of the digital age, Computer Assisted Instruction (CAI) [1–3] is proposed to improve the performance of the teacher's instruction by using the computer as a tool to identify and satisfy the requirement from various learners. In general, the design of CAI program is guided by the stimulus-response cycle based on the behaviorism [4]. The computer is used to instruct, test and provide the feedback to the learner.

Subsequently, the e-learning is proposed to represent the more extensively applying the information and communication technologies , especially the Internet, on the learning. The other theories of education, such as constructivism [5,6], are involved in the design of e-learning application. The constructivism considered that the learning is a self-directed and creative process in which learners construct their own knowledge through their real life experience, such as Fig. 1. It is the best way to learn the knowledge of the specific domain via experience from the specific corresponding context. The prior knowledge of the learner can help the learner as the schema of the similar context to explore more experiences. It is one important function of the instruction to improve the experience accessibility of the context to the learner. In classical classroom, it is difficult to provide the accessibility for the learning of tourism. This paper proposes a tour guiding system which applies the virtual reality technology to improve the accessibility of tourism.

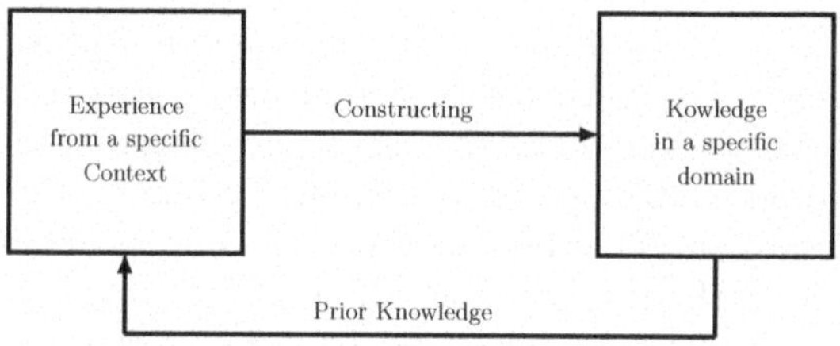


**Fig. 1.** Learning model of constructivism.

The virtual reality (VR) [7] tries to provide closely real experiences by a virtual way. For this goal, VR uses almost all of the current multimedia technologies, such as image, video, sound and text. In this paper, we mainly use the 3D-panorama technology to build the tour guiding system. Interactivity is an important characteristic of VR. VR can not only provide the closely real experiences of the specific context, and VR can change the scene or the viewpoint as the user's wish. In contrast with the traditional video clip, VR can provide more real experiences due to the interactivity. In the past, the VR is directly running on the desktop, laptop, or the other device due to the performance issue. At the moment, the web-based VR technology can be already used to construct a more interactive VR learning environment. The interactions are not only between the VR system and the learner, and among the group of learners.

The remainder of the paper is organized as follows. The related works are in Sect. 2. Section 3 introduced the design of our system. The implementation and experimental results are in Sect. 4. Conclusion is given in Sect. 5.

## 2 Related Works

Geneviève Lucet [8] has proposed a VR application which can discover the knowledge about the cultural heritage by building the 3D representation. This work focus on the building process, and pays less attention on the application of the 3D model. A Collaborative Learning Environment with Virtual Reality (CLEV-R) is proposed by Monahan et al. [9] CLEV-R is a web-based system which uses VR and provides social interaction facilities to support collaboration learning among learners. In essence, the CLEV-R builds a virtual campus in the cyberspace to support the social interaction among learners.

Huang et al. [10] have proposed a work about the influence of the virtual reality learning environments on the learners' attitudes. This work is guided by the constructivism and emphasizes that the VR simulates the real world to trigger the imagination of the learner. Furthermore, this work shows that the effectiveness of the VR in e-learning. Another work is proposed by Jou et al. [11] to illustrate the learning performance of technical skills in the VR learning environment. It shows that the VR can provide more practical trainings and significant assistance to the learner of technical skills.

## 3 System Design

This paper proposes a tour guiding training environment with the VR 3D-panorama technology. The purposes of design are to satisfy the requirements of applications in the classroom and the scenic spot. Figure 2 shows the scenario of applying the proposed 3D-panorama training system on the training of tour guiding in the classroom. The 3D-panorama training system can provide the simulated but close to the real scene for the practical training of tour guiding. The learner can easily do more practices to improve the guiding skill in the classroom.

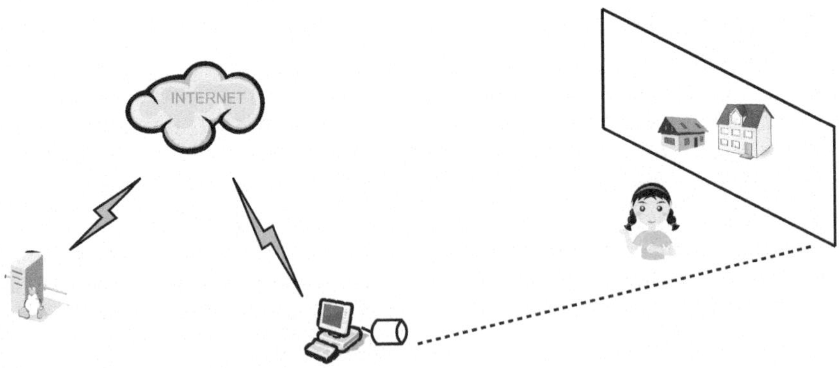


**Fig. 2.** The application of the VR 3D-panorama training system in the classroom.

**Fig. 3.** The application of the VR 3D-panorama training system in the scenic spot.

The second scenario of applying the proposed 3D-panorama training system is shown as Fig. 3. The web-based training system can be accessed by using the smart tablet with the mobile Internet. In the real scenic spot, the 3D-panorama training system can provide the information-rich content for the training of tour guiding.

## 4 Experimental Results

The proposed 3D-panorama training system has been implemented in the cloud of Tajen university, Taiwan. At present, the 3D-panorama training system contains many scenes of the Hakka culture. The 3D-panorama training system is currently used to support the training course of tour guiding in the Department of Tourism Management, Tajen University. Figure 4 shows an example of the 3D-panorama training system about the tour guiding of training house in Hakka region.

The subjects in this study are the undergraduate students who major the Tourism Management in Tajen University, Taiwan. The objective is to investigate (1) whether the 3D tour guiding system can enhance the understanding of the subjects upon the 3D-panorama technology, and (2) whether the 3D-panorama system can assist the learning efficacy in the tour guiding course.

(a) (b) (c) (d)

**Fig. 4.** An example of the 3D-panorama training system.

This study investigated the undergraduate students in the Department of Tourism Management. The valid response are 79 questionnaire, including 29 males and 50 females. We use 5-point Likert Scale to measure the attitude of agreement. Each response obtains a corresponding value to measure the degree of agreement of the response. In this study, the response of **Agree** or **Very Agree** are classified as is consented to the content of the corresponding question.

At the aspect of network using behavior, there are 87 % of subjects often using the Wifi in university, 78 % often using 3G network, 63 % of subjects have purchased online, 93 % can search for lecture materials on-line. Furthermore, 100 % of subjects are used to browse interesting topics on-line which shows that it is common for students to use mobile device on-line and have the habit to surf the Internet frequently.

As to the on-line applications, there are 68 % of subject usually use video service such as Youtube; 37 % of subject use Wikipedia oftenly; 96 % of subjects constantly use community websites, such as Facebook or Google+; 78 % of subjects play online games regularly; and 54 % of subjects regards Internet is the mainly learning tool. This investigation shows that students have the habit to use and learn from Internet.

In the investigation of the integration of 3D-panorama system into the tour guiding course, there are 97 % of the subject are interested in the tour guiding course; 94 % of subjects believe that modern tour guidance must include new technology equipment as a supplement. Nonetheless, before the investigation is conducted, only 37 % of subjects claim that they have a clear understanding of 3D-panorama system. While after this study and experience practice, 100 % of subjects regard they have sound understanding of the system. Furthermore, there are 73 % of subjects regard themselves have the ability to manipulate the 3D-panorama system as well as explaining the material at the same time. In this investigation, we find that 87 % of subject think that the 3D-panorama system have obvious value-adding to the tour guiding course; 83 % of subjects will like to apply 3D-panorama tour guide system to practice tour guidance; 87 % of subjects regards that this 3D-panorama system provide telepresence to the tour guidance; 72 % of subject regard the 3D-panorama guiding system makes her like the tour guiding course much more.

## 5 Conclusion

This paper proposed an application of the VR 3D-panorama technology on the training of tour guiding. The web-based 3D-panorama training system can be applied in both the classroom and the scenic spot. The 3D-panorama training system has been already implemented in the cloud of Tajen university to support the training course. In conclusion, this study shows that the introduction of the 3D-panaroma system in assisting tour guiding course can improve the study effectiveness of students.

**Acknowledgment.** The authors would also like to thank the Hakka Affairs Council, Taiwan for the support to this paper.

## References


1. Suppes, P., Morningstar, M.: Computer-assisted instruction. Science **166**, 343–350 (1969)
2. Carbonell, J.: Ai in cai: an artificial-intelligence approach to computer-assisted instruction. IEEE Trans. Man Mach. Syst. **11**(4), 190–202 (1970)
3. Anderson, K.: Computer-assisted instruction. J. Med. Syst. **10**(2), 163–171 (1986)
4. Gredler, M.: Learning and Instruction: Theory Into Practice. Prentice Hall Higher Education, Upper Saddle River (2008)
5. Riegler, A.: Constructivism. In: L'Abate, L. (ed.) Paradigms in Theory Construction, pp. 235–255. Springer, New York (2012)
6. Driscoll, M.: Psychology of Learning for Instruction. Pearson Education Limited, Boston (2005)
7. Craig, A.B., Sherman, W.R., Will, J.D.: Chapter 6 - education applications. In: Developing Virtual Reality Applications, pp. 189–237. Morgan Kaufmann, Boston (2009)
8. Lucet, G.: Virtual reality: a knowledge tool for cultural heritage. In: Ranchordas, A.K., Araújo, H.J., Pereira, J.M., Braz, J. (eds.) VISIGRAPP 2008. CCIS, vol. 24, pp. 1–10. Springer, Heidelberg (2009)
9. Monahan, T., McArdle, G., Bertolotto, M.: Virtual reality for collaborative e-learning. Comput. Educ. **50**(4), 1339–1353 (2008)
10. Huang, H.M., Rauch, U., Liaw, S.S.: Investigating learners attitudes toward virtual reality learning environments: based on a constructivist approach. Comput. Educ. **55**(3), 1171–1182 (2010)
11. Jou, M., Wang, J.: Investigation of effects of virtual reality environments on learning performance of technical skills. Comput. Hum. Behav. **29**(2), 433–438 (2013). <<Advanced Human-Computer Interaction>>.

# Author Index